THE STORY OF
WORLD ROWING

By the same author:

Henley Royal Regatta
The Oxford and Cambridge Boat Race
Boating

THE STORY OF
WORLD ROWING

Christopher Dodd

STANLEY PAUL
London Sydney Auckland Johannesburg

Stanley Paul & Co. Ltd

An imprint of Random Century Group

20 Vauxhall Bridge Road, London SW1V 2SA

Random Century Australia (Pty) Ltd
20 Alfred Street, Milsons Point, Sydney 2061

Random Century New Zealand Limited
PO Box 40–086, Glenfield, Auckland 10

Century Hutchinson South Africa (Pty) Ltd
PO Box 337, Bergvlei 2012, South Africa

First Published 1992
Copyright © Christopher Dodd 1992

Set in Sabon

Phototypeset by Intype, London

Printed and bound in Great Britain by
Mackays of Chatham PLC, Chatham Kent

A catalogue record for this book is available
from the British Library

ISBN 0 09 174610 8

For Thomi Keller

Contents

Who, what, where, when, and why

THE story of rowing came to be written because Thomi Keller wanted his 'rowing family' to have its own story. Keller was president of the International Rowing Federation (FISA) for thirty-one years, a period during which its activity grew both in breadth and depth, thanks in great measure to his energy and leadership and his championing of the athlete's cause in a sports world invaded by commercialism. FISA's main concern is competition sport, but Thomi loved all aspects of messing about in rowing boats. He was on first-name terms with most of the international athletes in his sport and could steer a course through the backwaters of rowing culture as deftly as through the treacherous currents of the Olympic estuary. His was sometimes a rasping voice from the bank, sometimes the essence of charm, and he commanded a loyalty and devotion which created a family feeling in rowing and saved it from shipwreck between the Scylla of politics and the Charybdis of show business.

He and I talked about the book for a number of years, and then at the 1988 Henley Royal Regatta, where Thomi was a steward and an umpire, he said, 'OK, let's do it in time for FISA's centenary in 1992.' On 29 September 1989, two days before I was due to start work, he died suddenly. He had run FISA virtually as a one-man band, and so many of rowing's best stories died with him, which is a further loss and sadness. His family telephoned immediately to ask me to carry on because they knew that this book had been dear to Thomi's heart, and so its existence is due to the support which his wife Dorry and his children Dominik, Adrian, Bettina, Anne and Barbara have given. Dominik Keller is well known in rowing as a photographer and he has been a generous and exacting helpmate on behalf of the family. In the extended family of rowing, dozens of people and institutions in many countries have assisted with information and hospitality, and they are listed in the Acknowledgements.

The Story of World Rowing set out to be a history, but it has not turned out quite like that. When I started work, the German Democratic Republic was the strongest rowing country in the world, and when I stopped, it no longer existed. The political and cultural map of Central Europe, if not its borders, had changed. The people of Leningrad have voted to call their city St Petersburg again. The Baltic states have won their freedom from the Soviet Union. Other Soviet republics are expressing dissent, and Yugoslavia is in turmoil as I write. And the tiny Kuwaiti rowing federation has been lost in the Middle East imbroglio. Sensible historians choose a date or an event at which to stop in order to put some distance between them and the present. But two things compelled me to bring at least part of the story up to 1991: the death of Thomi Keller, whose thirty-one years at the helm represent a generation of development that changed rowing from the inside, and the reunification of Germany just before the world championships in 1990, which brought to an end the life, if not the influence, of the world's most phenomenal rowing power.

For the rest, I decided to spend as much of the available time as possible on the countries and topics about which I knew least and about which the least is known in the populous European and American rowing centres. I also wished to avoid – as did Thomi – either a chronological story or a country-by-country directory. The scale of the project, the time available, and source material in many languages left me dependent greatly on the goodwill and talents of translators, correspondents, authors and enthusiasts. The aim has been to expose the roots of rowing as a recreation and a sport and to trace its main developments through the people who have had the greatest influence on it, whether they be rowers, coaches, boat-builders or officials. In addition to rowing's place in sport and life, I have also intended to show its fun and character. Inevitably, selection has coloured the record here and there; inevitably, some people will feel left out; inevitably, some will feel misjudged; inevitably, memories are fickle; inevitably, omissions and reinterpretations will come to light too late for this volume. Such judgements, errors and omissions are my responsibilty; I am satisfied that all my helpers have tried their hardest to be accurate. For the sake of ease of reading, proper names of institutions have been anglicized and modern placenames given in the text.

The book is divided into five parts which can be taken separately or together. Book One visits the ancient Greeks, the Vikings and the Venetians, three representatives of eras when rowing was the most important and sometimes the only form of transport and the only method of waging war. All three have echoes in the twentieth century. A fourth chapter sketches traditional forms of rowing which still take place. Book Two follows the development of the oar-powered ship from commercial craft to racing shell. Book Three starts with the trainers behind the top-level athletes of the 1990s and traces the innovators in styles of rowing back to the adoption of the sliding seat, a development which was in the nature of a quantum leap – the small step with big consequences – between traditional and modern rowing. Book Four attempts to explain why rowing as a recreation and a sport began in Britain and travelled with its pioneers to many parts of the globe, outlining how the natives adapted and influenced it. Book Five examines rowing's place as a founding Olympic sport and its growth as a competitive activity, particularly in the Keller years from 1958 to 1989. At the back of the book is a chronology of rowing's technical developments and growth, a glossary of boatbuilding and rowing terms, including some that are redundant, and a conversion table. There is a chapter-by-chapter guide to main sources and further reading and a broadly based bibliography. Lastly, the index groups topics and countries so that readers with specialist interests can follow them and no doubt spot inconsistencies.

The story of rowing has been a pleasure as well as a privilege to write, and I can only hope that readers will get as much enjoyment out of it as the author. In my history of Henley Royal Regatta I floated the notion of a Great Enclosure in the Sky where rowers congregate after they pass life's finishing post. For sure, Thomi is there among the family that he did so much to foster, and this book is our memorial and our thanks to him.

PART ONE
ROOTS

1

THE GREEKS

FROM the crest of a hill on a still summer evening, the only motion on the shimmering Aegean is a dark wooden ship etching a great chevron on the surface of the bay and sparkling a light-fantastic dance of sunbeams. The sole sound is oars in unison, the shush and thwack of 170 looms rattling against 170 wooden pins, arranged in three files, perfectly together. The ship is *Olympias*, a *trieres* of the Hellenic Navy, rowing home to Poros. Her *trierarch* in his starched white uniform stands alone on deck. Her sails are furled; her painted eye can just be made out above the waterline; the upward sweep of her stern is like a great hand cradling her steersman. Her bronze ram is partly submerged. She is awesome. *Olympias* is coming home nearly two millennia after the Greeks won a battle decisive for European history at Salamis. Her crew break into 'Jerusalem' in time with their rhythmic strokes, astonishing for locals who hear it from the shore: for the crew are British and they sing an English anthem. Their ship is the living solution to a fantastic detective story solved by modern scholars: *Olympias* is the link between the art and science of pulling for military and commercial enterprise, and pulling for pleasure.

At Salamis early on the morning of 20 September 480 BC, 271 of these ships, a third of them from Athens, tackled a fleet of around 800 similar vessels owing allegiance to Xerxes, Great King of the Persians and just about everywhere from the eastern Mediterranean to India. The consequential rout of the Persian mercenary fleet saved Greece from Persian rule. A future democracy and a future civilization were safeguarded by a highly developed, vicious, efficient, beautiful, swift deterrent, fuelled by muscle and unsurpassed teamwork.

The story of *Olympias* began at a dinner party in the Lake District of England in 1982, hosted by Frank Welsh, an author and banker. Guests began to discuss the *trieres*. Although thousands of these ships and variations on them had been built, no hulk had ever been found; nor did details of their construction or design survive into the Middle Ages. No rower left an account of how to pull them or what life was like aboard. Yet there is plenty of literary and historical evidence that they existed and that they were the most powerful ships of the ancient Mediterranean cultures. They had puzzled scholars and romantics for hundreds of years, not least the classicists and ship designers of the nineteenth and twentieth centuries. The possibilities were clouded by later Mediterranean rowing systems such as those in Venice, and imagination ran riot in movies like Cecil B. de Mille's *Cleopatra* in which the slave-driven monster is grandiose in both size and impossibility. By 1982 received opinion was either that a three-level system of rowing was impossible, or that the Greeks achieved it by using oars of varying lengths.

But a few scholars, notably Professor John Morrison at Cambridge, were convinced that received opinion was wrong. Morrison had come to the conclusion that a ship with oarsmen seated in three tiers and using oars of the same length was not only possible, but fast. He based his theory on two pieces of evidence: a carved stone naval inventory from the middle of the fourth century BC found at Piraeus, which recorded the number of oars and their spacing; and the remains of a *trieres* shed of the same period at Zea, near Piraeus, which gave him the maximum overall dimensions of the ship. A *trieres* had been rowed by 170 oars, and had a maximum length of 37 metres and a width of 5.5 metres. Any arrangement of oars other than in three tiers would have meant that the ship would have had to have been longer than 37 metres.

Morrison had spent a lifetime developing his theory and his views were known to Charles Willink, one of the guests at Frank Welsh's party, because Morrison had taught him classics at university. Over dinner, Welsh suggested that the only way to prove Morrison right was to build a ship. He set about doing so, and that is how the Trireme Trust came into being, and how, five years later, Professor Morrison came to be sitting in the *trierarch*'s chair being pulled across the bay with his lifetime's scholarship beneath his feet.

The architect of the reconstruction of the *trieres*, which is usually known by its Roman name of trireme in spite of the fact that the

Greeks perfected it first, is John Coates. A former chief naval architect for Britain's Ministry of Defence, Coates was already collaborat-
ing with Morrison on a book about triremes when Welsh bowled
them over with his scheme. Using Morrison's data, Coates was in
the process of drawing the lines of the ship and working out the
rowing arrangements. Morrison had discovered other details about
oar ports and such from studying sculpted reliefs, Greek vases decorated with ships and literary sources.

Herodotus, a historian at work in the second half of the fifth
century, mentions that a guard found asleep had been punished by
having his head put through an oar port, so Morrison knew that
the ports had to be at least head-sized; he had also discovered that
those on the bottom tier had been fitted with leather collars to
prevent water getting in. Forty years earlier he had come across
another clue in *The Republic*, where Plato describes a shaft of light
binding the heavens together 'like the *hypozōmata* of the *triereis*'.
The *hypozōma* was two lengths of twisted rope low down inside
the hull, attached at stem and stern and kept taut by a twisting
device in the centre. Coates deduced that because the ship was very
long for its depth, the hull would be under enormous stress, and
hence the need for a *hypozōma* to prevent the ship from breaking
her back. He also worked out that the tiers of oarsmen had to
overlap one another, otherwise the vessel would have been top-
heavy.

Coates and Morrison examined the remains of merchant ships
of the period to see how they had been constructed and studied
contemporary accounts of voyages and battles to find out how the
ship was required to perform. They built a mock-up of a segment
and displayed it at the National Maritime Museum in Greenwich,
inviting anyone interested to attend a seminar. Many suggestions
came out of this. The most exciting was a letter from a man in
Perth, Australia, in which he described how he had been shipwrecked
off Lesbos in the Aegean during the Second World War. While in
hiding he had carved model boats for the local children and someone
had shown him a very old pewter model of a galley with oars
arranged in three tiers. He enclosed a drawing from memory, and
Morrison found himself looking at a smaller version of his trireme,
adapted for river use. The Australian had returned to Lesbos after

the war to find that his protectors had been shot by the Nazis. The pewter model has never been traced.

The mock-up and seminar were followed by the construction of a 'trial piece', a segment of one side of a ship which seated fifteen oarsmen. It was built in Coventry by craftsmen using ancient Athenian methods, and was tested by students from Warwick University and Worcester. It was displayed at Henley Royal Regatta. Greek scholars and government officials had become interested at the Greenwich seminar, and the success of the trial piece convinced their navy, their ministry for cultural affairs, and their national tourist organization that the project was worth backing. Coates, who had a lifetime's interest in wooden boats as well as designing fighting ships, tackled what had taken the ancient Greeks hundreds of years to evolve. He produced 150 pages of specifications and drawings of what he was convinced would turn out to be a fast trireme, very close to the descendant of the oared ship invented in Corinth in about 650 BC.

Olympias took shape at the Tzakakos yard in Piraeus, with Coates trying to keep an eye on her progress during frequent visits from his home in Bath. In 1987 she was launched and tested by a crew of Greek rowers and Hellenic Navy conscripts. She was then taken to Poros for sea trials with a volunteer, mostly British, crew. These lasted for two weeks. On the last day the crew rowed her down the straits between the town quays and the mainland, an incredible sight for the descendants of the victors of Salamis, with forty members of the Trust on deck. The untrained crew, more used to sliding than fixed seats, achieved a sprint speed of 7 knots (13 kilometres per hour). Thucydides' account of the 340-kilometre voyage from Athens to Mytilene in 427 BC gives the time for the trip as just over twenty-four hours, implying an average cruising speed of 7.5 knots. In 1988 an international crew improved the sprint speed to 8 knots. In 1990 a hand-picked crew with greatly lightened oars achieved 8.5 knots consistently, and reached 8.9 knots maximum.

Below Decks

The Trireme Trust's programme has uncovered much more than the design of a ship which Coates describes as reaching the optimum within the limits of the materials and techniques available and without the benefits of present-day knowledge of hydrostatistics, stability of ships, structural mechanics, physiology or physics. Another classicist, Professor Ford Weiskittel, rowed on all three tiers during the first trials and says, 'If you can imagine 170 rowers dripping three to four litres of sweat apiece per day, it will come as no surprise that the trireme was a little fetid at the end of two weeks, the woodwork of the ship whitened by the salty perspiration.' The crew filed on board carrying their oars, sheepskin cushions and water bottles, just as the ancients did. At first they had to learn that each set of three rowers – *thranite* (top file), *zygian* (middle), and *thalamian* (bottom) – has to find water in a tight sweep, having no more than a yard of space inboard in which to move, and that they must not foul one another. Only the *thranites* can see what is happening. Graeme Fife, also a veteran of this crew, wrote:

> In this period of trial and error, oars crack together, get hooked over each other as one poaches another's water, then crash down on a third in the effort to get clear. Any more of this and we'll all be nervous wrecks; call it *trierititis*. The important thing, it's said, is not to think about it . . . Try not to *think* about it? This boat is crammed full of undergraduates, graduates, researchers, retired academics and opinion-rich racing oarsmen. Tell a seagull to give up flying!

Fife goes on to discuss bladework and technique and then describes, for him, the *pièce de résistance*, the full-tilt swerve:

> The boat gathers speed, the helmsman shoves the rudder blades hard over, and one side of rowers takes the boat on, the other side resting. The boat runs through 180 degrees in about one and a half times its length, taking not much more than a minute to complete its manoeuvre. It leaves a smooth, hook-shaped scar in its wake as evidence.

No wonder that the ancient Greeks, for many of whom pulling an oar was as much a part of life as eating and sleeping, took rowing seriously. One wrote that the Athenians, because of their overseas possessions and the public offices they held abroad,

> learn to use the oar as second nature, both themselves and their attendants. In fact when a man is often at sea he must of necessity take an oar himself and likewise his slave, and learn the language of the sea. The majority are able to pull an oar when they first set foot aboard a

warship, having had the preliminary training man and boy up to that moment.

Pericles told the Athenians: 'The fact is that sea power is a matter of skill, like everything else, and it is not possible to get practice in the odd moment when the chance occurs, but it is a full-time occupation, leaving no moment for other things.'

During the century and a half that triremes policed the Mediterranean, Athens had up to 40,000 professional oarsmen who were paid a drachma a day under service. Many earned bonuses on top. Ships were privately owned and leased to the government in time of war, and there was fierce competition on the Piraeus waterfront to hire the best men. There was rivalry among the *trierarchs* (commanding officers) and much debate about how to keep the crews' morale high and avoid desertion. What becomes clear is that a slave-based society, a society which forced men unwillingly to the oars, could not have produced the results achieved by Athens and the other Greek city-states. Teamwork and mutual support made a fast ship, not an atmosphere of grudge between crews and hierarchy such as the later French galleys suffered before their demise at the beginning of the eighteenth century, manned as they were by Turkish mercenaries, common criminals and Huguenot slaves. 'The ancients,' Fife wrote, 'talked of oar banks beating like wings; of the *trieres* as a bird of prey . . . I have to confess that every time we row out, it's the Battle of Salamis again; and every time my admiration for the Greeks who rowed that fleet under Themistocles increases. How did they do it?'

Frank Welsh concluded his account of building the trireme thus:

> The Athenian trireme, like the long-bow and the Kentucky rifle, was a weapon of democracy, in much the same way that cavalry has always been the arm of an aristocracy, and artillery that of a monarchy. Later galleys, larger and heavier but slower, may well have been pulled by slaves, but the fast trireme needed just such an independently minded, noisy, opinionated a crew as we had, quite unintentionally, provided.

The common people who served in the *trieres* brought Athens her power. 'In this way an authentic aspect of Athenian life had been re-created, and not the least aspect, either. Whatever interesting points emerge from future work on the ship, our understanding of fifth-century Athens has been vividly clarified.'

Olympias and Latsis

What of the ship itself? When Welsh floated the idea of building it, Coates and Morrison said that they thought they knew enough to make a start. Fortunately for them, the archaeologist Honor Frost had made underwater excavations near Marsala in Sicily in the early 1970s for the Society of Nautical Research in London. This turned up crucial evidence about the construction of lengthy oared ships in the ancient Mediterranean. Coates says, 'Clearly the trireme capped an impressively determined and sustained development effort in ancient Greece and possibly other parts of the Mediterranean beginning some time in the seventh century BC . . . Its development provides further evidence that the technology of ancient Greece reached a level generally unsurpassed until the latter part of the eighteenth century.' In about 482 BC Athens, with a population of about 250,000, built some 200 *trieres* in two years, an enormous and expensive undertaking. They were a considerable advance on their predecessor, the two-tier fifty-man *pentecontor*, although the latter continued in service widely. What the *trieres* gave the Athenians was speed. 'Triremes would have been some 30 per cent faster under oar than a *pentecontor*,' Coates says. 'They could have overtaken any other existing type of ship.' How the jump was made from the *pentecontor* with two files of twelve and thirteen oarsmen on each side to *trieres* with three files of thirty-one, twenty-seven, and twenty-seven is not known. A *trieres* carried a captain, about twelve sailors, and fourteen soldiers and archers. The purpose, then, was clear: sprint into attack, ram and retreat. The priority was the engine. Marines and fighting men were kept to the bare minimum, just enough to defend the steersman and the crew. The difficult part was to find out how the 170 rowers could be fitted into such a confined space and row effectively.

One important lesson was that a *trieres* carried very little or no ballast. Vernard Foley and Werner Soedel published findings in 1981 emphasizing that the trieres was extremely light for its size. During the reconstruction it was found that ballast was not required for stability, confirming contemporary accounts of stricken ships being towed away, which implies that they did not sink. This makes it unlikely that a *trieres* will ever be found on the seabed. Also vital

to the reconstruction were Frost's excavations, because they revealed
that previous attempts at depicting or reconstructing *triereis* – such
as the cumbersome creation built for Napoleon III in 1860 – were
wrongly based on ballasted timber ships or medieval galleys. Traditional wooden-ship construction works from the inside outwards,
starting with a frame composed of keel, stem and stern post, and
ribs, to which are attached planks on the outside, strengthened by
longitudinal members inside. But until the latter half of the first
millennium AD ships were built from the shell inwards. The technique is not fully understood but, according to Coates, the *trieres*
started with a keel, on to which planks were fastened in upward
progression. These were secured to one another by hardwood tenons
set tightly in mortice sockets and locked into place by a peg at each
end of the tenon. This laborious method meant that the hull was
very strongly jointed, and so thinner planks could be used. A frame
and ribs were not essential for holding the planking together. Large
longitudinal and transverse timbers were not required. The result
was a ship which could hold 170 oarsmen plus crew plus fighting
men and had a small enough displacement to balance it at the correct
waterline when fully loaded. The 'wine-glass' form of the hull gave
a small cross-section area below the waterline, reducing the displacement to about 40 tons for a ship with 30 metres or more of waterline.
A flat-bottomed hull of the same beam and draft would have had a
displacement of at least 70 tons. The length and form of the hull
were found to be well suited to overcome the main component of
resistance, the viscosity or frictional drag of water. Coates says: 'The
ship's length, together with its speed, determines the interaction of
the bow and stern waves and therefore the wave-making resistance.
It is remarkable that the trireme's length is such that its wave-making
resistance is increasing only slowly at just about the maximum speed
(from 9.5 to 11 knots) at which the ship can be expected to be
propelled under oar for a short sprint. To achieve the next slow
increase in wave-making resistance, I calculated that it would be
necessary to build a ship about 50 per cent longer, with a crew of
some 250 oarsmen; what is more, the gain in speed would be slight.
In any case the endeavour would come to naught for lack of the
longitudinal bending strength necessary to keep such a long ship
from breaking apart. The trireme was just the right length to achieve
the greatest speed in a practicable ship.'

The hull section and method of construction were found to satisfy several other requirements of buoyancy and stability. Among them was the important clue to the arrangement of oarsmen: the hull section had just enough flare so that each file of oarsmen was outboard of and higher than the one below it. It was found that by angling the seats of the top and bottom files a few degrees inboard all oar blades were evenly spaced. The top file had outriggers. This arrangement allowed all oars except for a few at the ends to be the same length. Information from the naval inventory found at Piraeus told the investigators that oars were 9 and 9.5 cubits long (15 and 16 feet). Details from the Lenormant relief discovered on the Acropolis at Athens and from the Ruvo vase found near modern-day Bari in the southeast of Italy enabled Coates and Morrison to work out the maximum length of swing of the handles and the maximum rate of about fifty strokes to the minute, from which they deduced that, to achieve the claimed speeds, the gearing – the ratio of the length of the oar outboard of its pivot to the length inboard – must be high, about three to one. They knew the width of hull at the waterline necessary for stability and the minimum height of the lowest file above the waterline for the oars to be workable. From the trial piece they discovered the maximum angle of incline of the top file of oars to enable the rowers to work them effectively (less than 35 degrees from the horizontal). These characteristics settled another old argument: the ship did not have to be augmented by sail to achieve its top speed. A *trieres* was first and foremost an oared ship. The sails enabled the crew to rest and to take advantage of a fair wind, but did not necessarily improve the pulling conditions.

One of the most important pieces of evidence concerning how the Greeks rowed a *trieres* was the Lenormant relief. At least one oarsman on the surviving section has his knees bent at the beginning of the stroke. Coupled with the knowledge that oarsmen were responsible for their own oars and sheepskin cushions, this makes it clear that the Greeks achieved some sliding on the seat. This had occurred to John Hale in 1971 when discussing his lightweight crew at Yale with his professor of Greek history, Donald Kagan. They considered the likely structure of the ships and studied their favourite sea battles, and concluded that, first, the outrigger, which was not found on Phoenician, Egyptian, Rhodian, Carthaginian or Sicilian triremes, seemed to enable an oar on the top tier to be handled successfully

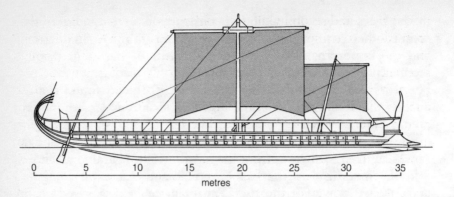

0 5 10 15 20 25 30 35

metres

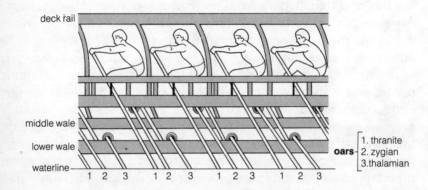

deck rail

middle wale

lower wale

waterline

1 2 3 1 2 3 1 2 3 1 2 3

oars
1. thranite
2. zygian
3. thalamian

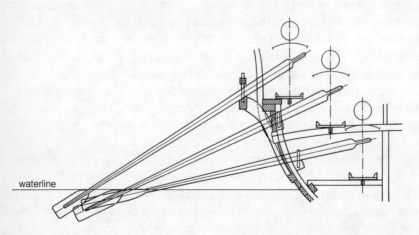

waterline

From top: John Coates's reconstruction of the trieres
The Lenormant relief explained – note oarsman with bent knees
The oarsystem of a trieres

by one man, and secondly, that the sliding cushion method of rowing enabled the oarsmen to achieve quicker starts, a unison of rating and quicker turning because one side could stop sliding. Enough momentum would remain after the turn to ram an opponent.

Apart from claims by classical writers the only statistic of performance available for fixed-seat rowing came from the US Navy's light racing cutters, which are a standard design and race over 3 nautical miles. A twelve-man crew was found to develop 2.05 effective horsepower or 1.53 kilowatts, an average of 0.128 kilowatt per man at 7 knots over 3 miles. The first *trieres* test crew achieved only half the effective power of the average cutter oarsman. If they had all been as effective as the US Navy men they would have moved the *trieres* at 9.3 knots with the twin rudders raised out of the water. The reason that they did not was their relative inexperience, their mixed abilities and fitness, and the fact that the first set of oars was too heavy. Weiskittel says, 'At the beginning, a minute of continuous rowing was a struggle, five minutes impossible. By the end, we were doing fifteen to twenty minutes nonstop, and nearly three minutes at full pressure.' It was worst on the top file as the oar was so heavy that it was harder to manage when it was out of the water than in. Coates recognized that to achieve the maximum potential of the ship it was essential to get exactly the right mass, balance, blade area and gearing. The oars had to be made using ancient technology too, from suitable timber without the benefits of weighting, modern glues or composite sections. In the literature there is mention of spruce, a light and relatively stiff wood. Oars are an afterthought to the oarsman's cost. 'Reaching speeds beyond 9.5 knots,' Coates said after the first attempts at rowing *Olympias*, 'will depend primarily on the quality of the crew and on arriving at the best design for oars . . . That such a search for the right oar design is necessary demonstrates the degree to which the trireme was refined to achieve its remarkable performance.'

In a sense that process took place during the first sea trials of *Olympias* off Poros. The Hotel Latsis, whose balconies and pavement terrace look out over the bay and the petty officer school with its jetty and chapel, was where the crew had their coffee and rolls at dawn. It was here that the professors and television crew lived in the stifling August heat. It was here that Coates and Morrison dealt with a thousand inquiries as the word went round the island about

the strange ship observed from the ferry. It was here that Welsh
brought the visiting Trireme Trust members and Rosie Randolph
administered the comings and goings of the crew, who lived a spartan life in the barracks at their own expense. It was in the bar at
the Latsis that peace was made between the navy men and the less
disciplined foreign guests who were manning their ship. It was here
that a man with an enormous suitcase arrived from the ferry and
introduced himself to Morrison as Darius Djafar-Zade, a Germano-
Iranian modelmaker of ancient oared ships who lived on Vancouver
Island, and Morrison shook his hand and said, 'Good heavens, a
Persian come to spy Salamis!' It was here that the pulling master,
Mike Budd, a doctor from Hereford in a red sunhat, would sink
into a chair with a beer and hear the reports of his section leaders.
After each outing the Latsis hosted informal seminars long into the
night, a *trieres* think-tank.

One of the greatest problems was transmitting orders through the
length of the ship. As far as is known the *keleustes* or rowing master
called the rating in ancient ships, but Budd's team found it necessary
to position somebody forward of the mast to relay instructions;
easily understood routines, such as the crew chanting the strokes by
numbers so that they knew when to stop, had to be worked out.
And it was round a table at the Hotel Latsis that the 'emergency
stop' procedure was devised, whereby a police inspector from Nottinghamshire would lie in the bilges with a whistle and blow it if
any *thalamian* caught a crab. Catching a crab on the bottom layer
risked being trapped between a beam and one's own oar handle but,
thanks to Peter Macleod and his whistle, nobody was. The *trierarch*,
Lieutenant Dimitri Papadas, would come to the hotel to watch the
video of the day's proceedings, and Yannis Manuelides, a navy
conscript with a Cambridge education, would perform another of
his diplomatic turns between his commanding officer Papadas, who
spoke no English, and pulling master Budd, who spoke no Greek.

The ship went out in the early morning and early evening to take
advantage of the cool of the day and to avoid ferries and sightseeing
yachts. In between, the sound of hammer on wood could be heard
as Paul Lipke, a boatbuilder and marine archaeologist from Massachusetts, mobilized his volunteers aboard *Olympias* to make repairs
to oar ports and tholepins. Colleagues from Bangor University recorded every detail of the ship and its movements. Owain Roberts,

the Welsh sailing master, conducted seminars on sail and ancient ships and had his chance to prove his points during the trials. Day and night the cast swirled about the Latsis and numerous tavernas, reassessing, re-forming, re-arguing, refreshing itself on kebabs, stuffed tomatoes, fetta and salads, on beer, retsina, orange juice and ouzo.

By 1990 there were firm plans to do the same thing on Drake's Island near the mouth of the River Tamar, just off Plymouth Hoe in England. The Trireme Trust has leased the island and its old naval battery and barracks to convert it to a trireme centre, including a taverna, and build two ships to be based there. The climate will not be as conducive as that of Greece, but Plymouth is much more accessible to rowers than Poros. The research goes on. The genius of Morrison and Coates has enhanced, and will further enhance, our understanding of three thousand years of history during which the oar was indispensable. Frank Welsh's discussion over the dinner table has help bridge the two-millennia gap between the zenith of oarpower and the age of the super-sleek racing shell.

2

THE VIKINGS

'IN the harbour of Gotland Vi so many ships lay at anchor that Orm was at first doubtful whether it would be wise to sail in. But they took down the dragon-head, set up a shield of peace in its place, and rowed in without any ship opposing their passage. The town was large and full of seamen and rich merchants.' Orm's men, according to Frans Bengtsson's saga *The Long Ships*, found much to marvel at, not least the houses, which appeared to be erected for the sole purpose of drinking ale, and the whores who walked the streets with rings of pure gold in their ears and asked a fistful of silver for their services. They were bemused by a man from 'the Saxon's land' who spent the day scraping beards from the chins of those rich enough to part with a copper coin, some bleeding as a result. These oarsmen from the mainland had never seen such customs or such riches.

The ship had twenty-four oars and a company of sixty-six, including Toke and Olof Summerbird and the eleven sons of Sone. It was bound from Skania, the southern tip of what is now Sweden but in AD 1000 was a province of Denmark, to recover Orm's inheritance, which was hidden below the weirs on the River Dnieper, a long way along the Viking road to Miklagard, the Norse name for Byzantium. Vi, now Visby, on the island of Gotland was the centre of the Viking world. There Orm had recruited a small, grizzled helmsman named Spof who had much experience of sailing east. Spof advised Orm to purchase a plentiful supply of strong Gotland ale to reward the men for their efforts on the great portage. From Vi they took the 'low road' to the Dnieper, which entailed crossing the Eastern Sea (Baltic), slipping between the south end of the island of Ösel (Saaremaa) and Kurland (Latviya) and into the River Dvina. From there they pulled upstream to Polotsk, on the way passing three ships from Gotland

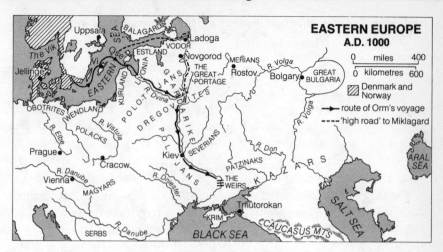

laden with fabrics, silver bowls, wine, pepper and slavegirls, one of whom was dangled naked over the side and offered to them for 12 marks. The slavers had come from Great Bulgaria (Tartarskaya) on the River Volga, so they said, and had rowed down the Volga to the Salt Sea (Caspian) where they traded with Arabs. Another ship returning empty to East Gutes gave an account of ambush and robbery at the hands of Meres tribesmen. Orm's men fished, hunted wild oxen, and traded shirts and shoes with the naked men of Polotsk, naked because they had not paid their taxes to the prince in Kiev. The price of non-payment was to lose their clothes and the services of their wives and daughters. Here Orm picked up a passenger, the scribe of the local chieftain, who had been entrusted to take a basket of criminals' scalps to Kiev to show the prince what a zealous lieutenant he had.

Where the river divided, Orm and his men took the Ulla, which brought them to the great portage. The men and their hired team of oxen struggled for seven days to haul their ship and its contents, which they put on an improvised cart, to the River Beaver. On the way three of the crew died when they were attacked by swarms of bees used by the inhabitants of a nearby settlement as their first line of defence. The rest had to sit in the lake for some time to recover from the beating they took from the bees. They knew that if they had attempted to enter the village at night, they would have been greeted by bears. From here their way was downstream between banks of broadleaved trees. The fish here tasted better. The Beaver took them into the broad waters of the Dnieper, joining the 'high road' from the Baltic favoured by the Swedes. The 'high road' ran along the coast of the Dead Land (Finland), up the Vodor (Neva) to Lake Ladoga and up the Volkhov to Novgorod continuing south to the great portage.

Once on the Dnieper Orm and his men passed four heavy-laden merchant ships home-bound from Krim (Crimea, on the Black Sea) to Birka (near Stockholm). They did not stop at Kiev, Orm retaining the scribe to act as interpreter for the potentially hostile tribesmen whom they anticipated meeting at the weirs. In any case, his basket of stinking heads had been lost to the fish, having been towed behind the ship. To cut a long saga short, Orm's party found their buried treasure.

On the way home they were attacked by Patzinak horsemen. The Vikings defended their cartload of gold, trinkets and silver coin by standing their ground and exchanging arrows with waves of Patzinak cavalry sweeping back and forth. The men who had stayed to guard the ship came charging to the rescue in the nick of time. The Patzinaks took hostages, Orm found an old friend in the Patzinak village, honour and valour won the day, and the Vikings rowed home to Skania to tell the tale. If the script is true, they had enacted the first Western, even if the location was in the East.

The saga of Orm was written in the twentieth century by Frans Bengtsson and serves to illustrate the harsh realities of the Viking Age and its adventurous, violent, rampaging, artistic, merchandising, colonizing, whoreing, boozing and wealth-loving oarsmen. Their name is from the Norse word *vik*, variously translated as 'creek', 'bay' or 'pirate'. They were prominent in the lands we now know as Denmark, Norway and Sweden from approximately AD 793 to the defeat of King Harald of Norway by King Harold of England at Stamford Bridge on 25 September 1066. Ironically Harold, himself the grandson of a Viking, died at the Battle of Hastings less than a month later when the Normans invaded England under William the Conqueror, who was also descended from a Viking. The Viking age was one of trading and a reasonably settled life, particularly in Sweden, where craftsmen fashioned goods brought from Eastern and Western Europe and even from India. In return they exported firs from marten, beaver and squirrel, ivory from walrus tusks, falcons for hunting, and amber from the coast for jewellery. The Vikings from Denmark and Norway travelled mainly to Western Europe, while Swedes sailed the Baltic, settled lastingly in Russia and mingled with the Slavs. They opened up the great trade routes to the Black Sea and Caspian, to the allure and riches of Byzantium, and into the Mediterranean. They were the catalysts in the break-up of Frankia, the great empire of Charlemagne, first Holy Roman Emperor, who ruled modern-day France, the Netherlands, Belgium, western Germany, Switzerland and Italy. They raided Lindisfarne on the northeast coast of England in 793, Weymouth and Jarrow in 794, Iona off the western Scottish coast and Rathlin Island at the northwest tip of Ulster in 795, and the Aquitaine coast of France in 799. They were unpopular visitors to Rouen, Paris, Antwerp, Hamburg, the coast of Spain and Portugal, Jerusalem, Alexandria and Constantinople. They acquired Normandy from Charles the Simple and colonized Ireland, much of the British Isles, the Faroes, Iceland and Greenland. They sailed to America, allegedly because of a navigation accident, and named it Vinland. In 1893 a replica Viking ship was rowed from Bergen to Newfoundland by twelve oarsmen, a gift from Norway to the great fair at Chicago. The voyage took forty days travelling at 11.5 knots. The Viking influence is still to be seen in the names, artefacts and images of all those places. They accomplished their travels because they had a superb tool: the wooden oarpowered ship.

The Travellers' Toolkit

Large Viking ships had sails as well as oars, but a remarkable study of boats by T. C. Lethbridge published in 1952 concludes that, despite sail having been used in the Mediterranean for over 2000 years, it was unknown to the Teutonic peoples in AD 400. The sail and yard were known in Egypt, Crete and Mesopotamia by 2000 BC. Lethbridge judges the earliest sail to have been seen north of the English Channel was that of the explorer Pytheas in about 320 BC. But 'if the Scandinavian Bronze Age vessels have had a similar place of origin to the war galleys of ancient Greece, the sail had not spread to this place of origin before the Scandinavian boatmen left on their migration to the north.' He finds no evidence that anyone used sails on the Atlantic seaboard before the Carthaginians destroyed Tartessus. He also concludes that Tartessan merchant ships were probably large pulling boats because Irish goldwork was known in Spain and the Levant by 1400 BC, and the Irish had connections with Denmark. His explanation for why no small Anglo-Saxon or Viking boat is known to have carried a mast is that the Teutonic people were habitual oarsmen, even though they may have been in contact with the single square sail and the long open boat. At any rate, the earliest known Viking boats which combine sail with oars are the Oseberg ship dated at AD 800 and the Gokstad ship, also from Norway, dated at AD 850.

Six rowing boats have been found from the pre-Viking period in England and Scandinavia. The Nydam boat in southern Jutland, Denmark (AD 400), and the Sutton Hoo boats found in England (AD 600) show evidence of being propelled by oars through grommets against single tholes. The Nydam is the oldest known Nordic boat and the 'earliest boat yet found specifically designed to be rowed, not paddled', according to Magnus Magnusson in his book *Vikings!* The Kvalsund boat from western Norway, dated AD 700, is the earliest Nordic rowing boat found with a keel. From the eighth and ninth centuries sail begins to feature in Scandinavian stone carvings.

The Gokstad ship from Norway is made of oak, 23.33 metres long, 5.24 metres broad and 1.95 metres from the gunwale amidships to the bottom of the keel. It weighed 7 tons and with an additional 10 tons of cargo drew about 1 metre of water. It was steered by a paddle on the starboard or 'steerboard' side, and has holes for sixteen pairs of oars. There are no thwarts, the rowers sitting on chests containing their personal belongings. Sixty-four shields were found with the ship, suggesting that it carried two crews. The longest ship mentioned in the sagas is the Norwegian King Ölaf Tryggvason's *Long Serpent*. It had thirty-four pairs of oars and carried 200 people.

The Vikings evolved ships tailormade for war, just as the Athenians had done. Their longships were distinguishable from their slow cargo or ferry craft. They could be adapted to carry two or three crews and cargo and/or plunder in various combinations. Longships could cross seas and oceans, but they could also operate effectively on the coasts, rivers and estuaries found in Northern Europe. And the combination of sail and oars gave the Vikings the speed and manoeuvrability to take Europe by surprise. The ships' shallow

Viking ship of the type found at Oseberg

draught allowed them to penetrate far inland and gain access to wealthy cities, Paris being an example. They did not require harbours, because they could be beached. They were landing craft for troops and horses, and could reach shallow parts of estuaries and islets where other boats could not navigate. They could raid swiftly, appearing as an unpleasant surprise round a headland or a bend in the river. Little wonder, then, that a longship was what every young upwardly mobile mercenary adventurer desired. Egil described it in his saga thus:

> My mother once told me
> She'd buy me a longship,
> A handsome-oared vessel
> To go sailing with Vikings:
> To stand at the stern-post
> And steer a fine warship,
> Then head back for harbour
> And hew down some foemen.

There was a spiritual element to the Viking tool as well. The many discoveries of buried ships suggest that they carried the soul to the afterworld. The origin of this may have lain in the idea of providing a boat for use in another world. It did not start with the Vikings, being a practice of people in the Eastern Mediterranean, notably Egypt, before them, and possibly going back farther than the Egyptians. It belongs to the rich array of superstition and ritual which attaches itself to boats. In the case of the Vikings, the outlines of some graves are marked by stone settings in the form of ships; others have ships anchored in burial mounds. The Arab traveller Ibn Fadlan described a Viking funeral in Russia in AD 922. The departed chief was accompanied by a slavegirl who answered the call for a volunteer; she was bedded by each of the other chiefs, and was then simultaneously strangled and stabbed before joining her master in the flames of his pyre. A pinch of salt should be added, however, for the raconteur, a diplomat attached to the Caliph of Baghdad, may have possessed a vivid imagination; and he may not have been witnessing a Viking funeral.

Replicas of Viking ships are preserved in several museums, notably in Oslo, Norway, and Roskilde, Denmark. At the latter are examples of a deep-sea trader, a merchant ship, a twenty-four-oar warship of the size used by Orm, and a ferry. Runic inscriptions tell us cryptically where the Vikings voyaged, where they traded, fought and died. But as with the ancient Greeks and their predecessors and heirs, the

Norsemen and the Vikings did not leave convenient accounts of how they actually rowed the ships. At a seminar on replicas of ancient and modern vessels at Roskilde in 1984, Einar Gjessing discussed the physiological background to rowing:

> Using their practical experience and common sense, the Vikings probably knew how to adapt the hull, the oars and the rower's posture to the most satisfactory compromise and how to give priority to certain properties such as cargo-carrying capacity, cruising speed and maximum speed, accelerating capacity and headwind rowing. Alternatively, they may have disregarded the short-term working capacity of the rower in favour of more comfortable long-term working conditions at a lower speed.

In the discussion that followed, Professor Bjørn Haslov said he did not know of any recorded material about rowing. 'I think it has something to do with its being an uncomfortable way of life to be an oarsman. There has not been any interest in rowing at all. Therefore nothing has been written down. I think that our problem is that we can never begin to understand the problems of rowing before we have prepared our bodies for it. For long endurance rowing you need a high oxygen intake. We also know that it is not possible to perform a correct stroke of rowing unless one's back is prepared for it, and that takes about four years. We also know that unless people have been together for some time, they cannot work together.'

Practical Muscular Christianity

The river highway east from Sweden took the Vikings past Finland. From at least the twelfth century the Finns, who originate from Eastern and Central European and Indo-European tribes, were hamstrung by the attraction of their piece of the globe to the Swedes on one side and the Russians on the other. Their homeland is flat and pocked with lakes, so many that it is estimated that there are half a million rowing boats in the country; the great majority of them two-man boats known as national boats in which one man rows and one paddles. There are also many Stone Age rock paintings depicting boats, in common with other northern forested areas of both the old and new worlds. In the late twentieth century it is still possible to find people practised in making log boats in Finland, and

there is considerable evidence of sewn boats, which scholars believe
are the link between the dugout and clinker construction of overlap-
ping strakes. One such find, the Mekrijärvi boat from North Karelia,
is called the 'five piece' boat because it is made from a hollowed-
out keel post, a hollowed-out stem post, and two side strakes, which
solved the problem of how to make stem posts.

Swedish influence over Finland led to a regular postal route
through the Åland islands between the two countries no later than
the fifteenth century. Large communal transports, later known as
church boats, were in evidence by the thirteenth century. And by
the seventeenth century Finland was the world's greatest supplier of
tar, which was brought from the distilleries by narrow *paltamo*
rowing boats. Add to these the inland and seagoing fishing craft and
it is discernable how deep are the roots of rowing in Finland. The
post boats were coastal fishing craft called *skötläggning*, crewed by
up to six men, and were also used for seal hunting. They were rowed
on ice by levering them along with the oars. In the far north of
Lapland there were narrower, longer rowing boats for the rivers. It
took ten to fifteen days to make up to fifty barrels of tar by dry-
distilling partly peeled pine logs. The tar boats developed in the
northern Ostrobothuia river system to carry twenty-five huge barrels.
These boats were 45 feet long, seven barrels being cradled on top
of two rows of nine. They were manned by a crew of three, one
man on each oar of a pair and the third on a huge steering paddle,
and they had a square sail to help them. These boats had 'washboards' made by sewing strakes onto their sides with withes to assist
them in the rapids, and they travelled up to 200 miles with their
valuable cargo. The people of Häme province had a large pulling
barge called a *uisko*. The first mention of a church boat comes
from the same region's assize records in the 1640s. At this time
churchgoing was compulsory, and the boats were used for taking
families to church from distant villages, sometimes in a relay of
boats, the worshippers disembarking and walking from one lake to
the next. Kauko Miettinen, who still builds church boats, says that
his grandmother told him they were used for bringing home the
Sunday shopping too; and from time to time they raced home,
against the clock or against a rival boat. Villages were required to
build boats as their contribution to the Swedish king's fleet. The
boats were sometimes built and operated by 'companies' whose

members shared maintenance. In Finland they were inland craft, medium-sized ones having ten pairs of oars and a rudder, although the largest known was 130 feet long with sixty pairs of oars, a beam of 10 feet, and could carry more than a hundred people. It came from Sääminki in eastern Finland. Swedish church boats differ in detail, for example by using a steering oar instead of a rudder. The Swedes claim that church boat rowing has been going on for a thousand years without a break. The species is also to be found in the far north in Lappland, which spans Finland, Norway and Sweden, and the earliest record of organized competition is in 1817. There is more on church boats in chapter 4. Meanwhile, let the claim remain on the table. We will visit the third great centre of rowing tradition and influence, Venice.

3

THE VENETIANS

WILLIAM PINARELLO has a desk in the Customs House on the end of the the quay which marks the meeting of the Grand Canal, the Giudecca Canal and St Mark's Canal. Pinarello has to step outside to see the pink of the piazza of St Mark's across water poppled with gondolas, and vaporetti and *motoscafi* plying their trade where the Grand mingles with the larger channels of the lagoon. Cruise liners creep into berths near the arsenal which gave Venice a fleet and an array of skills with which to dominate the Mediterranean for centuries. Ships are banned from the canals under measures to stop Venice sinking into her own lagoon. A car ferry is the largest vessel to sail the Giudecca and the St Mark's canals which separate the city of the sea from the islands of Giudecca and S. Giorgio Maggiore.

Part of the Customs House remains a customs house, but the tip of the building is the home of Bucintoro, which claims to be the oldest among the forty or so rowing clubs of Venice. Pinarello is president. Canottieri Bucintoro, founded in 1882, takes its name from the Doge's gilded barge which, propelled by forty-two oars and 168 oarsmen, supported a huge image of the winged lion of St Mark and Justice, fine of figure, sword and scales in her hand, beneath a sumptuous red canopy. The first Bucintoro was launched in 1311, others in 1520, 1605 and 1727. Each year on Ascension Day the Doge and dignitaries were rowed out to sea for a ceremony commemorating the defeat of the Dalmatian pirates in the year 1000. The Doge cast a gold wedding ring from his finger into the waves and addressed the sea: 'We espouse thee, O Sea, in token of our true and perpetual dominion over thee.' Hundreds of ships, galleys, gondolas and brigantines witnessed the ceremony and rejoiced. Bells rang out, cannon sounded, musicians played, the people sang. It was, perhaps, a ceremony in the nature of a regatta, though the great salute to the sea and the state did not run to races. The Bucintoro ventured out on ceremonial occasions until Napoleon's men burned the last one early in the nineteenth century. To the French it was a symbol of the Venetian power they had destroyed. Some of them thought the Bucintoro was made of gold. For days its ruins smouldered as soldiers sought in vain to catch the melted 'precious metal'. After the Austrians entered Venice in 1814 the hulk was first used as a coastguard battery ship and then as a home for convicts.

At first the Bucintoro Club concerned itself with traditional Venetian rowing, but soon adopted *voga inglese* as well, one of only five Venetian clubs so to do. Its small office is hung with pictures and trophies recording a distinguished history. Its traditional boats are kept round the corner in a large stone warehouse, many of them built by Enzo Fagherazzi in the club's workshop at the rear. The club's modern racing boats are housed in another boathouse at the other end of the Grand Canal, where the water is flatter and so better for rowing. 'There are too many engines,' says Pinarello, a retired banker, as he looks out of the Customs House, 'and there are too many tourists. Tourists are the new barbarians.'

It was not 'barbarians' who eventually destroyed Venice's power, but more the pull of the New World slowly dragging the epicentre of economic power from the Mediterranean to the eastern seaboard of the Americas. Venice was built by people who retreated from Goths and Huns to the islands of the northeast Adriatic and developed a swampy maze into the city in the sea. She became a massive naval power and unrivalled trading city-state; the ebb of her power and influence has left an enchanting monument where streets are canals and where water is the essence of life. Oarpower was the foundation, and oars and rowing boats still compose part of her commercial traffic and underpin her recreation and sport. There are no playing fields squeezed between her cobbled alleyways and squares. Palaces and churches, coffee houses and hotels spill their clients into ferries and aboard gondolas for destinations unattainable on foot. 'We are born in boats, we marry in boats, and we die in boats,' Pinarello says. A water-bound way of life is as total and as natural here as it is now unnatural anywhere else, at least in the developed world. Little wonder that *regatas*, an evocative word given to us by the Venetians, attract thousands of spectators and hundreds of boats, and that the best performers are named Kings of the Oar and are treated as such. A hundred thousand people will watch the top men performing to the tune of 40 million lira a year, the top women to 10 million.

Oarsmen and Their Ships

From 1200 to 1500 Venice was the dominant power in the eastern Mediterranean, and hugely influential for long periods before and after. The Venetians had no land to live off or control; their countryside was the sea, and on it they bettered the Dalmatian pirates, the rival Italian mercantile cities of Amalfi, Pisa and Genoa, the Ottoman Empire and the Crusaders. They developed independence from the Byzantine Empire and, together with Florence, became the middle men between Byzantine East and European West. They beat pirates by force and kept others at arm's length by diplomacy. Above all, they secured their position by the longship and the round ship, and then by a hybrid of the two. The latter were privately built sail-powered broad-beamed merchantmen which voyaged to the Black Sea and to Britain, trading in silver, copper and cloth from the British Isles and Flanders, wine from Crete, and Egyptian cotton, grain and sugar. The longships were sleek warships which went under sail or oar and which could outmanoeuvre any round ship. They were built in the Venetian state Arsenal, a huge industrial complex to the east of the city. Towards the end of the thirteenth century came the great galley, a huge merchant ship with the shape of the longship but with greater depth and width. Built in the Arsenal, the galleys were operated by the state and later used as warships. With them the Venetians milked the treasures of the East.

By the sixteenth century, while most Mediterranean galleys were rowed *al scaloccio*, the Venetian war galleys were rowed *alla sensile*. The former means that all the men on a bench pulled on the same oar. The Venetian way was for three men to share a bench each with his own oar. There were twenty-four or twenty-five benches on either side of the ship. The oars varied in length from 31 to 33 feet. Early galleys had two oars to a bench, and then the number was increased to three, four and five, but the three-oared ships were the best.

Like the Greeks – and the Indonesians, who developed long-hulled *praus* with two or three levels of oars – the Venetians did not leave much evidence of their method of galley rowing. Naval historians confirmed the system with the help of Christoforo Canal's *De La Militia Marittima* and a painting by Vittore Carpaccio. The oars were pivoted on an outrigger running the length of the ship about 3 feet from the gunwale. For cruising at 3 or so knots the men were seated, but for sprinting they stood with one foot on a rest and hauled themselves back onto the seat to take a stroke. The carvel-built galleys were 17 feet wide and about 137 feet long, with a draft of 5 feet, displacing only 200 tons, and they could achieve about 7 knots at a rating of twenty-six strokes per minute. Their design reflected the most favoured form of combat: their role was to ram an enemy ship and cripple it at the same time by firing a point-blank salvo, and then board it with fighting men. Thus the galleys had an iron-shod ram above the waterline, a gundeck at the bow which carried a large central-line gun, a couple of half-culverins and four swivel-mounted cannon. There were swivel guns at the stern, too, to repel boarders. Above the gundeck was a platform for archers and musketeers.

The war galley had one sail; the great galleys built at the end of the fifteenth century had three, and oars were the secondary source of power, only used when the ships neared port. They carried up to 200 men plus twenty to thirty bowmen. Later, bows were replaced by heavy-calibre matchlock guns called harquebuses. Galleys often travelled in convoys to deter pirates. In 1509 a fleet sailed from Southampton to the heel of Italy in thirty-one days.

As the maritime empire moved through the centuries, so the lot of the oarsman deteriorated. When the Venetians first used galleys officers were drawn from the nobility, sailors from ships' carpenters and other craftsmen, and oarsmen were conscripted or hired as mercenaries. In emergencies oarsmen were recruited by lot, one, two or three being drawn from each group of twelve able-bodied citizens. Wages were paltry, much lower than earnings for unskilled labouring in the Arsenal, but on board the ship was a spirit of cooperation, with sailors and oarsmen helping out the soldiers and vice versa. Officers had no great advantage of expertise over the men. With

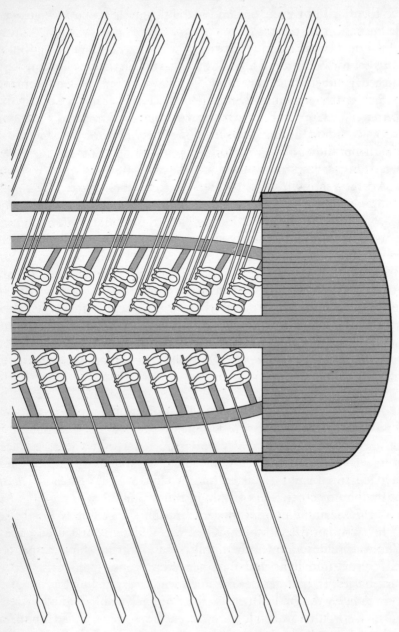

Rowing alla sensile, *the system used by the Venetians* (top)
Rowing al scaloccio, *the system used by other Mediterranean galleys*
(bottom)

specialization, however, came a hardening of the strata of society. The invention of the mariner's compass in the fourteenth century opened up new possibilities but also required expert knowledge; as the crossbow became more powerful, the requirements of armament changed. Soldiers, moreover, had to provide their own equipment, whereas oarsmen, unlike their Athenian forebears, did not. Hence the rowers fell in status even though their wages rose. Desertion became common. In the 1350s Admiral Nicol Pisani tried to improve the oarsmen's diet by asking for salt pork on three days a week and cheese and sardines on other days, but the Senate rejected his proposal, presumably mindful of costs. The conscripts were allowed a bundle of possessions and booty in wartime, but their life became less conducive to effective rowing. By the end of the sixteenth century, things worsened. Debtors and criminals, their heads shaven, crewed the galleys, manacled to benches until release or death. They wore a uniform of cap, shirt, linen trousers, knee-length tunic and cloak, a different colour for each galley. The 'volunteer' category of prisoner, who were mostly debtors, were allowed to walk the deck in leg irons, to wear a moustache, and to eat the sailors' diet of biscuits, cheese, beans, salt pork and wine. They were sometimes set free to fight. The *condemnati* were those under death sentence or criminals who were commuting, say, a five-year gaol sentence to two years in the galleys. They had the worst rations: 30 ounces of biscuit a day and water. In port and in winter they were given bean soup with oil every other day, but only received meat and wine four times a year on religious and state festivals. In the event of offences on board, the galley warden was supervisor, judge and executioner.

The oarsmen had tasks other than rowing to perform. They were responsible for stitching sails and clothing, softening the tallow for the oarlocks, handling mooring ropes, ringing the bell for morning and evening prayers, and, according to the seventeenth-century chronicler Pantero Pantera, forming a band of eight trumpeters 'for the comfort and lightness of spirit of those aboard'. Hell on the water hailed by fanfares.

The mighty Arsenal also reflected the levels of Venetian society. The idea for it came from the state enterprises of Byzantium, the name from the Arabic *dar-sina'a*, meaning 'a house of industry', for Venice was not the only place to build large fleets of ships. The Arsenal was situated on the twin islands of Zemelle. By the end of the fifteenth century it had grown into a 60-acre dock and factory capable of building 116 galleys simultaneously. Inside its 50-foot crenelated pink brick wall were stone sheds for shipbuilding, plus an oar-making room large enough to hold 2500 people for meetings of the Great Council when the Doge's palace was gutted by fire in 1577. There was a vast hall for rope making, and another for masts and spars. All manner of armament was fashioned there by thousands of *arsenalotti*, skilled craftsmen who held considerable social status and could pull muscle in labour disputes. Their wages were regulated by the state and they had ceremonial duties. They could buy some commodities at preferential rates and lived with their families in houses inside the Arsenal. But they were not allowed to leave and work in private industry.

By the end of the fourteenth century there were 16,000 *arsenalotti*, and the Venetian republic had 36,000 seamen manning 3300 ships. There was rigid quality control and inspection by the elected lords and commissioners, men who had proved their worth in the service of the state. The key men were the foremen of carpenters or ship-wrights, naval architects who chose timber and supervised construction. They were responsible for trying out other kinds of ship, like the 158-foot five-men-to-a-bench galley designed in 1525 by Professor Vettor Fausto, who worked as a designer at the Arsenal. It raced against a conventional galley in 1529, proving that five men with an oar each could share a bench and win a trial. But the ship was found to be unseaworthy in service off Crete.

The admiral of the Arsenal took responsibility for the outfitting production line. Hulls were built and laid up in dry dock, while fittings were stockpiled and numbered according to galley. When required, hulls were floated into the central basin where they were fitted with rudders and masts, and then towed along the canal towards the Arsenal gate. As they passed warehouses on either side they received ropes, food, armament, ammunition and, finally, oars. The Spanish traveller Pero Tafur witnessed ten galleys emerge in this way in six hours.

Great attention was given to timber. Oak from the Italian main-land or the Istrian peninsula at the head of the Adriatic was used for ribs, keels and planking. It was soaked in seawater until required. Bracing timbers were made of larch, masts and spars of fir, and oars of beech from Croatia.

Galleys apart, there were other oarpowered naval ships for other tasks: the 100-oared *gatti*, the light transport *ganzaruoli*, the *panfili*, the *marraani*, the *dromoni*, the *chelandie*, the *cursorie*, the *panzone*, the *roscone*, the *olcadi*, and the *asiri*. In the sixteenth century came the eighteen-oared *fregate*, or scouting vessel, the twenty-eight-oared brigantine with a cabin in the stern, and the *galeas*, which had thirty guns, sails and 343 oarsmen. The latter type took part in the Spanish Armada in 1588, beaten by storm in the Bay of Biscay early in the proceedings. If they had reached the shallows off Calais they might well have done serious damage to Admiral Drake's English fleet.

It is hardly surprising that this city of the sea which rowed herself into history gave the regatta to the world. The earliest reference to a *regata* is on 16 September 1274, but Venetian tradition has it that the true regatta is linked to the Feast of St Mary on Candlemas Day, held on the 2 February until 1379. This date commemorates a raid in 942 when pirates from Trieste mingled with the crowd in the church of San Pietro di Castello during the annual celebration of marriages, at which girls met their grooms, relatives and friends. The brigands carried off several brides and their dowries. The Doge Pietro Candiano III organized the pursuit, which resulted in the death of the pirates two days later. The Doge decreed that twelve poor girls should be married at the state's expense each year. They were carried in procession along the Grand Canal by two fifty-oared craft. Pace del Friuli refers to this event as a race in Latin verse in about 1300, the first account of a regatta.

The Venetians can prove the existence of true competitive events after this date. In 1315 Doge Soranzo issued a decree in 1315 that on the feast of St Paul (25 January) a regatta should be run for youths in fifty-oar boats. A decree in 1531 ordered the Arsenal to build twenty-five racing craft for races to be held four times a year. The course was from Porto di Malamocco to the Customs House, and six crews were drawn by lot from among 4000 men; prizes ranged from 200 ducats for winners to 40 ducats for sixth place. At this time the term *regata* seems to have meant both a single race and a collection of races including the festivities surrounding them. From time to time there were special regattas in honour of individuals, such as that for Marquis Nicolo d'Este di Ferrara in 1369, or the six regattas held on 17 May 1569 for Archduke Charles of Austria, which included races for women. Women began racing in

1493 when forty-eight of them competed in twelve-oared craft in honour of Eleonora d'Este and her daughter Beatrice. Men and women, the former naked, competed in regattas for Queen Anne of Hungary in 1502. In 1607 the counsellor of the King of Spain, Don Sebastian Cortizzos, was honoured with seven regattas, and on the 25 June 1686 the Duke of Brunswick sponsored eleven. The eighteenth century saw many such events, the heroine of the century being Maria Boscola who began winning races in 1740 and finished with two wins in 1784, forty-four years later. In 1751 eight noblewomen raced along the Brenta from Venice to Padua.

During the Renaissance regattas were organized by associations of young noblemen, but from the mid-sixteenth century the government appointed specific noblemen (*direttori di regata*) to supervise them. Most of the events mentioned above were part of a religious or civic occasion, but regattas also developed as challenges between gondoliers and boatmen in a variety of rowing boats. More than half a dozen traditional annual regattas still take place in Venice, the largest and best known being the Regata Storica, and several types of boat are used besides the gondola.

The characteristics of Venetian rowing are that the stroke is performed standing up and facing the direction in which the boat is travelling, and that the oar is not locked into the *forcole* or oarlock. The method evolved because in narrow and crowded canals it is necessary to see where you are going and to be able to retract the oar quickly. In many places there is not enough room for two oars. Shallow and sometimes rough water requires small boats which can be turned and beached easily. The *caorlina*, for example, is the classic cargo boat for confined waters, 9 metres long by a little more than 1 metre wide and rowed by six oarsmen. The *sandolo*, of similar dimensions, is the most common craft in the lagoon, a solid fishing, transport and racing boat. The *mascareta* is a lighter version of the *sandolo* and much favoured by women for racing: it is 8 metres long by 1.18 metres wide. The *gondolino* is a racing version of the gondola, weighing only 1.6 cwt against 3.2 cwt for the gondola. It is very fast and difficult to handle. The *pupparin* is 9–10 metres long, with a sharply pointed bow and a squared stern like the *sandolo* and the *mascareta*: it is rowed by one or two men. Frederick Rolfe (1860–1913, alias Baron Corvo) described a *pupparin* in *The Desire and Pursuit of the Whole*:

Directly after luncheon, the two went to the squero of Grassi by Sanzani-polo to get a pupparin. A pupparin is a smaller bark than a gondola, six to eight metres long against the other's eleven and without the twisted-up steel-armed fore and aft. It is flat-bottomed, like a gondola; and has the same curious but calculated curve in length, the same excess on the right which balances the weight of the gondolier poised high on the left. Its prow is sharply beaked: its poop (from which it takes its name) is pertly spread and tilted like the tail of a merle at moments. Crabbe's pupparin was very long and slim: it would carry one passenger in ease with three oarsmen at pleasure.

He was pleased with the look of this slim ship. It was black and smart and polished, and promised speed. Grassi had pitched and tallowed it without, and painted it within; and had fitted it with new gleaming-white floor-boards, and new oars and forcole nicely oiled and brown. It had none of the rumpled carpets or greasy brass-work or dusty cushions or funeral palls beloved of Venetians, but just a very low cane arm-chair which could be thrown about and used or not used. High on the prow rose a thin bright brazen rod, surmounted by a hollow orb, and bearing the miniature vexilla of the Royal Bucintoro Rowing Club in red silk and gold . . . Otherwise the bark was bare, built for use and stripped for speed.

The gondola is the classic Venetian boat, still plentiful on the canals, carrying tourists and doing ferry duty, although much less common than in its heyday in 1600 when there were 10,000. The six teeth on its ornamental metal beak represent the districts of Venice. It is rowed by a single *gondoliere*, draws little water and turns easily. It is 11 metres long, 1.37 metres wide overall, 0.96 metres wide at the hull, and 0.52 metres high amidships. It acquired its aura of melancholia, mystery and adventurousness partly from the fact that it is black, an austere livery imposed upon it by decree in the seventeenth and eighteenth centuries to cut out ostentatious competition between noblemen. But some have a gilded prow and richly carved decoration.

The American writer Mark Twain, travelling on a grand cruise through France, Italy, Greece, Russia and the Holy Land in 1867, was enraptured by the gondola, just as thousands have been before and since. He described it as 'as free and graceful, in its gliding movement, as a serpent', its sharp bow and stern sweeping upward from the water like the horns of a crescent. And the gondolier is a picturesque rascal for all he wears no satin harness, no plumed bonnet, no silken tights. His attitude is stately; he is lithe and supple; all his movements are full of grace. When his long canoe, and his fine figure, towering from its high perch on the stern, are cut against the evening sky, they make a picture that is very novel and striking to the foreign eye.

Twain took off along the waterways:

> Sometimes we go flying down the great canals at such a gait that we can get only the merest glimpses into front doors, and again, in obscure alleys in the suburbs, we put on a solemnity suited to the silence, the mildew, the stagnant waters, the clinging weeds, the deserted houses, and the general lifelessness of the place, and move to the spirit of great meditation.

Twain confessed that he studied the gondolier's marvellous skill more than the 'sculptured palaces we glide among. He cuts a corner so closely, now and then, or misses another gondola by such an imperceptible hair-breadth that I feel myself "scrooching", as the children say, just as one does when a buggy wheel grazes his elbow.' He observed closely the gondolier's art:

> The stern of the boat is decked over and the gondolier stands there. He uses a single oar – a long blade, of course, for he stands nearly erect. A wooden peg, a foot and a half high, with two slight crooks or curves in one side of it and one in the other, projects above the starboard gunwale. Against that peg the gondolier takes the purchase with his oar, changing it at intervals to the other side of the peg or dropping it into another of the crooks, as the steering of the craft may demand – and how in the world he can back and fill, shoot straight ahead, or flirt suddenly around a corner, and make the oar stay in those insignificant notches, is a problem to me and a never diminishing matter of interest. But he makes all his calculations with the nicest precision, and goes darting in and out among a Broadway confusion of busy craft with the easy confidence of the educated hackman. He never makes a mistake.

The present shape of the gondola came about in the 1880s when Domenico Tramontin found that by making one side larger than the other the vessel would turn on its own axis and move faster. His descendants build gondolas in three different yards, keeping the craft alive. At the recently restored San Trovaso yard on the Dorsoduro, Nardo Ettore makes and repairs them. Two hundred and eighty pieces of timber cut from elm, oak, lime, walnut, larch, fir, cherry, beech and mahogany comprise one gondola. Walnut is the favoured wood for the *forcole* or rowlock, which resembles a gnarled arm with a tightly clenched fist on it. Ideally it should be cut from one piece, and there are fifteen models for different classes of boat, made in specialist workshops like that of Giuseppe Carli. Walnut lasts a long time if seasoned for six months and causes little wear on the oar. Pear is also good, though liable to split if not seasoned thoroughly. Cherry is the third choice of timber for the *forcole*, used with variations on all the traditional boats.

The traditional regatta course is on the lagoon immediately in front of St Mark's and the Grand Canal. The starting rope is the *spaghetto* opposite the public gardens; the turning point is marked by the *paletto* , a pole in the centre of the Grand Canal; and the finish is marked by the *macchina*, a wooden structure on a raft, carved, painted and gilded, which also serves as the prizegiving pontoon.

Thousands of spectators gather in boats and beside the canal, and a pre-race procession is led by a fleet of *bissone* or long boats. These were used to carry noblemen armed with bows, whose job it was to clear the course by pelting unruly spectators with terracotta shot, normally used for hunting coot.

Notoriety and Legacy

Venice's decline as a grand maritime and commercial power left the city to bask in her glory, a colourful compote of medieval achitectural styles, domes and spires, churches and palaces, courtyards and canals, alleyways and coffee houses, a masked ball for playboys and courtesans, a canvas for painters, a resonant auditorium for composers.

Venice swooned to Vivaldi and basked in Canaletto, and claimed a five-star entry in the Grand Tour guide for Europe's cultured classes. She also attracted more humble tourists, particularly the English, whose romantic poets and writers flocked there. And one thing the Venetians borrowed from England was the English style of rowing, where you sit down and face the back. English influence was first seen in the oldest of Venice's present-day clubs, the Bucintoro and the Querini, where the modern style of rowing in English boats was introduced alongside traditional rowing in the 1880s. In Bucintoro's case it was Count Piero Venier, who returned from a visit to England enthused with what he found. His club began to attract notorious foreign members, too, including James Gordon Bennett (1841–1918), founder of the Paris edition of the *New York Herald* (now the *International Herald Tribune*). His business flare bought him the steam yacht *Lysistrata*, largest ever built on the Clyde in Scotland, and he moored her in St Mark's basin to host lavish receptions. He spent $30 million on sporting trophies, donating several to the Bucintoro. His prizes appear in Naples rowing circles, too.

Even more notorious was the eccentric, impoverished English sponger Frederick Rolfe (1860–1913). Variously a gifted musician, painter and writer, he became a 'defeated man of genius', according to his biographer A. J. Symons. Known as Baron Corvo, he was a homosexual in Victorian England, which was not a ticket for an easy life. He had failed to become a Catholic priest or to find a career in schoolmastering. His odd-job life produced some brilliant literary work which brought him no income, and ended with his death in Venice after a long love affair with the city and several of its gondoliers. He wrote a homily to Venice and the Bucintoro club in *The Desire and Pursuit of the Whole*, published posthumously in 1934. At one time he lived at the Bucintoro or squatted in its boats. His election to the Bucintoro came about after he fell overboard in the Grand Canal while rowing a *sandolo* in the Venetian style, and swam under water some distance from the boat before coming to the surface with his pipe still in his mouth. Back in the boat, he refilled the pipe from his waterproof rubber pouch, asked for a light, cried '*Avanti!*', and went on his way. His sang-froid and his aquatic fervour gained him membership. For all his reputation as a master of the insult and in Symons's words, his 'knowledge of the dark byways' of Venice, the Baron had a humanitarian side. After the great earthquake at Messina in December 1908 he used the Bucintoro's fleet to tour the city and hustle for food, clothes and building materials for the sufferers. He also provided convalescent patients at the English hospital with sunshine and fresh air by rowing them about.

If Venetians have not played a large part in international rowing, this is partly because they have the rival attractions of their own style of rowing and its accompanying prize money, sponsorship and vast crowds. Rowing remains poplar in all its forms, the Vogalonga being a comparatively recent addition to the regatta calendar. This is a 30-kilometre race for anything moved by oars. It starts from the Bucintoro and St Mark's, moves round the lagoon in a figure of eight, and returns to the Bucintoro along the length of the Grand Canal. The Venetians have a unique place in the story of rowing: they rowed themselves into their own history and gave the world the *regata*. Even in a world now plagued by motorboats, the gondola holds its own. The culture of the oar that is Venice's own is underpinned by family rivalries that reach back for generations. The treasures are in the hands of William Pinarello and the rowers, from both the Venetian and English disciplines, of Canottieri Bucintoro and the other clubs of the lagoon.

4

TRADITIONAL ROWING

'To my mind,' wrote T. C. Lethbridge in *Boats and Boatmen* (1952), 'the boat is man's greatest triumph over nature. With it, taking his life in his hands in a splendid gamble, he forced his way into every corner of the globe. It was not comparable to trudging across the continents beside a pack-pony. He was risking his life from the moment he pushed his boat down the beach, whether he was just going fishing, or off to investigate that unknown blue streak showing against the cloudbank on the horizon. Without the boat, there would be no history of Britain. Everything that came to Britain had to cross that strip of water, which still separates us from the land mass of the great continents. You could not walk round it. Nor could you walk into America from Asia. Therefore I believe the boat to have been the most important invention that man has ever made. You can eat food raw, you can walk thousands of miles without a cart, but you cannot populate the globe without a boat. The whole story of man is one of struggle to free himself from the tyranny of his environment. In this struggle the boat has played a dramatic part.'

And so has the oar, the lever which made much of the boat's work possible. As Tennyson said in *Ulysses*, let us

> Push off, and sitting well in order smite
> The sounding furrows . . .

Here is Arthur Grimble arriving at Ellice Island (Tuvalu) in the Pacific from a steamship which took him there as a British administrator in 1914:

The swells got steeper where the bottom rose towards the reef. As their racing slopes snatched up our stern and tossed it high, the oarsmen fought to keep pace with the forward 'scend of them, and the boat drove on, impossibly tilted, into valleys that forever fled away from under the plunging bows. But the bronze giant at the steer-oar stood easily poised on the tiny locker-deck behind us. His bare feet braced against the gunwales, he swung in lovely rhythm to the heave and thrust of the seas upon his oar, and sang aloud for the joy of his mastery as he brought the boat swooping like a gull towards the boat harbour. His voice cut across the crashing diapason of the surf with the gay challenge of a clarion. When we came to the very edge of the reef – so near it seemed nothing could stop our onrush into the maelstrom – he called all of a sudden, 'Easy!' The crew lay on their oars and waited. The passage into the boat harbour, a narrow channel blasted through the reef, was a few lengths ahead, its entrance wide open to the giant seas. The lesser surfs were breaking short of the entrance, and the backsuck from the brimming harbour basin – we could hear it snarling – fought their furious invasion to make a hell's cauldron of the passage. No boat could live in that raging battle of waters. The only safe way in was to ride on the crest of a wave so big that it would sweep the boat well down the passage before being undercut by the backsuck. We lay rearing and plunging while the steersman picked his wave. It came, house-high: 'Pull!' he yelled as its forefoot lifted the stern. We shot forward; the crest swung us towering; the crew spent their last ounce of strength to hold it; we held it – we were riding Leviathan – we were flying – we were half way down the passage. The crest began to topple and foam overside. The wave hollowed itself for breaking, and the boat's nose was pushed out into the void over its forefoot. There was a sizzling downward rush through ruin as it collapsed; the sea came boiling in over the gunwales; the life went out of the boat; we were labouring, half waterlogged. But we were safe in the still water of the boat harbour.

Spanish Traineras

There was a gentle sea for the grand finale to the season as *Koxtape* and *Sanpedrotarra* set off from outside the fishing harbour at Getaria for Donostia. Thirteen men strained in each *trainera*, *Koxtape* from San Juan wearing Leander pink and steered by Juan Maria Lujambio, the rival crew from San Pedro in purple and steered by Juan Carlos Fontan. They were almost swallowed up by steam from a naval vessel among the flotilla of boats ranging from trawlers to inflatables which gave chase.

The race to Donostia, better known outside the Basque country as San Sebastian, is 9 nautical miles, for which the record is one hour five minutes. Traditionally it takes place between the two fastest crews in the regattas for *traineras* held in San Sebastian's scallop-shaped bay on the first two Sundays of September. *Traineras* are 12 metres long. *Trainera* oarsmen sit alongside each other in pairs, while the thirteenth man changes sides if called upon to do so by the cox. The cox is also the trainer, commanding from the stern with his long steering oar. On this sunny and breezy occasion the contest is between two villages which can almost shake hands across the steep sides of the narrow harbour entrance to Pasajes de San Juan, which is the fishing and car export port of San Sebastian. Hundreds of their supporters are present in the pink-and-purple-bedecked pursuing flotilla. There is wine on the bridge of the trawler and beer on the deck. There are hampers of tapas, and a great many photographs are taken. Round the cliffs and along the quay at San Sebastian bookmakers do business, for the backbone of *trainera* racing is betting. Thousands of pesetas change hands on a race, some of it through official channels where punters must place boats in the correct finishing order, but most of it through 'on course' bookies where there are no rules. The oarsmen are paid by their clubs, and some crews may be sponsored for as much as 5 million pesetas.

Racing *traineras* is a tradition which began formally in 1879 when the town of San Sebastian organized a regatta as a tourist attraction. But betting on Sunday competitions between fishermen began at the end of the eighteenth century. At that time there was whaling in the area, in addition to the twenty-man fishing boats and smaller, faster craft used for bringing the sardine catch quickly to market. These sardine boats were manned by thirteen men with a cox. There were also sixteen-oar pilot boats, often pulled by women or mixed crews, which raced to ships to secure towing contracts. After 1910 steam power diplaced oarpower for fishing, but San Sebastian was a royal resort and popular with English tourists, and the regattas satisfied the Basques' twin passions for gambling and tough physical competition. By the 1920s rowing was mainly for gambling and pleasure. The weight of the boats had been reduced from 500 kilos to 200 kilos. Racing spread along the whole of the Spanish north coast, so that now there are *traineras* at about thirty-five clubs in Cantabria, Asturias and Galicia, as well as the Basque country.

The boats are made of Canadian cedar. Traditionally black-hulled, they are now painted in club colours and sponsors' logos. Before the steam trawler, boats were privately owned and manned almost exclusively by fishermen, owners dividing the winnings among the crew. But now that fishermen stay at sea for several weeks on end, farmers, landlubbers and students have taken up oars and villages sponsor their own boats. The club at Orio, for example, has 500 members, of whom seventy are active at the oar. The land on which the large boatshed and gymnasium are situated was donated by a supporter and is near the mouth of a river, so their two *traineras* can go to sea while their 'Olympic' crews can slide off upstream. Olympic rowing was introduced to the area in 1949 but has never had the appeal of *traineras* among the Basques. *Traineras* regattas take place on rivers, in harbours, and at sea from June to September. The races are rowed in four lanes round a stake, 1.5 nautical miles each way. At the start the cox holds a rope attached to a stakeboat or hung from an overhead wire. The boats always turn (*ciaboga* in Spanish, *ziaboga* in Basque) anti-clockwise. The bow oarsman uses a short oar to help the cox steer, while the *babor* side holds water and the *estribon* side rows normally. The cox's steering oar is tied to its pin or *tolete* by a rope called the *estrobo*. These boats are capable of rowing in heavy seas, for which they are fitted with 'false bows' or a *palka*, a sock-like breakwater which fits over the real bow. The knack is to raise the rating high when a wave lifts the stern in order to ride its crest. In calm water the cox stands down in the boat and keeps his blade out of the water, while in rough seas he stands up and digs deep. It is exhilarating to watch and to row. The technique is sometimes learned in *batels* or traditional coxed fours, progressing to *trainerillas*, which have six oars.

San Pedro and San Juan, meanwhile, are creaming along the rugged coastline while crowds gather at every vantage point around the bay at San Sebastian. On this occasion the weather gives the boats a trouble-free run. There are few opportunities for riding crests and few incidents of helter-skeltering into troughs out of sight of the spectator fleet. The pinkos arrive first in 1 hour 8 minutes 40.91 seconds, San Pedro following them home in 1 hour 9 minutes 28.07 seconds. A throng welcomes them at the harbour, and, after breath is recovered and boats secured on trailers, the prize is handed over at the yacht club.

That evening the street is quiet in San Pedro. The rowing club is a cosy building facing the quay. The floor is red-tiled, trophies and photos line the walls, men prepare dinner in the kitchen, a gourmet repast. San Sebastian's other passion is its stomach and the C. R. Sanpedrotarra is no exception. In the city there are numerous men-only dining clubs with seafood a speciality. At this rowing club there is evidence of family participation. The valiant crew have not yet appeared, and this is an occasion to take the ferry to San Juan and leave the losers to turn their grief into resolve to win next year.

San Juan is dripping with pink, flags hanging from windows and bridging the narrow streets and terraces. Half the people are wearing the colour as they promenade along the tree-lined terrace which overlooks the harbour mouth and the half-erected new boathouse belonging to their rivals, ominously facing the narrows from the other shore. 'They speak to each other, but be careful if you want to marry a girl from the other side,' said the ferryman. All was set for a perfect evening in the tapas bar followed by seafood supper, made all the better by the feat of the crew of the *Koxtape*.

A Catholic Collection

The maritime museum in Barcelona is housed in the fourteenth-century naval dockyard, which is now separated from the old harbour by a highway. It is a perfect setting for its Catalan boat and model collection, which includes a full-size replica of Don Juan of Austria's elaborately adorned galley *Real*. The original was built in the yard and saw service at the battle of Lepanto in 1571, its massive oars pulled by a crew of 256. Ceremonial flagships and royal barges were used from Spain to Thailand. Various kinds of barque survive in the Arabian Gulf, such as the sixty-man boats of Qatar, where crews from Doha and Al-Khawr race on the anniversary of the emir's accession. Twenty-metre fixed-seat *hawaris* with crews of forty-eight, two to an oar, can move at 30 kilometres an hour, faster than a racing eight. Ceremonial boats which can still be seen in museums include Napoleon I's twenty-eight-oared *canot*, complete with cherubs, sea serpents and cabin ceiling in gold relief, and built in twenty-one days for a review in Angers in 1810. Neptune is on the bow and the oars have white looms and blades, each blade enhanced by a carved gilded fish. It can be found in the maritime museum in Paris. On the Thames in Britain the City livery companies and noblemen with houses on the river had barges with their own uniformed crews, and so did the Lord Mayor of London and the monarch. Several can be seen at the National Maritime Museum in Greenwich.

Such specimens rarely venture onto the water, but ordinary workaday boats or derivations of traditional boats are to be found in many parts of the world being used for pleasure and for sport. Around the coasts of the British Isles are longboats on the Welsh coast in Pembrokeshire, seine boats in the southwest of Ireland, and racing gigs on the northeast coast of England and in Cornwall and the Scilly Isles. The Clyde and the Forth in Scotland have jollyboats, and other variations are to be found off the Donegal and Antrim coasts of Ireland. There are rowing clubs along the south coast of England which use boats which are basically sea-going versions of racing shells.

The Irish seine boats, originally designed for seine-net fishing but now blessed for speed when they are launched, have six oars with two men on each and race a triangular course round two buoys. Racing dates from the beginning of the twentieth century, with a revival in the 1950s, and these fast boats can be found at Valencia, Castlemaine, and on Waterville Lake in Kerry. On the east coast of England Whitby Friendship Amateur RC (1879) is the best-known club for gig racing, situated in the home town of the famous Pacific explorer James Cook. In 1872 there was word of a club called the Jet Workers' Amateur Boat Club. Hartlepool, Blyth and Scarborough have been or are involved in coastal rowing, and there is a rival club in Whitby called the Fishermen's.

The Cornish and Scilly Isle gigs are six-oared boats with a history of piracy as well as pilot service. The gig was originally a four-oar harbour and inshore craft light enough to be launched from a ship's deck by two men. They were craft of Nelson's era and ancestors of the racing eight. In Cornwall the first six-oared side-seated gig can be traced to 1791, built by Peters of St Mawes at the behest of a clergyman and probably used as a lifeboat at Padstow. The Peters family built gigs into the second half of the twentieth century. Narrow-leaf wych elm was used for the clinker planking, mature timber seasoned for five years in mud and usually lasting much longer than the keels and timbers, which were made from American elm. The expert sawyer who cut the planks each year used to arrive at the Peters yard from Penryn by hand-powered paddle boat. Gigs were fast and suitable for any weather, ideal for carrying pilots to ships, the first pilot to reach the ship securing the contract. They were also efficient at smuggling cargo between the Scillies and Brittany, rowed 'cut-throat', that is, with an odd number of blades, having an extra one on the leeward side when the wind was on the beam. The government prohibited the construction of eight-oared gigs in the 1860s because they could outpace a Revenue cutter. Professional gig racing began in the 1840s and thrived until the twentieth century. Revival came during the 1960s, and new boats have been added to the fleet alongside surviving nineteenth-century craft. The *Newquay* has records going back to 1813, and was still racing in the 1980s. Championships are held over a 2½-mile triangular course. In 1981 a crew from Newquay won the New York International Lifeboat Championship. American gigs appear to be based on the New England whaler and have a wider beam than the Cornish, allowing a crew of eight double-banked.

Pilot boats were also the forefathers of pleasure rowing in San Francisco. The South End Rowing Club (1873) and the Dolphin Swimming and Boating Club (1877) were founded just as engines were supplanting oarpower in the race to greet ships sailing in from the Pacific. Rowing had been the obsession of the waterfront for many years. In 1888 Henry C. Peterson backed himself in a race for $2500, which represents three years' wages for a working man at that time. Bets totalling hundreds of thousands of dollars were laid on some crew races. The West Coast Whitehalls used by the pilotage and chandlery companies were slightly deeper and narrower than the East Coast models which were common in New York. The San Francisco clubs now keep their shells on Lake Merced, but they have a variety of boats for use in the salt water of the bay, including their own hybrids of shells and Whitehalls and some boats bearing a resemblance to Cornish gigs. In 1915 two carpenters who were employed making hardwood interiors for San Francisco cable cars made a two-man boat called *Viking* which earned a reputation as a very fast boat before it was added to the Dolphin club's fleet. In 1980 the South End club ordered a replica called the *Valhalla*. The clubs cater for all generations and indulge in swimming, running, cycling and handball, but their main purpose remains rowing.

In Newfoundland traditional boats are rowed on Quidi Vidi Lake. The ports of Gloucester, Massachusetts, and Lunenburg, Nova Scotia, have held international dory races for years. The revival of interest in traditional salt-water rowing is illustrated by the Atlantic Challenge in which crews from Boston, Massachusetts, and Brest and Douarnenez in France race in ten-oar replicas of the Bantry Bay gig. This was a French naval gig captured in Bantry Bay during Wolf Tone's ill-fated invasion of Ireland in 1796. The original can be seen in the Irish National Maritime Museum in Dun Laoghaire, Dublin.

In Norway traditional fixed-seat rowing was much more prevalent than the imported English type well into the twentieth century, and on the lakes of Finland what are known as national boats, manned by one rower and one paddler, outnumber racing shells by thousands. Of the estimated half million rowing boats in Finland, only a few are sliding-seat shells. Church boats (see chapter 2) are among the oldest forms of rowing boats in Scandinavia. Swedish church boats have twenty oars with a steersman who uses a paddle. The most famous area for them is Siljanssockharnes, where there were sixty boats in the 1850s. Finnish church boats have fourteen oars and are steered by a rudder as well as a paddle. Kauko Miettinen is the last church-boatbuilder in Finland, turning out twenty each year. He builds them at Sulkava where his house overlooks the lake which hosts the Sontupitäjä long-distance race in which both church boats and national boats take part. Miettinen is a third-generation boatbuilder. He revived the trade in 1970, after a seventy-year hiatus, steamboats having killed off the long-distance efficiency of church boats and gasoline their short-distance usefulness as working boats. Nineteenth-century boats are still in use in parts of west Finland. Revival came in the 1970s in villages, and then company sponsorship promoted more activity. Miettinen receives orders at the rate of thirty a year, but he can no longer cope with that many. The size of the boats is determined by the maximum permissible length on a boat trailer. Races from Finland to Sweden in higher-sided boats attract up to fifty entries, and Finns have rowed from Helsinki across the Gulf of Finland to Tallinn in Estonia.

Naval gigs and variations on them are still occasionally used in the age of nuclear-powered ships for fitness training, competition and ceremonial duties. In 1990 the Soviet navy was using them in Leningrad, and a couple were spotted by the author scudding across the bay in the sunset at Napoleon's former prison island of Elba. They turn up on the Thames manned by cadets and by policemen for charity events, and something resembling a gig usually appears at traditional boat rallies. Australians row fixed-seat surf boats in the Pacific rollers, a sport with roots in lifesaving. Fixed- and sliding-seat *yolas*, a competition offshoot of the gig, are found as racing classes in several Mediterranean countries, notably Spain, Italy, France, Portugal and Gibraltar, and were in use in Switzerland until the 1980s.

Malta has a long tradition of rowing going back at least to the seventeenth century and the Knights of St John; in 1642 a petition from the people of Cospicua requested permission to race on the feast of Our Lady of Rosary 'as the people of Senglea hold theirs'. The earliest record of racing is a marine police note of 1826 which outlines four competitive events for four-oared fishing boats, two- and four-oared passenger boats, and four-oared caiques. There are now two large regattas each year, the National Regatta on 8 September and the Freedom Regatta on 31 March. These have five boat classes in which six districts – Kalkara, Cospicua, Marsa, Marsa-mett/Valletta, Senglea and Vittoriosa – compete. The unique feature of Maltese rowing is that it combines the Venetian and English styles. A four-oared fancy boat (*dghajjes tal-midalji*) has two men sitting in the bows facing the back and pulling and two men standing in the stern facing the front and pushing. Passenger boats (*dghajjes tal-pass*) with two or four oars and the two-oared caiques (*kajjikki*) have the same arrangement. Only the two-oar-with-cox (*frejgattini*) has both rowers seated and facing the back. Fancy boats and passenger boats are sharp at both ends with high stem and stern posts, while caiques and coxed pairs have square sterns. Oars are attached to olive-wood tholepins with a grommet. Both regattas take place against the magnificent backdrop of the Grand Harbour, where the ancient fortress of Valetta faces the twin peninsulas of Senglea and Vittoriosa, protected by the massive fortifications of the Cottonera Lines. The National Regatta was introduced in 1824 on the feast of Our Lady of Victories. The course is 1040 metres from the New Quay to the Customs House. The Freedom Regatta, first held in 1979, starts at the Customs House and runs 1130 metres up the deep blue Dockyard Creek between Senglea and Vittoriosa.

The Boat as Freedom

Some of the greatest pleasures of rowing have nothing to do with competition. Rowing caters for the lone voyager, the explorer and anyone who just wants to mess about in a boat, as well as for the competitor. Martin Cobbett, for example, a journalist writing in the nineteenth century, extracted the greatest dose of pleasure from Henley regatta simply by getting there:

> I . . . do it in my own way, which is to scull myself up, working the old skiff from bridge to bridge – Maidenhead to Henley – from an early start . . . that is, without an ounce of unnecessary weighty lumber, gratings, carpets, the board up forrard, the cushions and rail, that among them make pretty nearly one man's work to tug along. Why ever on earth people want to clutter up a boat and weigh her down with a cargo of lumber I can never make out. No more pleasant journey than this is to be found on the Thames . . . After you get past Boulter's [Lock] you get the sort of Thames I like. Nobody could possibly help admiring Clivedon, its hanging woods, diversity of foliage, and air of peace . . . but the Thames I care for most has very low banks, so that you from your boat can see across the meads, and mark all manner of vegetable, insect, bird, and beasty life, not forgetting the sleek cows or scenty hay . . .

Five men who rowed from Oxford to London in 1875 in a hired skiff loaded it with all the things which Cobbett despised. They had a short mast to which a towing line was attached, two pairs of sculls, one pair of oars, two boathooks, a stern cushion, two stretchers, two pads, three pieces of matting, two feather pads, a bow lounge board, bow cushion, two one-gallon cans, two pannikins, two windlasses, five rollers, a box of grease, a ball of string, lantern, matches, soap, Ordnance maps, tarpaulin, flag, rug, spare cord, six fenders and, most practically, a Dutch cheese.

At the other extreme are the loners who cross the Atlantic or the Pacific, driven by the fascination of the oceans and the challenge of conquering something because it is there. And there are those like Jill Fredston and her husband Doug, who rowed and paddled, she in a single and he in a canoe, from Blanc Sabron up the coast of Labrador to Cape Chidley in 1989:

> Suddenly we had about twenty whales making false charges at us from

varying directions; our eyes got bigger and our strokes got harder as we watched fins slice towards us at high rates of speed. There wasn't much we could do so we hung as close to the shore as we could, just on the backside of the five-foot waves that were breaking on the rocks . . .

They had encountered mincke whales protecting one of their number which had been gashed by a fishing boat's propeller. There is an old saying, according to Fredston, that God made Labrador in six days and on the seventh threw stones at it. For one period of twenty-three days in this landscape of fjords, waterfalls, jagged peaks and rugged headlands they saw no man, boat or aeroplane. They set foot on white sand beaches named *Wunderstrand* by the Vikings, and could sometimes see the bottom at a depth of 40 feet. They met fishermen, Naskapi Indians and Inuk; caribou, seals and birdlife. They spent four days stranded on a small island in rough seas while successfully avoiding the company of a large polar bear who shared their habitat.

And then there are the drifters and the dreamers:

Around here we usually think of rowing as a solitary art: a Sunday afternoon in spring drizzle out by the channel buoy with a gull or two, or possibly once every three years a harbor seal playing tag with your oar blade; an evening's sculling for bass up by the trestle just when the leaves are turning green and the grass begins to smell, or inside the cove itself in midsummer ghosting through the reeds for blue crabs at midnight with a gas lantern; a dawn run in October to the mooring to rescue something from the approaching storm. But this was to be a festival, a public display of drifters and dreamers who still preferred oars over pistons or even genoa jibs.

Stephen Jones was reflecting on a dripping foggy morn in 1970 as, in the company of two friends, he pulled a Whitehall against the tide on the Mystic River to a small craft conference rowing workshop at the Mystic Seaport museum. This unbecoming title masked a rally, since established as an annual event, of traditional rowing boats at Mystic where John Gardner, dean of small-boat writers and guru of the oar, presides over the workshop. For two days pulling boats of all descriptions from peapods to Saint Lawrence skiffs, from dories to Biloxis, come together, while their owners and restorers breath sawdust and varnish, try out each other's boats, and listen to lectures by builders. America has turned to oar and paddle and wood for pleasure, and revived maritime traditions along her coasts and on her lakes.

Peter H. Spectre, who writes the 'Waterfront' column in *Wooden-Boat* and much else besides, notes that during the Napoleonic Wars Horatio Hornblower made his escape from France with two companions by stealing a tiny rowboat on the Loire and making for the sea. Indeed, the rowboat is freedom for Spectre. As a small boy he discovered 'the ability to walk down the road to the harbour or the shore and step into a little boat without any preparation whatsoever, sit down on the thwart, slide the oarlocks into the sockets, cast off the painter, put the oars into the oarlocks, take a long pull, and be free.'

PART TWO
BOATS

5

WORKBOAT TO RACING BOAT

WHERE people and water mix, small boats have evolved. Their form, construction and means of propulsion are affected by the task expected of them, the materials available from which to build them, and the environment in which they are expected to work. Britain, a set of islands with a long and varied coastline and extensive inland waterways, is a particularly rich hunting ground for those in search of the oarpowered vessel, and the man who has made the most comprehensive study is Eric McKee. He wrote *Working Boats of Britain* (published in 1983) while a research fellow at the National Maritime Museum in Greenwich. At the end of his journey round coasts and up creeks he concluded that, even if oars are no longer the prime mover of a boat, they continue to be the cheapest and surest standby in the late twentieth century. They are also very versatile and can be adapted to almost any boat.

McKee took his lead from Professor Filgueiras's *No crepusculo das embarcacoes regionais*: 'If, in broad terms, the study of Man's implements of work gives a fair measure of his technological and social development, then boats are a particularly important source of material for such evaluation.' McKee believes that once man has developed an implement for a particular purpose he does not alter it until a situation arises that proves it is inadequate, even if he has the means to do so. This is not to be confused with an implement staying the same because the means of improvement are absent. Many aspects of boat shape and structure have changed over the years while others have stayed the same, so he identified both states of affairs as open to investigation.

McKee logged and attempted to codify the countless types of

small boat and the multiple variations in how they were built. Each coastline, and in some cases each beach, caused variations in the shape of fishing boats. In the eighteenth and nineteenth centuries more than a hundred ports required boats for pilots, and Britain's place in the world as a huge naval power and the pioneer of industrialization led to immense activity in building small boats for servicing ships of the line and the merchant fleet. Fishing on inland waters gave rise to boats with woven frames and hulls of hide, sometimes with flat bottoms. One of most enduring inland craft is the coracle, a light round boat most common on the River Severn, which can be rowed or carried by one man and is excellent for fishing and poaching. On rivers, particularly those which bisected large towns and cities, rowing boats were the main means of transport before the steam age.

The problem encountered by McKee is that the labelling of types of boats is random; like irregular verbs in a foreign language, they must be learned. Some names originate from a boat's place of origin, some from its use, and some from its shape – but many names do not. McKee identifies the Baldie as a boat emerging in southeast Scotland in the 1860s at the time when Garibaldi was uniting Italy. It is a variation of a fifie, which was named after Fife. Trying to tie down the ancestors of a boat built solely for pleasure or competition can, therefore, be misleading. There are many boats whose names do not describe their function, and there are many different kinds of boats bearing the same or similar names which have little in common, such as punts, cobles, skiffs, and yawls or yoles. In many cases the name is borrowed from another language, 'punt' and 'yole' being found in Dutch and Spanish respectively. A further difficulty is that for the last century and a half most instruction books on competitive rowing have been written by members of the intelligentsia who have indulged in the sport. They have also written the dictionary definitions of boating, often restricting this to their own experience. Thus the *Concise Oxford Dictionary's* description of a punt as a 'flat-bottomed shallow boat, broad and square at both ends, propelled by a pole thrust against the bottom of the river' applies to, among others, the obscure and threatened species of pleasure craft found at a few places such as Oxford, Cambridge and Stratford-upon-Avon, but ignores types of punt that are rowed. More seriously, the competitive freshwater rower decribes using one oar (sweep) as 'rowing', and using two oars (or sculls) as 'sculling', whereas the saltwater rower in Britain describes working a pair of oars as 'rowing', working one oar as 'pulling' and working one oar over the stern with both hands as 'sculling'. The thwart or seat is 'single-banked' if there is only one man on it and 'double-banked' if there are two. To describe oarpowered sea-going vessels as being rowed, McKee says, is a misnomer: rowing is the one thing that could not have been done with them. However, because modern rowing uses the freshwater terminology, this book does likewise. Here, generally speaking, 'rowing' means using one oar and 'sculling' means using two.

Gigs, Galleys, Wherries, Skiffs

Many of the hundreds of sailing and rowing boats mentioned in McKee's book made the transition from commercial to pleasure and competition use. The best known among the boats used primarily for rowing are gigs, galleys, wherries and skiffs. Gigs and galleys are similar; they are pulling boats with a rudder and a sail, and were used by working boatmen and the Royal Navy. However, any light narrow boat with four or more oars and a small high transom is liable to be called a gig – or even a lighthorseman, a name applied disparagingly to a boat used to pilfer from lighters (barges) in the Thames. Galleys are larger than gigs and are associated with the southeast coast of England where a few, like those from Selsey, were 40-footers with eleven pairs of oars. Gigs are found in the extreme southwest; they are almost 30 feet long with five or six oars. Appledore on the north coast of Devon had one 32 feet long with eight oars. This was the length of the naval galleys when they went out of service during the First World War, while naval gigs were 30 feet long and of carvel construction, the planks laid diagonally to the line of the hull. They became obsolete after the Second World War. McKee says that the magnificent Norfolk and Suffolk beach yawls, now extinct, were once the East Anglian equivalent of galleys and gigs, and are an example of the catholic application of the terms 'yawl' and 'yole'. T. C. Lethbridge in *Boats and Boatmen* says that they were claimed to be the fastest open boats ever built, employing a crew of twenty or more for use from gently sloping beaches to get pilots or assistance to vessels.

Multi-oared working boats were effective into the wind because they were long, light and narrow, but working boats supporting large crews were looked upon with suspicion because they were fast and associated with smuggling. In some cases they could not be operated legally. In 1722, long before the ban on eight-oared gigs referred to in chapter 4, Parliament ruled that any boat with more than four oars along the Dover Straits must be forfeited. Clan chieftains on the west coast of Scotland owned galleys and often displayed fanciful heraldic versions of them in their coats of arms. But multi-oared boats were also life-savers: the Royal National Lifeboat Institution, formed in 1824, was casting around for the most suitable design for its work by the middle of the century. Its early boats were traditional twelve-oars which were found to be good for getting off a beach in bad weather. They were manned by highly paid crews of volunteer fishermen.

Life-saving found an early rowing heroine, too, in Grace Darling, daughter of the keeper of Longstone lighthouse on the Farne Islands off the Yorkshire coast near Whitby. With her father she rescued five people from the paddle steamer *Forfarshire* in 1838 using a type of fishing boat known as a Northumberland coble, her father then returning to rescue four more. Cobles were also responsible for popularizing coastal rowing on the North Sea when crews from Blyth in Northumberland and Staithes in Yorkshire raced in the 10-mile Great Coble Race from Staithes to Whitby in 1866. The Staithes men won £100 and the championship of the North Sea in 1 hour 25 minutes.

The inland waterways produced their own boats too. In the days when good roads were few and far between and were often impassable in winter, rivers and canals were the natural arteries. Kings, bishops, noblemen and city merchants would move about on the Thames in multi-oared barges, competing to clothe their oarsmen in grand livery, and sometimes to arrive first. Some of these boats had many oars, but particular interest falls on the eight- and ten-oared versions as progenitors of the racing eight. Gilbert Bourne advanced this theory by careful observation in his *Textbook of Oarsmanship* (1925), in which he tried to discover why the more popular six-oared boat gave way to the eight-oar early in the development of competitive rowing in Britain. There is little doubt that it was the boys of Westminster and Eton schools, particularly the latter, who introduced rowing to the universities of Oxford and Cambridge. Eton has records going back to 1760 in which longboats are mentioned, and a ten-oar called *Monarch* led the college's annual fete day, the Fourth of June, in 1798. The ten-oared royal barge of George III, who showed special favour to Eton, attended the Fourth of June in all her magnificence. She was re-equipped as an eight-oar by Edward VII and, when taken down river to London after the First World War, covered the 4¼ miles from Mortlake to Putney on the ebb tide in twenty-eight minutes. At that time Oxford and Cambridge Boat Race eights did the reverse course on the flood tide in approximately twenty minutes (fifty years later they can achieve seventeen minutes in fast conditions).

Bourne provides a drawing and statistics of a similar barge belonging to the Duke of Newcastle which was built in 1760; it was clinker-built, 43 feet long, 6 feet wide, made of oak, with eight oarsmen stroked on the port side, which was unusual in those days, and had a high poop on which sat the coxswain behind a canopied cockpit which accommodated eight passengers at a squeeze. It was a typical river craft, Bourne says, not betraying the characteristics of sea boats that can be discerned in the royal barge. The duke's barge closely resembles pictures of the earliest boats used by Oxford colleges in 1815 and by Oxford in the first University Boat Race of 1829. Bourne says:

> The eight-oared boat was the aquatic equivalent of the coach and six; costly to maintain, splendid in its equipment, and appropriate only to great persons. Without doubt the owner . . . manned her with a picked crew dressed in his own livery . . . Many a time a nobleman must have noted with satisfaction that his boat 'did beat every boat that it came alongside of', and in days when men were ready to lay wagers on every event there must have been much rivalry, and considerable sums of money must have changed hands.

The young spurred on the transformation from grandeur to speed.

> If . . . the eight-oared barge was the aquatic equivalent of the coach and six, a six-oar would have the rank of a coach and four, a four-oar of a carriage and pair, and lesser craft would represent the one-horsed carriages of humbler folk. The young bloods of Eton and Westminster,

schools for the sons of the noble and mighty, were familiar from their childhood with the rivalry between the eight-oared galleys of their parents, and in their expeditions, processions, and contests would naturally attach to a ten-oar or eight-oared prestige belonging to the splendid turn-outs of royalty and the nobility.

As they grew up and transferred their rivalries to the universities, what more natural, asks Bourne, than that they should carry their school traditions with them? Besides, Oxford and Cambridge had rivers running past their colleges' backyards. A year after Durham University first admitted undergraduates in 1833, students were rowing in local regattas. Similar motives were at work in the London rowing clubs which existed at this time, according to memoirs of Westminster boys who set forth on the Thames from steps by the Houses of Parliament. Westminster launched their first eight in 1820, though it seems to have been a heavier cutter than the boats used at Eton.

For the rest of the population of London the wherry was the principal Thames passenger ferry. It was the London taxi of the pre-steam age. It can be seen in countless paintings and prints of the eighteenth and nineteenth centuries. Wherries took actors and audiences from Westminster on the north bank to the theatres of Southwark on the south bank, conveyed passengers to ships in the Pool of London by the Tower, and rowed diners to public houses in Greenwich during the whitebait season. Before steam, the Watermen's Company had 10,000 men under licence to work its exclusive control of craft on the Thames between Gravesend and Richmond.

The wherry had an exceptionally long straight overhung stem which enabled passengers to keep their feet dry when stepping ashore at places where there was no jetty; its stern was rounded. It was sculled by one or two watermen or rowed by two. Larger versions, 27–28 feet long with a beam of more than 5 feet 6 inches, could take a three-man crew either working as three scullers or randan style, that is with a sculler in the middle and the other two with one sweep each. A mast could be stepped for'ard.

The first paddle steamer appeared on the River Clyde in Scotland in 1812, and they were commonplace on the Thames by 1840. Steam was the enemy of the watermen, but not the only one. Every new bridge reduced their work, and the rapid spread of railways hit the river and coastal trade at the same time as the introduction of iron

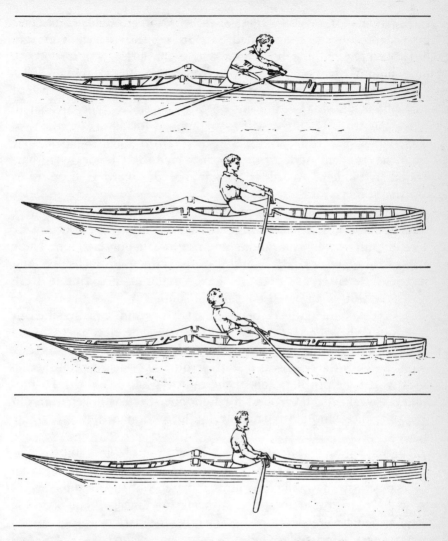

*Top to bottom: The beginning, middle, and end of the pull, and the return
of the sculls. From* Walker's Manly Exercises, *1834*

in ship construction changed the skills and methods of the boat- and
shipyards. The adage of the seafaring British was that 'before, we
had wooden ships and iron men but now we have iron ships and
wooden men'.

The wherry begat variations. There were slimmed-down clinker racing boats of several types, such as whiffs (outrigger sculling boats), rum-tums (a club-owned standard version of a whiff), wager boats (a light sculling boat with outriggers and a waterproof silk inner lining), best boats (developed from wager boats), funnies (clinker outrigger single-person double-enders, mostly found up-river), and cutters. 'Randan' came into use to describe a type of boat in 1884, but from 1828 the word was applied to the arrangement of oars, taken, according to the *Shorter Oxford English Dictionary*, from the 'randem' style of driving in which three horses were harnessed in tandem. An older meaning of the word is 'riotous or disorderly behaviour' (1662).

The term 'skiff' has many meanings: Ryde and Cowes skiffs were watermen's boats, 15 feet long and very beamy. Naval skiffs were 16 feet long, rowed as a randan and rigged as a gunter sloop. There are several types of coastal and saltwater skiffs used for fishing, and several different types of boats have similar names. But in fresh water the skiff is an oared boat much slimmer in beam than a Ryde or a Cowes skiff, halfway between a wherry and a racing shell. It superseded the wherry for hire and for play. The elegant craft used by Jerome K. Jerome's heroes in *Three Men in a Boat* (not forgetting Montmorency the dog) was a skiff. Jerome's book was published in 1889 when the proliferation of the railways had made the Thames valley a weekend playground for Londoners. It has never been out of print since, and skiffs still ply for hire, though they are a rare species.

The recreational skiff developed from about 16 feet until it was almost wherry-sized. It had less overhang to the bow, and a raking stern post with a small transom that flared out of the topsides aft to make more room in the sternsheets for luggage. The working arrangements were developed efficiently: the oarlocks were spread as far apart as possible, while the waterline beam was as minimal as possible. Then some were fitted with outriggers and sliding seats, and spoon blades with copper tips were adopted to improve leverage in the generally calm non-tidal water on which these boats served. McKee observes that the pressure to lighten boats has taken the structure of the wooden wherry and the skiff – which originally may have been a combination of dugout and rafting style of construction – to the limits of possibility. The tholes of the 1873 skiff *Nancy* in the National Maritime Museum at Greenwich are an example of fine engineering. All parts of the wooden oarlock were interchangeable and replacements could be made in no time. Georgia or pitch pine was often used for the keel of a skiff, mahogany being the usual wood for the strakes or clinker planks. Some had a small lugsail on a short mast to assist fair-wind passages. Scrolled ironwork was common on hire boats to support the arm- and backrests of the rear seat. Small drawers under the thwarts held goose grease for the leather buttons on the oars. Some privately owned models had leather fenders, velvet cushions and gold-leaf decoration.

In the main these boats marked the transition from craft designed primarily for transporting goods or passengers to those used for recreation or sport. Similar adaptations occurred in other parts of the world, sometimes in response to purely local conditions and requirements, sometimes influenced by developments in Europe. In Tigre, for example, the rowing centre of Buenos Aires, there are hundreds of boats which bear more than a passing likeness to a Thames skiff regularly in use in the delta of the River Plate. Many were built in Britain in the early part of the twentieth century, and their lines are not always ideal for the river waters churned up by fast passenger and cargo launches. A day spent on the delta will reveal all the stages in the transformation from wherry and galley to sculling boat and shell, and there are skilled men at work in the clubs repairing and replenishing the fleet.

Garden Place of the Great Spirit

A quarter of what we know now as Canada is water. Indeed, a sixth of the earth's fresh water is contained in Canadian lakes, ponds, streams and rivers according to John McPhee, whose classic book *The Survival of the Bark Canoe* is a homily on a small boat. The canoe in various guises evolved to serve the hunting and transport requirements of the indigenous population. McPhee calculates that someone setting out to paddle from the Atlantic to the Pacific would have to carry the boat for only 13 miles, and he sets the scene which greeted the white men who blew into Canadian waters from another world.

> They looked in wonder at such canoes . . . for nothing like them existed in Europe. There was eloquence in the evidence they gave of the genius

of humankind. The materials were simple [cedar, birch, maple, strips of basswood, spruce pitch] but the structure was not. An adroit technology has come down with the tribes from immemorial time, and now – in the sixteenth, the seventeenth century – here were bark canoes on big rivers and ocean bays curiously circling ships from another world. Long-boats were lowered, to be rowed by crews of four and upward. The sailors hauled at their oars. The Indians, two to a canoe, indolently whisked their narrow paddles and easily drew away. In their wake they left a stunning impression. Not only were they faster. They could see where they were going.

As McPhee points out, while the white man farther south began to eliminate the red man, the northern waterlands saw a partnership between red and white in hunting furry animals for profit, involving the Indian willingly in his own destruction. Four-man 36-foot canoes which carried 4 tons were made for the fur trade. They were called *canots de maitre* and were paddled by *voyageurs* who were mostly from the east of Montreal and who sang *chansons* of the Loire Valley as they traversed the territory of the fur companies, wearing brightly coloured sashes, plumed hats and billowing shirts, their paddles painted in primary colours. The companies eventually set up their own factories to build these big canoes. The Hudson's Bay Company boats bore the legend 'HBC' on their transoms, which came to stand for 'Here Before Christ'. Their prototypes were too.

The canoe was master of the terrain, although variations like the flat-bottomed York boats of the Hudson's Bay Company showed European influence. These were rowing boats developed in the early years of the eighteenth century by the HBC's Orcadian carpenters – descendants of the Vikings – to bring large loads from the trapping stations to the lakes and ports on the St Lawrence River during the short summer season. They were 30–40 foot double-enders with four or eight oarsmen, and showed their Nordic influence in their lines. They were taken in flotillas to the portages or carries, where their combined crews dragged and pushed them across the rollers. They were more efficient than the overgrown freight canoes, more seaworthy on stormy lakes, and capable of carrying larger loads. They had a sail for fair wind. In 1775 Samuel Hearne, who explored the inland water routes for the company, addressed the problem of replacing the canoe with a craft more suited to the company's trade and employees. He wrote in his journal:

> The only method that remains is to try what can be done in light shells made of wood after the canoe form; I am apt to believe that expert wherry builders could make vessels . . . so portable that two men may carry them one-fourth of a mile at least without resting . . . taking great care to avoid all superfluity of wood and iron.

This is the earliest reference to a 'shell' found thus far.

Hearne's father was the secretary of the London Bridge Water Works Company, so the young Londoner would have been familiar with wherries and gigs. He volunteered for the Royal Navy at the age of twelve and saw service against the French in the Bay of Biscay during the Seven Years' War. He seems to have arranged for light 'skiffs' to be built in England for assembly at York Factory (now Toronto), but the company history says that the HBC men refused to man the ungainly craft. Meanwhile the Orcadian carpenters learned more of the art of canoe building. Materials to build canoes were transported to their treeless northern bases, while York boats continued in service.

In Canada rowing really came into its own in the Garden Place of the Great Spirit. This is the Indian name for the Thousand Islands, an area of some 1800 islands stretching 50 miles eastwards on the St Lawrence from Lake Ontario. The river is 12 miles wide where it leaves the lake and enters rapids at the other end of the islands. Here was good fishing for muskelunge, pike, pickerel, bass and perch, and here, after the American Civil War, the wealthy of the northern cities found a playground. Summer mansions and luxury hotels proliferated, and a thriving business for fishing guides grew up, centred at Gananoque on the Canadian shore and Clayton on the American. The realization of Webster's *New Collegiate Dictionary* definition of a skiff, 'a light rowboat', has been attributed to Xavier Colon of Clayton in 1868. His boat was a light clinker-built double-ender which could be rowed from the bow seat by a guide, leaving plenty of room for passengers and cargo. Versions up to 23 feet long were sailing models as well; they were boats that handled smartly on all points of sailing without a rudder, 'as far as we know the only craft so sailed', according to John Gardner of Mystic Seaport museum.

Colon's boat evolved by trial and error from the experience of the St Lawrence fishing guides, and it was the design which Gardner, a great expert on North American boats and their lines, identifies as resembling in all essentials the boats which were to hold sway in great numbers until fishing declined, the wealthy migrated to the Caribbean in summer, and fast launches ran booze across the border during Prohibition. Dwight S. Simpson, an eminent naval architect and wooden-boat expert, claims that the true St Lawrence skiff 'is about the best small boat ever developed for more or less open water'. Their crews sailed and rowed the Great Lakes and the St Lawrence and handled what could be very rough water. As far as is known, they did it without fatal accident. According to Gardner, 'A 150-pound man can stand on the gunwale of a skiff of intermediate length in smooth water without putting it under.'

Simpson brought his designer's eye to bear on the skiffs:

> I was surprised to find that the skiffs of most of the old builders, while sharp at both ends, were not really 'double enders', the after body being decidedly finer than the fore body . . . Owing to this difference the boat obtains the best possible trim – down slightly by the stern . . . whether loaded with one, two, three, or four passengers. This makes her row easily.

In *Building Classic Small Craft* Gardner argues that the St Lawrence skiff owes its shape not to the birch canoe or its variations, or to the pleasure canoes of the Thousand Islands, but more to the eye and experience of shipbuilders and craftsmen with European ancestry or influence:

> While the lines of the skiff above the water do resemble the canoe, there is a marked difference below the water. The lines of the skiff show a rather considerable angle of straight deadrise, which the Indian birch does not have and cannot have on account of its manner of construction. And this amount of deadrise, which allows good bearing in combination with fairly deep displacement, is a critical factor in the skiff's superior performance, as it is in the Whitehall boat and other planked boats with similar underwater lines.

Gardner reckons that Colon did not devise the perfect skiff without prototypes or precursors, but no plans, models or accounts, let alone boats, have been found. But Gardner comes up with a significant observation recounted to him in a letter by Bertha Fry Hall, daughter of Lucien Fry of Fry and Denny, skiff builders in the 1890s. She wrote: 'We were in Norway a number of years ago and visited the museums housing the Viking ships. They are mounted on supports;

and as I stood at the bow looking aft, the lines were identical with those I had seen so often in my father's boat factory.' The Norwegian double-enders have lines strikingly similar to Colon's skiffs, Gardner says, and they were superlative rowed sea boats 'whose lines have not been improved upon in more than a thousand years.'

The Forest Guideboat

In New York State the process of evolution was also at work. In *The Adirondack Guide-boat* Kenneth and Helen Durant write:

> It may come as a bit of a shock to some to realize that one of the world's most exquisitely contrived boats, approaching the rowing shell and the violin in delicacy, was built and perfected in the north woods first by unknown woodsmen who had struggled under their burden on the carries, and later by the guides and local carpenters.
>
> Fashioning their craft in obscure little shops, the individual builders searched for their materials in the nearby forests. They examined and tested the lightness, strength, and variety in the curves of the spruce roots bending from the stump, and uncovered a secret that launched a thousand boats.

The Adirondack region is huge and, like the Thousand Islands, was a place where Americans from the burgeoning East Coast cities sought refuge and solitude in the woods, lakes and mountains, often 'going wild' for their summer vacation. There were virtually no roads except to those villages which had developed as resorts, and a thriving business opened up for guides for both the hotel-based tourist and the more adventurous. The Adirondack boats first appeared between 1825 and 1835 and achieved perfection between 1890 and 1900 before going into decline with the changing fashions of the twentieth century. They were light enough to be carried by one man, were smooth-skinned, double-ended or with a small transom, and looked like an Indian canoe. To an Abenaki Indian, Mitchell Sabattis, is attributed the 'invention' of this boat, and he certainly built fine Adirondacks, but the Durants say there is little but legend to back this up. It is also not known who developed the double-ended version that eventually prevailed, travellers in the 1860s describing being rowed in 15-foot boats 'sharp at both ends'. The historian of the Adirondacks, Alfred L. Donaldson, alleges in *A*

History of the Adirondacks (1921) that Caleb Chase of Newcomb was responsible for most improvements to guideboats, implying that he built the first double-ender. Donaldson attributes the reduction in weight, which was the final improvement, to Willie Martin of Saranac Lake. This was achieved by bevelling the strakes and fastening them with tiny copper tacks instead of heavier nails or rivets. This was the secret of a smooth skin. Whoever did what, there is no doubt, say the Durants, that the construction methods of the canoe and the guideboat are incompatible. The canoe builder starts with a flexible sheath folded and sewn or gummed, into which he forces a frame and thwarts. The guideboat builder starts with a frame of bottom board, two stems and ribs fashioned from natural crooks. This is covered by thin planking and propelled by oars, not paddles. The Adirondack museum exhibits a Maine wherry, a bateau and a dory, types of rowing boat which it claims have kinship with the guideboats.

Roving Eye and Belief Within

In his exhaustive investigation into the search for speed under sail (1967), Howard I. Chapelle says that it has been the fashion to picture the American designers and boatbuilders as primitive artisans, isolated from European development and knowledge, dependent wholly on their natural intelligence. But this is not the case. It must be remembered, he says, that 'ships themselves are the best and most common means of conveying information on their design to a foreign area. The copying process thus began in ancient times.' And, so far as America is concerned, the constant movement of English shipwrights to the American colonies brought the most advanced English ideas to American shipyards. Dutch, French, Spanish and other European ships traded in large numbers as well. It was a different set of economic, material and geographic circumstances that New World shipwrights had to take into account as the heirs to techniques of the Old World, techniques well documented from the end of the seventeenth century. Even so, the sailing-ship designers were forced to rely on visual methods when comparing new designs with existing successful ships of about the same size, because there was little recorded information. Also, successful design for speed was both an art and a commercial advantage, and so designers were loath to part with their knowledge except to their own apprentices. Secrecy does not beget how-to-do-it books. In the case of small-boat designers, documentation was almost nonexistent and visiting examples were much rarer. 'Father and son worked together. Thus the art is passed on,' say A. W. Brøgger and Haakon Shetelig in *The Viking Ships*.

The builders of gigs and galleys, the refiners of wherries and Thames and St Lawrence skiffs, the fashioners of Adirondacks and countless other oarpowered boats used hearsay and eye, their own pulling experience, and the tools and the materials to hand to change and perfect their boats. Just as the lakes and coasts of Britain and America are awash with small boats designed to meet local conditions and made from local materials, so are other parts of the world. For example, Kauko Miettinen, the builder of Finnish church boats, uses no plans, but relies on tradition, familiarity and templates. He could make one of his 12-metre boats blindfold. He starts by laying the keel, which together with the stem and stern posts requires twelve parts. He then uses a template to build up the sides, made of plywood strakes, in clinker style. Frames and ribs of Central European ash are then steam-bent to shape and inserted. Traditionally, strakes were made of matured pine and the frame of juniper, but pine is difficult to get and cutting juniper is no longer allowed in Finland. Foot stretchers and metal tholepins are added, and seats are individual, a departure from the traditional benches. Oars have straight blades made from two pieces of spruce.

The men who looked for speed in rowing boats worked from instinct, inspiration and eye. It is the new materials of boatbuilding that have brought plans and moulds and mathematics into the art.

6

NINETEENTH-CENTURY INNOVATORS

FROM the summit of the Abbey Church in Hexham, Northumberland, you can see the confluence of the South Tyne and the North Tyne rivers. Its inhabitants claim Hexham is the 'heart of England' because it stands midway between the North Sea and the Solway Firth and halfway between the English Channel and the Pentland Firth. Where the pebbly shallows and the rocky beds of the Tyne become tidal, 19½ miles before it reaches the North Sea, stands Tyne Amateur Rowing Club's boathouse. The club was founded on another site in 1853. Its modern building has a stone head of the god of the Tyne on the wall, a face with three strands of plaited beard surrounded by trade emblems such as picks, shovels, fish, nets and wheat. This dazzling river was famous for salmonries in the days before coal became the dominant industry of Newcastle-upon-Tyne and the region.

Not far below the boathouse the Tyne story is one of steelworks, of vast armament, shipbuilding and engineering factories stretching to the quays of the city and the bluffs of Gateshead on the southern bank. By the beginning of the nineteenth century an authority on nautical matters reported that ignorance, inattention and avarice had converted the Tyne to a 'cursed horse-pond'. A surveyor said that in some parts 'there was not water enough, when the tide was out, to cross in a sculler'.

After 1836 Newcastle Corporation made the Tyne more navigable. Shipbuilding and heavy engineering thrived as the nineteenth century drew to a close, and for 10 miles between Newcastle and the sea the river flowed 'bearing on her toil-stained breast the dark hulls of a mighty navy from the furthest ends of the earth.' Fishing fleets sailed from North Shields, and foy boats, black-hulled with elongated black and white checkers round their gunwales, rowed out to sea to pick up ships and pilot them to their moorings. Barges plied the river, drifting on the tide with the aid of long oars on their bows.

Beneath the bridges of the city, which include the Tyne Bridge (1928), the prototype for that of Sydney Harbour, and along miles of banks and docks and creeks, men built and worked wooden boats to service commerce through the age when sail power gave way to steam and then to diesel. In plotting the Tyne as a rowing man's river, the challenges and skills come from shipwrights and ferrymen, foy-boatmen and keelmen (the local name for those who work on barges), pitmen or coalminers, and builders of working boats who looked to the water for their recreation. They held regattas from Tynemouth to Hexham, raced in handicaps and took side bets, cheated and sought fair play, and took summer trips to Durham where the River Wear curls round the cliffs which bear the cathedral and university, or to the idyllic Talkin Tarn in Cumbria. Their influence came from competitiveness, skill and sometimes genius. Their technical developments profoundly affected events such as the world professional sculling championship, the Oxford and Cambridge Boat Race, and regattas such as Chester, Durham and Henley. In the mid-nineteenth century rowing was followed widely in England, and Tyneside names like Clasper, Taylor, Swaddle and Winship were etched on the history of racing boat design. Tyne competitors made their names also, becoming famous across the Atlantic and receiving heroes' acclamations, decent burials, and lasting memorials after they were laid to rest.

Four things changed the working boat to the racing shell: the outrigger, the sliding seat, the swivel oarlock, and the abolition, or at least the bringing inboard, of the keel. The men of Tyne were involved in at least three of them. Harry Clasper worked in the coal mines and as a cinder burner at the coke ovens before becoming a wherryman (boatman) on the Tyne when he was about twenty. He and his five brothers – Robert, William, John, Richard and Edward – were all rowers, William and John drowning in rowing accidents. Crews made up of Clasper brothers became well known, and Harry was a champion in the 1850s. But when he first formed a crew there was no such thing as a racing boat, at least not on the Tyne. Boats were designed for carrying cargo and/or people. Harry began to experiment with the shape of the hull and to shed weight to give the crew the best possible leverage when rowing. One of his first attempts was *The Five Brothers* in which he and his family won Newcastle's Barge Thursday gala race for several years. He fitted outriggers to a four in 1845, the same year as J. W. Conant, a student at St John's College, Cambridge, used them on his sculling boat at Henley. In 1846 both Oxford and Cambridge used them in the Boat Race.

Clasper was not the sole inventor of the modern outrigger. The first appeared in 1828, according to Robert S. Hunter in *Rowing in Canada since 1848*. It was made of wood and fitted to a sculling boat called *Diamond* by a Tyne boatbuilder named Ridley to the design of Anthony Brown of Ouseburn. In the same year Frank Emmet of Dent's Hole on the Tyne made a similar design and his *Eagle* appeared in 1830 equipped with iron outriggers. In 1838 George Steers, the son of an English shipwright who had emigrated to America, built a four-oared outrigger weighing only 140 lb and drawing only 4 inches of water. It seems to have been unreliable. Steers became a famous naval architect and in 1851 designed the schooner *America* which defeated the British yacht *Titania* off Cowes and started the America's Cup. Another claimant is the Englishman Samuel Welsencroft who built a racing single with outriggers and an inboard keel in 1844. He tried to make the skin from one piece of wood but it split while being bent.

It was Clasper who seems to have taken the outrigger to a state reliable enough to be trusted by oarsmen. It changed the equation between beam and leverage and enabled boats intended for racing to be made narrower and lighter. Eights grew to 66 feet in length, with a beam of less than 2 feet. Before he died of 'congestion of the brain' in 1870, Clasper was hailed in Newcastle as the 'father and teacher of modern aquatics'. His stone effigy stands beneath a canopy of carved aquatic plants and boatbuilder's tools in the graveyard of Whickham parish church overlooking a beautiful stretch of his river Tyne. His widow, daughter Dorothy and two sons John and Henry moved to Putney in London and set up in boatbuilding.

In 1854 Matthew Taylor of Ouseburn on the Tyne built a four-oared smooth-bottomed boat for Royal Chester Rowing Club. He did it by bringing the keel inboard. Taylor, a ship's carpenter and professional sculler, went to the amateur club as paid trainer. In 1855 the club used his boat to win the Stewards' Challenge Cup at Henley Royal Regatta and in 1856 Taylor built an eight in which they won both the Grand Challenge Cup and the Ladies' Plate. Oxford won the 1857 Boat Race against Cambridge in a Taylor boat, with some advice from him on how to row it. His own seventy races taught him to advise oarsmen to feather low in calm water and to get hold of the water at the beginning of the stroke instead of finishing it with a great wrench. Under the Boat Race rules professionals were barred from coaching, so the Oxford president A. P. Lonsdale, who had paid for the eight himself, engaged Taylor 'not to instruct us in the art of rowing but to show us the proper way to send his boat along as quickly as possible'. In the next year Taylor supplied the boat in which Cambridge won, and he obtained further orders from Oxford, Chester and Eton College.

Taylor's boats were regarded as revolutionary. They were 55 feet long, about 10 feet shorter than keeled eights at that time. This made them lighter. Their greatest beam was 25 inches and was placed well forward, further reducing surface resistance (skin friction). The savings of weight and friction by having the keel inboard were greater than those achieved by the outrigger. According to W. B. Coventry in *The Racing Eight* (1922), Taylor solved the problem of skin friction for boats with fixed seats with remarkable accuracy. Coventry says that prejudice against Taylor's boats was caused by lack of understanding of the relationship between the shape of the hull and its surface resistance, or wetted surface. 'With a given displacement, the shorter the boat and the greater the draught, the smaller is the resistance,' Coventry says. The later development of the sliding seat made the calculations different. But Taylor made his mark. It is not certain, however, that he was the first builder of a boat without a keel outside its skin. The design of the first Taylor-built boats at Chester has been claimed for J. B. Littledale, a member of a wealthy shipbuilding family in Liverpool, who was the club's captain, stroke and benefactor. Bourne in his *Textbook of Oarsmanship* says that Littledale had attempted to adapt the lines of the *Great Eastern*, which was propelled by paddles and at the time the longest steam ship afloat, to racing eights. Littledale certainly worked closely with Taylor: boatbuilders who work independently of clients and rowers work at their peril, as we shall see.

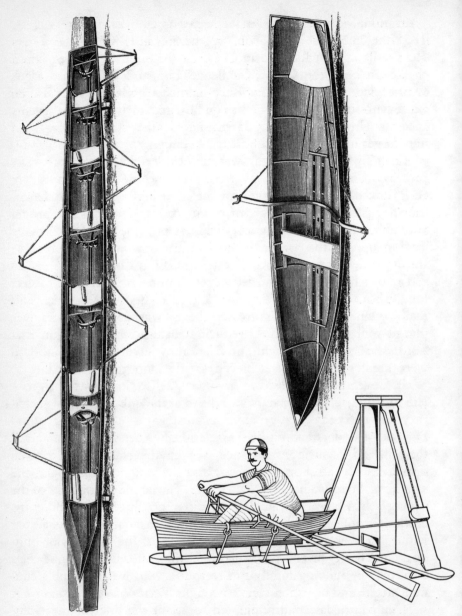

A 12-foot gig (above) and a six-oared shell from the Waters, Balch catalogue, 1871 (Troy, New York)

A nineteenth-century rowing machine from Victor Silberer's Handbook of
Rowing, 1897 (Vienna)

Several authorities cite Harry Clasper as the first builder of keel-less boats. Sir Theodore Cook, in *Rowing at Henley* (1919), says 'the keel-less hull which Harry Clasper used for his cedar skiff when he raced Coombes on the Tyne in 1844 was in fact the prototype of the boats which Matt Taylor so enormously improved,' and he quotes a letter from Harry's son Jack claiming that he steered his father in a crew at the Thames Regatta of 1849 in which they 'used the same smooth-bottomed boats as are in use now'. C. M. Pitman, in *Record of the University Boat Race* (1909), says that that first keel-less four was built by Harry Clasper in 1847 and used by Oxford to win the Stewards' Cup at Henley in 1852. This is challenged in Robert F. Kelley's *American Rowing* (1932) by the Seattle boatbuilder George Pocock (see chapter 8) who says, 'My father insisted that it was his uncle Bill Pocock who built the first keel-less boat . . . This Bill Pocock was rowing coach at Westminster School . . . in the days when a coach had to stroke the crew. He did not make any great fuss over his boat until Clasper of Newcastle-on-Tyne came out with a similar keel-less boat and claimed authorship of it. This Clasper had been in London when Bill Pocock was building his boat.'

Buckskin and Butter

The men of Tyne do not have first claim on the sliding seat or the swivel rowlock. The swivel, which followed the introduction of leather to cover the button of an oar in 1870, is claimed by the American Mike Davis in 1874. His device is a bracket mounted on a pivot which holds the oar, and it was to replace the fixed tholepins in the gunwale or on the outrigger. It quickly became universal for sculling boats on both sides of the Atlantic. But the swivel only made real sense once the sliding or moving seat came into use; even then, many English clubs continued to use fixed pins in larger boats well into the twentieth century.

There were attempts at sliding on a fixed seat long before anybody made a moving seat that worked. There is evidence that the ancient Greeks slid on sheep-skin cushions in their *trieres* (see chapter 1). Many, including men on Tyneside, have attempted to slide by greasing fixed seats with lard or tallow. In the 1860s the boatbuilders

Waters and Balch in Troy, New York, were offering 'The Plain Slide Seat fitted with Sidebars' made of a thin plank of close-grained cherry, up to a quarter of an inch thick, 16–22 inches long and 10 inches wide. The surface was highly polished and it was greased, as were the oarsmen's pantaloons, which were 'reinforced with wash-leather'. The arrangement was known as the 'buckskin and butter' plan.

In 1863 a Dr Schiller of Berlin made a slide using small wheels, but Herbert Manchester in *Four Centuries of Sport in America* (1931) attributes the invention to the American professional sculler Walter Brown, who made one in about 1861. However, the earliest claim was in 1857: 'The first sliding or moveable seat of which I believe there is any record was attached to a novel single scull-craft which I built in Chicago in the year 1857, called the *Experiment* . . . as an *experiment* I did not consider the craft or the seat a success,' wrote John C. Babcock to Waters Balch on 14 December 1870. Babcock was captain of the Nassau Boat Club in New York and a champion oarsman and sculler. His letter claimed that Brown considered his 1861 slide to be 'sanguine of success' but he abandoned the idea until 1870, when he had 'taken to it again and taken out letters-patent in July or August claiming it as his invention'. Babcock gave details of his own:

> The slide was used for the first time by a crew in May last [1870] at the opening season of the Hudson Amateur Rowing Association at Pleasant Valley. I had it attached to a six-oared gig, and with a green amateur crew from the Nassau's made the first trial before a large and critical audience. I deemed it, that day, a decided success, anticipating more difficulty than I found in working the crew in a first attempt. The crew . . . seemed to apply more power in their work, though their form was far from perfect. The opinion of those most competent to judge of the effect of the slide on the speed of the boat was against it, as it seemed to check headway at every stroke on the recovery, and the boat to take a series of leaps instead of that steady headway so essential to speed.

Babcock then tested the slide with a trained crew against three of the best Eastern crews, and beat two of them. The seat was a 10-inch-square wooden frame covered with leather and grooved at the edges to slide on two brass tracks fastened on the thwart, allowing a slide of 10–12 inches. The tracks were lubricated with lard and gave a 'rowing' length of slide of up to 6 inches. Babcock's letter concludes:

> The slide properly used is a decided advantage and gain of speed, and the only objection to its use is its complication and almost impracticable requirement of skill and unison in a crew, rather than any defect in its mechanical theory. When we take into consideration that the best oarsmen in the world, the Tynesiders, slide, when spirting [*sic*], from four to six inches on a fixed seat, the moveable seat can only be considered as a mechanical contrivance, intended for a better accomplishment of the sliding movement in rowing.

He had, of course, identified the huge obstacle that the slide was to introduce to the customary way of rowing:

> It requires more skill to use the seat properly than it does the oar, thus making it doubly difficult to perfect a crew. The tendency of the beginner is to slide too much and at the wrong time . . . It is as fully, if not more important, that the crew should slide together, as it is that they should row together, and it is doubly more difficult to do it.

Slides are the most far-reaching of the technical changes in the racing boat during the last century and this. It took many experiments to find the right materials from which to make them. Glass, various forms of wheels, rails and travellers made their appearance, including a ball-bearing-mounted slide which blew up under the sculler W. Sweetman at Henley in 1868, the shot showering over his opponent. It was several years before rowers learned how to use them properly. The slide made effective rowing the province of the tall and lean rather than the short and wide of physique, and it started a great debate about technique, the echoes of which could be heard even after the Second World War. But once Babcock made the slide reliable, clubs were swift to adopt them. Moving seats were used by Yale in their race against Harvard in 1870, and Harvard adopted them two years later. In England sliding seats were used with spectacular success at Henley in 1872, and by both crews in the Boat Race in 1873. Babcock's innovation also threatened Matt Taylor's notions of hull shape, because slides required larger staterooms for rowers, and thus longer boats.

The Music of Water

The eye and skill of these practical men were recognized by the amateurs of the day, those who, by definition, did not work with their hands. A. A. Casamajor, a great amateur sculler from London RC, wrote in 1858: 'at the job of combining the practical skill of the waterman with the mental intelligence of the amateur Matthew Taylor has no equal among amateurs.' Theodore Cook, who was a biographer of the painter J. W. M. Turner, said of the Thames boatbuilder George Sims: 'As he did it, the thing savoured of Turner's notion of perspective, a realization of what should be, without any knowledge of what must be. There was that strange sympathy in the boat builder which was in Matt Taylor, and in the Claspers too, and which is outside all calculation.' Other Tynesiders such as Swaddle and Winship were to make their mark in racing boats. They possessed the accuracy of the eye to see and of the hand to fashion exactly what was in their minds, and one finds the same uncanniness among men who have continued in the twentieth century where these left off in the nineteenth.

One who sought knowledge of what must be was Gilbert Bourne, who was a superb oarsman at Eton College and then at Oxford and spent many years coaching and designing boats while teaching at his old university. His *Text-book of Oarsmanship*, published in 1925, has many pages on the evolution and dimensions of eights. He begins by pointing out that boatbuilders are jealous of the secrets of their craft, just like shipbuilders. He says that a rowing boat is quite different from a vessel propelled by sail, screw or paddle wheel because for at least two thirds of the time – remember, he is writing in the 1920s – the oars are out of the water. He explains the paradox that the boat loses speed when the oars enter the water and gains speed when they leave it, and rejects the mathematician's argument that a boat would be faster if one pair of oars was always at work. This was actually tried in the thirties by F. E. 'Twolegs' Hellyer at London Rowing Club, using six men in an eight. Called syncopated rowing, it failed. Bourne discusses skin friction, the wetted surface area, the two waves set up by the bow and stern, the relationship between the distance which the boat moves with each stroke and the length of the wave, the relationship between camber and speed, and the difference between a good crew's 'best speed' and their fastest speed. He considers the geometrical wild goose chase of the 'harmonic correspondence between the waves created by a boat . . . and the rhythm of the oarsmen's movements'. Not forgetting, also, a crew's preference for one boat over another because it feels good or because it has already won a race.

Bourne traces the movements in the design of eights since Taylor's 57-foot boat for Oxford in 1857 began a trend towards shorter and wider (25 inches) vessels. As we have seen, after slides were introduced in 1873 eights grew a little longer to give oarsmen more room, but the beam was reduced, thereby causing greater depth, allowing greater displacement for heavier crews. Boatbuilders' attempts to reduce depth to the smallest possible made many crews under-boated. Swaddle and Winship's boat for Oxford in 1878 was 57 feet long, only 22 inches wide, and shallow in depth. Oxford won four out of five Boat Races in her, but in 1883 changed to a larger boat made by J. Clasper, and won again. Bourne, who rowed in both boats, says the Clasper was no faster or less comfortable than the Swaddle. Meanwhile Clasper had made short broad-beamed flat-floored boats for Oxford in 1882 and for Cambridge in 1883. They were rejected by both universities. Clasper therefore moved away from the boats he himself favoured to longer shells, until both crews used his 62-footers in 1896. Eights grew even longer after that, returning to the dimensions of those before Taylor had brought the keel inboard.

If he knew of developments across the Atlantic, Bourne does not mention them. While he is complaining of secrecy among the builders, Waters, Balch's illustrated catalogue of 1871 opines that length and lightness are best. Describing fifty years of development, it says:

> Today, four athletes, of 150 to 160 pounds weight each, propel a shell of 17 inches beam, 41 feet in long, and weighing but 94 pounds, at a rate of nearly nine miles per hour over a six-mile course, and single sculling boats of 9½ inches beam, 31 feet long, weighing 25 pounds, and carrying a single oarsman of 140 pounds weight, are driven with comparative ease at the rate of eight miles per hour in smooth water.

These weights are remarkable when compared with Vespoli USA's 1990 ultralight coxless four, which is 44 feet long and weighs 115–120 lb, or with a 27-foot sculling boat weighing 31–33 lb. The

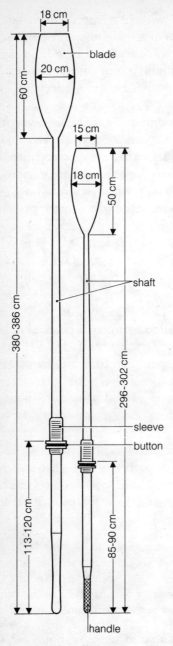

18 cm

20 cm

60 cm

blade

15 cm

18 cm

50 cm

380-386 cm

296-302 cm

shaft

sleeve

button

113-120 cm

85-90 cm

handle

Oar and scull (1990)

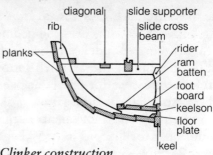

diagonal

slide supporter

rib

slide cross beam

planks

rider

ram batten

foot board

keelson

floor plate

keel

Clinker construction

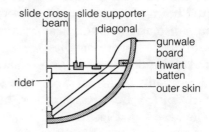

slide cross beam

slide supporter

diagonal

gunwale board

thwart

batten

outer skin

rider

Shell construction

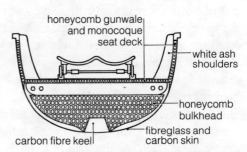

honeycomb gunwale and monocoque seat deck

white ash shoulders

honeycomb bulkhead

carbon fibre keel

fibreglass and carbon skin

Carbon/glass laminate construction

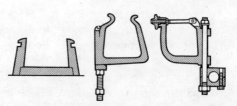

Rowlocks: left to right — fixed pin, swivel and adjustable swivel

Waters catalogue almost certainly refers to the ultralight paper boats mentioned below. It is also a coaching manual and almanac of clubs in North America, and runs to nearly 500 pages. It gives copious details of fittings and parts of boats, including the 'traveller', which enabled an oarsman to steer a coxless boat. It discusses English as well as American builders, and includes detailed cross-sections and lines of racing boats, including a four used by the Tyneside crew in a race at Lachine in 1870. At this time competitive rowing in America was almost entirely restricted to fours or sixes, both without coxes and therefore subject to much fouling, so the lines of the boats in the catalogue would not have been much use to Bourne who was preoccupied with the eight. Eights were introduced to the United States in the Harvard versus Yale race in 1876. Why it took so long for them to become popular and why American colleges and clubs persisted to row without coxes in sixes are mysteries.

The Waters, Balch catalogue also describes boats with skins of paper, which was the fad of the period and thought to be the material of the future. This came about because George A. Waters, a paper-box manufacturer, repaired a wooden sculling boat by literally papering over the cracks. The task was completed successfully with waterproof varnish. Cheered on, he and his father Elisha attempted to make a paper shell by taking a wooden boat 30 feet by 13 inches and using it as a mould. They covered its entire surface with small sheets of strong manila, glued together and superimposed in layers so that the joints of one layer were covered by the sheet above, until they had a paper shell one sixteenth of an inch thick. The fabric was dried and removed from the mould and fitted with a wooden frame. The skin, which was extremely stiff, was then waterproofed. Boats were also made using unbroken sheets of paper from stem to stern, and the process was then extended to using a single layer of pure unbleached linen stock as an alternative to manila. The method was adapted to gigs, whiffs and canoes. Remarkable strength, lightness and ease of repair were claimed for these prototype moulded boats, and the scullers of the day rushed to use them. The boats had a few seasons of glory, but their future became waterlogged. Paper boats did not spread to the Old World and they soon fell from grace in America. A manila boat required perfect and lasting waterproofing to maintain its rigidity and strength, and its frame did not have ribs to strengthen it. Compared with manila, a skin of wood, which contributes to the strength of a boat, is easier to maintain and less at risk when being transported or carried to and from the water.

Meanwhile in England competition and commercial matters were influencing development as well as notions of design. The first is well illustrated by the Harvard four who came to England to race Oxford in 1869, a momentous event in the development of international rowing which, some accounts say, brought threequarters of a million people to the 4¼-mile course from Putney to Mortlake. Harvard had two boats, one a 49-footer built by Judge Elliott and the other a shell made by an Englishman in New York. Elliott, who accompanied the crew, also brought a kit for a third boat, which he assembled with the aid of two hired hands once he arrived at Putney. But Harvard wanted the best even if it was not American, and they ordered the best that could be provided by Salters of Oxford, Jewitt of Newcastle, and Clasper of Newcastle. Messrs Searle, boatbuilders on the Thames, also provided their best boat for the Harvard trials, which were won by Elliott's kit.

Bourne identifies Swaddle and Winship and J. Clasper as the leading builders by 1880, at least so far as the Boat Race clubs were concerned. Competition took its toll of design developments when one of Swaddle and Winship's employees by the name of Halford set up his own business in Gloucester in about 1881 and began to make broader-beam boats than those produced by his old firm. They proved very fast but were of flimsy construction in a bid to undercut the prices of competitors, and Halford went bankrupt after two or three years. Swaddle and Winship collapsed a little later, leaving the field to Clasper.

Bourne conducted an experiment which shows what was happening in rowing while eights were growing in length. He compared the speed of boats in the finals of the Grand Challenge Cup at Henley from 1886 to 1913 and found that there was 'progressive deterioration', while a similar comparison for the Diamond Sculls showed that scullers were getting faster. Over the same period eights became longer and narrower, while sculling boats became shorter and wider. Bourne also notes that the Belgian crews from Ghent who won the Grand in 1906, 1907 and 1909 used short, 58-foot boats. Longer slides were becoming common by 1886.

In 1901 Dr Edmond Warre, headmaster of Eton, designed a 56-foot boat with a maximum beam of 27 inches which became known as Warre's Snubby. It had a wide floor as if two concentric circles were inside it side by side, and very little camber. Bourne says that if paddle boats were the ancestors of the Taylor boats, the same was not true of the Snubby. Its shape had more in common with the Royal Navy's torpedo boats and light cruisers. This was because back in 1880 Warre had asked Sir Nathaniel Barnaby, Director of Naval Construction, to design a boat for the Eton crew. This was a failure, but an 1882 design which combined features from Barnaby and from Swaddle and Winship was a very successful craft. Bourne coached crews in it and concluded that this progenitor of the Snubby 'was the making of the crew'. It was not until the 1920s that the shorter eights found favour.

Bourne was probably not the first, and certainly not the only, designer to conclude that if 85 per cent of a boat's resistance is due to skin friction, then the shape of hull most conducive to speed is the half circle. He also identified why such a shape is almost impossible to row. Round-bottomed boats are unstable because the rowers must be seated high up in the boat to enable them to pull. A semi-circular section leads to a very long, very narrow, long-waisted, deep boat, the depth being half the width. This was the sort of boat defeated by the Taylor-Littledale developments of the short, the broad and the shallow in 1856. Designers must accept that the centre of gravity of a loaded boat is higher than the centre of buoyancy. Beam can help stability, while steadiness is promoted by a 'generous allowance of flat or only slightly curved floor', Bourne says. The conundrum facing them all, from old Harry Clasper to the boatworks of Messrs Empacher, who were on top of the world in 1990, is the compatibility of steadiness with speed.

Bourne tackled it by making models of various hull shapes and testing their resistance by towing them on the river by means of a silk line on a light trout rod. Models were also tested at Sir John Thorneycroft's tank on the Isle of Wight. The outcome was a boat in which the broadest beam was well forward of the middle. The intention was to increase displacement and minimize the wetted surface area. It was successful, but nevertheless a boat for experts, being difficult to row and thus requiring experienced crews with good technique and enough time to get used to it. It won the 1923 Boat Race and the 1924 Grand. Sister boats achieved honours too.

That was the extent of Bourne's considerable contribution in the

area of boat design. One other notion that he examines turned out
to be an interesting aside on developments in the twentieth century.
Dr Warre and Professor Bourne were strict adherents of what
became known in England as the Orthodox style of rowing. By 1900
this was under attack by 'naturalists', the arch priest of whom
was Steve Fairbairn (see chapter 12). Meanwhile Warre attributed
post–1900 'decadence' to the prevailing types of boat, and Bourne
agreed with him. But, Bourne says, Warre

> cannot follow his flights of imagination into the realms of music with
> the accompanying theories of harmonic curves, of boats seven octaves
> long, and so forth . . . The analogy of music cannot be exact, for aqueous
> waves behave quite differently from aerial waves. Sound waves, whatever
> their length, travel at approximately the same speed . . . in water the
> long wave travels faster. Undoubtedly there is music in rowing. But it
> is the music of water, not of air.

Coffin, Barrel and Spade

Ezekiel Page of New York and Boston advertised a million feet of
oars, sweeps and sculls in the catalogue of the Great Exhibition in
London in 1851. Two immense factories employed the latest steam
machinery and over 200 men making 8000 feet of oars per day,
supplied rough or finished. These were workaday oars. Way back
in 1773 the Swiss Leonard Euler wrote that experience shows that
'the blade of an oar used by one man should never surpass half a
square foot, in order that the oars may not be too heavy for the
management of the rowers.' When the design of boats grew more
refined, people experimented with oars. Typical nineteenth-century
oars were 15 feet overall with a blade of 4 feet 6 inches, 4½ inches
wide, and hewn from solid wood. A year before the Great Exhibition
Edward Ayling set up a boatbuilding business in Putney, and by the
end of the century it was concentrating on making oars, with
Edward's son George in charge. At about this time Edmund Norris
introduced the French technique of splitting timber to re-form it and
reduce weight, and Aylings followed suit.

Meanwhile Bourne's *Text-book of Oarsmanship* examined
inboard and outboard measurements, thwartship distances, distance

Shaping amateur rowing I: Henley Royal Regatta in 1908

Shaping amateur rowing II: the Oxford and Cambridge Boat Race,
Cambridge winning in 1930

LEFT: Members of the British Boating Club at Xochimilco, Mexico, posing with Zapatista guerrillas billeted at their club, 1914

BELOW: Regatta belles at Shanghai, 1930s

BOTTOM: Members of the S. Sabba della Ginnastica, Trieste, 1924

OPPOSITE PAGE: Cardinal W. T. Heard, who rowed for Oxford in 1907, with Britain's eight at the Rome Olympics, 1960

The Royal Army Medical Corps, winners of the Challenge Fours at Lucknow, India, 1912. Mrs Gratton was the cox

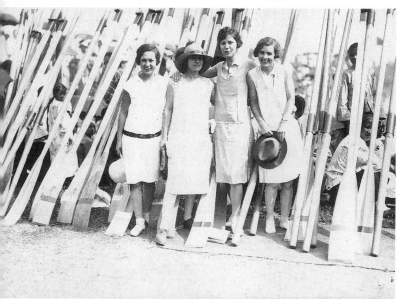

ABOVE: Al Ulbrickson coaching at the University of Washington in 1950

BELOW LEFT: Hiram Conibear with the Letter Men, 1910

BELOW RIGHT: George Pocock, boatbuilder at the University of Washington in the early 1970s

OPPOSITE: The boathouse at Jesus College, Cambridge, Steve Fairbairn's old college, in 1897

The teachers: Steve Fairbairn (*left*), Karl Adam, (*top right*), Thor Nilsen (*bottom right*)

1st May Boat 1897

Joe Wright whipping the 1920 Varsity into shape at the University of Pennsylvania

BELOW: *left to right*: The coaches: Charles Courtney (Cornell), Joe Burk (Penn), Harry Parker (Harvard)

OPPOSITE ABOVE: Venice remembered: the Italian rowing club at Tigre, Buenos Aires

OPPOSITE BELOW: President Castro has a coaching lesson at Varadero Regatta

Eights from the air

of the oarsman from the work, etc. 'Whatever the length of the oar its balance is of the utmost importance,' he wrote.

> Nothing is more stimulating to good oarsmanship than an oar which seems to take hold of the water of its own accord at the beginning of the stroke and swings back on the feather with the ease of a pendulum. The balance of an oar is not simply a matter of its gross weight nor of the excess of weight outboard relative to the weight inboard . . . The two things that are of real importance are 1) the moment of inertia of the oar about the button; 2) the distance of the centre of impact of the blade from its tip. It would seem if one is right the other will also be right.

He concluded that, when it came to the shape of blades, Ewing McGruer had it right in *Coaching for Young Crews by an Old Blue* (1921): 'The correct blade is that which has its area concentrated near the tip. Barrel-shaped and coffin-shaped blades are wrong in principle and have nothing to recommend them.' Barrel blades had the greatest width at the outboard end and were used by Oxford to win the Boat Race in 1890. In 1885 Eton won the Ladies' Plate with coffin oars designed by Dr Warre. The greatest width was at the inboard end of the blade. 'In my rowing days,' Bourne says, 'old Edward Ayling was a past master in the art of making well-balanced oars . . . Of late oar-makers have concentrated their attention on devising double-girder, tubular, boxloom, and other patent oars of very doubtful value, the balance of which is often extremely faulty.' Aluminium was tried by Ellis Ward in Philadelphia some time between 1879 and 1914, probably with the help of the Galanaugh dockyard whose aluminium eight was tested by Cornell in 1892.

Between the two world wars George Ayling's son Frederick introduced the weighing and balancing of every oar so that the customer could buy matching sets. Experimentation continued after the Second World War. Aylings, now with Frederick's son Peter making the running, were involved in the development of 'spade' blades, the most familiar shape today, with Oxford's coach 'Jumbo' Edwards. His blades were 20 inches long with a maximum width of 8 inches, while Geoffrey Page's for Thames Rowing Club were a few inches longer with a similar width. Synthetic materials and the American company Dreissigacker dominate the racing-oar market in the 1990s (see chapter 9). Their sweeps are between 378.5 and 386 cm long

(12 foot 5 inches and 12 foot 8 inches) with a blade 20 cm wide by
58 cm long. Their sculls are 296–302 cm (9 foot 8.5 inches–9 foot
11 inches) with blades 17 cm wide by 49.6 cm long.

7

TWENTIETH-CENTURY INNOVATORS

In 1872 Friedrich August Stämpfli built a giant skiff seating twelve oarsmen for a Frankfurt rowing club. Stämpfli came from Neuchâtel in Switzerland but had moved to Hamburg to learn the shipbuilding trade, afterwards moving around the shipyards and boatyards of Germany. He had the inquiring mind of an inventor, becoming a keen amateur photographer with a camera he made himself. In the 1890s he moved to Zürich and bought a house on the shore of the Zürichsee, where he built experimental steamboats which ran on naphthalene. These were not a success. Two of them exploded, and one man was killed. In 1896 August started a business with his son Alfred making sailing boats, motorboats and commercial craft for trade between the lakeside villages and the city. By then there had been a proliferation of local rowing clubs, mainly to serve the needs of foreign students and business men in the city. The earliest was the See-Club (1863). Rowing had also spread to Geneva, Lucerne and Basle. Most of the racing boats were brought from England.

It was Alfred who first started to make racing shells in 1912, using designs by his father. August, the Hamburg hydrodynamicist, decided that the optimum shape for a hull was a half circle, but he also knew that such a shape was impossible to row. The Stämpflis experimented and altered the shape according to what their eyes and their instincts told them. In later years laboratory tests produced the same results, to Alfred's immense joy. The shape of hull which he and his father had hit upon is basically the one made by the company in the 1990s.

From the very beginning Stämpfli insisted upon the best materials

August Stämpfli's twelve-oar, 1872

and the best workmanship. Only perfect cedar boats left the yard, after meticulous attention had been given to their finish. Alfred became a great rowing enthusiast, taking his own boats out on the lake, observing the crews and cultivating many friends in the rowing section of the Football Club of Zürich. In the thirties he allowed FC Zürich to use part of his premises as a boathouse, and every day he saw their crews go out in his boats. The club's coach Arthur Dreyfus and his men reported back: a bit of lift here, a strange wake there. Alfred and his son, also named Alfred, listened to criticisms and suggestions and adapted the boats from the findings of the research laboratory right on their doorstep.

The football club's goals were high. 'Turi' Dreyfus had his sights on Henley and the 1936 Olympics in Berlin, and he looked to the writings and successes of Steve Fairbairn, an Australian coach living in England, to help him. He was in frequent correspondence with Fairbairn, and translated Fairbairn's *Some Secrets of Successful Rowing* into German (see chapter 12). Dreyfus made his crew study slow-motion film of the Fairbairn-style Pembroke College four who set a record at Henley in 1934. When the FC Zürich eight went to Henley in 1935 they had an electric alarm fitted by No. 3's seat so that the stroke's commands could be relayed by the coxswain to the bow section of the crew. Alex Homberger, who was in the crew, remembers a 'horrendous race' in the first round of the Grand Challenge Cup when they were beaten by 3 feet. Their conquerors were Jesus College, Cambridge, Fairbairn's old college. Jesus helped the exhausted Zürichers to carry their boat to the rack. The following year Zürich beat Leander to win the Grand, and Alfred Stämpfli was at Henley as part of FC Zürich's backup team. He was also at the Olympic regatta in Grünau, Berlin, later in that year, where the Swiss failed in their main goal (see chapter 13).

Homberger remembers Alfred as 'Father Stämpfli', a good father to the club family. In a letter to the author he wrote;

He was a soft-spoken gentleman and a true artist in the art of boatbuilding. He would listen positively to any suggestions our crew had to make regarding possible improvements in the design of racing shells. Since I was at that time in engineering school this was of great interest to me. First, enlarge the cross-section of the oar in the oarlock area, reduce the 'angle of attack' of the blade to the waterline by half, from approximately 10 degrees to approximately 5. This would reduce the lifting component of the oar in the water. Secondly, eliminate the flat broad design of the rudder and replace it with a streamlined section flush with the flare of the hull at the stern. This resulted in a streamlined contour of the stern of the boat to the very end of the rudder. Thirdly, change the design of the hull by flaring it in with the washboard resulting in a flush cross-section of the boat. This resulted in increased stiffness, torsional and bending rigidity with only a nominal increase in weight.

Homberger says that Stämpfli usually listened to his suggestions, said next to nothing, and then incorporated them in his next boat.

One minor change Stämpfli made in the coxless four was to fix up the foot-steering for the stroke instead of the bow man on the theory that the stroke had a much better view of the stern wake. A turnbuckle was added to the steering cord to adjust it to zero when the foot-steering device was locked. This eliminated steering off course by accident when the steersman was concentrating on something else. Homberger says, 'We actually rowed many races without using the steering at all, but rather by adjusting starboard or port power by simply observing our course.'

The success of the Zürich crews at Henley, in the Olympics and European championships meant success for Stämpfli boats as well. Orders came from Germany and other countries, and the Stämpflis planned an export drive. Then the Second World War brought rowing to a virtual standstill, isolating Switzerland and closing the order books. Boat orders dwindled to a trickle and Alfred switched to producing skis for the Swiss army. He tried to keep his workforce together, perhaps eight or ten people, and in the tradition of the company made very good ash skis with hickory linings. At the end of hostilities in Europe his skis had a high reputation and he considered changing the emphasis of the company to winter sports equipment. But the late forties produced a boom in boat orders. John B. Kelly Sr, a Philadelphian building contractor and the 1920 Olympic sculling champion, brought his family to the workshop by the Zürichsee and bought a boat for his son, John B. Kelly Jr. John Jr won the Diamonds at Henley in 1947 and 1949 and the European title in the latter year.

Alfred Jr took over the business in 1948 and in the fifties more and more customers came from neighbouring countries, particularly Austria, France and Germany. In 1956 he made an experimental plastic sculling boat. Such a craft was a diversion: it was heavy, and the glue did not bond the two layers of the 'sandwich' together properly. The company forgot about plastic and carried on in wood. In the first world championships in 1962 six of the seven gold medals were won in Stämpfli wooden boats, and Alfred Jr was asked what he would do if he were to win all seven. 'It would mean that we would have to work even harder to stay there,' he said. In 1965 Oxford won the Boat Race in a Stämpfli, and the Harvard coach Harry Parker was so impressed with it that he ordered one for Harvard. Then Columbia, Princeton and the Massachusetts Institute of Technology had to have them, and the beautiful boats of Honduras cedar with ash shoulders and pine frames made Stämpfli a worldwide name. It was about this time, though, that Honduras banned the export of cedar, heralding future problems for all boatbuilders. And other designers, particularly in Germany, were at work.

The Glass Casket

In 1947 Willy Empacher opened his new workshop on the outskirts of the village of Eberbach which nestles in the wooded gorge of the River Neckar, to the east of Heidelberg. Eberbach's previous claim to fame was that Queen Victoria of England had been conceived there. Empacher came from Königsberg (now Kaliningrad) on the Baltic where he had trained in the shipyards before setting up a boatbuilding business in 1923. By 1927 he was building clinker boats for schools and for the East Prussian rowing federation, but his venture into rowing boats was not financially successful. During the Second World War he worked in the shipyards, and in 1944, as the Soviet army moved into East Prussia, he fitted out two small barges with supplies and fled with his family. It took them four weeks to pole themselves by canal and river to ice-bound Berlin, and they eventually reached Hamburg. Empacher worked for the British until 1947. Making boats was forbidden in the British zone at the time, although one of his activities was to convert naval launches into pleasure speedboats for British officers. His former partner in Königsberg, Willi Karlisch, settled in the same area at Mölln, not far from Ratzeburg on the border with the Soviet zone, where Karl Adam was germinating a future force in German rowing (see chapter 12). Adam and Karlisch were to form a partnership somewhat akin to that of Dreyfus and Stämpfli before the war in Switzerland. But Empacher's search for a place to set himself up again took him to Eberbach, where he found a 350-year-old boathouse.

Empacher attracted three of his former employees to Eberbach, including Gustav Neumann, who was the finest boatbuilder he knew. They obtained plenty of repair work from the clubs in the area and started to make fishing and pleasure boats. Neumann persuaded Empacher that there was a future in rowing boats because they were cheaper than sailing craft; Willy, knowing nothing of racing craft, went to Mannheim regatta to study the products of Pirsch, Perdes and Deutsch, the finest Berlin yards. He then reproduced a Pirsch boat so exactly that even Friedrich Pirsch thought it was one of his own with someone else's nameplate on it. 'I would be an idiot to copy a bad boat. If I copy I only copy the best,' Empacher told him, and they had a drink on it.

The first Eberbach boat was launched in 1948, and soon Empacher's were building clinker B-class fours in mahogany for the German market. Willy himself became an accomplished builder: the last boat he made with his own hands was a single for Mr Leitz of the Leica Company in 1978.

In 1948 Leo Wolloner, a refugee from the Sudetenland, joined as an apprentice. Neumann taught Wolloner to build clinkers. Clinker eights were in production by 1952, the year in which plywood came into use. They also built motorboats with Volkswagen engines for use by coaches. Then, in 1955, Wolloner made a launch from glass fibre (Gfk) and polyester, a process developed with the help of the BASF chemical company. This was followed by a prototype touring boat for two scullers. Ten people were photographed aboard it to show that it was strong and safe for children. In 1956 a training boat was made in glass fibre, and two years later Empacher's wood-shop turned out their first boat made of three layers of cedar ply sealed by a vacuum process. While Willy's son Dieter, who had started at his father's yard at the same time as Wolloner, moved to the Hamburg shipyards, Wolloner stayed in Eberbach, his mind fertile with ideas, always trying things, always watching how the boats moved on the Neckar.

Meanwhile, in 1949 Klaus Filter, an oarsman from Magdeburg, went to work under Max Niebeling at Pirsch's yard on the River Spree in the Soviet zone of Berlin. Niebeling, who had made the boats for the 1936 Olympic team, was master boatbuilder while Pirsch ran the business. In 1955, the year in which Niebeling died, the East German government set up their elite multi-sports clubs and began their relentless drive for international recognition (see chapter 11). At about the same time Pirsch moved his business to his home district of Spandau in the western zone of Berlin, but his old yard continued under East German management for a while, and Filter stayed on there. Good wood – Honduran and Brazilian cedar – became increasingly expensive and difficult to obtain in East Berlin. So Filter and his colleagues began to search for substitutes, and they found one with the help of East Germany's aircraft factory at Dresden. At the Olympic Games in 1960 the German coxless pair came fourth using what Filter describes as 'the first truly plastic boat'. He made it of glass fibre honeycomb bonded by epoxy resin. All the materials were manufactured in East Germany. Maybe, Filter says, his boat was before its time. Then the aircraft factory closed down. Nobody quite knows why, but Soviet jealousy of its technical expertise is suspected. When aircraft manufacture stopped, so did research and development.

Partly as a result of this, the authorities decided to convert the Pirsch factory on the Spree to a research centre for the development of materials and a factory to supply equipment to East Germany's national teams. It opened as the *Forschungs-und Entwicklungsstelle für Sportgerate* in 1961, starting with between twenty and thirty people working on projects for several sports. Filter, who had studied physical culture and naval architecture, was ideally suited to take charge of the rowing side. They began by reducing the length of the eight to reduce the wetted surface area and friction resistance. Theo Körner, the national rowing coach, was enthusiastic and cooperative in teaching people how to row the shorter boats, and by 1966 – the year in which the Democratic Republic (East) began to compete separately from the Federal Republic (West) – his team were trying out plastic boats with a hull shape close to the 'perfect half circle'. Filter says that scarcity of wood continued to be the main reason for the introduction of plastic.

Meanwhile, developments in the West Germany were coming to fruition. The wooden sculling boat used in 1968 by Joachim Meissner, the silver medal winner at the Olympic Games in Mexico City, was made by Empacher. It was the first craft from the yard at Eberbach to be associated with an international medal. And Karl Adam's West German eight won the gold medal at the same regatta in a wooden boat by Karlisch. Karlisch had shaped the stern of his boat like a canoe, and he did away with ribs by cold-moulding the hull from three veneers, the inside layer applied diagonally in one direction, the middle one laid over it with the grain in the opposite direction, and the outer layer laid fore-and-aft. The boat had shoulders for the outriggers, diagonals and crossbraces. Its gunwales had no structural purpose, serving only as protective strips for resting the boat on the rack. It was a beautiful, polished specimen of cabinet making, and the apple of everyone's eye.

In 1969 the East German women's double scullers used a plastic boat by Filter in the European championships. A year later Wolloner tested honeycomb construction using epoxy resin on the Neckar, fully ten years after Filter's first plastic experiment and fifteen years after Wolloner's prototype glass fibre boat. He found that it was good. Again, the technique and the materials were borrowed from the chemical industry.

Wolloner had not been idle in between. In 1960, when Stämpfli of Zürich were becoming the brand leader in both quality and medal scores, Wolloner designed a wooden 'dolphin' boat which was a variation on the hull shape that was to become the hallmark of Empacher. He continued to experiment with the hull shape, and in 1971 Empacher pulled off a marketing coup by promoting an international race in Heidelberg sponsored by Martini-Rossi with an eight as first prize. The Soviet Union won, and a relationship was born with a new and valued customer. Then in 1972, before the Olympic Games in Munich, there was great excitement when Wolloner unveiled a plastic eight-oared dolphin boat developed in coop-

eration with Ciba-Geigy, manufacturers of epoxy resin. The industrial designer Luigi Colani produced a rival boat for the West
Germans to test. His was a sensation. Its tubular frame was made
of titanium and criss-crossed between the staterooms. The sides
consisted of a Perspex framework perforated with large holes to
save weight, and covered by an outer skin made of two layers of
silk fibre. You could see through it. Outriggers and rails for the seats
were welded on at a standard height, and seats were mounted on
ball-bearings. This caused one of many problems: as soon as the
boat bowed, the rails, which were far apart, moved fractionally
apart, causing the seat mounts to jam. To solve this, wooden-moun-
ted runners were fitted closer together. But these changed the height
of the seats, so that the outriggers were now at the wrong height.
Wooden blocks had to be fitted to the upper surface of the three
titanium tubes which formed the outrigger in order to raise the
work. Reputations were at stake as the two boats were tested on
the Bodensee by the defending Olympic champions. First they preferred one, then the other, finding favour and fault while newspaper
reporters, some of them former international oarsmen, issued glowing testimonies to Empacher or Colani, followed by denials the next
day. The tests were inconclusive. The Colani boat was certainly
sensational and was christened the 'glass casket', but eventually it
lost the trials to Wolloner's Empacher. The crew thus found the
boat they wanted, but they lost their title to New Zealand. However,
the West German coxed four became champions using a Wolloner
boat which weighed only 59 kilos and sported a black hull. The
East Germans won three gold medals, including the coxless four in
a plastic Filter shell. According to Filter, the East Germans were in
plastic production 'to keep the prices down, while the others were
in production to keep prices up'.

In 1972 too carbon fibre was included in the list of materials for
possible use at Empacher. In 1973 Peter-Michael Kolbe of West
Germany used oars with carbon strips in them. In 1974 Jerry Sutton
was approached by the British company GKN with the intention of
making oars which were stiffer and lighter than conventional ones
by using carbon strips. GKN were interested because the pressure
to which the oars were subjected gave them information for their
research into carbon and its applications. The two worked together
for nine months, and the oars were used by the British eight in the

world championships and in the Olympics two years later. They were very expensive, but they made Sutton's name as an oarmaker.

In the first half of the 1970s, Karlisch were testing wooden hulls, having made an eight weighing 100 kilos. In 1972 Filter was experimenting with sliding-rigger boats in which the seat was fixed while the outriggers and foot-stretcher moved together, and he was using carbon in oars by 1976. Experiments using carbon fibre for a boat came to fruition in Britain for their Olympic crew in 1976 (see chapter 9). On the day they decided to row in a plastic Empacher, but they were at the start of something big.

During these years Leo Wolloner was endlessly fascinated by the possibilities before him and tirelessly pursuing his hobby of talking about boat design. He filled his drawers with books and papers about boats, ships and hydrodynamics. He tested the flexibility of oar blades; he tried out a slide for coxes, and rudders with two blades that could be raised from the water; he experimented with titanium and with various designs of fins; and he tested fish slime. Through all the developments ahead, he is probably the most tireless and most successful innovator. He made Empacher's plastic products reliable, and played a full part in giving the company on the Neckar its prime position in the world market for racing boats.

8

ATLANTIC TREATISE

GEORGE POCOCK remembered his upbringing among the ruling classes: 'There were absolutely no power tools, no machinery of any kind. Everything was done by hand, and to me the smell of the wood was sweeter than any perfume: Norway pine for the stringers, white ash for the ribs and shoulders, and Spanish cedar for the skin and washboards.' He remembered looking out of the window of his family's apartment above one of the Eton College boathouses and seeing the yard full of desperate men, journeymen boatbuilders answering an advertisement placed by his father Aaron, the manager of the school's boathouses. This was in the first decade of the twentieth century, when Edwardian England was feeling the pinch from other developing nations. By 1979, more than half a century later, the *New York Times*'s reporter was aghast at the mess of plastic which he found at the Eastern Sprints regatta: 'The aesthetics of this garbage is terrible. What more handsome place could an oarsman ever find than a boathouse filled with the magnificence of the Pocock products from the bright of the varnished Northwest woods in shells and oars which did not change for five decades, as perfect were they for this sport. And they may be still.'

George Pocock's description of his job was 'boatbuilder', but he was also philosopher, adventurer, teacher and soothsayer. His story turns from the advantages and disadvantages of England's class obsessions to a life of fulfilled hopes and aspirations on America's frontier. Born an Englishman, he died an American, but in a sense he was born an American and died an Englishman. He benefited from England's tradition of craft and graft but suffered hard times after the Victorian boom years and, had he stayed put, would probably have been frustrated by the lack of mobility through English society's class structure. But in 1911 George and his elder brother Dick set sail on a cattle boat for Halifax and British Columbia. Fate enabled them to use, to profit from, and eventually to prosper by the skill of their hands, and to be immersed in what George perceived to be the ultimate art form. 'When you're rowing well, why it's nearing perfection,' he wrote, 'and when you reach perfection you're touching the Divine. It touches the you of you's which is your soul.'

Once they had left the nobs of Vancouver behind them and moved, at the beckoning of one Hiram Conibear, to the thrusting society of the USA's northwest corner, they became naturalized pioneers. Dick was to go to Yale on the East Coast to build boats, but George, in his quiet way, became the philosopher-king of Seattle and then of the United States. Dick Erickson, Washington crew coach until 1988, said of him, 'As one learns to row, and we are always learning, the fine subtleties of matching wood with athletes emerge. There is a specific purpose for not only each piece of wood, but for its source and its shape. It is all designed to be useful, helpful, and, yes, aesthetic.'

The Pocock family were steeped in boatbuilding. George was born on 23 March 1891. His maternal grandfather Vicars had spent seven years building racing boats in Germany and had also constructed portable boats for Stanley to cart around the Congo when searching for Dr Livingstone. His father Aaron was a journeyman boatbuilder on the lower Thames before he came to Eton in 1901, one of four men employed on piecework by the then headmaster, Dr Warre, to increase the fleet of England's best-endowed rowing school to 650 boats. Aaron became manager two years later. George's uncle Fred had a boatbuilding business in Cambridge, but the two branches of the family had fallen out. As a teenager George just failed to get into the polytechnic and so instead became indentured to his father for five years, building and rowing boats and teaching the sons of the wealthy how to scull. That was how he met Tommy Sopwith before Sopwith became one of the world's leading aircraft designers; Anthony Eden before he became Prime Minister; J. B. S. Haldane before he became a Fellow of the Royal Society, a Communist and an Indian citizen; Prince Prajadipok before he became the last absolute monarch of Siam (now Thailand); and the sons of the shipowners Cunard and Holt. The single that George and Dick built for Holt was an extra-wide, shallow-draft shell tailored to fit the portly lad; it was known as Holt's War Punt.

George's biographer Gordon Newell observes that in the water-orientated milieu of Eton watermanship was the great equalizer. George's middle name was Yeoman and he had a deep interest in history and literature, seeing the monarchs of Europe coming to Windsor Castle on state occasions, sculling himself 7 miles down-stream to Runnymede where the barons had forced King John to sign the Magna Carta in 1215, and walking to Stoke Poges to muse under the great yew tree in the churchyard where Thomas Gray had written his 'Elegy' and found his last resting place. George ventured farther afield too. His father's advice on how to learn to scull was to go to Putney and watch Ernest Barry, the world professional champion. If you follow Barry, 'nobody will beat you,' Aaron told him. George remembered watching Barry come down in perfect form and then suddenly slump. What impressed George, he told his own son Stan years later, was that there was a man who could discipline his actions to such a degree that he should be sculling perfectly up to the instant he passed out. That lesson became central to the Pococks' aim: the most vital thing is form, and form must be kept at all costs. Ernie Barry once let young George try his boat, *Gertrude Charlotte*. George liked the boat but found Barry's sculls very stiff. 'I like stiff sculls,' Ernie told him, 'because I become unconscious much quicker and then I can row for ever.' The Pocock interpretation of this was that stiff sculls enabled Ernie to get his second wind quickly. In all his admiration of Barry, the one thing that George never did was to adopt stiff sculls. and Stan is scathing about the development of stiff oars in the 1970s, 'when everyone threw their brains away in this country' (the USA).

Aaron had some tips for his sons too. 'Think positively all the way to the finish line,' he told them. 'Never let a negative thought enter your mind . . . especially if you are behind.' And his advice about building craft was sound also. When George was seventeen his father entered him in a professional race at Putney and told him to build his own boat for it: 'I will give you one bit of advice,' Aaron said. 'No one will ask how long it took you to build it, they will only ask *who* built it.' George made the skin out of a fine Norway pine plank and the washboards from mahogany, which gave a distinctive pale hull and dark upperworks, the reverse of the normal Eton craft. And he won the final and the princely sum of £50, his dad winning £200 on a side bet.

Eton, Windsor and Old Father Thames were a boy's paradise, but there was no work for men. By 1910 there was no work for Aaron either, after he became a victim of the reorganization of the boat-houses at Eton. Mr Churchill, the rowing master, had offered to buy the boathouses and the entire fleet and turn them over to Aaron, but the manager declined on the grounds that the ancient buildings were in danger of collapse and he did not wish to take on the liability.

George and Dick, meanwhile, tried for jobs in London to no avail. So they decided to seek their fortunes in Australia in the knowledge that rowing was popular there. Just before they booked their passage, however, their sister Lucy's suitor told them that his brother was earning £10 a week cutting down trees in a place called British Columbia, and this is why the brothers booked steerage on the Allen liner *Tunisia* to Halifax, Nova Scotia, with rail connections to Vancouver. The total fare was £15, and George still possessed £30 of his racing winnings, which, after paying his ticket and outfitting, left him £5 with which to begin a new life in Canada. He intended to make a small fortune and come home in 1912 to win the Doggett's Coat and Badge, the professional race which brother Dick had won in 1910.

George's departure was a wrench:

There was no hope of making a decent living in England, so it had to be. There were tearful farewells at the London station where we boarded the train for our port of embarkation, Liverpool. My one special chum of many years, Jimmy Ottrey, was there to wish us Godspeed also. Many years later, Jimmy sent us a clipping of a BBC programme entitled 'What's wrong with British rowing?' conducted by Jack Beresford, a famous amateur British oarsman, in which he said, 'We never should have let men like the Pococks get away from England.' But in the year of 1911, it seemed, only our loved ones were aware of our departure, and there was nothing but fond memories to keep us in the land of our birth.

After steerage to Halifax and an even less comfortable transcontinental ride in a colonist train with only their own basket of provisions to feed them, the Pocock brothers found a clean room with

a Vancouver family for $2 a week, had their first baths and shaves
for two weeks, and feasted at a café on soup, fresh grilled salmon,
vegetables, dessert and coffee for 25 cents apiece. They marvelled at
the size of the city, its expanses of salt water, its timbered hills and
snow-capped mountains, a raw place with a thrusting population,
quite unlike the soft greenery of the gently flowing Thames. Dick
found work on a construction site and George began repairing boats
at Vancouver Rowing Club, being paid $40 a month. The boats
were in frightful shape, and so was the accommodation, a shed with
no cooking facilities. He left for a logging camp, then a sawmill,
then a shipyard, where he lost two fingers of his right hand in an
accident. This put paid to his dream of returning to England to race
for Doggett's in 1912. But things took a turn for the better when a
Mr Hudson, who had rowed at Cambridge, arrived in Vancouver
and was instrumental in the Vancouver BC placing orders for two
sculling boats from the brothers for $100 apiece. Furthermore, the
club had just completed a new boathouse and its old one, on a float,
was moored nearby. The old structure was sold to the brothers as
a workshop for $100, 'provided that said boathouse was removed
at least 100 yards away from the rowing club's buildings.' The
Pococks used the boat order as collateral to borrow $100 with
which to acquire their offshore floathouse, and they anchored it off
Deadman's Island.

The upper storey was living quarters – a bedroom with a primitive
wood stove. The Pococks bathed by diving into the water from
their bedroom window and carried drinking water from the public
fountain in Stanley Park. There was no electricity. The lower floor
was not long enough to house an eight, and work, they soon found
out, was governed by the elements.

We discovered that our shop was controlled by the tides. At high tide
the workbench was level, all was well. But at low tide, resting on the
sloping beach, the shop listed at a 25-degree angle, one end high, the
other low. We couldn't seek deeper anchorage. Farther out there was
the danger of rough water from sudden gales. Rough water would make
exact measurements impossible. And even the difference of a width of
a hair – three thousandths of an inch – would mar our work. We had
no money to go elsewhere. Accordingly, we had to adjust our working
hours to the tide. We stopped when the workbench went off an even
keel and tried to make up for lost time when the shop was afloat.

When the first single was complete the brothers took it to the club for inspection by the committee. They stood by, petrified, as members examined the skin. A hundred doubts and fears beset them. When one committee man wondered out loud how the boat would act, Dick said, 'Take it out, George, and show what it can do.'

George said, 'I sat down and shoved off. Our career was at stake . . . Slowly, then faster, I rowed, thanking the Lord we came from a family of scullers and that, at seventeen, I had won the Sportsman's Handicap. Half a dozen times I tore up and down before the watchful committee. Out on the float I awaited the verdict. It came in the form of a cheque for payment in full. God bless the committeemen, every one!'

The Tokyo Tearoom

The Pococks completed their first order soon after, but not before they had woken one morning to look out and see the Canadian Pacific steamship dock approaching. Their floathouse had slipped anchor and set sail across Coal Harbour. It cost them $2 for a tow back. Their reputation spread and their order book began to fill: lapstrake practice boats for James Bay Athletic Club of Victoria and Prince Rupert Rowing Club, and three fours for Kelowna, an inland town where British oarsmen were starting a club on Okanagan Lake. Then, on 24 May 1912, Vancouver BC held its first eight-oared race, for which Hiram Conibear brought the University of Washington crew from Seattle to the Indian River. On a rough, windy day shortly after the race, which was won by Washington by 2½ lengths, the Pococks looked out from their floathouse and saw a well-dressed man trying to row a skiff towards them. He lacked skill, to put it mildly, crabbing and catching the water with a mis-turned oar and making a lot of leeway. When in hailing distance, the brothers harpooned his skiff with their long boathook. The stranger climbed out of his boat and said, 'My name is Hiram Conibear. I am the rowing coach at the University of Washington in Seattle.' This was pre-legendary Conibear, the man who, on a whim and a prayer, was to build a crew programme that gave rise to the 'Conibear stroke' and changed the sporting map of America (see chapter 14). On that stormy day in 1912 only George and Dick Pocock had seen the

Conibear stroke, and they both concluded that it was under the influence of drink. But it wasn't, and they were to be ensnared by Conibear's charm and vision. Even if the dollars were elusive for a long time, the self-styled coach enticed the Pocock story round another important historical corner. For Conibear knew he needed them; but he could not have known what a key role George was going to play in American rowing knowledge, or that a Mr Boeing was going to hire the talents of an Eton shell-builder to enable his aeroplanes to walk on water.

The attraction of Seattle for the Pocock brothers was that Conibear promised orders for a dozen eights, fifty shells, a never-ending production line of crafted boats to satisfy the burgeoning American market. He was going to create a crew programme which would put the University of Washington in the mainstream. The Englishmen had never built an eight, and they summoned father Aaron, who was still out of work, to come and help them. It was not until Dick had moved to Seattle, while George finished off one or two jobs in Vancouver, and Aaron was on the high seas with his daughters Lucy and Kath, that it became clear that the only confirmed order was for one eight. Conibear knew that he needed a dozen, but his programme did not have one dime to rub against another. When he had used a piece of spruce to sketch out a map showing the university boathouse on Lake Union and the proposed ship canal linking it to the much larger Lake Washington, he had spared the Pococks the details. The building he had acquired for them on the untamed wooded campus – where there was only a handful of permanent buildings – was a rickety structure built in a day by Japanese labourers for an international exposition, and it was known as the Tokyo Tearoom. True to form, it had no power. When he learnt the news, Aaron Pocock said, 'You must remember that Mr Conibear is an American.'

Conibear had been a professional cyclist and trainer to the track team at the University of Chicago before becoming rowing coach at Washington when the programme was introduced there in 1904. He knew absolutely nothing, and tried to make up for it by giving it everything he had on a small salary from the Associated Student Body. He investigated the science of rowing by manipulating a human skeleton, and hit the university's alumni with fund drives. His persistence and charisma gradually brought dividends. In 1913 a Washington crew went to the great intercollegiate race at Pough-keepsie on the Hudson for the first time, and came a close third, ahead of their West Coast rivals. In the same year the Pocock family wrapped up their remaining orders in Vancouver and moved to Seattle, all except Aaron, who was homesick for the Thames and returned to England via the Poughkeepsie regatta. The crew's success brought alumni money rolling into Conibear's boat fund, and a women's programme was started with Lucy as coach. She also cooked for the men's crews' training table and at the University Way restaurant. Orders for boats from other clubs began to arrive at Seattle.

Unfortunately, however, Conibear was a great meddler in campus politics; he also perpetrated classic blunders such as arranging for privately owned trees to be felled because they obscured the view from his spectator train beside Lake Washington. He set off a Key-stone Cops drama in 1912 when he arranged – for the good of the spectators – a regatta in which the second race followed the first immediately, but in the opposite direction. Somehow both races, with attendant flotillas of motor launches, started at the same time, the fleets meeting in melée in the middle.

Politics began Conibear's downfall and tragedy completed it. In 1916 he was fired, along with Gilmour 'Gloomy Gil' Dobie, the football coach. Dobie went because his fame and popularity exceeded that of the university president, Dr Henry Suzzallo, who was set on making Washington one of the nation's great institutions of higher learning. Hiram Conibear was caught in the crossfire and told to go. But after intervention by Rusty Callow, the president of the Associated Student Body, he was allowed to stay if he promised to keep out of campus politics and to go East for six months to learn how to row. George Pocock told his son Stan that when Conibear returned to the boatshop after his enforced education 'there was fire in his eyes'. The next day Conibear was killed by falling out of a plum tree in his backyard while picking the last fruit. The moral: never go for the last dollar. The Pocock future was once more in doubt.

Red Cedar and the Red Barn

One day in 1916, however, Dr Suzzallo brought a visitor to look around the boatshop. The visitor studied the shells and then asked the Pocock brothers to come and see him. He left his card: 'W. E. Boeing, Hoge Building, Seattle'. Early in 1917 they were building pontoons for Boeing seaplanes at the Red Barn on the Duwamish River. By this time the Pococks had applied for US citizenship and volunteered for the draft, but a general turned up at the Red Barn and, in a voice that brooked no argument, told George, 'You can be of far more use to the war effort right where you are.' The brothers built 150 sets of pontoons before a single airframe was assembled. Before long George was foreman of the assembly plant and introducing machine-tool efficiency to the Boeing enterprise. He toured the country studying aircraft manufacturing plants and his studies on the East Coast led him to the conclusion that

> we had far better material for planking these flying boat hulls than the white pine all the East Coast plants were using. That material was vertical grain western red cedar. It is the wood eternal. It never rots. That material does not shrink in opposite weather conditions, wet or dry. Western red cedar (*Thuja plicata*) is lighter too. I knew it would make a far better hull and the Navy, after much correspondence, agreed to let us use it as planking for the Boeing HS–2 hulls.

At the end of the war Boeing order books were cut by half and the reduced workforce turned to building umbrella stands, telephone booths, hat racks, library tables and bedroom suites. The Red Barn went back to being a boatshop. Then Boeing and the Pococks built a prototype Speed Sea Sled, a powerful motor launch, the first of ten. At first they did not sell. But this was Prohibition time, and once it became clear that they could out-run Coast Guard patrols on Puget Sound, the remaining stock was sold in a day. The brothers' workmanship was instrumental in persuading a visiting Congressional committee to place an order for twenty pursuit planes with Boeing. From here, Boeing never looked back. But rowing too was picking up after the war. Ed Leader, a Washington oarsman who succeeded Conibear as coach, landed the more prestigious post at Yale, and he asked George to go with him. George, who had just got married, did not want to leave Seattle. It was Dick who went off to New Haven with Leader, and in December 1922 Rusty Callow, who succeeded Leader at Washington, enticed George away from Boeing and back into the boatshop.

Callow was the son of a Manxman who had hewn a homestead out of the rain forests of the Olympic Peninsula in the state of Washington. The Callow boys – seven sons and four sons-in-law – often went camping in the Northwest wilderness and invited their male friends along. George became one of this group. He described the camps as joyful gatherings, an amazing mix of professional men, politicians, clergy, loggers and labourers, a fellowship inconceivable in late-Victorian and Edwardian England. Rusty was 'a true Christian gentleman' in whom George put his trust and found that it was honoured. From Conibear to Boeing to Callow, George Pocock had discovered the New World's frontier and its spirit. In 1923 he travelled to Poughkeepsie with a shell called *Husky* and a crew who won the Intercollegiate Rowing Association championship. Many of the people they beat did not even know where Seattle was, but after that everybody knew who the Huskies were. George, who savoured Longfellow's 'Let us then be up and doing . . . learn to labour and to wait,' did not have to wait long before his order book was full. Twenty years later every shell at Poughkeepsie was a Pocock shell. In addition Joe Burk, the Pennsylvania sculler whom Stan calls an 'incredible man, sure didn't like to parade it', used a tailor-made Pocock shell weighing 29½ lb to win the Diamond Sculls at Henley in 1938. There was still scepticism among the East Coast press and the smart set that rude mechanicals from the Northwest could make decent boats. Burk's victory brought the comment from George that 'an ultra-conservative opinion might be that this did not prove that the boat was any faster, but it proved there was nothing wrong with it at least.' The wood eternal, the western red cedar which he had begun to use instead of Spanish cedar in 1927, he had also found on the frontier. In the thirties he introduced a less expensive model made by laminating two layers of cedar together over a mould under pressure. Later he was to experiment with glass fibre.

While the craft and the beauty asserted itself across America, the talk in the boatshop convinced generations of young men that Washington was the fount of all rowing knowledge. One returned from a regatta and said to George, 'There's some other joker making oars out there!' He was incredulous that the world contained another boatshop. Stan Pocock recalls that, during his days studying civil engineering at Washington, oarsmen simply did not talk to the coach. You *did not* talk to the coach. But in George's boatshop you could chew over the world after the outing. And it was George who kept an eye on the junior boats, George who corresponded nationwide with coaches and riggers who used his boats, George who went with shells and crews to the Olympics in Berlin in 1936 (where Washington won gold in the eight), to the Henley course during the London Games of 1948, to Helsinki in 1952, to Lake Wendouree in Melbourne in 1956 . . . It was George who rode in the launch when coach Al Ulbrickson, dubbed 'The Dead Pan Kid' by the *Seattle Post-Intelligencer*, had a problem, so that the men knew there was going to be a change in the line-up; and it was George who was asked to demonstrate the stroke in his sculling boat by coaches at a loss to make their charges see the light. And the Husky alumni, disciples of an art form brought to them courtesy of three generations of English professional scullers and labelled and packaged by Hiram Conibear, spread out and took over the Ivy League and more besides.

To date the Huskies can claim thirty-nine coaches after Conibear sent into the American college system. Many were outstandingly successful, among them Leader, who took Yale to the Olympic gold medal of 1924. George said of one of Leader's crews, 'The hallmark of a good crew, viewed from a distance, gave the impression that they had stopped rowing; then suddenly the oars would strike.' Essentially the English Orthodox stroke which was king at Eton and in England when George was a boy had been honed into a truly American Orthodox by the enthusiasm and naivety of Conibear underpinned by Pocock's experience, common sense and feeling. Chapter 14 tells the story of the college coaches.

The magazine *Northwest* said of George in his later years: 'He bears a striking physical resemblance to the poet, Carl Sandburg; the same craggy features, a not-quite unruly shock of white hair, the indifferent gait of a man utterly confident in his command of a medium. And, yes, one might say that both men, in their different ways, are brothers poet laureate.' But by then the kingdom of wood was under threat. Boatbuilders in Europe and America were experimenting with aluminium, plastic, kevlar and carbon fibre. The watchwords were lightness, ease of maintenance, and mass production economics, while for the oarsmen beef seemed to be more important than physique and the art of rowing. George died in 1976, before the space-age materials had reduced western red cedar to a curiosity. But wood is not totally dead yet in the rowing business, and George's essential philosophy – that there are no fast boats, only fast crews – holds good. His son Stan, who has sold the still-thriving business to the former international oarsman Bill Tytus, says that modern boatbuilding is beset by a mad rush to eliminate weight. He cites the opinion of oarsmen who assume that plastic boats are faster than wooden ones. 'Once a coach sucks into that, he's got a major problem – gutless wonders allowing themselves an easy row in a wooden boat because they don't believe in their own ability to beat a plastic one.' On physique he cites the Soviet crews who visited Seattle in 1987; the Washington men were shaped like isosceles triangles with the sharp end at the feet, while the Russians were less developed in the shoulders but more in the legs. 'They' – the latter – 'knew where the power lay.' And on technique he points to the British coxed four at the Los Angeles Olympics in 1984 who came out of the early-morning mist on Lake Casitas to overhaul the Americans and take the gold medal. Both were using German plastic boats, but the Americans had 'cling film' riblets on their hull, the latest high-tech theory developed by Boeing and NASA for reducing the wind resistance of space craft and the water resistance of hulls. 'The British four was the loveliest sight I've seen in the last 500 metres of a race, riblets or no riblets,' he says.

In a lifetime that brought the skill and technique of the Thames to the heady frontier of the Pacific Northwest, and that combined wood and athletes in an aesthetic whole, George Pocock found a poetry and a philosophy stronger than the 'beef and technology' school. He brought some good from the Old World to the New, found a Christian and spiritual home for himself and his family, and taught the Old World some New World tricks. *Sports Illustrated* once quoted George Yeoman Pocock as saying, 'In a sport like this – hard work, not much glory, but still popular in every century – well there must be some beauty which ordinary men can't see, but extraordinary men do.'

9

PLASTIC TO HEAT CURE

THE shape of the hull and the nature of the material from which it is made are not the only matters that have concerned inventors and manufacturers. The quest for speed has inspired examination of the motive power: training, fitness, technique and physique of the engine, and the tools which he or she is given to do the job. For example, in 1972 Klaus Filter and his laboratory in East Berlin experimented with a sliding-rigger boat in which the seat was fixed while a unit linking the outriggers and the foot-stretcher moved up and down in the boat. Like the sliding seat itself, this device was an example of an idea ahead of its technology. The earliest patent on record for sliding outriggers was taken out in Austria in 1898. But there is a suggestion that John Babcock, who is credited with developing the first successful sliding seat in 1870 (see chapter 6), was trying to find a way of moving the oarlock. He wrote to the New York newspaper *Spirit of the Times* on 14 December 1872: 'the rowlock should be moved six inches back and forwards each stroke. As this was impractical the idea of moving the seat occurred to me.'

The idea behind moving the rowlock is to reduce the movement of the centre of gravity each time the crew, who weigh perhaps five times more than their boat, take a stroke, thus causing the bow and stern to dip alternately into the water. The movement of the centre of gravity is considerable: a 27-inch slide plus the swing of the rower's body. A sculler must move his whole weight about 3 feet, half with and half against the run of the boat. Sliding forward to take the next stroke robs the boat of momentum (mass [weight of boat plus crew] × velocity), whereas sliding astern adds to the boat's speed. In 1954 Ted Poynter of Bedford Rowing Club in England designed a sliding-rigger double sculler, using metal runners along the side of the boat, and tried it out at Henley. Unfortunately the boat suffered damage and he and his partner had to withdraw. It was more than twenty years before the Germans were able to apply the strong, light materials originally developed by the aircraft industry to the sliding-rigger, and a while before scullers adapted to them. The Finn Pertti Karppinen, who won the Olympic sculling title in 1976, was in a sliding-rigger double scull with his brother by 1977, but their coach, Bo Gammels, did not take a liking to it. Then Empacher developed a sliding-rigger boat used by Peter-Michael Kolbe to win the world sculling title in Munich in 1981. With the sliding rigger there is only a slight reduction in drag, but it is enough to make a significant difference over 2000 metres. In 1983 all six finalists at the world championships used sliding-rigger boats. After that sliding riggers became ineligible for competition on grounds of expense.

Another attempt at reducing skin friction was banned after 1984. Skin friction on a hull arises from a thin layer of water known as the boundary layer, of which there are two types. The laminar boundary layer has a smooth steady flow; the turbulent boundary layer has a chaotic flow. The laminar boundary layer produces less skin friction than the turbulent one. A shell's boundary layer is laminar near the bow but becomes turbulent a little farther aft. If the transition can be delayed, the laminar flow area is increased and drag reduced. The above analysis was provided by Alec N. Brooks, Allan V. Abbott and David Gordon Wilson, three American academics who studied speed of water craft. They calculated that the propulsive efficiency of rowing (the ratio of useful power output, the product of the average thrust and the velocity, to the human power input) is between 65 and 75 per cent. In other words, a third of the rower's output goes into creating disturbances in the air and water. Despite outriggers and slides, they concluded that oars and paddles are basically drag devices because they generate thrust by slipping backwards through the water. Slippage can be reduced by increasing the size of the blade, but only to a limited degree because of practical constraints. Also, aerodynamic drag caused by blades when they are out of the water can be significant. One piece of evidence they cite is that three riders on a propeller-driven catamaran proved to be faster than 'a three oarsman shell' in a 163-kilometre test on the Thames in England in the 1890s!

Reduction of drag has been sought in other ways. The laminar boundary layer can be extended by injecting long-chain polymers or 'slippery water' into the boundary layer near the front of the craft. This has been banned on various grounds, including that of polluting the water. A slippery-water substance called Polyox which contained methylated spirit was tried out on the Thames in the 1960s by Geoffrey Page, the Amateur Rowing Association's technical officer. The Polyox was reckoned to be worth up to ten lengths for an eight on the 1 mile 550 yard Henley course. Page and the ARA persuaded the international rowing federation (FISA) to ban their discovery immediately on the grounds that it was a pollutant, as well as being expensive. In 1972 the Russians, with one eye on swimmers who were experimenting with coating their bodies, were trying out 'fish slime' with the help of Leo Wolloner of Empacher. Fish slime was a product of Bayer Leverkusen. It was banned by FISA before the 1976 Olympics in Montreal. During the Olympic regatta, however, a Soviet official detected traces of fish slime, recognizable by its sweet taste, on the hull of Kolbe's boat. Wolloner, deputed by FISA's president Thomi Keller as his technical adviser, instructed Kolbe to stop using it; at the same time he told the Soviet official that if Kolbe was reported, Wolloner would reveal that Soviet boats had used fish slime at a previous championship. That was the end of the matter, and the end of fish slime.

Another experiment was conducted by the Flight Research Institute in the United States in 1984. A sculling boat was covered with plastic skin in which grooves or 'riblets' had been formed, spaced three thousandths of an inch or 80 micrometres apart. Subsequent tests showed that the shell's maximum speed was increased by 2 per cent, or about four boat lengths over 2000 metres. It appears that the grooves stabilize the laminar boundary layer. The American coxed four at the Los Angeles Olympic Games put up an excellent performance using the skin, which came to be known as 'clingfilm', but they were nevertheless beaten by the British in the final. Since then this substance has also been banned by FISA. Again, the ground was cost at a time when the federation was trying to reduce the expense of rowing and make it more attractive to countries where modern rowing was in its infancy.

In principle the racing boat of the 1990s has not changed dramatically from that of the 1890s. It has sliding seats and fixed outriggers, a smooth bottom, and is not coated in chemical substances or equipped with a slippery-water tap. But plastic and alloy are king. Melch Bürgin, who took over Stämpfli in 1983, admits that the Swiss company shunned plastic for too long. After their early flirtations with plastic, Stämpfli made a policy decision to stay with wood. It lasted until 1989. The notice etched in brass on their door reads: 'If God had wanted us to have fiberglass boats He would have made fiberglass trees.' Bürgin now makes 'one-piece' plastic sculling boats which have a cockpit integrated with the hull. He does not use honeycomb, believing that where you can get air you can get water. He claims that his boats will last longer than other plastic boats, but that remains to be seen.

Bürgin was a Zürich sculler who used Stämpfli boats and learned his trade from the Stämpflis. Although his plastic boat was 'designed by computer' in Helsinki, he maintains that you cannot test a rowing boat without rowing it. It takes a long time to find out which boat is best. 'Hydrodynamical questions are like walking a tightrope. A small change can be completely disastrous. Put a boat on the water and it tells you what is going on if you just listen. Watch it with your eye, look how the waves are doing.'

Bürgin says that Stämpfli's real difficulties started when cedar from Honduras became difficult to get in the mid-sixties. Stämpfli buy a tree at a time. When a trunk arrives at the yard it is cut into planks 80 mm thick and these are stored for three years. Then the planks are cut into 5 mm boards. Even when Stämpfli could obtain Honduran cedar, they found it sometimes contained bullets fired in the civil war, and these wrecked their saw blades. The company turned from Honduras to Brazil, but Brazilian cedar is heavier. This occurred just when other companies had found a way to make plastic boats lighter. Bürgin says, 'Modern athletes want light boats, even if the lightest boat is not necessarily the best thing.' Eventually they found a suitable African wood, ayus. They now use ayus for the skin, pine for the frame and ash for the shoulders. They claim that they can make wooden fours which are lighter than plastic fours, and in addition tailor a boat to the sculler or crew to achieve the optimum distribution of weight. They also claim that a wooden boat will stand ten years of heavy use if it is maintained properly, as against probably four years for the average plastic boat.

For Stämpfli the future may lie with plastic, but the Stämpfli heart still beats to the skill of a builder like Gennaro Acttio fashioning a wooden single in Bürgin's workshop. It is company policy, Bürgin says, to introduce the client to the builder, and clients are encouraged to visit the shop during the course of the work. The frame is made first, then fitted to the keel. Washboards, ribs and templates for the skin are then added. The skin is first varnished in 4-metre sections, then fixed to the frame. Decking, track for the seat and foot-stretcher are then attached, and the last coats of varnish applied. The boat is fitted with Stämpfli-made outriggers. Stämpfli craftsmen claim to be able to recognize their boats years after they made them.

In 1989 Empacher made about 500 boats. More than a third were built of wood. For the ply skin they use Lebanon or Honduran cedar if they can get it, or African koto or wawa. Canadian or Alaskan spruce is used for the keel, and French ash for the shoulders. Christian Kulmey-Becker of Empacher's woodshop says that their wooden boats are about 5 per cent heavier than the plastic ones. They are trying to reduce the weight of an eight to 100 kilos by experimenting with mixtures. The first two layers of the ply skin are diagonal, while the third or outer layer is straight, just like the Karlisch. The finish consists of one coat of resin and two of lacquer outside and in; the inside of the ends receives only two coats. A sculling boat is made of three layers of 0.8-mm birch plywood in four stages: the spruce keel is laid, the plywood skin is added, coated in resin, and then given a cedar veneer using vacuum treatment. The boats take between 85 and 90 man-hours to make and weigh 17.5–18 kilos. Empacher are experimenting with a mixture of carbon and kevlar which will reduce the weight to about 16 kilos. Their method of testing is to make three boats and lease them to customers with an option to buy. They are asking the same question as Bürgin of Stämpfli: 'Does the rower like to sit in your boat?'

So wood is not yet finished. Plastic does not always beat wood for medals. Eton College Boathouse in England will make traditional clinker racing boats to order, and there are other yards building in wood or in mixtures of wood and plastic. But the cost of wood, the development of plastic, and the preference for plastic among the top racers have combined to make plastic the brand leader.

In the late 1970s Empacher's plastic hulls were finished in yellow. They became the hallmark of the company and began to dominate world markets during the same period as Filter's boats from the people's boatbuilding factory (VEB) in East Berlin were winning the most international medals. But the East German crews had no choice over whose boats to use. Only Filter's were on offer, and government support precluded survival in the marketplace. Whenever East European countries had a choice, they bought boats made in the West. Eventually Empacher became market and medal leader.

Another company prominent in the sixties and seventies was Donoratico, makers of fine wooden boats, in the Italian village of that name. Donoratico was started by Count Gaddo della Gherardesca, a parquet-flooring and radio-toy manufacturer, to make fishing and rowing boats. They then started to build catamarans, and took over the Carlesi racing boat company in the 1950s. Donoratico's name in racing boats was established by Commendatore Rodolfo Calvello and enhanced by an engineer, Marcello Beucci. Lido Filippi was employed there, and in 1969 he made a prototype sculling boat and had a mould made of it in England. The mould was in three sections because the drying oven could not take a complete boat. The parts were assembled with great difficulty. Like Stämpfli, Donoratico left their plastic boat on the shelf and carried on building in wood. By 1971 60 per cent of the boats in the European championship finals were Dons; New Zealand were using Dons for training but Empachers for racing. In 1975 Donoratico learned something of Empacher skills when they hired a former employee from the German company. His usefulness was cut short when he was found with his hand in Donoratico's till. Two years later Filippi, by his own admission, undertook some industrial espionage which resulted in his being caught in France while taking measurements of an Empacher pair. He left Donoratico around this time and set up on his own, founding the Filippi Lido company in 1980. It started by making wooden boats, but carbon and epoxy-resin construction began in 1984. Two years later Donoratico, which the count had converted into a workers' cooperative, failed. Its boats and remains were taken over by Filippi. In the same year the Italians used a Filippi eight to win the world lightweight title, and in 1988 the Italian quadruple scullers struck Olympic gold in a Filippi. The Filippi hull shape now owes something to Filter's work in Berlin.

Meanwhile, technology had transformed oarmaking. For high-level competition, wood is almost finished. Many companies experimented with carbon in the seventies. Wolloner of Empacher was

driven to distraction by the famous German crew known as the Bulls
of Konstanz, who delighted in breaking his prototype carbon blades.
But carbon became an essential element in the manufacture of stiffer
and lighter oars. In 1974 the English manufacturer Jerry Sutton cut
grooves into his oars and bonded carbon bars into them. This
enabled slimmer looms to be used, thus losing weight while retaining
stiffness. Aylings, with a company called Reredos, marketed an oar
which had an aluminium shaft, pressed plastic blade and a conventional wooden handle. In America the Dreissigacker brothers, Peter
and Dick, were winding glass and carbon fibre together, a technique
which they marketed in 1977 and which made them the world's
largest suppliers of blades. Their objective was to produce an oar
which minimized the energy lost to wind resistance, bad handling
(that is, poor rowing), and propulsive inefficiency in the water. They
have developed a range of blade shapes and shaft specifications, with
the emphasis on lightness, durability, and easy replacement of parts.
The most recent experiments with oars concern the angle at which
the blade is set on the shaft and there is renewed interest in the
'mutton leg' oar in which the blade parallel to the water instead of
in line with the tilting shaft.

In Britain, Aylings no longer make the oars they were once famous
for, but have moved back into boat production, taking over Carbocraft and using the hull shapes of Empacher and Yachtwerft, the
new name for Filter's outfit in Berlin. Some companies, like Sims of
Twickenham, continue to use only wood, and they maintain a steady
market among schools and clubs. But by the 1980s there were
probably more small builders of plastic boats than of wooden boats
in Britain. Moulding by American companies such as Vespoli, Van
Dusen and Schoenbrod has forced Pocock to turn to plastic. The
latest change, however, has come about through baking.

The Heat of the Kitchen

One who has achieved the transition from hydrodynamics to chemistry is Bob Janousek. By way of some broken riggers at the Olympic
regatta in 1976, a probe into the properties of rigidity, a management
lesson through bankruptcy, and some help once again from the
aircraft industry, he is a baker of boats in Byfleet, southwest London.

A graduate in physical culture from Charles University in Prague, Bohumil Janousek came to England to coach in 1969. In the 1990s he cooks boats for a living.

Before we learn how, however, we must consider anew the aims and problems that beset designers. In rowing hulls we are concerned with rigidity; rigidity is affected by both torsional and longitudinal flexibility, of which torsional is the more important. Torsion is the twisting by which, for example, a boat can be down on one side in the bows and the other side in the stern, or down on one side in the bows and stern and on the other side in the middle. Longitudinal flexibility is the lengthways bending in a straight line from bow to stern. Boats are often tested for longitudinal rigidity when they are on land, but this reveals nothing very useful. When a boat is afloat the water supports its entire length. It is in this situation that rigidity needs to be tested. Oars involve similar problems. Until the coming of carbon fibre, the quantity and quality of wood used in an oar were the only factors determining rigidity.

New materials opened up a new field. The shaft of an oar needs to give a little to absorb the impact of a sudden force on the human body when locking it into the water at the beginning of the stroke. But in the case of boats it was thought in 1976 that 100 per cent rigidity would be ideal. Janousek says, 'At Carbocraft, the company established to use carbon fibre in manufacturing boats, we gradually increased the proportion of carbon in the structure until we arrived at an almost 100 per cent carbon honeycomb shell. Then we found that people couldn't row it.'

In 1990 there were basically three materials used in the manufacture of plastic boats. These were glass fibre, which was the first wood substitute (after paper and aluminium), carbon fibre, and a nylon fibre called kevlar. All come in the form of woven cloth and can be laminated together in layers using polyester or epoxy resin. Polyester is good for solid laminating but is too brittle for bonding layers of foam or honeycomb. Epoxy resin is more flexible and better at bonding fibres with a small contact area. Each of these materials was developed in the aircraft industry, each has certain characteristics – kevlar is tough, while carbon is light and stiff – and each can be used in an almost infinite number of combinations with the others. 'The weaves, the strengths, the thicknesses, the materials have an infinite variety, as do the bonding substances,' Janousek says. 'What we have to do is simplify the choices before us to what is relevant, both in achieving the kind of boat or oar that we want, and in the cost of producing it.'

All this he has learned since the winter of 1975–76 when a former oarsman, John Vigurs, approached him with an idea. How would it be, Vigurs asked, if the British eight could go to the Olympics in Montreal in a revolutionary light, stiff boat moulded from carbon fibre? Would he be interested in trying it? Janousek as principal national coach of the Great Britain team was sceptical. He had a small squad of oarsmen and his sights were on two gold medals, one for Chris Baillieu and Mike Hart in the double sculls and one for the eight. He had formed a nine-man squad for the eight in 1973. In 1974 they had won the world championship silver medal in a wooden cold-moulded Karlisch boat; in the 1975 championships they competed as two fours both of whom finished fourth. For the Olympics Janousek had ordered a new plastic Empacher with a wooden frame.

Vigurs, an electronics engineer, proposed to borrow the aircraft industry's monocoque type of construction, which is essentially a tube with bulkheads in it. The three parts of the structure – hull, staterooms and decks or canvases – are each moulded in one piece, thus dispensing with a frame while retaining rigidity. Carbon bars had been developed by Courtaulds in the early 1970s for the turbine blades of Rolls-Royce aero engines, and a scientist at the Royal Aircraft Establishment had then succeeded in making carbon fibre which could be woven into cloth. Janousek agreed to lend Vigurs a boat from which to make a mould and told him that if he was going to test the product he would need it by 15 May. In truth it was the last thing Janousek wanted just before the Games, for which his crew were favourites and the competitors most feared by the German Democratic Republic. And something else exciting had already happened. Leo Wolloner had asked him to visit Empacher urgently and incognito. When Janousek arrived in Eberbach, Wolloner told him that if he could wait for delivery until March he could have the first Empacher eight to be made by honeycomb sandwich. Janousek said they could wait. When the boat arrived she was black and beautiful.

The Vigurs hull was made at British Aerospace in Weybridge and christened *Carbon Tiger*. It passed its first test when it fell off the vehicle that was taking it to be fitted out. It landed on the road undamaged and was light enough to be picked up by two people. Vigurs made all the fittings himself. In June Janousek and the crew tried it out in secret at Thorpe Water Park near London. They had no intention of being drawn into the kind of public trials which the Germans had undergone four years previously with the Colani and Empacher boats. The Vigurs boat, also sleek and black, seemed to move as fast, or perhaps a little faster, than the Empacher. 'In that situation, when you know already that things are very close,' Janousek says, 'you can't help thinking what if this boat works and could give us a few hundredths of a second in Montreal? So we decided to take it. At the very least we could use it to psychological advantage.'

They used both boats at their training camp on the Wellington canal in Canada. *Carbon Tiger* proved slightly faster than the German boat. Janousek never said which boat he would use. He didn't even tell his crew. Then, a week before the Olympic regatta, one of the carbon boat's specially designed riggers broke. It was welded together by a local blacksmith. Then another snapped, and then another. This was enough for the Czech in charge of Britain's rowing. The risk was too great. But he kept quiet about the breakages, made no announcement about the boats, and kept the world guessing. Eventually he told the crew that they were going to row in the Empacher but that they must tell no one. Speculation continued even after the heats. They led the final until the East Germans caught them in the dying moments of the race. Meanwhile Baillieu and Hart took silver medals in the double sculls using Vigurs's *Carbon Cub*. Carbocraft opened for business and Janousek accepted a job in sales even though other countries were trying to tempt him to take charge of their international rowing.

At first he had nothing to sell. While Jerry Sutton went into serious production with carbon-reinforced wooden oars and the American Dreissigacker brothers hitch-hiked around Europe and began to develop their all-carbon oars, the men at Carbocraft set out to stiffen their monocoque model so that there was absolute torsional and longitudinal rigidity. The only additional strengthening required was shoulders to take the strain of the outriggers. By 1977 they had arrived at a completely rigid boat made out of a carbon-honeycomb sandwich. The process was cold-moulding, which entails lining the mould with layers of fibre and saturating it with epoxy resin at room temperature. There is only limited time before the resin cures itself and becomes unworkable, so men have to work quite fast to apply it at the saturation stage. In the heat of summer the hardening process speeds up. If you are not quick you end up with resin in a partly cured state before the vacuum pressure can be applied, which means that the layers of fibre are glued together rather than bonded. Successful curing is an equation between temperature and time.

It was this stiff second prototype and the reaction of those who tried it out which sent the men at Carbocraft back to first principles of rigidity. 'If you kick it,' Chris Baillieu said of his boat, 'it kicks you back.' The ultra-stiff boat provided no cushion against a battering from rough water. It reacted sharply when the crew made a mistake. It had no feel to it. It was uncomfortable for the rowers. Janousek thought this through. 'A flexible boat will cushion the effect of rough water, and will cushion the results of technical shortcomings of the crew. If somebody makes a mistake, a flexi-boat will react softly, whereas a solid boat will do something abrupt.' He examined what rowers meant by 'feel', and identified it as the chain from oar to outrigger to boat which transmits what the boat is doing. He concluded that the three links in the chain should be closely matched in rigidity. Total rigidity of any one part deadens the feeling that the rower gets from the movement of the boat, and so the crew cannot feel the boat's reaction to what they are doing. Having arrived at that point, the remedy was straightforward. They reduced the amount of carbon in the boat until they arrived at the optimum compromise between rigidity and flexibility. They stopped when the testers said the boat was rowable. And they retained the shoulders, the strengthened joint between the outrigger and the boat, which were important for both strength and transmission of feel. Now the boat spoke to the crew when the going got tough. And this was really Carbocraft's contribution to design. 'It wasn't design,' Janousek says. 'It was evolution.'

Carbocraft were then able to produce reliable, fast, light, strong boats, and their black hulls became more familiar. But commercially they began to run before they could walk. The company looked into sailing boats and cruisers and catamarans, and overstretched itself as the leisure boating industry in Britain took a disastrous economic dive in the early years of Mrs Thatcher's government. The company collapsed in 1981, although the rowing boats were profitable. That part of the company was sold to its production manager, Tony Howarth, and later passed to the oarmakers Aylings, who began to make cold-moulded boats under their own name.

Before the collapse, however, Janousek had got wind of a new process of lamination used for Concorde in the development department of the British Aircraft Corporation at Weybridge. This was heat-curing, which Carbocraft tested in 1979–80. Janousek thought it would have advantages over cold-moulding. He decided to set up a 'bakery'. In February 1981 he was cooking boats in Shepperton Marina, later moving to an industrial estate in Byfleet. He trod slowly and softly at first. The technology and the materials were expensive, and although he had known little about business or production management or chemistry before he went to Carbocraft, he now knew that control of these was the secret of success. By 1988 he was taking a boat out of the oven every working day and making the full range of racing boats. In 1990 a very early model returned for a re-spray and he found that its rigidity had not changed. He hopes he has found a way of making boats which will retain their racing qualities for twenty years and possibly more.

Heat-cure is used for both aircraft and the cockpits of racing cars. In rowing boats it was first used by Van Dusen in the United States for the hulls of singles in the late seventies. Van Dusen adapted the technique from a helicopter manufacturer. But Janousek and his new company Janousek Racing were the first to apply it to the monocoque boat. Its advantage is that it has great rigidity due to the strength of the bond. Addressing once more the old rigidity–flexibility equation, Janousek identified three variables: first, the nature of the raw material; secondly, the nature of the honeycomb sandwich; and, thirdly, the monocoque structure. With the well-proven monocoque and honeycomb structure, it is the quantity of the bonding that determines long-lasting rigidity. Having arrived at a recipe by mixing materials of varying densities in various thicknesses, Janousek found the process was easier and less labour-intensive than cold-moulding. The bonding resin is distributed evenly by a machine which saturates the fibre, and will only cure when heat is applied. The pre-pregnated cloth is then cut into the required shapes, laid in the concave mould, a vacuum bag is put over the mould and sealed, and as air is sucked out, atmospheric pressure forces the material to the mould. Then the material is cured for approximately an hour and a half at 130°C.

The hull is released from the mould, bulkheads and shoulders are bonded onto it, followed by pre-moulded staterooms and canvases. A boat can be made in six days. The bonding is six times stronger than that achieved by the cold-moulding process. In fact, it is now stronger than the materials from which it is made. 'If you hit something,' Janousek says, 'you will knock a hole in it, but you won't delaminate it.' In other words, the layers of fibre will not peel apart. Forty-two per cent of the boat's purchase price is the cost of the high-tech materials, but this is offset by reduced labour costs.

A wooden boatbuilder retains the ability and the privilege of taking a look at a sculler or a crew and making a boat to suit their build, weight and preference. On the face of it a plastic manufacturer is stuck with what comes out of his mould; each boat is just like the one before and the one after. But this is not strictly the case. Janousek says that because the moulds are expensive, you first have to figure out the most advantageous shape of hull. There is a family resemblance to all the hulls, whatever their size, that come out of his oven. But by using two or three moulds and removable aluminium inserts, boats can be baked to suit crews of different weights. For example, there is one mould for a sculling boat broadly suitable for scullers up to lightweight men, and a second for heavyweight men. Three sizes of boat can be made from each of the two moulds using inserts which progressively reduce the size of the hull, while maintaining the same triangle of measurements formed by the distance from the waterline to the seat, the seat to the swivel, and the swivel to the waterline.

Besides the larger companies, there are many small manufacturers of boats and fixtures and fittings who cross an idea with their technical knowledge or practical experience in a boat.

Graeme King is making a valiant attempt in Putney, Vermont, to keep wood in eights. Having applied number-crunching to the hull shape, he has come up with a very light craft which has fins projecting at 45 degrees, one on each side under the No. 3 seat, to aid stability. But in the late twentieth century there are considerably fewer people and companies who begin from first principles than there were in the nineteenth. What is passing with the decline of wood is the possibility of equipping oneself with a few handtools and building a boat more or less anywhere. For plastic you need chemicals, moulds and specialized tools.

This is a long voyage from the days when people looked to the rhythms and currents of water dynamics to aid them with flying machines. It is a long way from young George Pocock, the Eton-trained boatbuilder, making wooden floats for Mr Boeing's aeroplanes so that they could land on Puget Sound, or Alfred Stämpfli Sr's 'webbed feet' for Swissair. Now it is the aviators grappling with air currents who make the waves that advance racing boats. Stämpfli's shop by the Zürichsee, Empacher's rambling sheds on the north bank of the Neckar, Sims's boatshed by the Thames, all retain the unmistakable characteristics imparted by lovingly acquired skills on a carpet of sawdust, to the sound of chisel and mallet, and in the aura of wood shavings and varnish. But in his hangar at Byfleet, which is near but not accessible to water, where rolls of woven fibre and tubs of resin stand by the moulds and vacuum bags and the oven, Janousek makes no claim to be either boatbuilder or designer. 'This is boat manufacturing, not boatbuilding,' he says. There is no hint of boatbuilding in his pristine white office either. No hint that this man is an Olympic medal winner or was a national coach whose crew came within two and a half seconds of being the fastest afloat. The pictures on his walls are of snow-covered mountains, clean and pure and white, the colour of the singles and doubles, fours and eights outside on the trailers, ready for delivery.

PART THREE
COACHES

10

THOR, GOD OF ENLIGHTENMENT

PIEDILUCO nestles in the mountains of Umbria. The village is strung along a lake, stone steps leading down between the houses to the water. More buildings cling to the hillside on the other side of the single street. The small square is open to the lake, the ice cream parlour offering the Italian version of snooker with a vista of the mountain on the far shore and scullers out at practice. There is little traffic and no hurry about Piediluco until you pass the rowing club and turn the corner leading to the countryside. There, set among lakeside trees, is a minimal modern building which is the Italian national rowing centre. There is a large boatshed, gymnasium and laboratory, as well as lecture theatres and offices. In the off-season rowers from many parts of the world are to be found in the local hotels and restaurants, enticed there by the development programme run by FISA (Fédération Internationale des Sociétés d'Aviron), and bringing a useful supplement to a village economy otherwise dependent on fishing and weekend visitors from Rome and the steel town of Terni.

From 1980 to 1990 the technical director of the Italian programme was the Norwegian Thor Nilsen. He is also the architect of the FISA programme which grew from a 1986 working party and is supported by Olympic Solidarity, the IOC's fund to further participation in sport. He set the Italians a new training system worked out in his previous job as technical director to the Spanish rowing federation, and their results have improved over the ten-year period, making Italy one of the strongest rowing countries in the world. The FISA programme has parallel objectives, but with different emphases. In the sporting sense it aims to help the less-developed and the smaller rowing countries to help themselves to increase their activities. In the educational sense it aims to spread the gospel of rowing as a highly beneficial activity for all ages and classes of society. In a political sense it aims to enhance rowing's standing in the international sporting arena and increase both the range of activities and the number of countries that take part. Over a few years it has made a good start by publishing coaching manuals simple enough for people with no previous experience of teaching rowing, or even of rowing itself, to learn how to coach. It has organized training camps for coaches and crews both in Piediluco and in Latin America, Asia and North Africa. And, recognizing that the cost and the quality of boats and equipment are key factors, it has organized boatbuilding seminars and courses in places far away from the European and American manufacturing centres, worked on standard boat designs to reduce production costs, and taught local boatbuilders how to improve their skills. As a result, activity has increased in Latin America, in a number of Asian countries and in some of the smaller European and Mediterranean states.

The programme outlined above implies standardization, reducing or eliminating variations in how boats are made and how they are rowed. Whichever way one looks at rowing's development, however, one finds strongly held opinions and practices handed down from generation to generation. How common the denominators that Nilsen and FISA have identified will remain is yet to be seen, but considerable achievement can be discerned arising from a background of much diversity. The great difference that Nilsen perceives between the accepted practices of rowing when he started out in the fifties and the Karl Adam era which took the West Germans to the top is one between hand-me-down coaching and coaching by lateral thinking. Of necessity an amateur sport has to rely on its own resources, and most rowing clubs initially produce coaches from among their own rowers and pass on accepted techniques from crew to crew. Of course, outside influences sometimes seep in and ideas jump from one centre to another through publications and migration. But tradition permeates the sport, and for the most part it breeds its own gurus and teachers. 'Coaching always came from within rowing, was based on personal experience and coxing. The traditional way to coaching was coxing. It worked fine for many

years, leaving you to try and develop something on your own,'
Nilsen says.

When Nilsen began to row at Baerum, near Oslo, in 1945, everything in Norway was based on Steve Fairbairn, the Australian whose
coaching career had been in England. Fairbairnism was an approach
to rowing rather than a style, a belief that pulling an oar should be
a natural movement. By the start of the Second World War it had
pretty well transformed English rowing after a titanic struggle with
the English Orthodox style, of which more will be said in chapters
12 and 14. English coaches sometimes visited Norwegian clubs, but
there followed a dose of Conibear style in the early fifties introduced
to Scandinavia by Gus Erickson, a Swedish American. Erickson,
having rowed at the University of Washington and having coached
there and at Syracuse University in New York, came to Sweden as
national coach. American crews had been very successful using the
Conibear style (see chapter 14), although Nilsen points out that they
rowed almost exclusively in eights and these were usually made up
of unusually tall athletes. The Swedes and the Norwegians used it
with some success until the end of the fifties, but it was less suited
to smaller rowers in smaller boats.

Nilsen rowed in the 1952 Olympics, suffered the Norwegian boycott of the 1956 Games, and coached for the 1960 Olympic regatta,
as well as being involved in a pile of Norwegian national championship medals and some Scandinavian titles. 'Rowing was a summer
activity only at that time, and I was doing other sport and coaching
other sport,' he says, 'so there were some outside influences, and
other coaches must have had similar experiences with running and
cross-country skiing. But this was not systematic.' He himself stopped serious competition in 1960. He took Norway into the international arena with help from abroad. He was assisted greatly by
Ivan Vanier, an Indonesian from the Netherlands who is a genius
of sculling. 'The technical changes made in Norway were based on
Vanier's inspiration. We had training and skiing and all that, but
we were not moving the boat as fast as we should. Ivan taught us
the art of technique. He saved us years of development due to his
knowledge, due to his feeling, due to his behaviour, due to his
enthusiasm.' Vanier coxed Nereus while studying psychology in
Amsterdam. He was already trained in physical education and began
to assist with coaching in the Dutch student tradition of passing

knowledge down the line. He says that he introduced more flexibility at the expense of lifting heavy weights into the Norwegians' training, and was surprised to see changes in technique taking effect in a year.

Nilsen was further helped by a lucky break. He came into contact with the fathers of exercise physiology, the Swede P. O. Astrand and the Norwegian K. Rodahl, who together wrote *The Textbook of Work Physiology*. 'I got a good back-door education. I had no degree in it. They had a lot of top younger people working with them. I was lucky. I had a direct door into all this research, all the knowledge I needed.' The rowers worked with the scientists and Nilsen paid his dues by passing on knowledge of general physiology learned from his own experience.

One of the things which Vanier brought to Norway was a hint of what came to be known as the 'international modern style' which evolved from Karl Adam, who was having even greater success in the Federal Republic of Germany than the Norwegians and Swedes were experiencing under Nilsen (see chapter 12). Adam was a mathematics teacher and he based many of his calculations on biomechanics. Nilsen's interpretation is that while Fairbairn focused on the body's movement in cooperation with the boat and the blade, Adam focused on the blade and asked what was the most effective part of the stroke. 'He asked, "How can I produce as much energy as possible on the blade?" He concluded that a certain arc is the most effective part, so he said, "OK, why should you do all this other bullshit if that is the most important part?" He arrived at shorter strokes, a higher stroke rate, applying more energy to each stroke, using the biggest muscles, the legs, with less bodyswing, bigger blades to catch the negative input we have with the catch, a quick catch. He studied the velocity curve of the boat . . . from a mechanical and mathematical point of view. Once everything was fixed, there was just one thing on which to focus; energy production . . . I think that was the way that Adam was thinking.'

Although Nilsen's Scandinavians won medals in fours and doubles, his ambition of gold was not achieved until Frank and Alf Hansen won the double sculls in 1975 at the world championships in Nottingham. And by then the rowers from the German Democratic Republic were in the international driving seat. They had risen to prominence as soon as they were allowed to compete under their own flag in 1966. They were already top of the medal table and going faster, and their crews made it look easy, which usually means that new tricks are being applied to something that is very difficult.

In common with other coaches outside Eastern Europe, Nilsen was stimulated by the professional full-time approach of the East Germans (see chapter 11). 'We knew we didn't have the time or the talent, so that means we had to be smarter, and I think that has helped us to develop. For me the East Germans pushed our sport a lot forward. Whilst they have been the leaders everybody wants to beat them. That's good. It's a challenge to beat such good people . . . All over the world we have athletes and coaches and federations who have been lifted up to take up the fight with them.' The East Germans changed the map by breaking the old tradition of passing knowledge down from coach to coach.

At the world championships in Nottingham in 1975 Nilsen's Norwegian double proved that a small country could target an event and win against the East Germans. When the Olympic Games came round in Montreal in 1976 Nilsen was being wooed by the British and the Spanish. His crew helpfully won the Olympic title. But Norway was not the only place where people could be found who responded to the challenge of the East Germans.

Britain Gets a Czech Mate

Britain, motherland of modern rowing, was a classic example of a country where everything was handed down, whether it was orthodoxy, Fairbairnism, or the stirrings of the modern international style. This was illustrated perfectly by a book entitled *Rowing, A Scientific Approach* published in 1967, two years before the arrival of Bohumil 'Bob' Janousek from Prague as national coach. It was an attempt by scientists to apply the principles of several disciplines to rowing. In his foreword the distinguished Cambridge coach Harold Rickett set out the problem that spurred the coaches of several schools to confer and float the idea of the book:

Coaches and oarsmen have made almost a fetish of clinging to the traditional, the proved and 'safe' methods that brought their forebears success. While we continued to beat the world in the sport we had introduced, this myopic complacency had some excuse. But now British oarsmen are becoming painfully aware that the success of overseas crews in international competition owes much to the fact that they are harnessing the fruits of scientific knowledge to improving the equipment and methods of their sport in a way that we have not . . . It is not that Britain has no scientists . . . The trouble lies, I suspect, in the attitude of mind of oarsmen and coaches, who have been brought up to regard rowing as a recreation for amateurs, and to consider outside professional help as suspect.

John Williams was even more forthright in his introduction, which was significantly titled 'Rowing – Art or Science?' It was an art, he said, that could benefit from some scientific study and application to improve it.

It is not many years since the Lady Margaret Boat Club [St John's College, Cambridge] and Cambridge University crews were carrying all before them both nationally and internationally. In those days the rivers of England were covered with crews all lying supine at the conclusion of each stroke, and these have been followed by the quasi-American, quasi-Russian and quasi-Ratzeburger [Adam], as if the outward form of rowing were itself the passport to success. Recently there has even been heard in Britain the idiotic idea of importing a German coach for the National Crew!

Williams was blind to the fact that the famous Cambridge crews did not always sweep all behind them at international level, certainly not when they met Americans or Germans. But, in turning attention to the sinking ship of British rowing, he acknowledged that there were lessons to be learned overseas. 'In the sport of rowing, science is still used far too little.' After producing evidence that, for example, Boat Race crews were not always using up-to-date methods of training, he wrote: 'It is not to be expected that any sensible individual would expect his own or his country's crew to take part in any competition under a built-in handicap of unsuitable equipment, of inefficient technique, or of dubious fitness, but this is precisely what is happening today.' He stressed the importance of the rational application of knowledge and experience of 'styles' like the American or the Ratzeburger, and of not relying solely on experience which can lead to the right conclusion for the wrong reason and result in its being enshrined in the lore of rowing without anyone understanding why or how it got there. The scientific approach is necessary, Williams said, because

> There is no single person directly connected with the sport today who is capable of handling by himself all the knowledge necessary for the full application of all the basic sciences in evoking maximum perform-ance from the oarsman . . . This book seeks to present not only what is known, but also what is unknown, of the behaviour of the elements of flesh, wood and water as they are combined in the practice of rowing.

The book looked at hydrodynamics, mechanics, biomechanics, physiology, psychology and mensuration. Among other things it set out the principles of the stroke for good rowing. Some of the authors' conclusions are interesting, especially in the light of what the East Germans were doing (see chapter 11). The design of a 'gentler' type of rigger which imposed virtually no sideways forces on the boat would enable a much lighter craft to be built; training must be fun, rating quality above quantity, and the rower must know why he or she is doing it; motivation is the prime factor in determining physical performance, and teamwork involves the integration of the crew's individual personalities by collective identification in a common cause; test results should be used to motivate the oarsman to achieve a higher standard of fitness to answer the question 'How am I getting on?'

The compendium was a useful investigation for its time. There was little else available in English and those who sought knowledge had to look elsewhere. The English sculler Penny Chuter found herself reading books by track athletes in the late fifties, and she trained with them too, sculling at Henley while Mary Rand ran along the towpath. Chuter also learned from her mother, who was a champion long-distance swimmer.

When Janousek arrived in London at the end of 1969 he brought three great assets: he was a medal winner, he possessed high-level qualifications in physical culture including psychology, and he was a foreigner, the latter essential at that time to cut through the entrenched stratification of British rowing society. He came from a system where state organization prevailed, and it was the countries where the state ran the rowing that led the world. The old ways, prevalent in Europe and the English-speaking world, of picking the fastest club crew and expecting them to win medals was no longer effective. Countries with many rowers needed to organize nationally, while those with fewer, like Norway and New Zealand, needed to identify events which suited the limited talent available. It was a lesson quickly taught by the East Germans and slowly learned by others, and one that set a remedial course requiring a decade of work for Western countries to make the grade. In his six years at the helm of British rowing, Janousek took the first steps towards organizing a national squad which was not under the umbrella of one club, and he produced a double and an eight who won silver medals at the Olympic Games. He also started a programme for educating amateur coaches.

Janousek, Nilsen and others like Rusty Robertson in New Zealand recognized that the East Germans were the model in the sixties and seventies because they had succeeded in combining a good training machine with intelligent selection of talent and high technique. In women's rowing the Romanians adapted the East German system, sending coaches to factories to test workers and inviting the best to training camps, thereafter offering an attractive package of sports training combined with education. 'If you do that you will always find some talented people,' Nilsen says. The task facing him was to answer these methods with the material and the system which he had at his disposal. 'Variations in body movement are very often related to the type of body you are working with. Tall people have less bodyswing and more leg drive. Most of the nations cannot select from a lot of people. The smaller have to build crews physiologically and technically. The art of coaching therefore becomes much more important to get results. On the other hand, if you are rowing 8000 to 10,000 kilometres a year you cannot expect each stroke to have technical quality because you cannot concentrate for such a long time. Some teams are not good bodymovers. They have bad coordination, but they have physical capacity to bang it through. Smaller outfits sometimes win through technical proficiency.'

Nilsen Takes on the World

In 1976 Nilsen decided to give up his career in marketing and become a full-time coach. He wanted to move to Britain, where Janousek had created a vacancy by becoming a boatbuilder. But the salary on offer was equivalent to that of a Swedish bus driver, and Nilsen had children at university in Scandinavia. Instead, he took up something which sounded crazy. Pedro Abreu, a Cuban living in

Barcelona, wanted to establish a Spanish national rowing centre based on the club in Banyoles. He offered Nilsen a good salary to run it and provided funding for the necessary equipment. Banyoles was ideal, a village close to a quiet lake with good weather conditions for rowing throughout the year. Dick Pieper, a German friend of Abreu, established excellent links with the local community, and soon Spanish oarsmen and women were being schooled academically as well as in rowing. Spanish results improved, especially among the lightweights, and the world came to beat on the door of Banyoles. Nilsen built on his reputation and soon, like most of the world's top scullers, the Russians and the British, the Italians and the Americans were training there in the winter. In Banyoles they were assessed as well as trained. A scientific approach to training aped the successful and secretive approach of the East Germans. The world was catching up through cooperation. By 1980 Nilsen, with the agreement of the Spanish, was looking after the Italian team, and he moved to Piediluco. Much of the international interest in his coaching and testing and research activities moved with him.

At Piediluco he introduced a systematic year-round training programme aimed at high performance in the international arena. He created technical, physiological and musculoskeletal conditions specifically aimed at developing athletes for rowing. These were supplemented with supervision of technique, observation of physical parameters and experience of competition. Preparation was for endurance, strength and flexibility; aerobic conditioning was emphasized rather than the interval training prevalent in Italian clubs during the seventies. Italian results improved from 1981.

The IOC's Olympic Solidarity movement made it possible for FISA to launch its development programme in 1985. When the programme started, Nilsen estimates that at least twenty-five countries had some kind of educational programme of their own. 'We looked at a lot of them. The point is that we were forced to present things in a simple manner so that people without a scientific background in exercise physiology and without much rowing experience could learn something and use it in daily work. I think that for each sixteen-page booklet we have collected material from 1000 pages to extract what is important. It is crucial to get the right practical information into these booklets. You can criticize: some federations have 150 hours of instruction for these matters, whereas our first level, apart from practical experience, lasts sixteen hours. With these sixteen hours you can go out and show people how to row and you can tell them how to train. That is the key point. If you are enthusiastic and intelligent you can create results.' By 1990 the booklets had been translated into eighteen languages. In the booklets the programme is set out clearly in three levels. The topics of the first level are basic rigging, rowing physiology, technique, training methodology, fitness training and learning methodology, and the other levels move on from there. They are the building blocks for the seminars and courses conducted by the programme's coaches. FISA also encourages countries to set up bilateral aid programmes.

There has been one important change in the eighties which has helped the development programme; indeed it may be the key factor. It is the willingness to share knowledge and the universal conviction that knowledge should be common and free. This has been encouraged by modern communications and much greater mobility of both athletes and coaches. But it is primarily a change of attitude. No longer is secrecy or exclusiveness or isolation seen as the only way or the right way. Openness is not born entirely of altruism, of course. Coaches realize that success requires good competition, and in the absence of the huge resources which have been available only to the now defunct Democratic Republic of Germany and a handful of programmes in other countries, high-level competition depends upon a broad base of rowing activity. Perhaps it is this factor which attracts brilliant minds to teach rowing and which keeps them in a sport which, in global terms, is small. 'Small is beautiful' has a rather special meaning in rowing. Nilsen knows why he has been in it a long time and devoted much of his time to it: 'You will always find people who have a different reaction, but our sport builds character because you learn little things that are important to life. You share responsibility, you have to work together, even as a single sculler, because you have to work with other people in the club. It is a team sport even for individuals. You cannot reach anything without hard work. You learn to make the best of yourself, to fight. All these things you learn from rowing. It's a value for life.' Nilsen tells of a Norwegian oarsman whom he coached who became an international lawyer and, years later, told him that when he goes into court he always has butterflies in his stomach: 'I am nervous but I prepare myself like I did when rowing, to go out and fight and take out the best of myself, to use my intelligence. I got this from rowing.' These things make coaching interesting because, Nilsen says, you have some influence on young people's development. 'Medals, we all want to be in the medals, but we cannot all be. But we can go out and make the best of ourselves. That's a coach. I think my best coaching had not been with the medal winners but with the people who have not got into the final but who have still reached something that seemed impossible, beyond their perception of their capacity. You can teach people to take out the best for themselves. I think that is one of the reasons why you continue with this stupidity.'

11

WORLD MASTER CLASS

HANS SENNEWALD rang down the curtain on the greatest rowing show on earth. He stroked the Germany East eight to a bronze medal on Lake Barrington on 4 November 1990. A month previously his country had merged with the German Federal Republic, so he became the last oarsman from a team formed by the German Democratic Republic's rowing federation to cross the finishing line. From Tasmania his team took home five golds, one silver and five bronzes. They first competed under their own flag in the world championships in 1966, and their combined men's and women's total for a quarter of a century of pulling oars in European, world and Olympic regattas is 153 gold, 74 silver and 42 bronze medals. From 1966 to 1990 the total number of golds awarded in these events is 334. Oarsmen from the Democratic Republic did not take part in the combined German team in the 1968 Olympics and, having been allowed into the Olympics as a separate nation in 1972, they boycotted the 1984 Games in Los Angeles. Their oarswomen won four golds out of six in the first women's world championships in 1974, and four out of six in the first women's Olympic regatta in 1976.

By any standard this is a stupendous achievement, a bruising superiority achieved quickly and sustained for twenty-five years. It was conceived by politicians and it was ultimately strangled by their unhappy subjects. Sport was a main instrument, perhaps *the* main instrument, by which the Communist government of the Soviet zone of occupied Germany created a national identity after the Second World War and stamped that identity on the world. This aim was multifaceted: the rulers of the Democratic Republic wished their country to grow as an equal to the Federal Republic. They wanted influence within the Warsaw Pact of socialist states, and to emerge from the shadow of their big brother, the Soviet Union; they wanted to be recognized in the United Nations and the Third World; and they wanted their own conception of socialism, of which sport was an integral part, to work. The successive governments of Walter Ulbricht and Erich Honecker put an unlimited price tag on achieving domination of Olympic sport and the worldwide recognition it was designed to bring to the German Democratic Republic. For them it was cheap. The programme was massive, thorough, secret and successful; in rowing it was supremely successful. It continued long after the identity crisis was over, sustained largely by the carrot of foreign travel and benefits at home held out to athletes and officials. Ordinary East Germans were not allowed out of their country on holiday, certainly not *en famille*, except to their unexotic Eastern European neighbours, and to Cuba. Belonging to a national team got round these restrictions. It gave one a privileged life during training and earned one respect, if not necessarily admiration.

From the outset the German trait of 'thoroughness' was harnessed for the cause. The investigation of dope was another, and the secrecy surrounding the methods by which they achieved their sporting superiority quickly led to accusations of drug abuse. The Democratic Republic's sports machine was regarded with as much suspicion as awe, and throughout its life its achievements were clouded by rumour and suspicions of evil and unsporting behaviour. The spoof British publication *Rowling* captured the mood in 1982 with a cartoon showing an East German oarsman in cutaway section. His limbs were reinforced with carbon fibre, his skull was solid hardwood, his backbone was cold-cured, his brain was a silicon chip, and his stomach was impregnated with kevlar. The question before us is whether the East Germans' domination of rowing was achieved by dope.

Matthias Schumann graduated from a sports boarding school to the Dynamo club in Berlin: he continued to attend high school three times a week and was allowed an extra year in which to obtain his high-school qualifications. He won a silver medal as a junior in 1976 and then a gold medal in the eight in 1978. He says that at that time it was the usual practice for oarsmen at Dynamo Berlin to be given weekly pills and fortnightly injections in the backside. They were told these would help their performance, but they were not told what they were taking. They were not necessarily being given illegal substances, for the East Germans were known to experiment with placebos.

Thor Nilsen is convinced that the Eastern European countries were experimenting with drugs in rowing at this time. 'Sure, they used dope when it was popular, but they found that it didn't help as much as they believed it would.' This is borne out by Hans Howald, a Swiss doctor who was in the chair of FISA's sports medicine commission for sixteen years until 1990, during which period one of his colleagues was Helmut Pohlentz, the East German team doctor until 1987. Howald is an outspoken critic of the use of dope and says that the East Germans may have experimented with small doses of steroids and blood doping from time to time, but he believes their success in rowing was due much more to the thoroughness of their training methods, research, selection of athletes, and incentives such as foreign travel and cars. 'It is too easy to say that their success was due to doping,' Howald says. 'They were good at all aspects. They selected fourteen- and fifteen-year-olds on a set of simple statistics of height, weight, and certain measurements of limbs. The sports which had the best medal records had priority of choice for tall boys and girls, and that is why rowing has done much better than volleyball or basketball or soccer. There were more medals achievable, particularly for women . . . If you take a 6-foot Prussian girl and get her to lift weights, she is bound to develop her muscles. Rowing is not an event in which you can expect much from dope. You cannot increase aerobic capacity by steroids. Huge explosive power does not get you far in rowing. The best thing we ever did was to increase the distance women row from 1000 metres to the men's distance of 2000 metres, which made it a truly endurance activity for women as well as men.'

Howald knew that in East Germany doping was widespread in sport. Much of the information came from Alois Mader, who defected in 1974 from the medical unit at Chemie sports club, Halle, where he worked with oarsmen. In his new career at the Cologne sports institute he revealed details of drug abuse and blood doping. Howald also learned that the control laboratory at Kreischa near Dresden conducted 10,000 tests annually. The testing was cast-iron. Every athlete was required to pass through the centre each time he or she left the country for training or competition. A positive test resulted in the end of an athlete's career, according to Professor

Herman Buhl, the head of research in the department of medicine and bio-science at the Research Institute for Physical Culture and Sport at Leipzig. On his own admission his department had conducted doping research at the behest of Honecker, who had taken over the leadership of the party from Ulbricht in 1971. In an interview with the author for the *Guardian* in March 1990, conducted on the day after East Germans voted for unification with the Federal Republic, Buhl became the first person working inside East German sport to admit to the doping programme. 'When Honecker and the party decided that East Germany must be the first in the world I had my orders,' he said. 'It is not possible to show you a piece of paper . . . the order is not written.' The seventy scientists at the laboratory spent fifteen years investigating the central nervous system, the respiratory system, muscle fatigue, the hormonal system and related matters. Six or seven of them worked for ten years on hormonal regulation. They charted how bodies work and enabled physical profiles to be built showing how an individual reacts to different training schedules, diets and pressure of competition.

> We can say how an athlete's insulin or cortisone or testosterone level changes when he trains in such-and-such a way, and so his physician or coach has information about the regulation of his system. After that the coach and physician can give him a special programme with substances and medicaments. But I cannot say what the dosage is. I don't know what a coach does with his athlete . . . it is a problem. When I get my orders, I must make the research and make the knowledge known. As a physician I would say: 'No, I shouldn't do this.'

Buhl stressed that his laboratory was under orders from the party: 'If I don't do this work I can go into the hospital or clinic, but my job at the institute is at an end.'

Buhl's laboratory worked directly with all the Olympic sports except rowing, which had its own medical laboratory in Grünau. He was quite clear that some East German medals had been won with the assistance of dope, though he could not speak for rowing. Testing took place only at Olympic and FISA championship regattas until 1980, when it was introduced to all international regattas. It was extended to cover round-the-year training in 1990. Until then, it was easy to avoid falling foul of such tests. An athlete who had been taking anabolic steroids, say, could be reliably clean before being dispatched to a competition. No East German rower tested by FISA was ever found positive. It was two rowers from the Soviet Union who were first found to have been taking steroids, caught by a test conducted by Howald at Mannheim regatta in 1980. 'If I had tested their whole team, they would have had no rowers at the Moscow Olympics,' he says. 'The doses were mild, about 10 milligrammes, which was thought to keep the body in shape. Weight-lifters have used twenty times that amount.' After this the British proposed that FISA stepped up testing, and they were strongly supported by East German rowing officials. The latter ran into severe criticism from their national Olympic committee for doing so. Since 1980 very few rowers have been found positive, and in 1990 all samples collected without prior warning in twenty countries, some visited more than once, were negative. So were the ninety-four samples taken at international regattas and the world junior championships, a high note on which Howald retired. Such results bear out Howald's and Nilsen's conclusions that, in rowing, dope was found to be wanting. 'We are lucky in rowing,' Nilsen says. 'We can get the same result without dope.'

Nevertheless, doping is a story that will run and run. The German magazine *Stern* reported in December 1990 that the entire East German men's rowing team at the 1980 Olympic Games were on the doping programme lists at the Leipzig Institute and the sports medicine centre in East Berlin. Every crew won gold, except the sculler Peter Kersten who took bronze. The women's squad for 1981 was also named by *Stern*.

A System of Sport

The suspicion of doping certainly spurred athletes in other countries to rise to the challenge emanating from Leipzig and Berlin, from Rostock and Potsdam. Some reacted by accusing the East Germans of cheating, others by taking greater satisfaction if they beat them without the use of drugs. But if the reality is that doping did not enhance the performance of East German rowers, other forces must have been at work. Theodor Körner was at the centre of the training, research and selection measures alluded to by Howald. He studied rowing in Leipzig from 1952 and was in the champion lightweight

eight there in 1953. He graduated as a physical education teacher in 1961 and took further study while working as secretary of the East German rowing federation and coaching at SC Motor Berlin. In 1962 he became director of training for the federation. He had been using long-distance work with his juniors and convinced the hierarchy that such an approach was an improvement on interval training, the repetition of sequences of strokes at various rates that was prevalent at the time. As the training system changed, Körner also started a research programme in physiology, biomechanics and, with Klaus Filter, boatbuilding. Constant tests and analyses took place to examine how the programme was working. By 1964 its benefits were visible, and by 1966 – the first year of competition under the black, red and gold tricolour with its emblem of hammer and dividers – the East Germans were at the top in both men's and women's rowing. 'To my last moment in the federation,' Körner says, 'I worked permanently with a scientific research programme to develop the training programme, training analysis and competition performance.'

A parallel step was to educate coaches in the new ways. All coaches were professionals, having been through a basic programme worked out at the Leipzig Institute to give them a thorough knowledge of performance training for rowing. They also sought talent to benefit from such a carefully prepared scheme, the best talent that their country could provide. 'The background of our results is the combination of having good men at the top, good ideas, hard work and hard thinking, and the money to do the work. New ideas in training are very rare, and new ideas are only good if you can reproduce the result. So we worked very hard to find out how to keep on getting good results. That is only possible with a scientific background. We made good results.'

The seed corn was to be found in the schools sports service, and representatives from the federation visited schools and applied their measuring tests to youngsters such as Matthias Schumann. There were 120 schools with rowing programmes. Those students who met the exacting standards laid down by the men with the tape-measures were invited to attend one of the twenty-seven sports boarding schools. Because of its success at winning medals, rowing had first choice of youngsters. Educational programmes were designed around the needs of the sport. In the boarding schools there was rowing every day, a total of thirty hours a week, with training camps before major competitions. Each boarding school was associated with an elite sports club. Some of these changed their names over the years, but at close of play in 1990 they were SC Dynamo Berlin, SG Dynamo Potsdam, ASK Vorwärts Rostock, SC DHfK Leipzig, SC Berlin Grünau, SC Einheit Dresden, SC Chemie Halle and SC Magdeburg.

Sport was the first priority for students on the elite programme. They were given extra time to complete college courses. Factories were compelled to support those athletes sent to work in them by releasing them for training, as were the various branches of state security (Dynamo clubs for the police, Vorwärts for the armed forces). Adult athletes were classified into the master class and class 1, class 2 and class 3, with more time allotted to training as students moved upwards. Class 3 athletes were district winners, class 2 county winners and class 1 national champions. Masters and class 1 athletes were expected to log between 1300 and 1600 hours of training each year. Assessments were continuous, academic standards sometimes exacting, and the failure rate high. The rowing system was eventually staffed by around 200 full-time professional coaches, plus administrative, service and medical staff. Under Helmut Pohlentz's sports medical programme doctors, including Pohlentz himself, were on duty from 6 a.m. All national and club coaches had to take four-year graduate training courses under the wing of the German Gymnastic and Sports Association, which also guaranteed and controlled their future employment and ran the postgraduate sports medicine service.

There was thus a career structure, indeed a total life plan, in sport. When fourteen-year-old Schumann passed into the system, with the approval of his parents, he was guaranteed state-funded care of body and soul for his working life, just so long as he performed to his potential, did what he was told and did not talk to foreigners. For the state expected him to grow up a good German, a socialist according to the creed of the Socialist Unity Party (known as the Communist Party in the West), a good athlete and a good sport. It expected his mentors to attend to his moral as well as his physical welfare. It spent a large portion of the gross national product on him. It set out to buy thoroughness to ensure that he won medals. That is why Schumann and his group of a dozen or so oarsmen at

Dynamo Berlin were addressed several times a year by their 'moral tutor', Wilfried Hofmann, about the politics of the Democratic Republic. That is why the security arm of the state, the Stasi, were ever-present among the rowing crews, with informers in the clubs and minders on tour. That is why some of the rowers defected.

Until the eighties the rest of the world saw only the results of the Democratic Republic's system. Certainly some of the ideas were taken up in part and adapted to other cultures. Certainly some of the coaching goals, stripped of ideological tint, will be recognized elsewhere. But the former socialist countries which adopted similar methods could not do so on the scale of Leipzig and Berlin, with the possible exception of the women's programme in Romania. For the system required not just money and thoroughness, but a structure backed by a political will to ensure that it was carried out. The background to this is the German tradition of linking sport and physical education to nationalism and political organization.

Chain of Command

After the Second World War the eastern zone of Germany had to be rebuilt physically, socially and politically, and this task first fell to Walter Ulbricht, a fanatical sportsman who had been a member of the workers' sports movement during the 1920s. Born in Leipzig in 1893, he was a founder member of the German Communist movement, and returned from the Soviet Union in 1945 to found the Socialist Unity Party which was in charge when the Democratic Republic was proclaimed in 1949. It was Ulbricht who called in Soviet tanks to quell strikes and riots in 1953, and he who erected the Berlin Wall in 1961 to stop the flow of defectors. It was also Ulbricht who saw sport as a means to world recognition. He charged Honecker, the man who was to succeed him as party chairman and therefore effectively the head of state, and his Free German Youth movement with the task of reorganizing sport. Honecker began by disbanding all existing clubs and associations because of their connection with fascism and replacing them with ideologically acceptable organizations. This was not necessarily a popular move with teenagers who were trying to get something started in their own backyard. Before being allowed out in a boat at his local club in Magdeburg, Helmut Pohlentz and his mates were required to do seventy-five hours of reconstruction work on the war-damaged boathouse. Then the government confiscated the club. 'You can imagine what we thought about that,' Pohlentz says. At first socialist principles discouraged competition; then, after trades unions and industry had been saddled with providing facilities and working with the Free Youth to encourage participation, the German Gymnastic and Sports Association (DTSB) was formed. It was created on the advice of the State Secretariat for Sport and Physical Culture. It was all-embracing and all-powerful, and ideologically firmly under the whip of the Party.

The DTSB absorbed existing elite sports organizations and assumed responsibility for everything connected with sport from the cradle to the gold standard. The sports boarding schools and the German College of Physical Culture (DHfK), founded in 1952, came under its wing, and it was given responsibility for the sports medicine service, the National Olympic Committee, the training of coaches and sports doctors, and the staffing of all the schools and elite clubs. The chain of command was like a Christmas tree with the Party's politbüro at the top. Directly under it came the state secretariat with responsibility for the scientific council, and the Leipzig Institute. The politbüro also had direct links with the council of state and the DTSB.

At the sharp end, the first post-war regatta in the Soviet zone took place on 4 August 1946. In 1949 the Eastern zone championships were held in Grünau, and in 1950 a meeting at Klingerweg boathouse in Leipzig founded the 'Rowing Section of the Democratic Republic' to spread interest and develop competition. The following year the first international regatta was held at Grünau, and in 1952 *Wanderruder* or pleasure rowing was reintroduced. Rowing was documented in a publication called *Wassersport* from 1952, the first of a series of official magazines which lasted until 1990. In 1953 the Rowing Section and the Federal Republic's federation began to talk. In 1954 the elite sports clubs were started, and 5000 copies of *Rudern (We Row)*, a manual by Werner Pfütze (Körner's trainer) and Ernst Herberger, were printed. In 1955 the Democratic Republic was admitted to FISA as an extraordinary member, on the stipulation that its rowers could only compete as members of a combined German team. Combined teams were formed from 1954 to 1964, at first by holding 'sudden death' selection regattas between the two Germanies. The last all-German championships were held in Grünau in 1957, each country winning six titles. Subsequently crews were selected by their performance at international regattas and elimination regattas between the two federations. When the East German Rowing Federation (DRSV) replaced the Rowing Section in 1958, it applied immediately to FISA for full recognition. This was the beginning of pressure which lasted until December 1965, when FISA's congress removed the 'combined team' stipulation. In 1965 the DRSV refused to take part in the eliminating competitions for the German team at Duisburg 'owing to constant interference and discrimination against Democratic Republic rowers by the Federal Republic', according to a research paper by Rolf Blanke of Magdeburg teachers training college. An English translation of *Rudern* gives a more moderate reason: 'The GDR crews did not participate because they were not allowed to enter the championships as an independent nation.'

Meanwhile the standard was rising. The first medals were won as part of combined German teams at the first European championships for women held at Bled, Yugoslavia, in 1956. In 1957 Vorwärts Berlin's coxed four won the European gold, and Achim Hill won silver in the single scull in both the 1960 and 1964 Olympic regattas. The women's European championships were held at Grünau in 1962. In 1966 championships for children, youths and juniors were held, and coaches attended the first FISA coaches' conference in Prague. The first teams went off to compete in East German colours, men to the world championships in Bled, where they won gold medals in three events, women to the European championships in Amsterdam, where they also won three. They rowed in boats and used sculls and oars made in VEB Yachtwerft Berlin, the former Pirsch yard where Filter was at work. Medals followed every year thereafter, including at the 1968 Olympics in Mexico City, where East Germans in the combined German team won the coxless pairs and coxless fours and West Germans the eights. Only in 1984 did they miss out when the Democratic Republic boycotted the Olympic Games. Juniors, too, began to win international medals. The first student championships were held in Halle in 1967, and in 1969 4000 rowers of all categories and ages took part in the first club regatta at Brandenburg on the Beetz-see. The second in 1973 attracted 5000.

A Bible of Thoroughness

Ernst Herberger and his team continually brought their manual, *Rudern*, up to date. It was not merely a how-to-do-it book but a textbook for coaches, instructors and sports teachers, emphasizing their role in education and starting out with the reasons why rowing is important. First, rowing has top rating for the overall development of the body because its sequence of movements uses all the main muscle groups. It develops strength, endurance and flexibility. Both sexes from childhood to advanced age can do it. The variety of boats gives athletes choices and enables them to match their activity to their physical and mental abilities. Collective training and competition, long-distance rowing and living together at the boathouse 'help form socialist sports personalities'. *Wanderruder* is emotionally stimulating and healthy. Rowing demands physical exertion and high powers of insight, readiness, reaction and intellectual qualities.

Rudern points out that at competitive level most rowers are active for seven to ten years and so decisive periods of personality development lie within the care of the coach. It is not hard to find rowers on whom a coach has been a greater influence than teachers, priest or parents. But *Rudern* says that it is essential 'to ensure an education which can create a socialist personality'. The instructor, therefore, 'must be conscious of the fact that all his actions, all instructions, and his social behaviour are registered and evaluated by the young.'

One of the twelve educational goals is 'discussion of day-to-day political events, explanation of the Party's and government's attitude, actions and decisions, and particularly the decision of questions concerning the policy of sport in the country.' The occurrence if not the importance of such discussion is confirmed by Matthias Schumann, who says that Wilfried Hofmann, the leader of his group at Dynamo Berlin, sometimes gave them socio-political lectures, speaking for two hours without notes. Schumann summarizes the message as lying somewhere between propaganda and bullshit.

The other goals in *Rudern* concern pleasure through success, discipline and diligence, duty to crew and club. As an example of decision making the editors cite Steve Fairbairn: 'The English [sic] coach Fairbairn once said: "Train in such a way that the athletes can train themselves. The coach is not the athlete's wet-nurse!" ' The coach must counsel private life and share responsibility for keeping performance in school or college at a high level. Parents should be invited for discussion evenings; 'the sportsman must be convinced that his performances and behaviour relate directly to the Democratic Republic's struggle for peace.' Anybody – and there cannot be many – who read right through this manual would be left in no doubt that the paymasters, Ulbricht and Honecker, called the ideological tune.

The manual then tells the coach how to school the will, that many-sided expression of personality. It is important, it says, not to underestimate difficulties or overestimate capabilities. Targets should be attainable within a reasonable time. Three recognizable attitudes towards opponents are then identified: 'I know my strength and will win in any case'; 'I know I will have difficulty beating my opponent but will give him the hardest possible fight'; and 'I am afraid of him'. The first is the right attitude for good crews; the second shows realistic evaluation; while the third shows that the oarsman has been racing too early and too often. Evaluation should be made after each race to cut out the excuses for losing, such as blaming the umpire, the starter, a bad lane, the cox, the man in front, the coach, the wind, etc. During the race, concentration is important. Not everyone has the ability to concentrate on rhythm, technique and one's opponent, so there must be systematic training in concentration. A dramatic example of the results of this kind of training was witnessed at Nottinghamshire International Regatta in 1975 when Ulrich Karnatz crabbed and broke his rigger in the eights final, which his crew were leading as they approached halfway. He threw his oar overboard, stood up and jumped out of the boat. The British and American eights on either side gained rapidly, while the seven-man crew hardly faltered. They recovered their equilibrium quickly and rowed to the finish as if their lives depended on it, and as if such a catastrophe had been rehearsed. The British crew eventually won by two seconds, but the East Germans fought off a strong challenge by the Americans.

The manual also turns its attention to individual and crew performance. The single,' it says, 'ruthlessly reveals all weaknesses.'

This is a truism known to nineteenth-century professionals, re-discovered by Karl Adam when he began working with schoolboys in Ratzeburg in the 1950s, and subsequently used as a gauge for selection in several countries. We know, *Rudern* says, that an individual in a crew is capable of performances he could not attain on his own. But the single requires the full application of the entire person. 'No one else can be blamed for failure. This education toward hardness and honesty in relation to self is an essential part of training. We consider that performance in the single is a valid criterion to be used for crew selection.' In the East German creed, it is the responsibility of the club to foster solidarity among single scullers: 'The crew is the basis for the education of the socialist personality. By it, we mean a group of people who voluntarily unite to realize common goals serving socialist progress.'

The thoroughness of the research programme is revealed when *Rudern* outlines the basic values of competitive performance. The time taken for men to race 2000 metres is between 5 minutes 30 seconds and 8 minutes 30 seconds, depending on the event and the weather. Thus, say Herberger *et al.*, rowing is neither short-distance nor long-distance; nor can it be compared with middle-distance running because the propulsion of the boat and the resistance of the water require the application of all muscle groups. 'In competition the oarsman is required to exhaust his physical and psychic potential fully and without pause.' The factors determining his performance are endurance, muscle power, speed of movement, coordination of movement or technique, willpower and concentration. Endurance, they say, plays a decisive role. They also identify facts revealed by the study of numerous competition results: when racing no oarsman has yet managed to travel the entire distance at a uniform speed; the highest speed, reached immediately after the start, is seldom attained or exceeded in the final spurt because at such speed the oarsman's aerobic capacity does not provide enough oxygen, so oxygen deficiency develops and inhibits performance. At the start the heart rate increases from 120 to 180 beats per minute, remains there until the final spurt, when it can reach 200, returning to pre-start level within three minutes. There is frequently a fall-off of performance over the first third of the course but this is not accompanied by a corresponding change in the heart rate. The antidote to this is to create a 'reserve' by developing respiration, heart beat volume, and rate of blood circulation.

Everything described above is from the chapter on training racing oarsmen. *Rudern* has twenty-one other chapters, plus appendices setting out everything required for successful rowing, from stepping into the boat to crossing the finish line, from first walking through the door of the boathouse to retiring as a coach. It is both catalogue and creed of everything that the system developed in its laboratories in Leipzig, its work in the schools and clubs, and its observations at the rowing academy in Grünau.

Escape

Sometimes the rewards of this regimen of seriousness came in the form of a visit to Henley Regatta in England, a totally different environment to other international regattas. Even the 'B' crews were sent to foreign waters at least once a year. Each year there was an altitude camp in Yugoslavia. But there was also the drudgery of many miles of rowing, which even coaches like Körner admitted was too much. As one Western coach commented, 'If you have people at your disposal for most of every day, you have to entertain them.' Sending them off in boats was the easiest solution. And the athletes learned to buck the system. For example, at the world championships in New Zealand in 1978, the British sculler Hugh Matheson found a flotilla of East German crews sunbathing on the bank on a tributary of Lake Karapiro. 'We're out of sight and radio contact,' they explained. This kind of avoiding action was much harder at home: escape from the secret underground pressure chamber used for altitude training at Kienbaum was impossible.

The system produced technically superb and powerful crews, prepared for almost any eventuality, and was very hard to beat. Among them were crews of scullers who won the quadruple event from its year of introduction in 1974 to 1982. It ensured a seemingly endless supply of graceful scullers to man the boats, and the sweep-oared crews often gave the impression of being relaxed and rowing well within themselves while stretching out a lead. Their opponents knew that this was not the case: every detail had been attended to, and that was why the East Germans were out in front. Bruce Grainger,

an English school teacher who trained under Adam before taking
Wallingford Schools to the top of junior rowing in Britain, was a
close East German-watcher. His conclusion is that the East Germans
realized that Adam was on the right course at Ratzeburg (see chapter
12), copied his methods and found that they worked, and then set
about improving them. They then refined their system by setting
numerical training targets. The top men's crews were chosen from
a pool of 100–125 seventeen- and eighteen-year-olds. The same
applied to women. Each of the eight elite clubs had to produce
between ten and twenty candidates, and each club had about twenty
coaches. Each centre also had a squad of about twenty-five fifteen-
and sixteen-year-olds, and below them a wide base of youngsters up
to the age of fourteen being taught to row and undergoing appraisal.
This, Grainger says, was empirical application of statistics. The
individual did not count. 'Take a population of a certain size and
you are bound to get suitable candidates coming out the other
side at twenty, twenty-two and twenty-four. They put tremendous
pressure on these people.'

Grainger also monitored changes in the way they rowed. 'In the
sixties and seventies they used a short slide technique where they
didn't use the legs so much, and they had a long reach with the back
and a lot of back draw movement. The theory is that the buttock
and lower back muscles have a greater proportion of aerobic fibres
and therefore are better for rowing. But at same time the West
Germans were using a very long slide technique, with their kneecaps
up round their ears, and somehow by accident the two extremes
seem to have merged together.'

The next stage came as a result of the East German 'telemetric
system' for studying performance in the boat. Crews were monitored
from a catamaran by measuring the force on the pin, the arc of the
oars, the force on the foot-stretcher and the speed of the boat. Total
propulsive force on the boat and the decelerating force could be
measured. The results could be superimposed on video pictures and
the crew could be coached there and then, while changes were
recorded for subsequent debriefing. 'It is not surprising that they
have produced many superbly technically coordinated and integrated
crews,' Grainger says. 'We do pretty well without this equipment,
but you begin to get an insight into just how thorough they were.'

Grainger became Britain's full-time coach for juniors and then, in

1990, performance director responsible for all the national squads. He and many other coaches outside the Democratic Republic were pulled along by the challenge emanating from Leipzig and Grünau. Margins narrowed even though standards rose. By the second half of the eighties the East German men were not winning quite as often or quite as easily, and it was then that the secrecy began to recede. Circumstances changed as well. Although foreign travel remained impossible for those not on teams, increasing international fraternization increased contact. Leipzig-trained coaches were sometimes sent out to help other socialist countries. And throughout, despite the presence of snoopers and Stasi informers, sharing a language and, perhaps, family ties with Federal Germany was a constant breach in the defences.

So in spite of the privileged life there were defections. Matthias Schumann was among them. He became a world champion in the eight in 1978 at Lake Karapiro, New Zealand. He was irritated by the rigidity of the system and the petty regulations, but his personal crisis came in 1980 when the Stasi ordered him to stop seeing his girlfriend. Her crime was to apply to emigrate using the legal procedure. Schumann crossed into Austria from Bled regatta, Yugoslavia, in June 1982. Within a year he had made a new life in sports journalism and earned a seat in the West German eight. When he met his former crewmates at regattas they cut him dead, but he understood the pressures that they were under from informants not to be seen talking to foreigners. For his part, Schumann refused to say anything about his life as an East German athlete until German unification in 1990. Werner Berg, vice-president of the German Gymnastics and Sports Association and of the rowing federation, was the Stasi presence in rowing, and he always travelled with the team, conspicuous by his lack of stature compared with the rowers. Western journalists would ask Berg technical rowing questions which they knew he could not answer. He had informers in every group of athletes. When Colin Moynihan, the cox of Britain's eight in 1980, 1981 and 1984, travelled through the Democratic Republic as a teabag salesman before becoming Minister for Sport, the first thing that the rowers did when he visited their centres was to tell him who the informers were.

There were other defections over the years. Dietrich Rose, who was to become an influential coach in Philadelphia, left for

Ratzeburg before the 1964 Olympics and tried without success to earn a place in West Germany's eight. One of the best things that happened to Pohlentz in 1990 was to be invited, along with other members of his club in Grünau, to the annual dinner of the Grünau escapees, who numbered at least fifteen.

Collapse and Legacy

The system fell apart as suddenly as the divided Germanies were cemented in unity. The process began on 9 November 1989, watched on television at an international coaches' conference by an incredulous Wilfried Hofmann, Schumann's former minder. Hofmann's career had progressed from manager of Dynamo Potsdam in 1958 to a top administration post at Dynamo Berlin in 1968, coupled with the presidency of the rowing federation from 1974. He was also chairman of FISA's junior commission, with Grainger as one of its members. He flew home to Berlin and its crumbling Wall next day. Before the end of the following March, East Germans were supporting the conservative Christian Democrats at the polls and faced a collapsing economy and a changing social system. The Stasi, the Party and its leader Honecker were discredited. The nation faded from the map on which its sportsmen had etched it, and neither the money nor the will to support them remained. Klaus Filter took his first foreign holiday in the company of his wife, and Dr Pohlentz and his family were able to visit relatives in Hamburg. The old incentive for young rowers was gone. In the tidy set of rooms at the dour headquarters of the German Gymnastics and Sports Association Hofmann was a sad, almost red-eyed realist. 'The training system is no good for the new political system. There will be less time for training, less money, new motivation . . . Coaches, sportsmen, and functionaries must find another way. The old system is finished.' And so was his job as president, his association being swallowed by the West German federation in December 1990. The Liebig café in the avenue at Grünau, scene of postmortems after many a championship, was alive with discussion of an uncertain future, for never had it been so important for crews to win to maintain their coaches' reputations as professionals seeking employment. By November 1990, when the world championships were held in Tasmania, the two Germanies were one. However, both Federal and Democratic teams took part for the last time, an arrangement agreed by FISA earlier in the year. The international federation could not anticipate the speed of political events. There were no fans to cheer the athletes of the East, but then there never really had been. One of the most telling things at the Olympic regatta in Seoul in 1988 was how the East Germans organized 'rent-a-crowds' of flag-waving athletes and officials whenever their crews were racing.

Just as East Germans turned against their sports stars in resentment at the resources that had been devoted to the elite and certain privileged sections of society at the expense of facilities for ordinary people, so the East German rowing machine commanded no sentiment among its peers. But it certainly commanded respect, as Grainger said at the close of 1990 championships:

> They have left us a huge number of technical lessons and tips on the actual business of rowing and training and all that goes with it. But they've also left us in the aftermath of the political downfall of the totalitarian system a warning about how sport can be misused. Instead of being sport for all in which everybody has a chance, it became sport as a political weapon, a political showcase and so on, and that's not what sport is about . . . But it's right to acknowledge the contributions of the East German crews, teams, coaches, organizers and co-workers over the years because they have set a tremendous standard for the sport . . . For the last seven or eight years crews from other countries have been able to match those standards, and I'm glad that this has happened because if we'd never met that challenge before the Berlin Wall came down we'd never have been able to turn round and say we can do it.

Grainger's sentiments are echoed by Nilsen and other prominent coaches.

He identified another aspect of the legacy, a further explanation of why the secret society began to loosen up:

> One of their motivations was to achieve world-class recognition by superb success in sport, but they suddenly realized that they had a highly marketable commodity in the form of knowledge about sport and sports coaching and training. Leipzig became a world-famous institution. In the last few years they were in a position to take a lead, they got new recognition as leaders in the world of sport through what they had to contribute to it in a positive sense, which was a curious irony really.

Only about twenty of the 200 coaches found work in the new united German rowing federation and half of those jobs were guaranteed only up to the 1992 Olympic Games. Several more left for foreign parts, including the chief women's coach Jürgen Gröbler, who went to Leander in England as the venerable club's first professional, a posting which raised a few eyebrows on the committee of a club where tradition is, outwardly at least, held much in awe. In 1991 former East German coaches were working in Australia, Austria, Belgium, France, Italy, the Netherlands and the United States. The future oarsmen and women have to adjust their way of life to one of part-time sport, even though the Federal German system funds high-class competitors quite generously. Certainly there are no longer guarantees of employment later. They can look back on a quarter of a century of unique achievement; we will look back farther, to the men who set the sporting parameters which formed the East Germans' first stepping stones to excellence, and who owed some of their own experiences to another extraordinary period of history in which German ideas were often in conflict with those more liberal and democratic ones held elsewhere.

12

ADAM AND STEVE

AFTER the Second World War the boys of the Lauenburgische Gelehrtenschule began rowing in the gigs which their fathers had hidden in the woods when hostilities began. The school is in a village on a small island on a lake in Ratzeburg, Schleswig Holstein, south of the Baltic port of Lübeck and east of Hamburg, the birthplace of German rowing. Ratzeburg is a watery forested rest home, an archetypical German backwater discovered by the English Romantic poets Wordsworth and Coleridge in the last century but left to its monastery, its farming and, latterly, to elderly Hamburgers who, surrounded by a nature reserve, take coffee and cake on a Sunday. After the war the island and most of the lake were included in the Federal Republic but are within sight of the East German border. The island village is connected to the mainland by two causeways.

From its foundation in 1896 the school used the lake for rowing, and its post-war director, Dr Tredup, was very keen to continue the tradition. In 1948 he asked one of his teachers, who had been a world student heavyweight boxing champion and a hammer thrower, to supervise the self-governing group of rowers. In 1960 Germany won the Olympic eights in Rome with a crew from Ratzeburg coached by their *Protektor*, whose name was Karl Adam. Until that year the blue-riband Olympic event had been exclusively in the hands of the Americans, except in London (1908) and Stockholm (1912) when Great Britain had taken the title. That first German win marked a revolution in rowing which was scarcely believable to people both inside and outside Germany. Inside Germany the men of Ratzeburg were regarded as upstarts, anti-establishment oarsmen who bucked the traditions of German rowing, a view shared by the men of Ratzeburg themselves. Outside Germany the only people who had heard of Ratzeburg were the long-deceased poets Wordsworth and Coleridge. Among rowers both inside and outside the country there was deep suspicion of a pugilist who had anything to do with pulling oars. It became media mythology that Karl Adam knew nothing about rowing and therefore must either be a genius or possess a dark secret or be having an extraordinary run of luck. He had appeared from the woods and was running on borrowed time.

In a sense all of these were true. At the school Adam taught mathematics, physics, philosophy and physical education, but he himself had been taught by rowers at college in Berlin during the thirties. And in the sixties, when his crews were top of the world, he was able to predict when and by whom their superiority would be defeated. He was a democratic coach, prepared to share secrets, but his main competitor was the Democratic Republic which, by the 1968 Olympics, was competing as a separate nation.

Adam was a war veteran. He had injured his left arm in the army, which he entered in 1938 after a year at Berlin's state academy for physical culture, where he won his heavyweight title in 1937. Although not a rower himself, he was taught by Dr Karl Feige and Hugo Borrmann. Borrmann made extensive use of the skiff or single scull and influenced future masters of the sport, but his ideas did not filter down to the clubs. In 1936 Borrmann became the first head of the rowing academy at Grünau. He also spent some months in London. Feige's book *Riemen, Skull, Paddel (Sweep, Scull, Paddle)*, published in 1939, was essentially a book of watermanship; a revised edition called *Natürliches Rudern* appeared in 1952. One of his dicta was that the best coach was a single, meaning that skill in the skiff was the basis of good rowing. Adam decided to try out these ideas. According to his own students at Ratzeburg, Adam was a good sculler, and when he became a coach he based selection for fours and eights on sculling. The lesson was to be taken up in other countries.

It was no accident that Feige's book came to be called *Natürliches Rudern*. 'Natural' methods of sport were developed in Vienna in the 1920s by Dr Marguerite Streicher and Dr Karl Gaulhofer. From 1890 there had been criticism of the narrowness of Austrian physical education according to the principles of *Turnen* (gymnastics) and demands to extend the subject from the *turner* style of exercises and elementary gymnastics on apparatus to include outdoor activities such as swimming, athletics, rowing, tobogganing and skiing. Some progress was made and cognisance was taken of the 'play movement' in Central Europe, Anglo-Saxon developments in team sports, and Swedish ideas in gymnastics. But the First World War effectively concentrated minds on other things. In 1918 the secondary school teacher Gaulhofer was made consultant for physical education at the Austrian Ministry of Education. He became a lecturer at Vienna University and from 1921 cooperated closely with Streicher, who taught gymnastics teachers as well as secondary-school physical education. Natural gymnastics became the basis of Austrian physical education until the 1960s, except during the Nazi period from 1938 to 1945. Its effect was to take the formality and rigidity out of *Turnen*, renouncing the old 'style' of skill training and teacher-led instruction in favour of more creative activity and outdoor pursuits allied with self-motivation and development of the whole being. Their ideas, which also drew on the earlier ideas of 'animated gymnastics' by Adalbert Slama, had considerable influence in the Netherlands, where Gaulhofer became head of the academy for physical education in Amsterdam in 1932. The ripples of the natural movement were to be felt in Germany, Britain, Spain, Portugal and Latin America. It transformed gymnastics during the twenties and thirties, even if, in Germany, it did not immediately change the militaristic roots and purpose behind the huge numbers who practised it and who were also manipulated by the 'Fatherland' philosophy of the National Socialist Party. As we shall see in chapter 13, the leaders of rowing in Germany mostly pulled with the Nazis.

The Call of Jesus

Meanwhile in rowing there was a similar 'doing what comes naturally' movement under way, this time rooted in England but with channels which led to Germany by several paths, including through Adam's teacher Borrmann. Arthur Dreyfuss of Zürich saw what was happening at a German regatta in 1933 when a four from Amicitia Mannheim who had finished second in the 1932 Olympics were beaten by Pembroke College, Cambridge. Dreyfuss had been asked to coach the rowing section of Football Club Zürich and he made it his business to find out who was behind Pembroke, an inquiry which led him to an Australian, Steve Fairbairn. Fairbairn was a member of a large Melbourne family who had sent a succession of sons and cousins to Jesus College, Cambridge. His eldest brother George had returned home in 1877 filled with enthusiasm for the English rowing style, a style which became known as Orthodox. Two years later the next brother, Charles, came back with similar views. Each entered controversy with self-taught locals, professional scullers and amateurs at their Melbourne club, and were converted back to the prevalent style of the Yarra River – whatever that was. As a schoolboy Steve would go rowing from dawn to dusk, the crew taking chops and billycan with them and stopping to cook their meals. They took turns at coxing and rowing in different seats: 'We never heard of a boy who could row on only one side of the boat,' Fairbairn wrote in his memoirs. The debate on the Yarra was between the rational and the traditional. Their era coincided with the introduction of the sliding seat on both sides of the Atlantic. Although the use of slides manifestly made boats faster, there was much controversy over the desirable length of slide when Steve Fairbairn arrived at Jesus College in 1881 – a college which had been so good at fixed-seat rowing in 1872 that their crew had beaten sliders at Henley. Fairbairn favoured a longer slide than his coaches, and he won the day in extending the Jesus slides from 8 to 14 inches. He also introduced a fifth stay on the iron riggers of those days to make them stronger, and made it easier to balance the boat by seating the crew along its centre. These were early indications of the independent thinking and preparedness to try anything new that was characteristic of many British colonials at that time. They were deeply respectful of Britain, which they regarded as their mother country, while being suspicious of the conservatism which was inbred in the comfortably off upper and middle classes of the mother country's indigenous population.

After rowing for college and university, Steve Fairbairn returned to Cambridge from Australia in 1904 and began to coach at Jesus. Although a small college of fewer than 300 men, Jesus soon had remarkable success. Other colleges invited Fairbairn or his disciples to coach, and they too achieved success both on the River Cam and at Henley. Jesus College won the premier event, the Grand, in 1908. Thus began an assault on aspects of orthodoxy which was to conquer

Dr Gilbert Bourne's cinematograph of rowing, showing part of the Ortho-dox stroke from catch to finish

Europe by the Second World War and to be the greatest influence on moving boats between the introduction of the sliding seat and Karl Adam's first outing on the lake at Ratzeburg.

The fountainhead of orthodoxy was the schoolmaster R. S. de Havilland (Havi), who coached the first eight at Eton College from 1893 to 1914, during which time his crews won the Ladies' Plate at Henley twelve times. Eton had resisted slides, partly because they had raised fixed-seat rowing to a fine art along their reach of the Thames at Dorney, and partly because slides were dirty, noisy and produced a 'deprecatory spectacle' of eight pairs of knees rising simultaneously into the air, according to one account. On the ten occasions during Havi's reign when Eton did not win the Ladies', all the crews made up of older and more mature college oarsmen who did win it had a majority of Old Etonians on board. There were seven Old Etonians in the British eight who won the 1908 Olympic gold medal, and six in the 1912 Olympic champion eight.

After the First World War the London clubs, infiltrated by Jesus and other Fairbairn college men, flirted with Steve. First Thames were converted, then London, and their results at Henley improved dramatically. Controversy raged in the press, the careful analysis exercised by some correspondents at times overshadowed by exaggeration heaped on exaggeration by both sides in the debate about form. Insults were voiced if not written, and the editor of the *Rowing Almanack*, Sir Theodore Cook, is said to have forbidden Fairbairn's name to be uttered in his office.

By this time Fairbairnism was labelled a 'style' or a 'method', but it would be more accurate to call it an approach to rowing, a state of mind rather than a set of rules. Fairbairn's son Ian, who was coached by de Havilland as well as by his own father and became a 'Fairbairn' coach himself, said that orthodoxy and Fairbairnism were not actually very far apart. He identified the essence of

Fairbairnism as the application of psychology to rowing many years before other English amateur coaches had thought of it.

Steve – as everyone called him – published his *Notes on Rowing* in 1904 and urged his oarsmen to read them repeatedly and study them every night. According to his great collaborator at Jesus, Freddie Brittain, he saw rowing in a different light from all other men, 'for he had made it his link with the metaphysical world. The longer he coached, and the more victories he won, the more he was haunted by a vision of something which he knew to be beyond the power of himself or any other man to attain or even to conceive – perfect rowing.' The orthodoxy that Steve's teaching was struggling against was a stiff-upper-lip style of rowing developed successfully for fixed-seat boats and then adapted to the sliding seat without, said its critics, enough thought about the fundamental changes that the slide demands. As Ian Fairbairn put it:

> The Orthodox ideas started from fixed-seat rowing and a consequent veneration of 'swing', and they thought of the slide as only an extension, however important an extension, of fixed-seat rowing; to Steve, in spite of statements about sliding being merely the prolongation of the swing, slide and leg drive were the source of power which fixed seats only served to dam.

Steve's own summary of the difference between his teaching and orthodoxy was published in his *Some Secrets of Successful Rowing* in 1930. First, orthodoxy taught the oarsman to open up the angle between thighs and ribs as soon as possible at the beginning of the stroke, on the front stop if possible; in shorthand, 'catch it with the shoulders'. Steve taught the oarsman to drive at the blade and let the body and slide take care of themselves. Secondly, orthodoxy taught a rectangular movement of the hands at the finish. Steve taught a rounded movement, 'just like turning the handle of a mangle'. Thirdly, orthodoxy taught a 'lively recovery'. Steve taught the oarsman to sit back at the finish, being careful only to flick his hands away fast and to be sure they were over his knees before he let his slide move. The Jesus or Fairbairn style, Steve said, is 'concentrating on working the oar, and natural body action'. This approach was often confused with sloppiness. Orthodox crews had the appearance of being drilled, aspiring to uniformity in the boat at all stages, whereas Fairbairn crews were taught that perfect togetherness of bladework was the only uniformity that mattered. They were taught to think about rowing all the time they were doing it, to concentrate on keeping the balance and making the blade effective, and – this is the crucial difference – to allow their bodies to behave in a natural and comfortable way. By concentrating solely on working the oar, the body movements were left to the subconscious which, with training, would take care of them, just as in learning to walk or run. An infant is not taught to walk in a series of discrete physical movements but is allowed to discover the whole process by trial and error.

The word 'natural' crops up frequently in Steve's world of rowing. There is no evidence that he knew anything about the work of Drs Streicher and Gaulhofer or the debate about *Turnen* in the Austro-Hungarian Empire. His method was learned from pulling boats on the Yarra in Australia and the Cam in England, from listening and talking to oarsmen on both sides of the world, and from watching people moving boats. As a young man he was an active sportsman in other fields, a good cricketer, footballer, tennis player, billiards player and dancer, the last an activity which he said was the highest form of sport. As an elderly man he was a delicate, perfectly balanced skipper. No doubt all of these and more contributed to the Fairbairn method of natural rowing.

In his introduction to the 1990 reprint of Steve's works, Geoffrey Page, whose father Freddie was a Fairbairn coach, describes Steve's understanding of the psychological side of coaching and his reliance on allowing the subconscious mind to solve problems as light years ahead of his contemporaries. Page describes the process thus:

> Put simply, it works like this: a physical action comes first through the eye and then is carried out by the various muscles necessary for the action. If you want to pick up an object, you first look at it and the sensory perception of the eye controls the muscular movement, all the necessary adjustments being made through the subconscious mind. Eventually, as a result of trial and error, movements that do not come off are rejected subconsciously, while the ones that succeed are retained. Sensory information from movements of muscles, tendons, and joints comes through various receptors which transmit information about position and movement, while the sense of balance is controlled through organs in the ears. The feedback of information from internal and external sources allows the body to establish the relationship of each of

its parts to the rest, so that it registers what it is doing without involving the conscious mind . . . It is important to realize that you can sense something without actually perceiving it. You perceive something only when you interpret sense impressions. Through experience, some groups of stimuli are eventually perceived as being more important than others and these are registered while the unimportant ones are ignored . . . The subconscious mind knows better than the conscious mind what it should do in any given situation and this is very important when applied to skills . . . Steve taught his oarsmen to think of the end product rather than a predetermined conscious pattern of movement. He asked them to concentrate on bladework linked to leg-drive and left them to work out how best to do it.

The records of Jesus, Pembroke, Thames, London, FC Zürich and many others show this methodology to be successful, but the results were not always pretty. This led the advocates of orthodoxy, who achieved very good results from 1870 well into the thirties, to accuse Fairbairn of bad practices. The charges were that he taught people to 'shoot their slide', to row with their eyes glued to their blade (thereby unbalancing the boat), and to start the stroke with bent arms. Steve did not teach any of this. What he *did* say was that the slide should be driven evenly, without check and without excessive speed; that, contrary to the Orthodox code of fixing your eyes on the neck in front, it was a good idea to watch what your oar is doing occasionally in order to learn how to control it; and that rigid arms at the beginning of a stroke do not help the rower to spring off the stretcher and drive the blade into and through the water – the essence of Fairbairnism. To achieve this the arms must be straight but elastic. So a Fairbairn boat at practice might contain a crew of different shapes and sizes wearing unmatched kit and watching their blades while using various body movements. But they would be concentrating on moving the boat and enjoying their work. Nowhere in the Fairbairn textbook is to be found a phrase like that emphasized in de Havilland's *Elements of Rowing* (1913): 'Now comes the really hard part of rowing', and later, 'REAL EFFORT' in capital letters. Steve's critics might interpret his crew as being lazy, but his creed says that although you cannot do anything at all if you cannot do it easily, it is mileage that makes champions. Rowing for Fairbairn was a strict discipline and a serious business, even if it brought a twinkle to his eye. He demanded plenty of hard work and fitness of body and mind as he marshalled his fleet on the Cam or the Thames. They may not have looked like ramrod Etonians, but they learned to move a boat.

For Steve, rowing was thought and discussion. As his son wrote in the introduction to Steve's collected rowing books, first published in 1951:

> Steve made allowances for an individual's physical limitations as Orthodox coaching seldom, if ever, did; and Steve produced the man with physical defects to the best of that man's capacity, often, again, with results that looked very odd. And it must be remembered that a large proportion of the men whom Steve coached had limitations. No crew was beneath Steve's dignity. He never took into account the possible effect on his reputation of coaching a crew however good or bad, however promising or unpromising. He required one thing only – that they should believe in him, and then he was ready and happy to coach any crew that asked him. He did not pick and choose whom he would coach: he felt it was part of his mission to coach everyman and he readily coached the halt, the maim and the blind, as well as women and children. He was more concerned to get the very best out of each man than to get together the very best men. And this was a great part of his achievement.

Steve died in 1938, and there were very few left in 1990 who had actually been coached in the boat by him. Alan Burrough, in his foreword to the 1990 edition of Steve's works, says:

> On his final visit to Cambridge, which was my very first week as an undergraduate at Jesus College in October 1936, he took me out in a tub pair. The following May the potential Jesus First May boat [the college's top eight for the May bumping races on the Cam] all went to his flat in London to gather round his bedside and take part in what was probably his last 'Chat on Rowing'. I recollect that we all returned to Cambridge full of confidence and determined to do as well as we were able. Who knows how much importance can be attached to our visit to London? Suffice it to say that Jesus retained the Headship of the Cam comfortably and went on to contest the final of the Grand Challenge Cup at Henley, being narrowly defeated by Rudergesellschaft Wiking, the leading German crew of that time.

That was in 1937. Rudergesellschaft Wiking were coached by Karl-Heinz Schulz, a newspaper proprietor and the head of sport at Berlin Radio. He taught Fairbairnism, and his 1936 crew represented

Germany in the Olympic Games, the only club crew to be selected for the national team.

The Olympic Games of 1936 are a story in themselves (see chapter 13). Here was a maelstrom of politics and prowess involving Nazis and the Jewish question, racialism, democracy versus fascism and motherlands against the Fatherland. When it comes to winning medals in Berlin and tracing the channels of communication between Fairbairnism and orthodoxy, between *Turnen* and fitness for the Fatherland, it is as well to note this list: MacIntyre, Tarryer, Kelley, East, Driver, Liddle, Heynes, Bubear, Brightwell, Sullivan, Cordery, H. Arlett, E. Barry, E. Phelps. They were all English or British Empire professionals, and they all coached in Germany or Austria between 1880 and 1936. There were probably more. Nine of them succeeded one other at Berliner Ruderclub. Sullivan and Cordery coached Germans and Austrians for the Olympic Games regatta held at Grünau, and Eric Phelps was employed by Georg von Opel as a coach but finished up coaching Beresford and Southwood of Britain for the Olympics. Whether they taught Fairbairnism or not, those of them who were around in the twenties and thirties were certainly intimate with his method. They came from a long line of professional scullers who knew and taught rowing, built boats, sculled and coached for cash when the opportunity arose, but who could not be classed as amateurs or go upstairs to an English clubroom unless invited under special circumstances. Many left their island fastness for work, and there was work in Germany. A peer of their class was a professional world champion sculler called Joe Sadler. Sadler emphasized good bladework and leg-drive rather than stylish body form when he coached gentlemen amateurs in the nineteenth century at Jesus College, Cambridge, shortly before Steve first arrived there.

The Rise of Ratzeburg

This was the background for the survivors of the Second World War who were returning to the water, whether it be to the 1948 Olympic Games at Henley-on-Thames or to revive club activity and teach a new generation who were dusting off the old equipment. Ratzeburg has one great natural advantage in that the low wooded hills which surround the lake always protect a part of it from the wind, so that suitable water – flat or rough depending on the conditions one expects at one's next regatta – can be found throughout the year. In 1953 the teachers at Adam's school and Walter Schröder, a former pupil, founded a club in the village so that the leavers could continue their rowing. The first man to achieve national success from Ratzeburg was Klaus von Fersen, who won the German sculling title six times in succession, the first being in 1955. He was Karl Adam's first real oarsman. Adam's next aim was to find someone for von Fersen to race, and Manfred Rulffs, another graduate of the school, fulfilled the role. The two men won the German double sculling title in 1955. The press attacked Adam on the grounds that von Fersen would be even better if he had a proper club and a proper coach, and later suggested that rowing, as opposed to sculling, was a different ballgame. In 1956 von Fersen failed to reach the Olympic final in the single. Critics accused Ratzeburg crews of bad technique and the German rowing federation offered the services of a coach, but Alfred Bloch, the Ratzeburg club president, refused. At home the crews continued to win races. Schröder went to Freiburg University where the running coach, Waldemar Gerschler, and the physician, Professor Herbert Reindell, were working on interval training. The British distance runner 'Galloping' Gordon Pirie was among the students there.

The origin of interval training is disputed, but it was developed by track and field athletes in the thirties and used to good effect by the Czech Emile Zatopek. The method is to run shorter distances than those required in competition, but more frequently and often at a higher pace. It is based on the principle that 'a chain is as strong as its weakest link', working at the weakest link of the heart. The effect is to increase circulation and build strength. After Adam applied interval training to rowing, he learned that he had been beaten to the draw by Mrs Gerda Stöck, who was married to the 1936 Olympic javelin champion and was teaching girls to row by the interval method in Hamburg.

By the time Schröder, who was the connection between Gerschler and Adam, left Freiburg in 1956, Adam was watching 10,000-metre runners and weightlifters; by now more than half his training programme for rowers consisted of interval training. For winter training he had introduced barbells. But Adam's third great innovation after the use of the single and interval training was a re-examination of the rowing movement. He found that Orthodox coaches taught the technical points of the stroke by describing the steps in great detail, laying down a set pattern of movements. He found that both Fairbairn and Borrmann had set out to subordinate outward appearances to developing a feeling for what Fairbairn described as the 'endless chain movement'. Adam then encouraged feedback from his athletes to apply cybernetics – the theory of control and communication in living organisms (from the Greek for 'steersman') – to rowing. Indeed 'cybernetics' was not in use as a word in Fairbairn's day, but Steve had often wrestled with problems of verbal communication. It was one thing, said Steve, to understand an idea or a way of doing something, but quite another to explain the same thing to two people. So Adam, like Steve, sought discussion and thought. He was, Schröder says, a democratic coach. He attempted to put his cybernetic concept of style into a sentence: 'A purposeful cycle of movements is not directed step by step by a preconceived notion but by being automatically directed by a sequence of acquired and memorized patterns known as feedback.' He did not accept that there was any fundamental difference between rowing and sculling.

Schröder weighed 80 kilos and stood 1.8 metres tall. Though small in stature he was winning five or six times in different boats each weekend. 'Normally,' he says, 'an oarsman's weakest link is endurance. We must have been very good in endurance.' By 1957 he was in a double scull with Rulffs or with Hans Lenk, another Ratzeburg oarsman. With Rulffs he won the coxless pairs at Hamburg in a boat rented half an hour before the race. It was their very first outing in a coxless pair, which is the most difficult boat to balance. Rulffs had never seen the steering mechanism before. In the double they came first in the German championships and fourth in the European championships. 'Interval training was the secret of our condition,' Schröder says. And Adam replied: 'If you can handle a single you can handle all boats.'

In 1958 five seventeen-year-old schoolboys from Ratzeburg were junior champions, and Schröder, Rulffs and Lenk were rowing in Kiel University's crew. Together they made up an eight, rented a boat at a Berlin regatta, and lost by not more than 4 metres after one training outing. Four weeks later they won the German championships using a Karlisch-made boat with the cox in the bow. The

80-kilo Schröder was the heaviest man. The crew who came second were 10 kilos per man heavier. Rulffs, Lenk and two Kiel students won the fours title as well.

In the following year Kiel's coach, Karl Wiepcke, again cooperated with Adam and formed an eight of Kiel students and Ratzeburg club oarsmen. Four were large, and the rest made up in technical proficiency what they lacked in size. They were unbeaten for two years. Adam made them row in singles, doubles and fours so that they would not forget how to lose. They won the European championships at Macon with twelve seconds of clear water. The Ratzeburg men were Schröder, Rulffs, Lenk and Moritz von Groddeck, a huge, amiable, powerful man who had been thrown out of his club in Hamburg for indiscipline. They were hungry for success, keen to prove Adam's ideas, and very anti-establishment. 'Two lengths is not enough' was their maxim. They wanted to pulverize the opposition. In that year only the coxed pair in the German team were not from the Adam school of rowing. In 1960 no doubling up was allowed at the German championships, and Ratzeburg won the coxed and coxless fours, the doubles and the eights. The second-placed coxed four went on to win the Olympic title, and then the Ratzeburg eight ended the Americans' run as Olympic champions. As Schröder, Rulffs and Lenk completed their studies, other oarsmen gravitated towards Kiel and Hamburg universities to be near Ratzeburg, still a small club but one with a coach who was gaining a reputation for himself.

In 1962 Ratzeburg's eight won the world championships. Two years later came a defection from the Democratic Republic, symptomatic of the magnetic field leading to Adam. Dietrich Rose appeared in West Berlin and went to Ratzeburg but failed to reach the first eight from a pool of twenty men. At that time the best eight scullers made up the first eight, although Adam would occasionally select from pairs if trialists had little or no experience of sculling. Everything depended on water work. On the evening before racing there was always a discussion on technique involving Adam and Wiepcke, the crew and the cox. Rose left the second eight for Philadelphia where he joined Vesper (see chapter 14). At the 1964 Olympics Vesper beat Ratzeburg's eight into second place, though not with Rose on board.

In 1965 Adam, who had turned down the offer of a coaching job in Cologne, became the first director of the new rowing academy at Ratzeburg. No longer a schoolmaster, he was now a professional. The federation had changed its mind about Ratzeburg rowing. Its president Walter Wülfing became a great friend of Ratzeburg. Indeed, it was he who persuaded the federation that continuous success depended on the establishment of the academy. That success continued with Ratzeburg's regaining of the Olympic eights championship in 1968. But Adam knew that his methods and his crews' success would lead to them being caught and overtaken. Adam was a pedagogue, a leader, and at times outspoken and stubborn. He had identified and examined the three components of rowing – style, stamina and strength. He had recognized technique as cybernetic rather than mechanical, and saw that both weight training and interval training were essential for achieving a gradual build-up of strength and maximum circulation, in harmony with recovery aided by sleep, relaxation and the right food. He championed the single and smaller boats. He thought about gearing and equipment, and cooperated with boatbuilders like Karlisch and rigger makers like the Matt Wood company in England to get what his rowers needed. He once sent Cyril Bishop of Matt Wood a specially made china figurine of the master rigger maker at work. Above all, Adam always supported the athlete, believing that sport was an opportunity for a person to find his or her personality. The real aim was to improve oneself. The group must use this growing time as an investment for the future. The graduates of Adam's methods say that he never used an athlete as a tool for his own profit, but taught by discussion between equal partners. He believed that first place by unfair means is second place. Unlike many coaches who develop ideas and keep them to themselves, Adam published, believing that this was the way to create better competition and to develop influence. But he also knew that by doing so he was reducing his chances of first place.

13
HITLER'S GAMES

WHEN George Pocock and Al 'The Dead Pan Kid' Ulbrickson arrived in Berlin in 1936 with the University of Washington eight, their first and deepest impression was the hold Hitler had over the people. 'Red and white flags bearing the Nazi hooked cross were everywhere, as were uniforms of all kinds,' Pocock wrote in his log. They soon realized they were up against governments: 'Hitler's Germany and Mussolini's Italy in particular provided total financial support to their Olympic athletes. They had the finest of equipment. In contrast the American shells, other than the *Yankee Clipper* [Pocock's shell for the eight], were very old and, I thought, in disgraceful condition.' The Americans' impression was that the German oarsmen were good on the water but arrogant off it. In the opening ceremony at the athletics stadium the Americans deliberately strolled out of step while removing their hats in deference to their hosts. 'It was a very small blow for freedom, certainly, but it somehow made us feel a lot better,' Pocock said.

This was going to be the largest Olympic regatta so far. The seven events attracted twenty-four countries and ninety-six boats manned by 348 oarsmen and coxes. It was held on the Spree at Grünau on a straight six-lane 2000-metre stretch of water, a stretch of similar size having being marked out at the top of the regatta course for practice. For the first time some of the German oarsmen had been prepared in a national squad system, and this had taken their opponents unawares. There was a thoroughness and purpose about their method. At Grünau there was no question but that the winning meant more than the taking part. The occasion was an unprecedented expression of German nationalism and patriotism, the culmination of a movement that had started well before the First World War.

The idea of German nationalism was firmly in place when the Archduke Francis Ferdinand of Austria was assassinated in 1914, which led to the First World War and resulted in all the professional English coaches in Berlin losing their jobs. The nationalist tradition ran strongly in rowing and led to 30,000 German oarsmen taking up arms against the English and French, whom the German rowing federation (DRV) described as 'indisciplined'. By 1915 4000 oarsmen had won the Iron Cross, and by 1916 four out of five oarsmen were in the war.

On 5 August 1915 the rowing federation began its campaign to persuade children to take up rowing. By 1917 pre-military training was under discussion in Germany. For the price of 1 Reichsmark children over fourteen were admitted to a new rowing programme, the aims of which were to abolish social ranking, involve all classes in character-forming activities and instil a love of nature, punctuality and discipline. Rowing was in gigs, and rowers were required to pass a style test and a medical before they were allowed to race. They also took part in swimming and received pre-military instruction, which included running, negotiating obstacles, observation and reporting back. The military drill proved to be unpopular, and so more racing was introduced. Through all this, however, the rowing federation continued to sit on its anti-egalitarian perch, equating the programme for juniors with professionalism, while its member clubs helped the war effort by raising 30,000 Reichsmark in a year for families of fallen soldiers and using their premises as food kitchens and convalescent homes for the wounded. Their members provided medical help and other social services for casualties of the war.

After the defeat of Germany in 1918 the federation continued to advance the cause of German-ness. When the Austrian federation merged with the German on 22 January 1921, the Austrian president Dr Reiffenstuhl said prophetically, 'We Austrians are members of the great German nation. Our country is in a terrible position . . . Political union is perhaps not possible in a time we can foresee, but there are signs that it becomes more and more the wish of the Germans in Austria . . . We rowers have done what is possible by joining the German *Ruderverband*. It is a forerunner of political union which Austrians demand.' Annexation of Austria – the Anschluss – came seventeen years later, on 31 March 1938.

The union of the federations, ironically, meant that the Austrian clubs had to accept Jews as members now that they were under German rules. In 1921 the German federation made a pact with German clubs in Czechoslovakia to form a common regatta organization. It tried to strengthen German clubs outside Germany with contractual links, an example being the Germania Club in Posen (in the Prussian part of Poland, now Poznan). German clubs in the Saar and the Rhineland turned their backs on fraternization with the enemy so long as troops were in occupation of territory which the Germans considered to be German. This resulted in the French taking over a club on the Rhine because it refused to admit French members.

The cause of German-ness was further advanced by the National Olympics, first proposed in 1894. The first meeting was in rowing and tennis in 1922, a *Volksfest* of physical power and skill of youth, expressed in German art, song and custom. The second meeting in Cologne, in the Rhineland, emphasized the cult of the spirit, the renewal of the body, and the rebuilding of self-respect. The third was in Breslau, Silesia (now Wroclaw, Poland), close to the post-war eastern border. The meetings were organized deliberately near Germany's boundaries to act as beacon for the 'occupied' Germans.

The thaw began at the Locarno Conference in 1925 when France moved closer to abandoning the Rhineland and Germany guaranteed the inviolability of the western border and agreed arbitration treaties with France, Belgium, Poland and Czechoslovakia. The sport of rowing made a gesture of reconciliation when the United States invited German crews to the Philadelphia regatta. 'America as the former occupying enemy state holds out its hand to German rowing sport,' said a headline in *Wassersport*. On 4 February 1926 a *Wassersport* headline greeted the exit of occupying troops from the Rhine with 'Köln free!' There was strong pathos in the writings of the federation when asking clubs to remember the dead through comradeship and faithfulness above all else. Memorial tablets on boathouses were to be honoured on memorial days. The promoted theme was spiritual union between today's youth and the fallen.

On 24 July 1930 Heinrich Pauli, president of the federation, wrote a piece called 'Freeing of the Rhineland' in which he congratulated sportsmen on the Rhine on their release from the pressure of occupation. His article was heavy with national metaphor and symbolism. A subsequent correspondent hailed the Reich of Hindenburg as the 'incarnation of German-made virtue, the guard of German honour', and recalled a regatta witnessed by Hindenburg. Dr Horst Überhorst, author of Germany's centennial rowing history *100 Jahre DRV* (1983), says that they were appealing to an emotion which encompassed unity of people without a homeland and the myth and tradition of a thousand-year fight for national identity. National Socialism emerged from the sublimation of party differences and fervour for the Fatherland. The implication was that Germany was surrounded by enemies. Conjuring a picture of enemies seems to have been necessary to persuade youth to make sacrifices for the leadership. The First World War had been a heavy burden and there was no feeling of guilt or thought of reconciliation. Paul von Beneckendorff und von Hindenburg, Posen-born hero of the Eastern Front and narrowly elected president of the Reich in 1925, was adulated as a substitute Kaiser, and the vision was one of future might and glory.

The National Socialist Workers Party became the second largest political party in September 1930, and it was Hindenburg who summoned Adolf Hitler to assume the chancellorship in 1933. Economic collapse was the cause; the middle-class unemployed were the party's strength. The National Socialists revolutionized the social structure in a way that had not been possible immediately after the First World War. They lauded the past while destroying its institutions. Other parties were dissolved by the Enabling Act of 24 March 1933. Institutions such as the church and the trades unions lost autonomy, and the systematic breakdown of the old social order included sport. The rowing federation appeared a willing partner, its president Pauli making ever more patriotic acclamations of loyalty to Hitler and toadying to the new sports supremo Hans von Tschammer und Osten. On 20 April 1933 Pauli sent a telegram to Hitler: 'The great leader of the national regeneration is greeted on his birthday by the DRV which is proud of its 50 years' work in education of German youth towards national feeling, thinking, and acting.' Pauli, a Prussian regional government official, was a bull-necked crew-cut rightist who identified with the national revolution. He was president of the rowing federation from 1926 and thereafter became rowing's spokesman until the destruction of the Nazis.

The federation celebrated its fiftieth anniversary on 19 March 1933 in Hamburg. There were more women than men at the party.

Four hundred and eighty-two of the 574 clubs were represented. (Their total membership was 100,000, compared with 1.6 million gymnasts in 12,000 clubs and 500,000 soccer players in 9000 clubs.) Six months later the Ministry of Education ordered clubs to ban Jews. On 4 May 1933 Tschammer attacked Marxists and Communists and called on sportsmen and gymnasts to work together for the people and the Fatherland. Dr Theodor Lewald resigned as president of the German Workers' Rowing Association. His crime was that his paternal grandmother had been born a Jew. The announcement was made by Tschammer's press secretary. The association was eventually dissolved. Lewald was also forced to part with the presidency of the German Olympic Committee in favour of Tschammer. Pauli, meanwhile, embraced Tschammer's guidelines. Soon leadership courses were arranged at rowing clubs on Wednesdays and Sundays. The summer programme included intensive *wander* and competitive rowing and monthly marching and military exercises. The winter programme contained long marches with backpacks, small calibre shooting, drill and monthly 'political' evenings.

Tschammer's move towards centralized leadership was in two stages, one each side of the Olympic Games. First, he insisted that all associations move their headquarters to Berlin. On 30 January 1934 the Reichsport association was founded, organised in sixteen new areas with twenty-five federations under its wing. Reichsport was intended as a great educational institution to put Nazi political thinking in the foreground for everybody in the youth movement. Thus political leaders in clubs became top dogs. *Wander* rowing was encouraged, as was association with Germans abroad and the singing of patriotic songs. In 1935 the Protestant and Catholic associations were absorbed into the Hitler Youth movement. On 28 January in that year all clubs were included in Reichsport. Pauli signed the order submitting rowing to it. His written explanation said that the federation no longer had its own laws but had an international role to play. In 1936 the little Prussian had to dissolve the federation that he had presided over. It became a committee appointed by men from Tschammer's department, and Pauli was appointed to it. By now he thought that all the workers in his federation were Marxists, but Tschammer told him to accept people who declared themselves ready to play their part in building the new Germany. The new order affected club life. The clubs had no role, and the annual rowing day was replaced by one of political indoctrination. Trustees of the rowing committee were appointed by Tschammer, and areas were created corresponding to those of Reichsport. A legal department was established to sort out inter-club quarrels. Every club had to set up a youth division. Hitler Youth navy departments were created and added to the summer rowing and winter land training programmes. Thus democracy in the rowing federation went down the Spree along with democracy in the Reichstag.

Roads to Grünau

The Games were awarded to Berlin in 1933, before the Nazis had total control. In 1936 they took place in an extraordinary atmosphere of German joy and triumphalism. Men like Lewald and Carl Diem had been preparing for the Games for years, ever since their plans for 1916 were thwarted by the First World War. The Germans had never won a track or field event, and their only rowing gold in the previous Games was in the coxed fours. The nation's athletes were prepared for winning, and the nation was led to expect them to do so. The Nazi Party, meanwhile, grasped the opportunity to use the Games as another exercise in pageantry, another Nuremberg rally to demonstrate to the *Volk* the superiority of the Aryan race. Meanwhile anti-Jewish legislation became part of the *Gleichschaltung*, the process of forcefully establishing the superiority of National Socialism and Aryan Germans by eliminating the opposition. Jewish businesses were boycotted in 1933, and in April of that year began the purging of 'non-Aryans' from the civil service, the universities, law and medicine. Intermarriage was forbidden, non-Aryan property was expropriated, and the Nuremberg laws of September 1935 deprived Jews and part-Jews of citizenship and civil rights. On 2 June 1933 the Minister of Education announced that Jews must be excluded from all youth, welfare and gymnastic organizations and clubs. Swimming resorts were declared off-limits, Jewish teams were forbidden to compete against Aryan teams and to compete abroad. By 1935 Jews were banned from all public and private practice fields. As we have seen, this extended to the *Mischlinge* or people of mixed blood such as Lewald, who was eventually kept on as an Olympic adviser after an outcry among his foreign friends in the Olympic movement. Diem, who with Lewald was largely responsible for bringing the Games to Berlin, was a scholarly German of the old school and a genius at organization. He believed in a new sports culture, and his research and education centre for physical education, lavishly equipped, was opened near the Olympic site. He was not pushed aside like Lewald even though his wife Liselott, an educationalist, was racially tainted because she had a Jewish ancestor. Diem was certainly not a Nazi. He was a silent opponent, avoiding almost all contact with the chancellor. But his Games, full of technical innovation and extending a warm welcome to visitors and foreign athletes, served the Nazi purpose nevertheless. Diem's triumphant athletic festival was also Hitler's.

Given the political build-up to the Games and the violent treatment handed out to Jews which was increasingly becoming public knowledge, it seems surprising that anybody agreed to take part. Certainly some on the political left in Britain urged a boycott, an idea dismissed by the aristocrats of the British Olympic Committee. There was opposition in some other countries, notably Sweden and Switzerland. In the United States a much larger protest movement forced the Germans to concede that Jews would be eligible for the German national team and would be welcomed as members of other teams. Basically, Chancellor Hitler stayed his hand until after the Games. Before the Games, the Americans put politics behind them and set sail on the *Manhattan*.

The cox of their four, Edward H. Bennett, described the voyage as

a zoo, an incredible spectacle. You had the walking team striding by, with that peculiar waddling gait. The boxing team, a bunch of lowlifes if you ever saw them, were shadow boxing on deck. The high divers were insufferably vain. They postured and posed on the diving board for an hour at a time. One of the weightlifters was even worse – on deck he wore a silk wrapper and a blue hairnet so the wind wouldn't muss his coiffure ... A backstroker on the women's swimming team, Eleanor Holm, had a fondness for champagne that ignited a minor brouhaha. Holm enjoyed roistering with journalists each night in the *Manhattan*'s first-class bar. But when one writer radiogrammed this story to New York, Avery Brundage, head of the US Olympic Committee, dismissed Holm from the Olympic team for 'breaking training'.

Meanwhile the threads of English and German rowing which

became intertwined at the Olympic course in Grünau led all the way back to Berliner RC, a top-drawer club founded in 1880 by Georg Wilhelm Büxenstein and attracting industrialists and professional men of the Bismark Reich. Like many others in the higher echelons of nineteenth-century Berlin society, Büxenstein was a Jew. He was a member of Berliner RC Welle-Poseidon, an exclusively Jewish club. Early in the 1930s Berliner attracted Herbert Buhtz from Magdeburg because he wanted the best available coaching. He was a student dentist and lived with other oarsmen in the imposing headquarters by the Wannsee, with its Emperors' Room hung with portraits and adorned with a silver bust of Hindenburg. The coaching staff list before the First World War reads: Tarryer, Kelley, East, Driver, Liddle, Haynes, Bubear, Brightwell, and Sullivan. All were Englishmen except Tom Sullivan, a New Zealander who had spent the First World War at the Kaiser's pleasure in a concentration camp in Ruhleben, where he organized physical fitness for the Allied prisoners to keep body and soul together. A giant from Auckland, he started as an amateur at North Shore Rowing Club and was apprenticed to the Logan boatbuilding company, which was known as New Zealand's finest. He became master boatbuilder to the New Zealand government in Wellington and represented Wellington at rugby. He won forty-four of his forty-nine races before moving to Sydney as a professional. He travelled to England in 1893, becoming the English sculling champion, but he never won the world title.

When it was suggested at Berliner that Sullivan should be re-hired after the First World War, the club was almost irreconcilably split, but the faction which saw him as primarily a sportsman prevailed, and he was in residence above the boathouse again from 1925. He had an international outlook, could not abide timidity, was incapable of lukewarmness, and referred to himself as 'old devil', saying he was a man 'only for big fish'. Buhtz, bored with his training routine of sculling round the island on which the club is situated, once put Sullivan to the test. One morning the coach, as usual, set his watch and saw Buhtz off, returning to the club for his breakfast. As soon as Sullivan was out of sight Buhtz swung round, sculled across to the other side of the clubhouse and lay down in his boat under a bridge for an hour or so before coming strongly home at the appointed time. Sullivan watched him return, asked him a few questions, then told him to take off his shirt. Sullivan had greased the slides that morning, and Buhtz's shirt displayed tram lines all down its back.

In Buhtz's time Heinrich Pauli was a member of Berliner, and so was General Daluege of the SS, like the rest of the membership ascending and decending the staircase decorated with the Star of David every time he went from social rooms to boathouse. Daluege tried to persuade Buhtz to scull for the SS, but Buhtz, by now a dentist and ambitious to be a professor, refused. No more was said about it. He found the atmosphere very difficult. He had to leave his job at the hospital because his professor told him that, regrettably, he was not allowed to promote anyone who was not a member of the National Socialist Party. Buhtz set up his own dental practice. Before the Olympics he was more or less ordered by Tschammer to try out against Gustav 'Gummi' Schäfer for the Olympic nomination, losing to him at Grünau because of wash.

From 1925 to 1936 Sullivan's pupils at Berliner were responsible for 224 of the club's 490 victories. Buhtz was one of his stars, winning the Diamonds at Henley in 1932 and coming second in the Olympic doubles in the same year. In 1934 he went for the Diamonds again. In the final he was in terrible pain because he had somehow damaged his back after setting a record in a heat. He blamed an uncomfortable car journey to Oxford with Sullivan as driver. He went on to win, but recollects that the incident was the beginning of the end of his career. Eventually adherence to orthodoxy forced Sullivan out of Berliner. He went off to the Lia club in Vienna in 1936 (and so eventually to another war spent in internment). When he left, Buhtz wrote of him in *Wassersport*: 'He was known as a master of the hard English school, of strict discipline and exact method of rowing . . . Any disobedience . . . resulted in the instantaneous dropping of the same person even, as once happened, when it endangered an ultimate victory in the Kaiser fours.' Berliner hired their first German coach and their first Fairbairnist, Fritz Gwinner.

Other English professionals worked in German clubs. The one-time world champion Ernest Barry was at Hellas in 1929. The journalist Hylton Cleaver reckoned that the best British coaches at the time of the 1936 Games were trainers outside Britain. 'Britain had not offered employment to one of them,' he wrote in his *History of Rowing* (1957). Dan Cordery, a professional from Putney, had flitted all round the world before becoming the German federation's

Olympic trainer in Berlin. From 1911 to 1913 he was with Berliner RV 1876, in 1919 at Sandefjord in Norway, in 1920–21 at the Scandinavian club in Buenos Aires, from 1922 to 1923 at Yale, in 1924 at St Michael's RFC, Limerick, in Ireland, and then in Dresden, Leipzig, Hamburg and Dresden again. He was known as 'His Master's Voice' and from April he ran a sculling school in Berlin and was in charge of Schäfer and the double scullers Willy Kaidel and Joachim Pirsch. Also helping at the camp was Eric Phelps, a brilliant sculler also from Putney, whose brother Ted won the world professional title in 1930. Phelps was employed as coach, chauffeur and handyman to Georg von Opel, an Olympic team aspirant, and he knew the German rowing scene well. He observed that Kaidel and Pirsch were very fast off the start, being able to catch Phelps and his partner in a minute after giving them a four-length start, which was almost unbelievable. But when Phelps spent three weeks sculling against Pirsch in singles he discovered that 'the bugger had no stamina'. Pirsch could not scull farther than 1000 metres, which meant 1500 metres at the most in a double.

Six weeks before the Olympics Phelps went to Henley, just to watch. There were no events there for double sculls, but his hero Jack Beresford was there with his doubles partner Dick Southwood, out every day pacing everybody. Phelps told them, ' "You needn't go to Berlin. Waste of time." To prove it I challenged them in a single, and in a borrowed boat I finished three lengths ahead after a minute. "No sculler beats a double scull, and I'm in a strange boat," I told them. That started Jack thinking. Southwood didn't think much, but he was horsepower.'

Beresford, who had won a medal in each of the four previous Olympic Games, was an inspiration to Phelps all his life. 'I paced him a lot. He was very vicious in the boat. He would give a sickly smile to the man next to him. He never knew what it was to pack up. He never knew what it was to let a man pass him.' Beresford's father 'Berry' was a Pole who had been caught up in disturbances as a boy and taken to England by his governess. He was himself a coach and oarsman. Jack had high Slav cheekbones, a magnificent torso and funny little legs. He once exchanged blazers with Johnny Weismuller, the Olympic swimmer who became the first Tarzan, and only had to shorten the garment's arms. The family firm made furniture and amunition boxes in east London. His partner Southwood was a jeweller.

Beresford asked what they should do. They had been coaching themselves for months. The first thing, Phelps said, was to get a new boat, for they were using one built for heavier men. Beresford's racing weight was 11 stone 4 lb. 'What we want is a knife in the water, not a balloon,' Phelps said. There were only six weeks to go; Roly Sims of Putney made a 'knife' in two and a half days for £50, according to Southwood. Phelps reduced all their habitual long-distance training to one, two and three-minute pieces several times a day. Some may have called that interval training.

The boat was shipped off to Berlin, but had not arrived when the crew settled in at the police barracks at Köpenick castle. After the opening ceremony Cordery lent them a training double. The next day it had disappeared. They were told that the Germans had taken it to replace another that had been damaged. Phelps loaned his single to Beresford and took Southwood out in a double whenever he could borrow one, and they resumed training.

The hosts were preparing crews for all seven events. Schäfer had been selected in the single sculls and Kaidel and Pirsch in the doubles. The German coxless four were coached by Wolfgang Freyeisen, who was unencumbered by scientific ballast, according to his biographer Carl Anton Rom. Freyeisen's father Georg was a professional coach who advocated the natural development of movement which differed sharply from Orthodox ways at a time before Fairbairn's style won the argument in Germany. Wolfgang believed in self-will. His crews went out after work and after dark, with double training sessions on Sundays and holidays.

The coxed four were Fritz Gwinner's, a post office worker before he became Amicitia Mannheim's self-made trainer in 1924. According to Carlheinz Neumann's assessment of Gwinner in the German centenary rowing history, Gwinner's crew were the first outside England to understand Fairbairn's teachings of natural rowing. This was when they were working with the Mainz trainer Josef Fremersdorf. In 1933 two of this Olympic crew were in an Amicitia four beaten by Pembroke College, Cambridge, at Henley, Pembroke being a 'Fairbairn' crew.

Henri Erb, a bank official who took up coaching with Mannheimer RC in 1930, was in charge of Willi Eichhorn and Hugo Strauss in the coxless pair. In 1934 he saw the Fairbairn light and trained them accordingly, substituting 10-kilometre forest runs for weight training. He accompanied them on his bicycle. Together they overthrew sixty years of strict orthodoxy at Mannheimer.

Gustav Gehrmann of Baldeneysee coached Gerhard Gustmann and Herbert Adamski, steered by Dieter Arend, in the coxed pair. Gehrmann followed Einstein's teaching that the joy of achievement and its value for society are the most important motives for life. He was the federation's choice to produce an Olympic eight, but his crew were beaten for selection by the Glider, a club crew from Wiking Berlin coached by Karl-Heinz Schulz. There were, as we can see, various paternity claims for Fairbairnism in Germany, and Schulz's was among them. For this economics student who became a journalist and broadcaster is claimed the introduction and evaluation of Fairbairn training methods. Certainly as a young oarsman of nineteen, Schulz met Fairbairn and began an exchange of views which taught him that Fairbairnism was a complete sports education. He adopted the Fairbairn maxim that 'kilometres make masters', believed in light weight training to strenghen wrists, and adopted long-distance running in forests. He instilled fighting spirit, agility and spiritual togetherness of trainer and crew, and at Wiking he coached two outstanding eights who raced each other frequently. The Wiking Glider were the only pure club crew to reach the Olympics in the German team, 'a blow for the Nazi selection system,' commented Buhtz, the Berliner sculler beaten by Schäfer in the trials.

Medals and Wreaths

Thirty thousand or, depending on your informant, seventy-five thousand spectators turned up for four days of rowing on the Langer See at Grünau. The course was buoyed straight along the centre of the river, and a temporary grandstand had been floated opposite the lawns which front the imposing boathouses, their numerous jetties giving access to the water. The boundary wall of this natural rowing stadium is the forest. For some on finals day – among them a twelve-year-old Swiss boy called Thomi Keller – this was simply the greatest regatta that they had experienced. For others, viewers and competitors, German and non-German, patriotism and national pride was

Regatta at Molesey by Alfred Sisley

Hommage to Sisley: Henley Regatta by Raoul Dufy

TOP: *Max Schmitt in a Single Scull by Thomas Eakins, 1871*

ABOVE: *The Great International Sculling Match by Thomas Hare, in which the English champion Harry Kelley beat the American champion James 'The Little Engine' Hammill in two races in 1866 at Newcastle-upon-Tyne*

OPPOSITE ABOVE: *The Thames at Erith by William Anderson, showing a wherry*

OPPOSITE BELOW: *'Mr Phelps' is prepared for a scull, watercolour by Julia Phelps*

GORDINNE, LIÉGE.

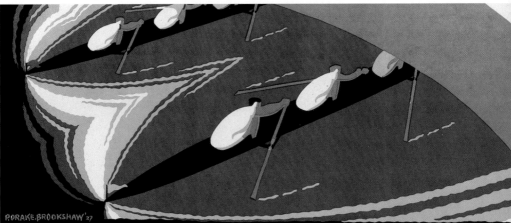

P.DRAKE.BROOKSHAW '27

SATURDAY MARCH 31ST - 9-45 AM
NEAREST STATIONS:- PUTNEY BRIDGE, HAMMERSMI
RAVENSCOURT PK, TURNHAM GREEN & CHISWICK
UNDERGROUND

OPPOSITE ABOVE: *Sculler and Woman in Plumed Hat by August Donnay, c. 1895*

OPPOSITE BELOW: *London Transport poster for the Oxford and Cambridge University Boat Race, 1928*

ABOVE: *Eights at Henley by Cosmo Clark, which is clearly not at Henley but on the tidal waters of the Thames*

BELOW: *Henley Regatta by Alfred de Breanski*

ABOVE: *Military Revue at Messina, Sicily by G. Vasari*

OPPOSITE ABOVE LEFT: *The Young Rower by Lancelot Glasson*

OPPOSITE ABOVE RIGHT: *Coming of Age of Louis XIII, 1614 by Rubens*

OPPOSITE BELOW: *John Biglow in a Single Scull by Thomas Eakins*

TOP: *Venice Regatta on Grand Canal by Canaletto*

ABOVE: *The Nottingham Boat Club, 1894 by Arthur Spooner*

at stake, as it was on the other side of the city in the great athletics stadium near the Wannsee. In the athletics events the Americans took their toll and kept the Führer's runners in their place. The stadium in the capital of the Aryan 'master race' turned out to belong to a black man, Jesse Owens, who won the 100 metres, the 200 metres and the long jump, and was a member of the 4 x 100 metres relay team for the Stars and Stripes.

For the competitors, efficiency in the organization was apparent. Martin Bristow, a member of the British team, said that the bus service from the police barracks was rigid and unalterable, so that oarsmen used their free public transport passes most of the time. Victor de Bisschop, the Belgian official who had travelled to the regatta in a coach converted to contain sleeping accommodation, was impressed by the arrangements for running the regatta. The starter was on the top platform of a large covered pontoon. Below him sat a radio officer who relayed the starting time to officials at the finish. Pontoons had been floated on the river by the army and were each manned by four soldiers to hold the boats at the start of races. Commentaries were given through loudspeakers for the first 1500 metres, delivered from a boat and a tower at the 1000-metre point, where a bell was sounded as crews passed. Another commentator was on the roof of the Viktoria club. Silence would descend for the last 500 metres. Bristow reported that everyone was friendly, and de Bisschop that German hospitality was unsurpassed. The crews set about image-making, the American four wearing feathers in their headbands like Indians, and the big Italian eight scarfs on their heads like pirates. Lawrence 'Monk' Terry, coach of the American coxed four from Harvard, helped Pocock to repair his eight, which had been damaged by a derrick when being unloaded. Terry had problems of his own. He had mistakenly rubbed his boat down with disinfectant intended for oar handles instead of sperm whale oil, and it had taken off the varnish. 'At least you will have the most sanitary boat in the race,' Pocock told him as they sanded the bottom, and applied paraffin wax to make it watertight. Terry was not amused. His four were used as a stalking horse by the Washington eight. Pocock and Ulbrickson thought they were good. In 1000 metres the eight could not get away. 'That ruined us,' said Bennett, cox of the four. 'Over-confidence. We were walking on air and could only go downhill from there.'

Downhill they went, like the Japanese eight who could rate 50 strokes to the minute but could not reach the final. Ulbrickson described them as 'Ducks trying to rise off the water'. Germans won the first five gold medals, to great acclaim from the crowd in the presence of the chancellor. As the two pairs, the two fours and Schäfer paddled away bearing huge victory wreaths, their team were on target for a clean sweep. The sun was in the hosts' and Hitler's heaven, even if the sky over Grünau was dark and sullen. As he left the changing room to go afloat for the double sculls final, Dick Southwood met a German who was a member of Thames, his rowing club in London. 'A good day for the Germans,' Southwood said. 'It will get better,' came the comradely reply.

Some days earlier, a British official had located Beresford and Southwood's boat in a railway siding somewhere between Hamburg and Berlin. It arrived just in time for their first heat. This had been won by the Germans, Beresford easing up when Kaidel and Pirsch came across into their water. Later he told his partner that it was better to enter the repechage than risk damaging the precious boat. Southwood noticed that the Germans took a stroke before Beresford and he had moved, and that the starter, de Bisschop, was none the wiser because his megaphone was so large that he could not see round it. The British won the repechage by streaking out to 1000 metres and easing off, posting a message to the Germans. Before the final Phelps told Beresford and Southwood, 'Don't let Fatguts out of your sight. They will be ahead, but I guarantee that after 1500 metres something will happen.' Southwood, the stroke, revealed to Beresford that he was going to start the instant the Germans squared their blades. On the start they tried de Bisschop's temper by going off just as he was calling them up. 'A bit of gamesmanship, I'm afraid,' Southwood said many years later. The British caused further delay by taking off their sweaters. They went off at the same moment as the Germans into the headwind, and led for the first 500 metres, according to Southwood. Then Kaidel and Pirsch moved ahead. But the Germans gained scarcely a length, and at 1800 metres, opposite Phelps's vantage point on the bank, the crews were level. They remained level for 100 metres and Beresford warned Southwood that he was going to shout because the two boats were converging. He shouted; the Germans moved away. Then Pirsch stopped. Kaidel went on sculling, but it was all over. Poles, French, Americans and

Australians were strung out way behind. Beresford and Southwood had won gold and stopped the German procession. At thirty-seven, Jack Beresford had taken his fifth medal in five Olympic regattas, a record unsurpassed.

This left the eights, an event won six times thus far by the Americans and twice by the British in Olympic regattas. Ulbrickson and Pocock were convinced that only Britain were capable of beating the Huskies, their crew from Washington. Pocock assessed Ulbrickson's men as a classic example of eight-oared rowing at its very best. 'To be of championship calibre,' wrote the wise boatbuilder,

> a crew must have a total confidence in each other, able to drive with abandon, confident that no man will get the full weight of the pull. Without this confidence, the men tend to 'row with the boat', meaning they will not pull faster than the boat is going. A good run between strokes is impossible under these conditions because the oarsmen have to rush up on the slide for the next stroke to attain a higher beat. The 1936 crew, with Hume at stroke, rowed with abandon, beautifully timed. Having complete confidence in one another, they would bound on the stroke with one powerful cut; then ghost forward to the next stroke with the boat running true and with hardly a perceptible slowdown.

The Americans had drawn the outside lane where the fierce crosswind was at its worst. They were lying fifth at halfway, but when they approached the finish line they were in a race with the leaders Germany and Italy. The immense crowd chanted '*Deutsch-land, Deutsch-land*' in time with the German stroke, whose crew, according to the *New York Times* reporter, were 'galvanized into action at the sight of Hitler on the boathouse balcony'. Meanwhile the Italians were rating well over 40 and the Huskies' coxswain Bob Moch was screaming 'Higher! Higher!' The *New York Times* reported that 'Courage boiled high and the gray, cold waters were churned into white-flecked foam by the fury of their efforts.' The Huskies crossed first, followed by the Italians. The Wiking Berlin crew came third, less than half a second behind the Italians. The British were fourth and the Hungarians fifth. The Swiss, in sixth place, learned a hard lesson. Arthur Dreyfuss had entered half of his brilliant eight from Zürich, the Henley Grand winners, in three events, and it proved too much for them. Hermann Betschart, Hans and Alex Homberger and Karl Schmid had already won bronze medals in the coxless fours and silver medals in the coxed. Wreaths were hung round the necks of the Americans and Moch was thrown into the Langer See by his crew, to the delight of the crowd. Ulbrickson was so overcome that he was 'completely at a loss for words', said the *New York Times*. But its reporter Arthur J. Daley found some for him nevertheless. 'He took one look at Morris, the bow oar, with a victory wreath around his head, and asked "Where did you pick up the hay?" ' 'Downstream,' came the reply.

That evening Pocock and Ulbrickson and their wives were taken to dinner at the Adlon Hotel by Royal Brougham, sports editor of the *Seattle Post-Intelligencer*: 'I don't remember what we ate, but I know what we drank. Hitler may have modernized Germany's highways, railways, and military forces, but we had yet to find decent-tasting drinking water. The Adlon, we found to our delight, served delicious, sparkling fresh water, and we couldn't get enough of it.'

Next day they went to the closing ceremony, but their hearts were not in it. 'We had won the gold . . . We wanted very badly to leave the screaming crowds of uniformed and regimented Germans, and breathe the air of freedom again.' They departed for Eton and Henley-on-Thames so that George could introduce the Ulbricksons to his old father, old friends, old roots and the first boat that he ever built. He took it out on the river, free as the air.

Much honour was satisfied at the Olympic regatta. The Germans won enough to show that the imperfect squad system which they had created was the future in terms of making national teams, despite Wiking's success at keeping the club banner aloft in the selection process. Steve Fairbairn could rest assured that his approach to rowing was winning the day. Cooperation and sportsmanship were alive in international rowing, illustrated by Cordery and other English-speaking coaches at work in Germany, a mite embarrassing from the political point of view. The overall result was satisfactory for Hitler, for the thousands at Grünau were spared the humiliation of the torrent of American victories witnessed in the track and field events. Now that the world and its press had gone home the Nazis could get on with their new social order. In 1938 came the Anschluss and the takeover of Sudetenland. The German-British non-aggression pact gave Hitler his greatest power. There was a night of anti-Jewish aggression and German troops entered Moldavia. The National Society for the Organization for Sport was founded within the Nazi party. In 1939 Tschammer's office became part of the Office of Sport of the National Socialist Workers' Party. All sport was thus organized through the party by a party hack who had little interest in it. The orientation was towards the political soldier, with emphasis on purity of race, leadership and military preparedness according to an ideological base laid out in Hitler's *Mein Kampf*.

There was a coda during the war that followed. Southwood met Cordery in Putney one day and asked him about the missing boat in Berlin. Cordery said, 'Mr Southwood, I was told to take it away and make sure you didn't get a replacement.'

Exodus

The 1936 Olympic regatta passed by some people who had played a prominent part in the Berlin rowing scene. Imagine a day in 1935 on the bank of the Yarkon River in the British Protectorate of Palestine. In peaceful countryside by the only river in the region to carry mountain spring water to the Mediterranean, twenty or so men are unloading large wooden packing cases. The men speak in German and are mostly tall and middle-aged. They take out fourteen sailing boats, more than thirty rowing boats, and the entire furniture of the Ivria Ruderclub, late of the Wannsee, Berlin, and then improvise a building from the containers. They are from the cream of Berlin society, leaders in education and industry, medicine and the professions. They are highly intellectual Jews, but not militant Zionists. They read the writing on Hitler's wall. Persecution was coming their way, and so they opted to move from their homeland to start afresh in the Promised Land with their families, possessions and their entire club – boats, chairs, tables and memorabilia. These twenty-five families left Germany under a government patriation scheme. They were serious people, and several were to become fathers of modern Israel, establishing hospitals, holding chairs in universities, and setting about building a new country while Hitler destroyed an old one. Professor Fischer, for example, introduced the study of pathology to Israel, Dr Hirschmann began Israel's textile industry. Professors Marcus and Sumner were top surgeons in Berlin and transferred their skills to Palestine. Their first act, however, was to erect their own club from the packing cases where their ship had dumped them. They named it Hashyatim (Tel Aviv Club of Sailing) because there is no word for rowing in Hebrew.

The leading light of this exodus was Dr Martin Hönig. He was the rowing coach and devoted all the hours God sent to the new club, providing inspiration for others. He visited the nearest secondary school and, not without difficulty, persuaded the principal that rowing would be a worthy activity for his boys. Hönig was allowed to pick the most promising athletes from the sports teams of the school and put them under the training regimen of the club's trainer, a former discus champion in Germany. Elkana Caspi, a fifteen-year-old champion 600-metre runner from Lithuania, was among the chosen, along with six of his friends. Others came from another school. Soon the waters of the Yarkon were worried by the oarblades of recruits, and soon the earnest Dr Hönig was a figure of fun in the town. His wife brought his lunch to him at the club. The boys mimicked him and called him a *yekeh* (square-bum) because he was so straight. Communication with him was difficult. He was a strict disciplinarian and hit out physically at detractors and miscreants. They marvelled at his dedication which at first they did not share. To him the re-rooting of Ivria and the nurturing of Hashyatim was a religious undertaking, a mission to which he was prepared to donate his life.

Then one day he did just that. His boys were thrashed by the club's old men in a four-oared race. Hönig, despite being forbidden to row by his doctor because of an enlarged heart, took the stroke seat in the boys' boat and ordered another race. He kept his pupils nose to nose with the other crew until there were only ten strokes to go. But in two strokes he crabbed and was projected into the water, plummeting to the depths like a stone. The boat lurched to a halt, but the coach did not break the surface. The crews dived for three hours trying to find him. His body was washed up near the sea three or four days later.

This was in 1941. Before the tragedy the boys had changed their attitude, becoming 'crazy and dedicated' rowers and taking on the crews of the British Police at Jaffa. The tragedy made them realize that Hönig had reached their soul. 'Dedication and hanging on is something he gave us,' Caspi says. They vowed that they would stick together and take over their coach's work, and in 1990 most of them were as good as their word, still involved in a club which thrives, with more than 300 members. They carried on where Hönig left off, organizing visits to the mountains in the belief that education was a part of rowing. Sailing had stopped in 1938 when all the dinghies were claimed by a flood, an annual November occurrence which the members did not know about until it was too late. Rowing had continued, and Hönig had inaugurated holiday and weekend trips to Lake Tiberias (the Sea of Galilee). Boats were stored there. Later the Geynosar kibbutz and the Deganya kibbutz began rowing there, though the latter stopped. A rival club was started in Haifa, also by Berliners, this time from the Poseidon Club. Later, the Yarkon River was killed for rowing when the waters were diverted for irrigation schemes, so Tiberias has become the centre of serious activity. The seed of the pioneers has borne fruit. But in one sense rowing in Israel owes a glance of acknowledgement to Adolf Hitler, who allowed a group of his talented countrymen to leave their homeland and probably saved them from a much worse fate.

14

CONIBEAR MYTH AND MAGIC

To swing or to slide: that was the question which faced rowing after John Babcock came along with a sliding seat that worked. Lighter boats, outriggers, and even opinions changed the way people rowed, but it was the slide that really marked the watershed between traditional and modern rowing. It took several people several years of experimentation before Babcock produced a reliable sliding seat by 1871, and it then took rowers a long time to learn to use it. Babcock tried the seats in a six-oar in the Hudson River Regatta in 1870. Yale tried them in the same year, and Harvard in 1872. At Henley Regatta in England the slide revolution arrived in a rush in 1872, initiated by London Rowing Club who had used them while beating the New York club Atalanta on the Thames. 'Instantly there was a run on slides,' W. B. Woodgate reported in his book *Boating* (1888). Crews were fitting slides in the week before Henley, and several indifferent crews won pots against better quality fixed-seat boats. Pembroke College, Cambridge, had slides on wheels, 'a mechanism which was soon afterwards discarded by builders in favour of greased glass or steel grooves or tubes, but which seems to be returning to favour in 1886 and 1887,' Woodgate wrote. Long slides were in use by 1885, at least in America.

Broadly speaking, slides meant that the length of stroke was increased and the power of the legs could be brought into play. Different sequences for harnessing the back, arms and legs to the oar now became possible, and these gave rise to different solutions evolved on either side of the Atlantic. English orthodoxy with its immense swing of the body took its style from the fixed seat and used the slide to augment this disciplined and difficult stroke. Dr Edmond Warre's *On the Grammar of Rowing* (1909) is the purest exposition of orthodoxy at the most influential school, Eton. Many of Warre's disciples were convinced that all oarsmen should be started on fixed seats. Warre reminded the coach that 'in teaching men to row, his object should be to teach them to economize their strength by properly using their weight. Their weight is always in the boat along with them; their strength, if misapplied, very soon evaporates.' His book was published at a time when his method was enjoying unprecedented success. Eleven different nations competed against the English at Henley between 1872 and 1914 and out of 119 attempts only fifteen won a Henley cup outright, about one in eight. The Belgians who had such success in England in 1906–9 were true fundamental Orthodox crews.

It was the Orthodox emphasis on long layback and sharp entries which Fairbairn challenged in England, while in America the question was posed the other way. Having taken their early notions largely from English books, American coaches sought to adapt the stroke to the slide and developed their own American Orthodox which had sometimes fictional and sometimes factual variations from college to college. Although some, like Princeton, had amateur coaches, colleges primarily involved in eight-oared rowing with professional coaches dominated the sport in the United States from the 1870s, and this put a different emphasis on the coaching methods and the motivation for success. The hand-me-down method of transmitting wisdom from crew to novice was not for Americans. They were instructed by paid trainers who were recruited first from among professional oarsmen and then from their own graduates. Many professionals took advantage of the natural laboratory that sculling provides to test a change in style. Until 1877, when launches became fast enough to keep up with crews, a coach without a towpath to follow on horseback or cycle either had to row in his crew or pursue in a single. Neither were Americans ensnared in class distinctions when defining an amateur. Although their ideas of fair play and amateurism were akin to those of the British, they said that anyone who played sport for no pecuniary reward and in his own time could enjoy amateur status. As long as he was not being given special privileges or time off by an employer, he was eligible.

Other practical factors were present in the American equation. There were virtually no secondary-school feeders comparable to Eton where a boy had time to master the exacting straight-backed bodyswing and the fixed pin. In most centres running, weights and some form of rowing by machine had to be substituted for work on the water because rivers and lakes are frozen from November to March. All these factors combined to make changes in the English import to suit American conditions, according to Tom Mendenhall, the American rowing historian: a shorter swing on longer slides; swivels instead of fixed pins; larger blades; centre seating and shorter oars inboard; fast hands out of bow, a low feather and often a slower entry. America was in a better position to exploit the long slide. The short rowing season of college oarsmen meant that they had less experience in small boats and learned less watermanship.

Harvard and Yale were responsible for changing the emphasis of college rowing from sixes when they adopted eights and excluded other challengers from their 4-mile race in 1876. Besides being the time of the new-fangled slide, this was also the decade when the increasing number of professional sculling matches and club regattas drew large crowds. It also marked the beginning of the slow rise of college rowing and the slow demise of club activity. Colleges wanted their own crews, and hired the men who could train them. The Canadian Ned Hanlan was the first professional sculler to make the slide really work, and his great rival, Charles Courtney from Union Springs on Lake Cayuga in upper New York State, became the first to take up college coaching when he was invited to go to Cornell in 1883. Jim Ten Eyck, known as the 'Fox of the Hudson', went to work at the Naval Academy and then Syracuse, as did Jimmy Rice at Columbia, both professionals. 'Mr Ten Eyck, the Chancellor wishes to put Syracuse rowing on the lips of the college world – make its name synonymous with victory on the Hudson,' said Hurlbut Smith when offering the job to Ten Eyck. As professional sculling declined in popularity at this time, partly because of corrupt gaming practices, so the pros moved into college coaching. But the man whose name became synonymous with a stroke that was to become internationally famous was not a rower or sculler. He was an adherent of physical training and conditioning which had a following in turn-of-the century America. Hiram Conibear's stroke was still making waves in Scandinavia in the 1950s, forty years after his colourful, energetic and controversial career at the University of Washington in Seattle ended when he fell out of a plum tree and broke his neck. After his death, Washington coaches conquered America with the Conibear stroke until almost every college had a coach from the Pacific Northwest and almost every crew had a boat built there by George Pocock or by his son Stan.

To Slide, and How

Before Conibear, though, the running was made by coaches at Yale and Cornell. After the slide, another innovator came along and produced the swivel oarlock. Michael Davis of Portland, Maine, who coached Yale from 1880 to 1883, was a professional oarsman by inclination. Born in Ireland in 1851, he found rowing in 'Montreal's winter port' where his family had settled. Just like its rival Boston, Portland had a large Irish community, and as a young man Davis helped out the social function of the Emerald Boat Club and Union Rowing Association where there was tap dancing, elbow and collar wrestling, boxing, catch-as-catch-can, and in 1876 an exhibition of hydraulic rowing machines. Retiring from professional competition in 1882, he set himself up as a rowing-appliance manufacturer. He experimented with steel clamps sliding on rails, light outriggers made of three iron rods, light crossbraces between the riggers, and a wind sail which contributed to a spectacular performance and spectacular defeat of Yale in 1883. This was a large sail mounted in the bows of a 74-foot boat. The oarsmen, who were seated in four cockpits, used a rating of 45–50 strokes per minute. The crew could not cope, and Harvard won by more than a minute. Davis's first swivel came in 1874 and he spent five years developing it. And he also toyed with the idea of putting the cox of his first Yale crew in 1880 in the bow, 'out of sight'. Some of his crew were less interested in reducing wind resistance than in getting rid of a 'nuisance'. They saw the cox as responsible for most of the sprints in a 4-mile race, all of which, 'except the final one, hurt the crew more than they benefited from it'.

In 1883 Charles Courtney began his association with Cornell which was to last for thirty-three years, somehow getting round the National Association of American Oarsmen's ruling, made that year, that people who rowed for money were excluded from racing or coaching amateurs, a ruling echoed by the Rowing Association of American Colleges. Born in 1849 at Union Springs, as a young man he built a canoe with a friend, inspired by John Macgregor's trip through Europe in the *Rob Roy*, the canoe he designed himself in 1865. Courtney won his first sculling race in 1868 using his canoe fitted out for oars, beating two scullers in paper boats made by Waters. Fortunately Courtney's opponents could not row, while he found out that he could. That began a long run of successes as an amateur followed by a period as a professional. He had the most important attributes of a coach, possessing great technical ingenuity and knowledge of equipment, and understanding the stroke and how to teach it. He had a realistic approach to conditioning oarsmen. As a carpenter by trade and a sculler he recognized the importance of marrying the rig to the rower. He tried to cure the characteristic dousing of the bow brought about by early slides by fixing the seat and assembling a sliding framework of stretchers, outriggers and oarlocks. After trying out slides on rollers, he then perfected the double motion slides which gave a smoother and easier stroke. An expert photographer, Courtney used photography to record parts of the stroke and persuaded a graduate to set up a machine which would show how the power was applied. This taught him that the body and legs must work together from the beginning of the stroke to achieve maximum power. Six feet tall, he was a big man with a square chin, and a strict disciplinarian who was attracted by the combination of moral character and bodily fitness engendered by rowing. He inclined to the straight back with a combined leg drive and swing. When his crew beat Bob Cook's Yale and Rudie Lehmann's Harvard by three lengths over 4 miles in 1897 he told the press, 'We know a little about rowing in Ithaca.' Under Courtney, Cornell won fourteen times at the Intercollegiate Rowing Association regatta at Poughkeepsie, and never finished lower than third in his other ten races. Negley Farson recorded his experience of being driven against Courtney crews by the old pro Ellis Ward, who was in charge at the University of Pennsylvania:

> For the score of years he was doing it old Coach Ward had the reputation of being the most man-killing rowing coach in the United States. He whipped his crews along like dogs . . . He was a man with one idea, and that was maniacal – to beat the crews of Courtney of Cornell; an ambition that nearly killed all of us, for Coach Courtney of Cornell was probably the greatest rowing coach that this world will ever see. A Courtney eight rowed like one man.

Meanwhile in New Haven in 1873 the captain of Yale, Bob Cook, decided that no one in America really understood rowing: 'I felt convinced that Yale had to go to school in rowing and learn her alphabet.' He spent three months in London, Oxford and Cambridge, and was coached by F. S. Gulston of London Rowing Club. He witnessed the experiment being conducted at the club in which a tub four was put on trestles and Gulston's strokes through the air were marked off to prove that even a very short slide of 9 inches adds about 18 inches to the stroke. That year both crews in the Oxford and Cambridge Boat Race had used slides and Cambridge lowered the record by half a minute. Cook was impressed. He returned home with a tub pair, and began the migration of the English Orthodox stroke to college rowing in America, just when the slide invented in America was about to cause a critical review of that style in the Old Country. Cook was a rare phenomenon in the United States, an amateur with enough spare time to coach. He was the main advocate of adopting the eight for the Harvard–Yale race, believing the six to be 'an unwieldy, fragile alternative'. He directed matters from his newspaper office in Philadelphia during the early months of Yale's season and then spent the last month before the Harvard race with the crew full time, winning fourteen out of nineteen.

The Heir of Heritage

In 1906 the University of Washington hired Hiram Conibear, former professional cyclist and trainer of the Chicago White Sox baseball team and the University of Chicago's track team, as an athletics jack-of-all-trades. With no experience at all, he thus became head coach for rowing on lakes Union and Washington, a programme which had been introduced two years before. He threw himself into it, borrowing a skeleton from a university laboratory to work out the positions involved in the rowing stroke and making graphs of his results. He improvised the recovery by keeping a bicycle wheel revolving by the tap of a hand, and the stroke by using a broomstick. He shouted and swore at his crews from a knoll on the lakeshore, and their successes against meagre opponents attracted some funding. Then in 1912 he lured the Pocock brothers, the English boatbuilders working at Vancouver BC, with promises of full order books and facilities beyond their dreams (see chapter 8). There is no question but that bringing George Pocock to Seattle was the wisest thing Conibear ever did. Conibear was fanatical about making Washington conquer the rowing world and was able to tap the English Orthodox tradition embodied in the Pococks, particularly George, who was to make his life in Seattle. Conibear sat at his feet and adapted what he learned to American physiques and techniques. He became the most famous coach in America.

The first real success came in 1913 when the Washington Huskies beat California and Stanford and were consequently invited to the IRA regatta at Poughkeepsie, the first western crew to reach the eastern seaboard. Farson describes the importance of this race in his autobiography:

> The ultimate triumph of rowing in the United States is to win the big Poughkeepsie boat race. Lose the Navy, lose Henley, lose all the dual races of a season; but win the Poughkeepsie race, and everything was all right. That was the only race that counted. It was like the final battle of a war.

Washington came third, behind Ten Eyck's Syracuse and Courtney's Cornell. The Conibear stroke was working well and attracting notoriety, although nobody knew what it was. It was impossible to define, one oarsman remarked, because it changed every year. Conibear's own definition was 'the stroke that gets you there'. Certainly there were Aaron, Dick and George Pocock genes in it somewhere. In 1917 rowing was suspended for the First World War and Conibear tragically fell out of his plum tree. Thereafter he lived only by reputation.

In 1967 Andra Zezelj, a Yugoslavian coach, subjected Conibear to a critical sandbagging in an article in a British magazine. It is time to brush off the cobwebs of legend, he said. He starts by demolishing the adulatory brigade, led by Conibear's student Al Ulbrickson who was the Huskies' coach at the Berlin Olympics in 1936. In the *Saturday Evening Post* of July 1937 Ulbrickson said that Conibear sat down and figured out the Conibear stroke on a piece of paper, the stroke used to win the Olympics in Berlin, the stroke used by himself at Washington and with minor variations adopted at Yale, Harvard, Pennsylvania, Cornell, California and

Marietta. The article claimed that Conibear had a hand in the design of the original two shells built by the Pococks for Washington in 1912, and that 'the general dimensions of racing shells remain very similar to those developed by Conibear.' But Taylor, Clasper and Swaddle and Winship of England built shorter, wider, flat-bottomed boats long before the claims made for Conibear in the design of such craft.

The main characteristics of the new stroke which brought comfort to crews, according to Zezelj, were a reduced bodyswing with no layback, a terrific arm and leg drive, and a long run of the boat between strokes. He then looks at coaching before Conibear. Samuel Crowther in *Rowing and Track Athletics* (1905) contrasted the styles of the Harvard and Oxford fours who raced in London in 1869:

> The Englishmen had a very long swing, caught with all their force, and recovered slowly, all the time keeping the back very straight. Harvard did not lay stress on the catch, but pulled the whole stroke through and finished hard, swinging little; their entire stroke was faster than Oxford's, especially the recovery.

Mendenhall says that in the middle of the nineteenth century oarsmen and coaches were articulating the Orthodox style, largely in reaction to the rather short swing and early break of the arms which the professional watermen had to use in much heavier boats. Zezelj reminds us that fixed-seat rowing is the province of the broad-chested physical specimen, demanding power from shoulders and arms. The slide favoured the long and lithe, those who can best benefit from leg drive. By the turn of the century shape was more important than weight in sliding-seat rowing.

After his study in England, Bob Cook tried the long swing and slow recovery with American rigging, but the result was too exhausting for the oarsmen. Harvard, meanwhile, retained a stroke dubbed 'jack-knife'. The English paper *Pall Mall Gazette* described the Columbia crew at Henley in 1878 as keeping their backs straight, 'but their swing has a wooden appearance . . . They hang at both ends of the stroke.' Unlike Harvard against Oxford, they won. Out of this American fluctuation of styles Zezelj deduces the reduced bodyswing. The New York paper *Spirit of the Times* set out the American argument in a discussion of the sliding seat:

> Few comprehended the best way to utilise the new invention. Some slid

and did not row; some rowed and did not slide; some rowed first and slid afterwards; some slid first and then rowed. But all tried to suit the new motion to their old style. No one grasped the basic idea that old traditions had passed. The cornerstone of the new teaching was the substitution of slide for swing.

The London paper *Land and Water* retorted that Englishmen would say that the difficulty was 'the art of adding the advantage of the slide to the swing without spoiling the effect of the latter.' In 1905 Crowther concluded:

> Thus it came about that our stroke had the slide as the basis and the English the swing. We steadily cut down our swing, and at the same time increased the number of strokes per minute, until we had forgotten the swing altogether and got all the force of the stroke from the legs. The oar travelled only through the arc of the greatest power.

R. P. P. Rowe and C. M. Pitman observed in their book *Rowing* (1898) that at Henley the Yale and Cornell crews appeared to row uphill because their slides inclined downwards towards the stern. Crowther recorded slides lengthening from 16 to 27 inches. When the Cambridge coach Rudie Lehmann arrived at Harvard in 1896 he found bodyswing sacrificed to piston action of legs on a very long slide. Partly under Lehmann's influence there was a move back towards the swing, but in 1898, at the IRA regatta at Lake Saratoga, Pennsylvania used the American stroke to set a record against the leaders of the Anglophiles, Cornell. Under Courtney, Cornell reverted to long-slide and leg-drive rowing in 1901 after three years of disaster. George Marvin, the bow of the 1897 Harvard crew defeated by Cornell, identified the magic of Courtney: 'The fundamental idea of the Courtney system for over twenty-five years was the mastery of the "recovery".' The skill, said Marvin, was not in driving the boat through the water but in keeping it running between strokes. 'You don't pull your oar through the water, you anchor it in the water and then drive the boat past the purchase your blade has made.' Courtney himself emphasized that 'the oarsman should have his oar in the water as long as possible, and the least possible time in the air. He should never over-reach, and should be equally careful to avoid going back too far at the end of the stroke.'

Twenty years after the slide came into use it would appear that a recognizable style had developed in America to make use of the

innovation, and that it was distinguishable from the English Orthodox, which persisted with swing. Its elements were in place before
Conibear began his coaching career. His part in its blossoming was
probably distorted by oversimplification in the press, for it is curious
that Ulbrickson's *Saturday Evening Post* piece does not mention
George Pocock, the man whom Ulbrickson always invited into his
coaching launch at Washington when something was up. The sight
of Pocock signified to Ulbrickson's oarsmen that there was a crew
change impending, and he was the man who built the shells in which
they achieved so much. But Pocock the philosopher-boatbuilder was
to be found in the boatshed; he was not employed to coach. Ulbrickson made amends later, saying in a testimonial:

> George Pocock has contributed more than any man that has been been
> connected with the sport in the past fifty years . . . more than all the
> others combined. He has given us constantly improved boats from year
> to year, which has meant that we were always rowing with the world's
> best equipment . . . Of equal importance . . . has been the impartial
> giving of his knowledge of rowing to all who sought his counsel.

Conibear had found that out in Vancouver in 1912. Things might
have been different if he had accepted an offer from Walter Camp,
the physical education director at Yale, to become rowing coach in
New Haven. But Conibear stayed in Washington and roamed the
campus collaring tall lean guys and sending them out in the boats.
He became, in Zezelj's words, 'the lucky heir of a rich national
heritage, through which he became famous'.

The Washingtonians

Ed Leader began the exodus from Washington to spread the Conibear word by going to Yale in 1923. An uncomplicated man, at the
start of his nineteen years there he explained that different crews
adhering to the same Conibear principles would appear to row in
different ways because 'somewhere in the mind's eye every crew
coach has a picture or vision of the perfect oarsman, his ideal, and
he is for ever trying to make the real conform to his ideal and in
doing so applies each principle in a different way.' Yale had been
in disarray since Cook departed in 1898, his legacy a stroke adapted

from the English style for the most important fixture, Yale's 4-mile race against Harvard. English coaches had been tried after the First World War, ending abruptly in 1921 when Guy Nickalls called the Varsity 'gutless'. When Leader was interviewed the alumni were anxious to recapture the Cook stroke, and Leader expounded the Conibear. The interview progressed to a good dinner and then to the chairman's apartment, where the latter demonstrated the Cook on his bathroom rowing machine, and Leader the Conibear. The captain elect could not tell the difference. Leader got the job. Dick Pocock joined him there in the boatshop.

Leader was born in Portland, Oregon, and he and his twin brother worked on fishing boats on the Columbia River to help pay their way through college. At Washington they studied law and were both outstanding athletes in rowing, baseball and football. As a student Ed worked as a bouncer in a dance hall. He became the first of a new breed, the college graduate who chose coaching as a profession. He selected crews by punishing programmes of seat racing, whereby two crews perform a series of races during which individuals are swapped over to try to determine which combination is the fastest. Leader was strict on training rules and proper diet, seldom offered encouragement, never praise. He regarded things Eastern as effete, regretting that his Yale crews did not as a matter of course spend the summer logging in the north woods as the Washington oarsmen did. During the 1924 Olympic regatta in Paris, where his crew won the gold medal, Leader stared in horror at the heap of lobsters specially prepared for their Fourth of July dinner by the proprietress of the François Premier restaurant. Ben Spock, No. 7 in the crew, said that to Leader lobsters meant the threat of shellfish poisoning. 'Take them away!' Leader cried. The journalist Bob Kelley labelled Leader the brilliant apostle of Conibear who had carried the true word across the country. But after great success at Yale in the twenties, things began to slide there in the mid-thirties. Harvard and others were winning, Yale men were breaking training rules and angering the Leader they respected but had little affection for. Some of them were dropped in acrimonious circumstances. Meanwhile young bloods like Ulbrickson and Tom Bolles were tinkering with the Washington style, and then Bolles turned up coaching Harvard and gained the upper hand. During the war Leader went to work for an oil company; he never returned to coaching.

Rusty Callow was from a large and devout Methodist family in Olympia, Washington, and spent his summers felling trees. He worked an 8-foot saw with his partner on the largest specimens and set a felling record of seven minutes on the Fourth of July 1915, just after his graduation from the University of Washington. The red-headed extrovert rowed, played football and threw the javelin at the same time as Conibear was establishing his programme at Washington. Callow taught history at the university until joining the Spruce Division in the First World War to run a logging mill. He married a girl from Conibear's women's programme. After the war and Conibear's death, Leader re-started the Washington programme, but when Leader went to Yale Callow was summoned from the bank where he then worked. For five years Callow's crews could do almost no wrong, dominating college rowing on the West Coast and scoring three first places and two seconds at the IRA at Poughkeepsie. And it was Callow who enticed George Pocock back from Boeing to re-establish his boatbuilding business. At that time Callow had little experience of coaching and no fascination with technique. But he was a catalyst and a manager of men. He asked his veterans to write down their descriptions of the Washington stroke, and Pocock's experience was always available to him in the launch and the sculling boat or on the machine. The serpent in this Eden, as Mendenhall describes it, came in the form of offers from outside. Harvard dangled a 56 per cent salary increase in front of Callow, which he refused. Their perceptive agent on the West Coast cabled back to the Crimsons: 'If impossible to get Callow, try Pocock . . . Success of this system for the past twelve years under three different coaches largely due to Pocock.' Harvard never asked George. But Pennsylvania got Callow.

The contrast between the open water and geographical isolation of Washington and the crowded Schuylkill River in Philadelphia was vast when Callow arrived in 1927. He was to stay at Penn in the cauldron of activity on Boathouse Row for nineteen years. On the short muddy Schuylkill, which he described as 'much too thick to drink, much too thin to plough', he introduced more layback and earlier use of the slide and concentrated on full power at low ratings to achieve good length at high ratings. Joe Wright, the Canadian who was reputed to be the only coach in North America who did not require a bullhorn, had invented lightweight rowing at Penn in

1925, and both light and heavyweight programmes attracted 250 or so men each year. Callow tried unsuccessfully to set up a residential crew house like Conibear's 1910 Varsity Boat Club in Seattle, and he never gave up on rowing at Penn. He made it rewarding and fun, and his men did not give up on him. He brought women into the boathouse in 1935. His instructions were always clear and explicit, judiciously dealing out praise and criticism. He could inspire the despondent, chew out the slovenly, and make light of drudgery. His voice, said Joe Burk, who was to succeed him at Penn, 'came from his socks', in common with most of the Washington coaches. 'If he had asked us to row over the Fairmount Dam we would have done so without question.' When he left Philadelphia for war work in Seattle he let rip at the city authorities for allowing the Schuylkill to become polluted. In 1945 the mood along Boathouse Row, the venerable line of clubs in Franklin Park, had begun to improve as a result of concern by the city fathers. In 1949 Penn celebrated their coach with a Callow Day, and two Penn oarsmen won the Diamonds at Henley – Joe Burk in 1938 and 1939 and Jack Kelly Jr in 1947 and 1949. Then in 1950, when he was sixty-one, Callow moved to the Naval Academy at Annapolis on the River Severn following the sudden death of his friend and Navy coach Buck Walsh. There were 9 miles of deep water available, sheltered creeks, elaborate equipment and disciplined men for whom fitness was already a requirement. His eight won the Olympic title in 1952, the seventh American eight to do so in succession. It was the sixth in succession to have a Washington coach, three of whom had rowed under Conibear and one under Callow. He took his adaptation of the Washington stroke – the Conibear-Pocock-with-added-layback stroke – to Annapolis. He concentrated on what happened at the blade while leaving the technical details of shells and rig to their builder, George Pocock. His Navy crews raced from 2000 metres to 3 miles in their season, perfecting the stroke at low ratings and learning to hold on to their power as the rate rose. From 1953 to 1955 the Navy Varsity were undefeated in thirty-one races. Callow logged their peculiarities and progress in an old cash ledger.

According to Mendenhall Callow the teacher, trainer, motivator and oarsman's friend sent more men into coaching than any other coach. He could echo the language of the logging camp on the water, while his discussion was peppered with Shakespeare and Plato. He was a Sunday-school teacher too, and a popular dinner speaker, and with his wife Dottie kept open house for oarsmen and their dates. In 1958 he answered the question 'Why crew?' in *Sports Illustrated* by invoking the similarities between scouting, another of his interests, and rowing: 'The good turn without thought of recompense; the ideal of helping others; from such sincere unselfish efforts come the real rewards of life.' He died in 1961.

The fourth man behind the meteoric rise of Washington rowing was Alvin Ulbrickson, stroke of the Varsity from 1924 to 1926. In his thirty-two years with the Huskies Ulbrickson's crews won twenty out of twenty-eight races against California, six IRA titles and the Olympics in 1936. Ulbrickson's father was Danish and his mother Welsh, and they lived on Mercer Island which was not connected to Seattle by a bridge when Ulbrickson was a lad, so he rowed himself a mile and a half to school and to his summer job at the saw mill. He was twenty-four when Callow went to Penn and Pocock recommended him for the vacancy because he was a good listener and a good leader. It was 1927; there were eleven eights working out of the Washington boathouse and 250 hopefuls trying out under his classmate Tom Bolles, the freshman coach. The first season belonged to Washington's main rival, California, who were under another Conibear graduate, Ky Ebright (Ebright's real name was Carol but he did not answer to it). Cal's Varsity crew beat Washington, all-comers at Poughkeepsie, and won the Olympic title in Amsterdam in 1928. At Poughkeepsie Ulbrickson was nicknamed the 'Dour Dane' by the New York papers which observed him wearing his felt hat with a towel around his neck and carrying a huge bullhorn. In 1930 he was still a young man struggling with an inherited stroke and little success, and at the end of the long train ride home from Poughkeepsie he was of the opinion that it was time to change the stroke. He and Bolles had started with what Callow had taught them, a style inherited by some of Conibear's oarsmen. According to Mendenhall:

> This included a hard quick catch with the shoulders with only two or three inches of the slide used before the body reaches the vertical, a zip out of bow [hands away] led by fast hands; on the recovery a quick slide decelerates toward the catch. The original Conibear stroke ran the danger of becoming stylised and split into catch, stroke, and finish, with an exaggerated swing forward and at the finish.

In 1931 a Seattle newspaper heralded five years of change with the headline 'They've Changed the Stroke of the Husky Crew', and Ulbrickson had to assure readers that the changes to the sacred Conibear were not radical. The forward reach was shortened and the back straightened, the arms broke a little earlier in the drive, and the oarsman sat straighter at the finish. The blade was hooked in and the legs alone began to move it. The finish was made smooth by rounding the shoulders slightly just before the blade came out, measures intended to prevent check on the boat at these two critical points. Thus emerged the shorter Conibear stroke. It dealt a blow to the Germans in 1936 and the crew returned to Washington complete save for the coxswain in 1937. They enjoyed an undefeated season, and Huskies won all categories at the IRA regatta.

In 1948 the Junior Varsity four won the Olympic trials after an intense week's preparation under Ulbrickson. He sent George Pocock with them to the Games in London where the rowing took place at Henley. They became the first Americans to win the coxed fours. But from 1951 to 1958 Washington struggled to keep up numbers, win against Cal, and maintain respectability among the East Coast giants such as Callow's Navy, Burk's Penn, Harvard and Yale. The 1958 crew, though, were fast, and Ulbrickson went for Henley's Grand Challenge Cup. Forty-seven thousand dollars were raised in Washington State to send them there, $10,000 of it by the sale of 'On to Henley' buttons. The trip cost $29,000, the change becoming an endowment for the crew. Royal Brougham of the *Seattle-Post Intelligencer* went too, sending daily dispatches of purple prose. At Henley they drew the favourites, the Trud club of Moscow, six of whom had been together for four years. Trud were six years older, 'burly and rawhide tough, battle-scared from nearly four years of naval warfare,' Brougham said. It was 'muscle versus skill'. Muscle won, and went on to win the Grand, but the State Department had arranged another race between the Huskies and the Bears in Moscow two weeks later. Brougham found out the secret of Soviet sport when he arrived there:

> No wonder Moscow's stars are great.
> Their ways are cute and clever.
> Their athletes never graduate.
> They just go on for ever.

The day after the American embassy had been stoned by a hostile crowd in a Cold War flare-up, 6000 people watched Ulbrickson's men avenge their Henley defeat by a length and a half. The Dour Dane decided to go out on a high. Early in 1959 he resigned his coaching post.

Ulbrickson, the fourth man, had an alter ego, however. Tom Bolles was his freshmen coach from 1928 until 1936 and was very much associated with the shorter Conibear stroke. They developed it together. Observing Bolles's Washington freshmen in 1936 Callow said, 'If there's a wind they'll go backwards.' Kelley called it 'more or less sitting-up rowing' in the *New York Times*. Frank Strong, captain of Harvard in 1949, said that Bolles emphasized a hard catch. 'We practised compressing like coiled springs at the forward end of our slides, then "exploding" into the catch and recovering with fast hands.' Bolles was born in Minnesota in 1902 and wound up reading history at Washington and paying his way by working at a filling station. He was president of the student body and his fraternity, and rowed in the same crew as Ulbrickson. He became involved with Harvard in 1935 and succeeded Bill Bingham as coach in 1937; he took a Washington cox, Harvey Love, with him to look after the freshmen.

The style Bolles and Ulbrickson perfected with, let us not forget, help from Pocock was intended to produce sustained power, unwavering and uniform for the whole distance. Bolles thought this was best realized at a racing rate of 30–32 strokes per minute in long races and a stroke or two higher over 2000 metres. He believed in holding the boat to a low beat while allowing the opposition a length lead and then, two minutes from the finish, raising the rate while maintaining power and accelerating past the other crew. Strong provides a vivid description of this method at work:

> None of us will ever forget the Adams Cup race against Navy and Penn at Annapolis in 1947. Close behind the stake boats was a Naval armada of destroyer escorts and gun boats loaded with spectators with steam up . . . With 'Ready All' these giants moved forward in line as if headed for a beachhead landing, cleaving the water behind into three-foot waves. Unfortunately, Harvard came down from its customary short ten-stroke start into a high beat of terrible proportion and promptly fell behind Penn and leader Navy by nearly three lengths. That Naval armada loomed high above us and our cox, Sam King, who was in the midst of

a colourful discussion with ex-Marine stroke Frank Cunningham. I doubt to this day that Sam was aware of these monsters drawing closer behind him. Little Frank dropped the stroke in a single long pause and we were suddenly together at 31–32. Partly due to our lower stroke and partly due to those threatening Navy ships, the Harvard eight took off like a streaker after Penn and Navy, catching Penn with a half mile to go and catching Navy just short of the finish line with an extended sprint. It was the most painful race I can recall.

Living dangerously brought Bolles a record over twelve seasons with Harvard of sixty-three firsts and fourteen seconds in seventy-nine races; three undefeated crews (1938, 1941, 1942); six crews who lost only one race; three Varsity firsts in the new Eastern Sprints event introduced in 1936; two wins in the Henley Grand (1939, 1950); and a Varsity score of eleven to one against Yale, whose Allen Walz-inspired high-rate beat Bolles once described as an 'eggbeater'. The lost one was the 1949 race in which the gap was two seconds. The crews were level for 2 miles. Allison Danzig's report quoted Bolles as saying: 'It was the closest four-mile race I have ever seen', and the end to the 'longest victory string in ninety-seven years'. Only Harrison 'Stork' Sanford's Cornell beat Harvard more than Harvard beat other Ivy League match opponents (Penn, Navy and Princeton). And Harvard almost beat California in the 1948 Olympic trials. Bolles achieved success by such training tactics as sending his crews out for a week during the spring vacation to row 15–20 miles in two outings, including a trial over his favoured selection distance of a mile and threequarters. He left the rig to Pocock; seats were raised if necessary and crews were as low as consonant with conditions. Bolles considered that the English he saw at Henley had nothing to teach. They were seldom in good physical shape.

Bolles, who had his doctorate in Latin American history at Harvard cut short by war service in Guam, surprisingly wrote little on rowing, even though he kept meticulous records and commentaries on his crews. In *Red Top, A History of Harvard Rowing* (1948) he blew the myth that West Coast crews were bigger than those from the East by finding height, weight and age to be very similar during the period 1923–48 except for a tiny height advantage to oarsmen from the West. He attributed Western superiority to style and self-confidence. Like most of the college coaches, Bolles thought the eight was the only boat. When he stopped coaching in 1952 to follow Bingham as athletics director at Harvard he remained involved in rowing, managing the 1952 and 1956 Olympic teams and chairing the Olympic Rowing Committee in 1964. He died in 1978.

Ulbrickson's alter ego thus dropped out of active coaching a decade before the Dour Dane himself. Watching Ratzeburg rating forty in 1963 Bolles said, 'Think what they might have done at a low rating.' He dropped out before new methods and equipment arrived. In 1959 Ulbrickson felt that the climate which the Washington ministry had done so much to create was changing. Races of 2000 metres were growing in popularity, at the expense of longer distances. The eight was losing its role as the measuring stick of success. New techniques were succeeding. Ratzeburg was the buzz word, but nobody in America knew what it was or where it was. Besides, students were finding new diversions and had other things on their minds. The Conibear stroke, longer, shorter, straight-backed or arched, had lost four of its famous five, even if many of their disciples were still playing on. The fifth man, the one who sat in the boatshed and only spoke if asked, the man of whom Bob Moch, cox of Washington's 1936 Olympic crew, said, 'In his presence Washington crewmen always stand, for he symbolized that for which God's children always rise,' the man whom Joe Burk described as 'a glowing beacon in the darkness of ignorance', was still there in Seattle, and still making superb boats – the design of which had been erroneously attributed to Conibear by Ulbrickson in the *Saturday Evening Post*. But it would not be many years before Pocock red cedar boats lost their pride of place in the American rowing firmament.

Strokes That Got Them There

Al Rosenberg led American rowing out of the Dark Ages, according to Emory Clark, Olympic gold medal winner in the eight of 1964. Writing in *The Oarsman* in 1974, Clark's assessment of the 105-lb former race-track cashier was that he introduced Americans to a new order and a place in the sun, if briefly. Rosenberg coached the Olympic eight in 1964, and Clark says that Rosenberg taught him that 'courage in the last 500 metres is to a large extent a function of proper training'. With a mixed bag of club and college oarsmen, whom he gathered at Vesper in Philadelphia, an Italian boat, German oars and 'European training methods', Al won the Olympics, recovering the title that the Americans almost regarded as theirs by divine right. The deities had let them down in 1960 when Karl Adam's German crew won in Rome. Rosenberg was doing it again when Clark wrote his piece. His 1974 crew won the world title, and he became US coach for the 1976 Olympics, when national squad rowing arrived in America, using 'sudden death' selection trials, a method dictated by the size of the country.

Rosenberg himself denied his reliance on European training methods in an *Oarsman* article. He claimed that Vesper's style was derived from the Syracuse coach Jim Ten Eyck through their former coach Jim Manning. Another style was prevalent in colleges at that time and was considered to be *the* American style and so, Rosenberg says, all other styles came to be regarded as something else. Vesper coaches were not Conibearians, nor were they Ratzeburgers. 'It is appalling to see so many aberrations of the so-called Ratzeburg style that are employed today, taught by persons who are either uninformed or lazy and who seem to equate 40 strokes a minute with a very complex style of rowing,' he wrote in 1967. He had some information readily to hand from Germany, for Dietrich Rose had moved to Philadelphia via Ratzeburg after his defection from the German Democratic Republic's rowing programme. Rosenberg went on to say that there were many styles, most of which had some merit, and they were dictated by equipment, personnel, weather, training and the coach's understanding of basic rowing principles. He proved it by dissecting the stroke:

> You can do one of three things on the slide during the recovery: (1) go at constant speed; (2) accelerate to the catch with constant speed thereto; (3) decelerate at the catch with relatively constant speed prior thereto. You can come away with the body from the bow [at the finish] either fast or slow, with any of the above slide options. You can row through the pin, up to the pin, or behind the pin. There are several methods of achieving body angle and swing using arms or body or both. You can swing the body forward and back or just in one direction. If you do either, you may or may not get any back thrust into it.

Any combination is possible, Rosenberg said. He maintained that it is the equipment that dictates the rating (see the Conibearians and their reliance on Pocock's boats and rig). He outlined his teaching at Vesper as (a) a constant recovery on the slide, body swinging slowly out of bow, reaching with both arms and body; (b) slide through the pin to the catch; (c) great emphasis on explosive initial use of arms and legs, breaking the arms slightly at the catch; (d) a quick back-thrust or lift; (e) moderate layback; (f) constant slide speed with body swinging slowly out of bow.

It may be extreme to call the period after the Conibearians the Dark Ages of American rowing, but it is certainly the case that the United States continued to be an isolationist rowing power until the Russians and Germans left everyone behind in the fifties and sixties. The Great Powers like Britain and America had been caught napping and were no longer great. The Americans awoke first.

Rosenberg did not come from big college rowing. He began steering Vesper the year he graduated from Temple University's pharmacy department and then returned to Temple to study law. He lived above Vesper boathouse and went on tour with the club to Egypt and Eastern Europe. While studying and working he also found time to introduce rowing to St Joseph's College in Philadelphia and to coach in Israel. A shrewd observer and fixer, he built up a network of rowing contacts on both sides of the Atlantic. In the seventies he studied psychology and in the eighties was working as a traffic court judge in Rochester, New York – one of his lengthy absences from rowing. His house there contained rare treasures of nineteenth-century rowing memorabilia. He turned up in Europe in the eighties with an ominous-looking crew in a black strip, reminiscent of New Zealand's All Blacks, but they turned out to be the Dirty Dozen, a rugby club from San Francisco whose wealthy sponsor had decided to give rowing a try and hired the biggest name in coaching he could find.

While Rosenberg was making things move on the Schuylkill, Joe Burk was in charge at Penn. A Callow man, Burk had become a superb sculler while at the university's Wharton School of Business. After winning Henley's Diamonds in 1938 (breaking the record set in 1905 by the Australian F. S. Kelly) and again in 1939 in a Pocock 'teardrop' boat, he skippered a PT boat in the South Pacific. On the way home from the war he met Tom Bolles in a barber's shop in San Francisco. Bolles, who was returning to Boston from his aircraft carrier, asked Burk if he had thought about coaching, and soon after 'Skip' Walz was on the telephone from Yale looking for a freshman coach. Burk moved to Penn when Callow went to Navy. Callow's low-stroke work was the basis of later high-stroke work, Burk said. He bowed to Fairbairn for slaughtering sacred cows and to Adam for re-thinking the training-technique-technology triangle. But, twenty-five years before Adam, he had come to the conclusion that 'the run on a shell should be kept virtually constant, with as little variation in speed at either end of the stroke as possible', according to Mendenhall. The way to achieve this was to shorten the stroke and increase the rating. Burk made sculling work for himself, but he reckoned that any reasonable sculling system could be successful if you believed in it 100 per cent. He was deeply loved at Penn, and was extremely innovative. At Yale he had persuaded the engineering department to build an ergometer, a rowing machine with adjustable resistance invented in Australia. He developed it further at Penn and his rigger, Wayne Neal, fitted a tachometer to the coaching launch to act as an 'accurate and unforgiving pacer'. 'Stay ahead or be inundated' was the advice to the crews. A Penn cox, John McGinn, made the 'Wizard', a black box or dynamometer for testing pressure on the oarlock. Later Burk introduced a points system of selection in which crews chosen by their stroke men took part in weekly intra-squad races. When a student named Harry Parker was stroking, his boat always scored well. Burk found that Parker kept a daily log of results enabling him to select the most effective performers, and so Burk changed his system to one of random selection for intra-squad races. In 1968 the final Olympic trial for the American eight was between Harvard and Penn. Harvard won by four tenths of a second in a photo-finish. Burk's only comment was: 'That's the way Olympic trials should be.'

Although Washington continued to turn out powerful fast crews and good coaches like Dick Erickson, whose voice comes from his socks in traditional manner, Parker has been the outstanding college coach from the moment he reached Harvard as freshman coach under Harvey Love, who succeeded Bolles there. Parker took up sculling during his three years in the Navy, who obligingly posted him to Philadelphia. He competed in the 1960 Olympics and met the great Russian Ivanov and the Pole Kocerka. He was coached by Burk and by reading everything he could find about sprinters and long-distance runners, just as the British sculler Penny Chuter was doing in England at the same time. Adam's success was up and running in Germany but his influence did not seep into America until Ratzeburg were persuaded to go on tour there by Burk in 1963. Performers and college-level coaches like Parker now rubbed shoulders with their contemporaries on both sides of the Atlantic more frequently, travelling to Henley with the Varsity and on European tours with the national team. The rowing family gradually became both wider and closer. With one eye on the Soviet and German crews, Parker changed the Bolles stroke at Harvard by dropping the fast recovery in favour of a hesitation at the finish and a slow-to-even speed up the slide. He adopted Adam's longer oars with the centre of pressure farther from the rigger, and a slightly shorter and wider blade. Oars for eights grew from 12 feet 1 inch to 12 feet 5 inches in 1961. He became a pivot of the national coaching team.

The Washingtonians would not recognize the American national scene in the 1990s. There is a national technical director, a burgeoning club scene, and a much wider college programme which is integrated with the national camps. Parker's Harvard crews have an almost continuous run of victories over Yale and many Crimson oarsmen have risen to the national team through the exhausting camp selection system masterminded by the emigré Pole Kris Korzeniowski. On success, Parker quotes the British oarsman Colin Porter's book *Rowing to Win* (1959) in which Porter says that successful coaches are people who have the force of personality to make things work. 'What I see at Harvard is the people who are in it, highly motivated and willing to work for it,' Parker says. 'Obviously the coach has some role in drawing that out . . . When you try to work people really hard' – such as in his legendary 'stadiums' which involve ascending and descending the stairways of the Harvard football stadium – 'it's important to make sure that you're getting the full benefit from that and not working them too hard . . . Unfortunately, that's not an easy thing to judge.' You have to live with injustices, too, like when the guy who has worked hardest and for whom it is most important to make the crew does not make the crew. Performance must be the only criterion. 'Even for people who are motivated, there's a pretty natural built-in resistance in the body to working hard. The coach has to help the oarsman overcome that.

It's probably not a good idea to trick them, because you can only get away with that so often.'

PART FOUR
COOK'S TOURS

15

MADE IN BRITAIN

EMPEROR Napoleon III's France showed off its sense of wellbeing by staging a world exhibition in Paris in 1867. The country was enjoying a period of industrial expansion. The French-inspired Suez Canal was almost complete under the direction of the engineer Ferdinand de Lesseps. France was prosperous and the previous fifteen years had seen an enormous road, rail, canal and harbour building programme and the reconstruction of Paris under its *préfet* Baron de Haussman to make it a world capital. So in July the capital was awash with visitors exploring the new boulevards and buildings, and the world had been invited to a regatta on the Seine. Ödön, son of Count Széchenyi, the father of Hungarian rowing, sailed the small paddle steamer *Hableany* from Pest to Paris to take part. The chosen spot was between the bridges of St Cloud and Suresnes to the west of the city and separated from it by the Bois de Boulogne, where the Seine was broad and almost straight. The *Manchester Guardian* published three reports from its 'Occasional Correspondent', which began:

> Paris has resolved to have a genuine regatta, and neither trouble nor expense have been spared to procure it. Splendid prizes, the most exalted patronage, reduced fares for the oarsmen, and free carriage for their boats, have been the baits held out to tempt competitors from every country. When to these are added the inducements which Paris itself at its carnival offers to every visitor, we cannot be surprised that the entries for the races have been larger, perhaps, than have hitherto been anywhere known.

The regatta was apparently half under French management and half under English, 'the rules and whole method of procedure of the two countries being very different'. The grandstand was erected halfway between the two bridges. The starting post was half a mile below St Cloud bridge and the course ran downstream past the stand to three buoys arranged in triangular fashion a quarter of a mile above Suresnes bridge. The course measured 2½ miles round the buoys and back to the winning post at the stand, or more than 3 miles if rowed all the way back to the starting post before returning to the winning post. The first day was cool with a gentle breeze and not much of a crowd, but the *Manchester Guardian's* correspondent encountered 'plenty of excited officials, and plenty of impassable *sergents de ville*'. The boating men wore high boots, long flannel coats and peaked hats. A prize of 1000 francs was on offer for the six-oared race and another of 500 francs for the sculls. There was a line across the river marking the start. This was released when a mortar was fired. In one case the line fouled a rudder. The six-oared race was well contested:

> The boats were inrigged, and the stroke rowed bow-side after French fashion. Paris, Brighton, and Boulogne started. Brighton passed the stand second in going down, but were outstripped by Boulogne, whom they fouled at the buoys. Paris thus gained a long lead . . . Thus Paris won every race. It is but fair to add that one of the Paris six is an Englishman, and three others, the Geslings, English by birth, though genuine Frenchmen by education.

The correspondent was Charles Prestwich Scott, a twenty-one-year-old student at Corpus Christi College, Oxford, who had been offered the editorship of the *Guardian* when he graduated. He was the owner's cousin. His visit to Paris's international regatta is believed to be his first assignment for the newspaper that he was to edit for fifty years.

Germania of Hamburg had also sent a crew to Paris and thus far they were spectators with little to be cheerful about. Their boat had been lost on the railway, and when they found it they were almost ashamed to step into it. Compared with the French and English gigs and outriggers, 'our Hamburg wherries and gigs with their thick strakes covered with oil paint and left on the water all day seem to belong to an antediluvian period.' But they observed the heavy broad boat with no straps for the feet or leather buttons on the oars which the 'Americans' had brought with them and reckoned that here was one crew they could beat.

The second day brought out the exotica, and was one which the English correspondent noted should make either English oarsmen or English boatbuilders reconsider the first principles of their art.

> Among the strange-looking people whom this regatta has brought together . . . were a certain crew of four sturdy New Brunswickers, who, having beaten everything on their own waters, had brought two home-made boats some thousands of miles to show the rest of the world how to row. With their flesh-coloured jersies, dark cloth trousers, leather braces, and bright pink caps, they were in striking contrast to their neat competitors.

These were the 'Americans' observed by the Hamburgers. At a very high rating they beat five other crews in their heavy 200-lb boat, and they were eating oranges as they crossed the finish line. The crew from the Rowing-Club de Paris discovered that the ingenious conquerors, whose 'long and lithe rowing had been the admiration of the connoisseurs', had coated the backs of their culottes and the wide benches of their boat with a thick layer of tallow which enabled them to slide without effort. The *Manchester Guardian* reported that they rowed without a cox. The bow oarsman Robert Fulton steered 'partly by an ingenious contrivance with his feet, partly with his oar'. Other accounts have Fulton at stroke. Wherever he sat, he and George Price, Sam Hutton and Elizah Ross won a second race, beating Germania and Boulogne and two English crews described as 'crack' – University College, Oxford, and London. The correspondent noted that the Brunswickers were in splendid condition and appeared heavier than their reported average weight of 11 st 5 lb, and that their keel-built boat stood up well in the bows and displaced wonderfully little water even though it was much too heavy. He noted their advantage in not carrying the dead weight of a coxswain, but if their opponents' boats weighed only 60 lb as he reports, then the Brunswick boat would more than make up for the lack of a steersman. (Sixty lb would have been incredibly light for a boat in 1867, suggesting that the newspaper committed a rare misprint.) Scott's final observation was that the New Brunswickers 'are not amateurs of the usual kind, being men to all appearance of much the same stamp as our English watermen.' His opinion of the latter was made clear in his next report when professional crews formed by Messrs Tagg, Caffin and Clasper lined up against Amsterdam, the Brunswickers having shunned another race and dismissed the Seine as a 'mud-creek'. 'At the start, the English watermen, as usual, stole a lead, cheating the Amsterdam boat of a clear length.'

Scott's last report for the *Guardian* noted that the general public paid almost no heed to the great regatta, that publicity for it was nonexistent, transport for spectators was difficult, and Emperor Napoleon had stayed away because Mexican republicans had assassinated Archduke Maximilian of Austria, thus shattering Napoleon's scheme for Maximilian to rule Mexico after he himself had been forced to withdraw by the United States. Scott's entreaty to English oarsmen and boatbuilders did not go unheeded; the crew from St John's in New Brunswick were the first coxless four seen in Europe, and next year Brasenose College were disqualified at Henley when their cox, Fred Weatherley, jumped overboard after the start of their heat in the Stewards' Challenge Cup. The man in the No. 3 seat, Walter Bradford 'Guts' Woodgate, steered with a wire and lever attached to his foot stretcher. He had also been in Paris and had taken a close look at the Brunswick boat. This started a process which resulted in the 'emancipation' of coxes from four-oared boats at Henley, as Woodgate described it later. The change came sooner for professional races in England, and not without steering problems, but a movement to restore coxes was resisted. Woodgate says in his book *Boating* (1888): 'Fortunately . . . oarsmen realized that it was better to attempt to raise their own talents to the standard required for the improved build than to detract from the build to suit the failings of mediocrity.' Henley had no events for coxed fours until after the Second World War, which was not encouraging for those many clubs situated on winding and busy rivers where steersmen are essential.

The Paris meeting took place just before the sliding seat became the most important change in rowing and just before other team sports, inspired and developed largely by the British, were to take centre stage for both spectator interest and participation by the new urban masses. Paris encapsulated custom and practice as Queen Victoria's reign in Britain climbed to its zenith of power and prosperity. Both amateurs and professionals rowed for money prizes, sometimes in the same races. Cheating and fouling were common and tolerated by some while disapproved of by others, and Scott attributed the lack of spectator interest partly to 'the exclusive and unconciliatory character which Englishmen unhappily not unfrequently display.' Innovation in boat design was abroad, and the sport had spread a long way from Europe's offshore island to the Continent itself, as well as establishing outposts among the fishing and hunting folk of North America's East Coast. English influence in the guise of oarsmen was present in French amateur crews. Special dress was required; officials proliferated; the social elite were associated with rowing even in their absence, and some sponsorship was available for boat transport and crews. Even if the course and the boats and the rules were different from those of the twentieth century, the sport which is known variously as 'modern', 'Olympic' or 'English' rowing was recognizable at the gathering of French, English, German, Dutch and New Brunswickian oarsmen between St Cloud and Suresnes in 1867. So what was special about British, and particularly English, society that its people should be the first to take to boats for pleasure, just as they were to be the first to take up many other modern sports?

Peace in Their Time

Rowing as a modern sport developed in England in the eighteenth century, was consolidated there in the nineteenth century, and by the early years of the twentieth had taken root in many other countries spread over five continents. Venetians may claim to have originated the regatta, but the British were the pioneers of moving across water while sitting down and facing backwards. It was they who produced two of the essential ingredients that distinguish modern sport from traditional or local sport. First, they codified the rules of racing; secondly, they determined who was eligible to take part by attempting to define the amateur and the professional. The first published laws of boat racing were drawn up in 1847 by representatives of Oxford and Cambridge universities and the principal London clubs and were adopted by Henley Regatta in the following year. The pro-am argument entered choppy water later.

The cause was the industrial revolution, a small phrase with very large implications. Horst Überhorst's centenary German rowing history says:

The development of modern rowing . . . with rules and organisation . . .
only becomes comprehensible against a background of social change.
With industrialisation competition became keener, the sense for technical
planning and organisation grew, leisure increased and heightened interest
in sports activities . . . The process was facilitated because England had
been spared the revolutionary developments that Europe experienced.
Social adjustment could be created in an evolutionary way between
privileged nobility and newly forming wealthy classes, with social
mobility based on democratic principles.

Britain was the first country to become predominantly industrial,
and this process brought with it enormous changes in population
and its concentration, in wealth and in social life, including sport
and entertainment. Britain was also strong abroad: naval supremacy
underlay the largest empire the world had seen, an empire created
by a variety of methods – commerce and trade, colonization, treaty
and protectionism, and piracy and conquest. British commercial,
trading and entrepreneurial interests were also evident in many countries which were not part of its empire, Argentina and China being
two good and very different examples.

To understand what happened in British society it is essential to
step back to the dawn of the industrial revolution. Although the
factory system gradually pulled workers into the cities, agriculture
remained the largest employer in Britain in 1850. But the increasing
size and number of the towns changed the opportunities for
recreation among all classes, and two particular developments speeded
things along: the railway and the newspaper. The first enabled players and spectators to venture farther afield than the next village, and
the latter informed them of what was happening on playing fields
and regatta courses in places far distant. Both conspired to encourage
sportsmen to find common sets of rules. It was one thing to walk
to a cricket match in the next village where everybody understands
the unwritten rules and customs, or to attend, say, a sculling match
the rules for which have been agreed by participants and backers.
But anything which casts its net more widely, such as a series or a
regatta, requires a commonly accepted code of conduct. Some rural
sports stayed the same, some adapted to a changing environment,
some new sports arose. The volume of sport increased, not simply
because of the growth of population, but because prosperity spread
gradually from entrepreneurs and financiers to skilled artisans, and

then to clerks and unskilled workers. As prosperity brought workers spare cash, the Factory Acts gave them leisure time. The opportunity to place a bet was also a significant factor, bringing both the prospect of making something for nothing and the danger of being ripped off by unscrupulous bookmakers and competitors.

Richard Holt points out in *Sport and the British* (1989) that it is important to consider what did not change when determining what did. He says that sports have a heroic and mythical dimension above the mere expenditure of energy determined by the physical environment. 'They are "a story we tell ourselves about ourselves", the nature of which may differ markedly between countries with broadly similar levels of economic development.' British society stamped its own trademarks on such development. With industrialization came huge enlargement of the liberal professions and the business community. Business and professional people aspired to the life style of the gentry, the old rich landowning aristocracy, whose sporting interest centred almost exclusively on four-legged activity and whose sons were educated at exclusive private schools and universities. The so-called public school system expanded greatly and evolved a philosophy of education peculiar to Britain. Not only did it seek new sports which were more appropriate to urban dwellers to replace the equestrian pursuits suited to the space of the countryside, but it also forged a view of moral worth, patriotism, even imperial fervour. Holt quotes the Hon. Edward Lyttelton, at the time headmaster of Haileybury:

> A boy is disciplined by athletics in two ways: by being forced to put the welfare of the common cause before selfish interests, to obey implicitly the word of command and act in concert with the heterogeneous elements of the company he belongs to; and, secondly, should it so turn out, he is disciplined by being raised to a post of command, where he feels the gravity of the responsible office and the difficulty of making prompt decisions and securing obedience.

Team sport was seen as particularly apt for forging the character of those who were to govern country and empire. The catchphrase was Henry Newbolt's line 'play up and play the game', emphasis being put on taking part rather than winning. These ideas were to affect the truly public education system which the beneficiaries of private education put in place for the lower orders. It was the products of the public schools and universities who usually codified the rules of sports which developed after rowing, and several sports which overtook rowing in participation and spectator appeal formed national associations before it. Examples are the Football Association (concerned with the round-ball game which became known as soccer) which started in 1863, the Amateur Athletic Club (forerunner of the Amateur Athletic Association of 1880) founded in 1866, and the Rugby Football Union founded in 1871. The rules of the Amateur Athletic Club were drafted by a Cambridge University oarsman, John Graham Chambers, who also drew up the Marquess of Queensberry's rules for boxing a year later. The Amateur Rowing Association did not come along until 1882, born of the Metropolitan Rowing Association which was formed in 1879 with the unrealized aim of forming national crews to ward off foreign competition. None of these national bodies, it will be noted, saw any need to include 'British' or 'English' in their title.

The Newbolt theme remains a cornerstone of the British attitude to sport, even if the concept of winning has held much more sway since the Second World War. It is an attitude which was successfully exported to many of Britain's overseas possessions, and is at considerable odds, for example, with the roots of sport in continental Europe, where the French and the German traditions have gymnastics at their base, the kind of gymnastics which the British would call 'drill'. This is the tradition which Baron de Coubertin set out to change in favour of English-inspired team sports in the *lycées* of France towards the end of the nineteenth century. His quest was largely unsuccessful. He obtained the idea from Rugby School and the educational ideas of its headmaster Thomas Arnold, and from observing Henley Royal Regatta at work. French noblemen like Coubertin who were attracted by the idea of English sport were looking for more than a sporting way of playing games from the public school education system. Harsh conditions in many English schools, often combined with more emphasis on playing hard than working hard, produced tough men who interpreted Darwin's 'survival of the fittest' to mean 'survival of the strongest'. In 1870, three years after the World Exhibition in Paris, the French lost to the Prussians on the battlefield. After that they wanted to create an elite who did not have, in the words of Coubertin, round shoulders and narrow chests.

The British, then, developed their play into 'a rule of life and a national code', according to a German visitor in the 1920s, and Coubertin saw it both as the source of Britain's imperial dynamism and the creator of solidarity between the upper and middle classes which assured political stability at a time of economic and social upheaval. Holt says that whether such claims were true is probably less important than that they were widely believed to be so, and points out that there is considerable evidence that the working classes shared this solidarity when it came to sport.

The Pros and the Elite

Rowing and sculling were present at the beginning of the industrial revolution, were one of earliest activities to acquire rules of racing, and one of the first to define the amateur – or rather, to distinguish between professionals and others. They broke down class barriers by doing so, and then re-erected them. Naturally, rowing development was coloured first by the availability of water, but it was also closely allied to economics and education, to gambling and gambolling. In some places, believe it or not, it held the largest spectator appeal before the boom in sport which occurred in the last third of the nineteenth century. And it was one of earliest sports to become international, not only being exported as an activity but indulging in fixtures across the English Channel or even the Atlantic Ocean before that century was out, as the Paris regatta of 1867 testifies.

The first reference to a regatta in England was by William Hickey at Walton-on-Thames in 1768. There was another in 1775 on the Thames at Ranelagh Gardens, London. The first recorded race in eights was between the *Chatham* and the *Invincible* crews, held from the bridge at Westminster to Richmond-upon-Thames in 1778 for 60 guineas (£63). *The Annual Register*, the newspaper which later became *The Times*, recorded that the race was against wind and tide: 'The bets at starting were much in favour of the *Invincible*, and continued so till they came off Sion House, when *Chatham* touched her in the stern, and drove her ashore, to the surprise of the spectators, the *Chatham* being 300 yards astern at Kew Bridge.' From their names the boats may well have been naval cutters, but it was the custom of the time to name crews after the boats in which they rowed. From the early eighteenth century there was racing between watermen, particularly on the Thames and the Tyne. A number of conditions combined to increase this activity as the cities grew. There were few bridges in London or Newcastle, both cities being situated several miles from the mouths of the rivers they straddled, so the demand for ferries was great. The road system was bad, especially in the winter, so there was much river and canal traffic. Erosion of the watermen's livelihood by steamboats, railways and bridge construction did not bite hard until the second half of the nineteenth century. Meanwhile thousands of men worked the rivers and ports, tens of thousands in London, both loading and unloading ships, ferrying passengers to and fro, and carrying out marine construction and repairs. The Watermen's and Lightermen's Company regulated employment in London from the sixteenth century and a long apprenticeship was required before it was possible to work on the tidal section of the river from Lower Hope near Gravesend to Teddington Lock. Noblemen had their own craft with liveried oarsmen, and wagers would take place between these and between the one- or two-man 'water taxis' for hire. Both cities had long commercial traditions connected with the water and generations of families to uphold them, and they threw up their fair share of the strong and the athletic. Betting on boat races grew, whether it was the copper of the workers or the silver and gold of the well-to-do. Purses were often held by publicans, many of whom were retired watermen. Organizing matches and other sporting activities was sometimes as much a part of public house life as serving drinks.

By the middle of the nineteenth century a race could be found on almost any night of the week during the summer in London. The Wingfield Sculls for the amateur championship of the Thames was held for the first time in 1830 and the first professional sculling championship took place in the following year. Neil Wigglesworth's introduction in *Victorian and Edwardian Boating from Old Photographs* records that between 1835 and 1851 there were 5000 sculling matches on the Thames, which averages five per week. At Newcastle it was reported that 130,000 mourners turned out in 1870 for the funeral of Harry Clasper, one of the heroes of the Tyne. Along the quays and among the shipyards the following for these men was phenomenal: they were championed by the city's songwriters and music halls. It was sometimes possible to view their races by train, as in 1846 when five trains on the Newcastle and Carlisle Railway followed Harry Clasper and Robert Newell. Many were innovators as well as great performers in crews and sculling boats (see chapter 6), and several have large memorials in the graveyards of Newcastle and Gateshead. Their following was fiercely partisan, so much so that Eric Halladay (*Rowing in England*, 1990) claims that the demands of the crowd burned some of them out by encouraging them to satisfy reputations and expectations by tempting them to race too often and for too many years.

Meanwhile the class system was working away at social gradations. A study of the northwestern county town of Lancaster in the mid-Victorian period illustrates this neatly, showing that archery and rowing clubs for the gentry, clergy, professions and merchants operated a black-ball system of entry. A cricket club aimed at the same kind of people started in 1841, and another was formed by skilled workers in 1859. The latter joined shopkeepers to play bowls on greens at inns. Lancaster's sports calendar included wrestling, racing, rowing matches, quoits and athletics until the 1870s. Holt detects a Europe-wide decline in patronage of popular recreation by the upper classes as their own culture became more refined and less militaristic. In England the country gentleman was eclipsed, the relationship between farmer and farmworker changed as social mobility changed, and the Church of England establishment, with the Queen at its head and manned largely by the younger sons of the gentry, drew back from its toleration of traditional recreational pursuits. These tendencies all contributed to the decline of patronage at the same time as the numbers, wealth and leisure time of the middle classes grew amidst complex and confusing cultural changes centred round the principle of *mens sana in corpore sano*. The Victorian elite was keen on public health, undertaking drives on dirt and disease in cities, taking to the seaside for its air and spa towns for its water, scaling peaks and introducing the world to alpinism. 'Character' was formed. This was done by segregating the sexes in schools; declaring homosexuality to be the opposite of manliness and, in 1885, making it a crime; and by promoting active religion, which gave rise to the phenomenon of 'muscular Christianity'. The effect of prolonging the education of an elite also prolonged childhood. The Victorians invented the teenager, a monster to be tamed.

Muscular Christians – a movement, not a church – tried to stop a drift towards Roman Catholicism on the one hand and to interest the industrial classes in religion on the other. Among their number was Thomas Hughes, whose *Tom Brown's Schooldays*, was an account of life at Rugby and became the bible of character formation. Much less well known is its sequel *Tom Brown at Oxford* which contains a heavier dose of morality in a less entertaining fashion. Its significance is that Tom, like his inventor, became an oarsman, and there are some fine racy passages describing his crew's exploits. Hughes became a kind of Christian Socialist, the muscular Christians tackling social problems in the cities and governmental problems in the Empire. Because rowing was prominent in a great many of the highest stones in the Victorian education pyramid, including the largest and oldest universities, it is not surprising that rowing men often turned up in influential and remote places, many of them wearing the cloth or dispensing medicine, law or money. Politicians and editors were frequently to be found in their number. Eleven of the eighteen men involved in the first Boat Race between Oxford and Cambridge in 1829 became priests, and one a lay preacher. Much later it was said of Charles Hose, a graduate of Jesus College, Cambridge, that his most striking achievement on joining the government service in Sarawak was to 'induce the pagans of Borneo to give up head-hunting as a method of settling tribal disputes and take to boat-racing instead'. Cecil Tyndale-Biscoe, who coxed Cambridge in 1884 and was a sort of elephant's mahout to Steve Fairbairn at the height of the latter's rowing fame, used his rowing experience as a means of inculcating manliness among his high-caste Hindu pupils. He wrote *Character Building in Kashmir*, and his autobiography is called *Fifty Years against the Stream*.

By the second half of the nineteenth century rowing was more and more identified with this elite class, while its working-class and professional roots slipped towards obscurity. The professionals had a slow and honourable death. The British elite isolated and ostracized them by worshipping an idol of its own making, a confusing god known as 'The Amateur'. One effect of this was to force professional oarsmen to seek fame and fortune overseas, where many of them found clubs and individuals prepared to pay them for their expertise. Shortsightedness, perhaps bigotry, at home paradoxically added to British influence in rowing abroad (see chapter 13). Professional rowing on the Tyne was moribund by the time Hitler's bombers destroyed the boathouse where the Newcastle Handicap committee boats were housed; on the Thames professionals were reduced to the echo of Doggett's Coat and Badge before the socialist countries of Europe and commercial pressure on sport forced 'professionalism' to become the attribute to which amateur sport aspired the world over.

College Crucible

Before we venture to cross the Channel to that isolated place which Victorian Englishmen knew as the Continent, we must first look at the quagmire of class and skill with which they surrounded the amateur. It shaped British amateur sport and had repercussions in the international arena. In Victorian times the unique English concepts of education and elitism penetrated many sports organizations, including the Olympic movement. In rowing, definitions of the amateur and rules of racing were sometimes adopted wholesale in other countries, occasionally taking problems with them. For example, Cork Harbour Rowing Club in Ireland modelled their regatta rules on the Oxford and Cambridge rules in the early 1860s, and when the Irish Amateur Rowing Association (IARA) was initiated by Irish university clubs in the 1880s, their definition of the amateur, unsurprisingly, was virtually identical with that of the Amateur Rowing Association (ARA). The IARA was not successful but the Irish Amateur Rowing Union (IARU) was founded in 1899 along similar lines and received a warm welcome from Rudie Lehmann, secretary of the ARA in London. By 1937 its definition had dropped any class-based references, and the IARU has remained the governing body for the whole of Ireland after British rule ended in the south in 1922. Rugby Union is the only other sport whose governing body in Ireland straddles the border between the Republic and the six counties still governed by Britain. Irish rowing teams often include crews from Northern Ireland and the Republic. When 'English' rowing was introduced to Norway, English rules went too, and the Norwegians found themselves in a pro-am argument as well as embroiled in the conflict between their traditional coastal rowing and the English style, the former with its roots in fishing and the latter imported by the business community. Less controversially, English clubs in far-away places like Calcutta, Gibraltar and Oporto affiliated to the ARA or achieved close relations with it.

In 1888 Guts Woodgate observed that the old theory was that an amateur was a gentleman and that the two were simply convertible terms. The first amateurs competed for money prizes. Until 1861 the winner took all in the sweepstake of the Wingfield Sculls, which was the amateur sculling championship of Great Britain until national championships began in 1972. In the early nineteenth century it was not unusual for gentlemen scullers to race for wagers. Leander, which claims without certainty but with considerable evidence to be the oldest club, beat Christ Church for £200 in 1828 and Oxford for a similar sum in 1831. Both crews had professional coxes in the latter race, and Leander habitually employed one. Cambridge were steered professionally in matches with Leander in 1837 and 1838. Oxford and Cambridge are collegiate universities, each made up of a number of colleges, and boat racing between the colleges became popular at both places immediately after the Napoleonic wars. They developed 'bumping' races in which boats were stationed at equal intervals along the bank and were started simultaneously by a gun. Racing took place over several days, and crews who bumped or touched the boat in front of them moved up in the starting order on the following day. After more than a century and a half bumping races attract hundreds of eights and are raced in divisions. They are held twice a year (called Torpids and Summer Eights at Oxford, Lents and Mays at Cambridge). By the 1840s the system of racing unique to Oxford and Cambridge was taking on its own discipline, a discipline which shied away from the use of professionals and from wagers and money prizes. This was partly because the students could not afford them, and partly because of the association with cheating which was widespread in regattas – witness Durham regatta's rules in 1837: 'In the case of skiffs fouling, all jostling is allowable which can be accomplished with the sculls in the rowlocks, and the rower on his seat.' Regattas at Durham, first held in 1816, were certainly lively. In 1860

Robinson endeavoured to pull right into Clasper's boat, but missing it the oars became entangled, when the former jumped out of his boat and tried to pull the latter out of his. Clasper, seeing that all chance of winning the race was gone, and that his boat was likely to be capsized in the struggle, hit Robinson on the head with his fist, and was just on the point of striking him with his oar when he found that his boat was fast filling with water and going down bow foremost, and to save himself he had to jump out and swim to shore. On arriving at Bow Corner, Bone placed his boat right across the river for the purpose of fouling Newby. Succeeding in his object both boats became entangled and immediately afterwards Newby's boat upset and, in tumbling out, its occupant seized hold of Bone's boat and upset it ... The race was ultimately won by Craggs.

Ten years after the Oxford and Cambridge Boat Race's inception in 1829, one of umpires, C. J. Selwyn, stated that 'watermen's ways are not our ways, or watermen's notions our notions'. He asserted that gentlemen should steer, fouling be abolished, and victory be its own reward. Even in the 1990s, when the race receives thousands of pounds worth of sponsorship for the clubs, the winning Boat Race crew are not allowed to look after the 1829 golden sovereign used to make the toss for stations lest they be tainted with winning money, albeit a loan. Back in the nineteenth century Brasenose at Oxford were the last recorded college crew to include a professional in their boat for a race, but Lady Margaret, the boat club of St John's College, Cambridge, employed one for training in the mid-forties, and Trinity Hall hired one in 1849. Oxford banned watermen coaching or training the university crew during the last three weeks before the Boat Race in 1841, followed by Cambridge in 1871. However, in 1857 Oxford engaged Matt Taylor to show them how to use the newfangled keel-less boat he had built at their president's expense. They also employed legal draftsmen: Taylor was there 'to show us the proper way to send his boat along as quickly as possible', not to instruct them in rowing. Each university acquired a high priest of gentlemanly amateurism. Cambridge's Tom Egan wrote that 'We ought to be able to point to our match crews and challenge the world to produce anything so uniform in motion, so polished in form, at once so speedy and so graceful, as one of those picked eights of the gentle blood of England' without threat of lowering standards by being tainted with watermen's practices. Arthur Shadwell of Oxford wrote the first competitive rowing manual in 1846 in which he described the moral and enduring effect of discipline. It involves the notion of principles which, when put into practice, enter into man's ways of feeling and thinking: 'Thus . . . they are much more than written law; they are not letter but spirit; and become hereditary guides of every successive set of men in the boat club, a wholesome pervading system of tradition and a standard which each man endeavours to act up to.' Never mind German tradition, the English cannot get away from discipline either.

Gradually the rowing interests took precedence over other river users on the Isis in Oxford and the Cam in Cambridge, although the behaviour of the students was often superior, arrogant and loutish. The muscular Christians among the dons were yet to assert their influence. Charles Kingsley and Leslie Stephen are alleged to be the founders of this movement, the former the Regius Professor of History at Cambridge who often cut his lectures short to go sculling, the latter a tutor and fanatical coach at Trinity Hall, a mountaineer, and one of the organizers of the first inter-varsity athletics match in 1864. They grasped the idea of educating the body as well as the mind, or in some cases only the body, admission to university at this time often having more to do with father's pocket than son's brain power; and, for some colleges, position on the river in the bumps seemed to assume more importance than academic record. For example, Dr Corrie, Master of Jesus College, Cambridge, held that 'much evil was connected with rowing' but his college eight stayed at the head of the bumping races on the Cam from 1874 to 1885. The place of games was supported from below by the public school headmasters, some of whom encouraged sport for disciplinary purposes. Rowing was at the root of it, and schools like Eton, Radley and Shrewsbury took to the boats with a vengeance. By the second half of the century rowing was an integral part of the games system at every public school which had a rowable river nearby, and naturally the university oarsmen graduated to teach rowing at them, some doing little else. A self-perpetuating system grew up among the gentlemen amateurs. From here, from the principles and enthusiasm of Egan, Shadwell and Stephen, arose what Halladay, in his exhaustive study of amateurism in rowing, identifies as the sport's praetorian guard, which was to lead rowing to absurdity before saving it from the brink of disaster.

Coincidentally with the two universities coming to terms with rowing in their own exclusive worlds, club rowing for amateurs was in a moribund state at mid-century. Its basis was, again, professional gentlemen working in London or officers of the Guards whose background was public schools and universities. The Cambridge Subscription Rooms is an example, the club renting a room above a boathouse at Lambeth, and hiring boats in which to row. The clubs' decline was caused by increasing traffic and pollution on rivers like the Thames and by the expense of rowing. This was to change during the 1850s and 1860s, but it was a mid-century vacuum which the praetorian guard attempted to fill. This was done principally through Leander, the only club in London to survive at this time in recognizable form, and achieved partly by opening a university membership. The emergence of a few new, large clubs for amateurs in London also reinforced the link between Oxford and Cambridge and Henley Regatta. The latter started life as a town enterprise in 1839, but rowing men gradually gained control of the stewards who ran it until they were in the majority in the 1880s. Their challenge cups became the trophies most sought after by the colleges and the metropolitan clubs, and their way of doing things fitted perfectly Selwyn's Boat Race notions that gentlemen should steer, fouling be abolished and victory be its own reward.

Facing Both Ways

By the 1860s, therefore, a group of oarsmen emerged who shared the rowing philosophy of the universities and the values of the rural gentry and the middle classes thrown up by the industrial revolution, a uniquely British pattern of life with a markedly English accent. Many of them then reinforced their social ideology with a layer of class consciousness on top of the clear-cut difference between themselves and those who took part in sport as a living or for monetary gain. Crucially, they singled themselves out as being above 'trade'. Their number included factory owners, proprietors of businesses and creators of wealth, but they kept those who got their hands dirty, however skilfully, at arm's length. A further complication came from across the sea, where values, customs and practices were different. A safe world was threatened by the arrival of foreigners to take part in Henley Regatta and in private matches. Many wished to repel these boarders entirely, while others took the view that if foreigners could not be stopped, they must be beaten. The invaders came from North America and from continental Europe, anxious to race on the waters of the country which had given them their sport. The question of who was an amateur was the crucial one of the last quarter of the nineteenth century. It was not resolved properly in Britain until the 1950s, after the British had twice hosted the Olympic Games and not long before the socialist countries of Eastern Europe created professional rowers in everything but name to compete on the world amateur stage. It was coming to terms with foreign crews that affected the early arguments and brought matters to a conclusion.

First, the attitudes. In 1835 the prominent sporting newspaper *Bell's Life* defined an amateur as anyone who rowed and was not a waterman or otherwise engaged in rowing as a living. In 1846 Lancaster Regatta asked *Bell's* for guidance about allowing a crew of tradesmen to enter a race for amateurs. The newspaper replied that on the London river many members of distinguished amateur clubs were engaged in trade, but that 'this does not include journeymen or mechanics whose crews are called "landsmen" to distinguish them from gentlemen amateurs and professional watermen. If the oarsmen concerned are master tradesmen, the decision should stand; if journeymen or mechanics, they should be defaulted.' As a result of discussion among London amateurs about the need for some sort of authority to tackle the question of definition, Josias Nottidge set up the Thames Subscription Club to run the Thames National Regatta in 1854. But two years later Nottidge and his friends put their energies into founding London Rowing Club, which was to grow quickly in membership and influence, offering low subscriptions and sending successful crews to Henley. The significance of the short-lived Subscription Club was that it proposed to include professionals in its projected national rowing organization. Three years after its foundation London RC started an annual race for apprentice watermen, but its main attention was reserved for drawing in the small near-bankrupt Thames clubs and forming representative crews from among them to race at Henley. There was resistance, but eventually many joined and the club became large, strong, influential on other rivers, and showed great interest in the rest of the world, welcoming foreign crews and meeting them on their own water. In 1861 the *Rowing Almanack*, published by *The Field*, a sporting competitor of *Bell's Life*, listed universities, schools and institutions as amateurs and excluded tradesmen, labourers, artisans and working mechanics. A year later it classified rowing clubs under the headings 'Gentlemen', 'Tradesmen' and 'Watermen'. In 1866 Edwin Brickwood, twice winner of the Diamond Sculls and rowing editor of *The Field*, who wrote under the *nom-de-plume* Argonaut, tried to define the amateur by restricting the species to officers of the army, navy or civil service, members of the clerical, medical or legal professions, members of the universities of Oxford, Cambridge, Dublin, London, Durham, Edinburgh, Glasgow, St Andrews and Aberdeen, the Queen's colleges in Ireland, the public schools, and members of any club 'not composed of tradesmen or working mechanics' which would be allowed by the stewards of Henley to compete for the Grand, Stewards', Silver Goblets or Diamonds Sculls.

The Amateur Athletic Club, started in 1866 by Chambers with two winners of the Diamond Sculls on its committee, added the exclusion tag referring to mechanics, artisans and labourers to its definition in 1867. 'Athletic' in this context refers to track and field. The rest of its definition followed Brickwood's closely, maybe because E. B. Michell, one of its 'rowing' members, was also a rowing reporter on *The Field*. A year later its headquarters in Pall Mall defined an amateur as a gentleman, but the lower orders could compete in its championships as long as they had never run in open or handicap races. Through the 1870s the cause of the gentleman amateur was trumpeted by Walter Rye, who proposed to an 1871 meeting convened to discuss an association of athletics clubs that membership should be barred to anyone who was not a gentleman by position or education. Rye's significance was that he represented Thames Hare and Hounds, the first cross-country running club, which had started in 1868 after a run which he organized in the previous year at Thames Rowing Club.

Thames RC began life in Putney as a recreation centre for workers in the rag trade, the London stores and drapers, but it soon became the chief rival to Leander and London in competitive rowing. Its membership went up-market too. In 1874 Agecroft regatta in Salford disqualified a winning crew from Bolton and Ringley on the grounds that they were artisans. In the lengthy correspondence in the *Manchester Examiner and Times* Bolton and Ringley defended themselves vigorously, saying that they had often visited their neighbours at the Agecroft club and that the latter knew that they were working men, that the crew had been coached on only three occasions before the regatta, and that they had returned the £10 prize which they had received before disqualification at Agecroft because to accept it 'would have forever excluded our crew from rowing in another amateur regatta.' They also posed the big question: 'If any gentleman would kindly give us a true definition of what an amateur is, we should feel greatly obliged, as we have always been under the impression that if a person did anything for pleasure and not for money, that person was an amateur, but if he should do anything for money, or in any shape for his living, he loses his title to be an amateur.' The Bolton men did not get their answer until after the Second World War.

By 1878 London RC members were worried about foreign relations and conduct. Having been beaten by the St John's crew in Paris in 1867, they had voiced doubts about the New Brunswickers' status; they then got themselves into a wrangle at Philadelphia's centennial regatta in 1876 when, having been fouled by an opponent without redress or sympathy, they withdrew. In April 1878 they called a meeting in Putney to discuss amateurism, attended by Oxford, Cambridge, Thames and Kingston RC. At this point in time defining the amateur was occupying some minds, but nobody in rowing had thought it necessary to define a professional, or to ban the mixing of events for professionals and amateurs at regattas, or competition between professionals and amateurs as long as it was not for money. But London RC's target for repression had become men who worked with their hands. The meeting decided an amateur must be a military or civil officer, a member of the liberal professions, or of the universities or public schools, or of any established boat or rowing club not containing mechanics or professionals. They then added some pernicious clauses, excluding those connected with stakes or money prizes, those who had rowed with or against professionals for any prize, those who had 'ever taught, pursued, or assisted in the pursuit of athletic exercises of any kind as a means of livelihood', those who 'have been employed in or about boats, or in manual labour', and anybody who works as a 'mechanic, artisan or labourer'. The Oxbridge-Henley viewpoint was taking hold.

At this period rowing was growing all over the country, but was regionally based. Clubs formed and ran their own regattas, some with other activities; and, outside London, the clubs' relationship with their own community and neighbours was far more important than being part of a national picture. Most did not aspire to row at Henley or travel far; many were more concerned with recreational activities than with racing and coaching.

Just after the April meeting Columbia College from New York won the Visitors' Cup at Henley, the first foreigners to do so. They lost a heat of the Stewards' at the same regatta to the Shoe-wae-cae-mettes, French Canadian lumberjacks from Michigan, who were eventually beaten in the final by London RC. The Shoes were suspected of not being true gentlemen-amateurs. It was hard to be French, Canadian and a gentleman in 1878. The following year the stewards of the regatta produced their own definition of the amateur, in terms of who was ineligible to be one. It followed the Putney model closely but left room for foreigners of the Columbia breed, if not the Shoes. But the stewards required legal evidence that foreign crews were amateurs in the spirit of the stewards' own definition, being worried by, for example, the habit of racing for cash prizes in France, a practice which was now frowned upon in England. In June 1879 there was a further meeting of the Putney group with the addition of Dublin University. The result was the foundation of the Metropolitan Rowing Association (MRA) to form composite crews to compete at Henley and fight off foreign challengers, and to maintain the standard of rowing throughout the country. The headquarters was London RC and the aims reflected the hopes of Nottidge and his London associates. By spring of 1882 the MRA had changed its name to the Amateur Rowing Association. In 1884 its members had drafted their definition, which closely followed Henley's but added 'and anyone engaged in menial duty' to the exclusion clauses. They also added guilt-by-association with a clause saying that nobody could be an amateur who 'was a member of a boat or rowing club containing anyone liable to disqualification under the above rules'. This was incompatible with custom and practice at many provincial and coastal clubs and regattas, particularly those in the Midlands and the West Country. The secretary of Tewkesbury regatta responded that certain practices may 'shock the feelings of the lavender-gloved amateur; but if rowing is to be encouraged, we must not be too thin-skinned'. Wargrave regatta, right next door to Henley, had no recognizable rules and allowed women to compete.

The ARA at first paddled softly, realizing that it was best to stay close to the Henley stewards but futile to steer clubs and regattas away from their own custom and practice. A blind eye paid dividends eventually as clubs and regattas were enticed to join, but the new governing body failed to settle the vexed question of amateur status. Rudie Lehmann, the ARA's secretary from 1893 to 1901, persuaded the association to adopt a positive definition of a professional in 1894, restricting the said class to those who made their living out of some form of rowing. So by now there were definitions of what an amateur was not and what a professional was, with a large no-man's-land in between populated by men who worked with their hands in non-rowing-related industries. They could be rowers but not gentlemen.

While the hardliners in the praetorian guard sniped at the softness of the ARA on this issue, the muscular Christian wing formed the National Amateur Rowing Association (NARA) in 1890, born out of indignation. Its leading light, Frederick Furnivall, wrote

> that for a university to send its earnest intellectual men into [a city] settlement to live with and help working men in their studies and sports, while it sends its rowing men into the ARA to say to these working men, 'You're labourers; your work renders you unfit to associate and row with us', is facing both ways, an inconsistency and contradiction which loyal sons of the university ought to avoid.

Furnivall was just such an evangelist of education. A Cambridge graduate, he taught at London Working Men's College and coached their boat club as well as working-class girls at the club named after him in Hammersmith. Several Cambridge-educated clergymen were involved in starting the NARA, as was the philanthropist Quintin Hogg, who founded the Youth Christian Institute which fathered the Regent Street Polytechnic in London. The NARA's definition excluded the true professionals but omitted any reference to menial and manual workers, artisans or tradesmen. A meeting between the two associations in 1891 failed to shift the ARA's uncompromising position. The NARA drew considerable support from members of the praetorian guard clubs, and the ARA had another look in 1893 when Lehmann did his best to persuade a subcommittee to rewrite the definition, being of the opinion that rowing required skill as much as muscle and that manual workers had no advantage of dexterity or fitness. Only two others on the committee supported change, although a satisfactory definition of a professional was introduced, applying it only to those who made their living at some form of rowing. Not being an amateur under the ARA's definition no longer branded one as a professional. It was a small move in the NARA's direction, condescendingly recognizing their kind as 'non-amateurs'. As the end of the century approached, there were ARA-type amateurs, non-amateurs who were not professionals, and true professionals. By 1895 the ARA settled down to discuss individual cases, pronouncing that a railway booking clerk was eligible but a printer's apprentice, an ironmonger and a tailor were not.

The establishment of the NARA split English amateur rowing into two camps. On the one hand the ARA and the stewards of Henley were rooted in a class definition of the amateur, while the former claimed to be the only authority empowered to endorse representative British crews, particularly when the Olympic movement came along after 1896. On the other hand, the NARA championed all non-professionals and arranged regattas and regional rowing associations for them. Some clubs ignored both camps for a while, some continued local traditional practice, and a few straddled both by forming crews which complied with one or other according to the event. On paper the relationship was frosty, but in practice the rowing community was usually friendly and cooperative: they lent their boats and shared officials and facilities. The NARA was more democratic and eventually attracted about a third of England's clubs. The ARA attracted most of the rest. The two associations went their own ways with occasional squabbles. The same differences of principle affected Henley, the best-known dispute being the banning of the Philadelphia bricklayer Jack Kelly in 1920, reasons unspecified, just before he won the Olympic sculling championship (see chapter 20). The 1928 Olympic champion Bob Pearce, from Australia, was barred from Henley because he was a carpenter, but when he returned in 1931 as a Canadian working as a whiskey salesman for Lord Dewar he was permitted to start and won the Diamonds. The final showdown came in 1936 when Henley banned the Australian Olympic eight on the grounds that Sydney policemen could not be true amateurs. It was a case, you could say, of discrimination against foot workers. The Second World War delayed settlement, but fusion occurred in hearts and minds by the time the

Olympic regatta was staged at Henley in 1948. When in 1947 both
the ARA and the NARA joined FISA, the international rowing
federation, British rowing was brought into Europe and the real
world. A few years later the two associations became one under the
ARA flag.

16

BIRTHPLACES AND CHANNEL CROSSING

BEFORE returning to the Olympics in chapter 22, it is as well to do what educated Victorians and the generations before them did. No preparation for life was complete without a Grand Tour, an extended progression through Europe's cultural capitals and the archeological centres of the Mediterranean. Thomas Cook eventually profited by adapting this for well-heeled tourists. We will take a Cook's tour of rowing's cultural centres, hopping in time and place to observe something of how British influence infiltrated other peoples and places, and how others adapted and reacted. The starting place is modern rowing's back yard.

In the early days of boating in the eighteenth century, says *The Eton Book of the River* (1952), not only the polluted and dangerous state of the Thames hindered its use, but there was no conception of a boat as anything but a means of transport. Boats were for conveyance or ceremony, and the book finds no evidence of rowing for sport at the school before 1775. A regular passenger service from Windsor to London by two- or four-oared rowing boats which carried five or six people under an awning was still running in the early part of the nineteenth century. To undertake a 45 mile journey under these conditions does not say much for the state of the roads, which were the only alternative means of passenger transport until the coming of the railways. In 1793 the Prince of Wales's birthday was celebrated by a regatta involving watermen near Eton. In the same year the Fourth of June, Eton's annual gala day, featured a regatta for the boys, one of whom wrote home to his mother that six boats turned out manned by boys with feathers in their caps.

Three or four years later he wrote that there were four eight-oared boats and two sixes.

Westminster School possessed a six-oar called *Fly* in 1813. The crew was made up of scholars. The Westminster records tell of adventuring on the Thames from steps in the shadow of the Houses of Parliament, opposite the King's bargehouse, and of fights with bargees. William Henry Lennox Lascelles Fitzgerald de Ros was among Westminster's oarsmen at this time, and he continued his education at Christ Church, Oxford, where he was the owner of one of three fours which were in use on the river. De Ros's family home was on Strangford Lough, a 20-mile sea inlet on the east coast of Ireland in County Down. In 1944 John McGifferd, a local farmer, made a remarkable discovery. At an auction of effects from the old house of the Bailie family he bought a four-oared boat found hanging in the barn. It was called *Royal Oak* and proved seaworthy, if rather leaky. McGifferd met an old man who swore that his father had been present when the boat had been hung up in the barn 110 years before. *Royal Oak* was used by fisherwomen for racing. It is made of pitch pine native to that part of Ireland, and is remarkably light, suggesting that it was built for speed. Two men can lift it comfortably. It resembles the type of sea gig used in Nelson's navy for carrying dispatches between ships in harbour. Such boats would have been suitable for speedy transport and weekend sport for guests at the great houses of Strangford Lough. It seems that Ireland was also a nursery of using boats for pleasure, and that de Ros, who became a general and governor of the Tower of London before his death in 1874, had a hand on the oar in both countries.

The 1990 *British Rowing Almanack* lists about eighty amateur clubs which were in existence by 1867, the year of the Paris world exhibition and international regatta. Leander, who moved from Putney to Henley in 1898, trace their foundation to 1818, and the smaller clubs from which Leander grew may be considerably older. Then comes Trinity College, Oxford, in 1820 and a string of Cambridge colleges, thirteen of them before the next club, Royal Chester (1838). By 1825 there are a few Oxford colleges and Guy's Hospital Medical School from Southwark, across the Thames from the City of London. Cambridge University Boat Club started in 1827, two years before the Boat Race, but although rowing was established earlier in Oxford than in Cambridge, the Oxford University Boat

Club dates only from 1839. The first Durham college boat club was University, founded in about 1836, and King's College, London, came along in 1837. Two more London medical schools were next to appear, St Bartholomew's in 1844 and St Thomas's in 1850. The rowing map fills out with clubs being founded in Henley (1839, the same year as the regatta), Worcester (Vigornia, 1841), Dover and Gloucester (1846), Burton-on-Trent (1847), Eton (Excelsior, 1851), Folkestone (1852), Tyne (Newcastle, 1852), and Boston in Lincolnshire in the watershed year of 1856 when London RC left the slipway. These clubs are not the complete picture: they are the survivors. In *Rowing in England* Eric Halladay includes statistics of the number of individual amateurs by area and amateur and professional clubs and regattas from 1834 to 1857. These were calculated by *Iota, The Boat Racing Calendar*, and do not include colleges, universities or schools, which for the most part lived in their own cocooned worlds of bumping races and matches against one another. There were professional or watermen's clubs in Bristol, Durham, Eton, Glasgow, Newcastle, Norwich, Oxford, Southampton and three in Manchester. Regattas are mentioned in places such as Talkin Tarn in Cumbria, Rudyard Lake near Leek in Staffordshire, Liverpool and Wakefield. Sixty amateur clubs are listed on the Thames, four in the Northeast, five in the Northwest, three in Nottingham, six in Worcester, and two in Norwich. They are a catholic group, many small and short-lived. They include the Grenadier Guards and the Coldstream Guards, the Phantom Crew, the Richmond Confidence Club, several more with classical names and several with names that sound like boats, such as Nottingham's Dreadnought Club, Nautilus and Sylph Club. The number of leading amateur competitors over those years is 176 at the Oxford colleges and 124 at Cambridge, thirty-two and thirty-five at Eton and Westminster respectively, and double figures for six of the twenty-nine Thames clubs listed. In other areas Durham does best with seventy-one, followed by Worcester with sixty-one and Chester with fifty.

There was also activity in Scotland. Loch Lomond regatta dates from 1828 and Dumbarton from 1829, and Oxbridge graduates formed the first amateur club in Edinburgh in 1846, called St Andrew. A national association, the National Amateur Rowers Association of Scotland, was formed in 1859 and included the

English club Tyne, but was not very active. National championships are traceable to 1881 when the Glasgow and West of Scotland ARA was formed. This eventually became the Scottish Amateur Rowing Association (SARA). Coastal regattas grew from 1860, and both professional and trades rowing developed separately from the amateur code. Some of the Scottish amateur clubs affiliated to the English ARA after its formation in 1882. Twenty-seven-foot jollyboats were used on the firths of Forth and Tay. While professional rowing died, the Scottish Trades ARA (STARA) was formed in 1920. Some of its member clubs dated back to the 1850s. The amateur-trades schism was healed before the Second World War, with crews taking part in the same regattas by 1938. Amalgamation of STARA and SARA came in 1947.

The post-Paris years witnessed an explosion of rowing clubs in England in parallel with the rapid expansion of other sports, particularly soccer, cricket and rugby football. This coincided with the time when the British Empire offered limitless opportunities to business men, engineers and adventurers and called for an army of civil servants, missionaries, soldiers and sailors to administer and police it, to tame it and minister to it. By the end of the century British engineers had built half the railways in Asia, almost all the railways in Africa, and linked the Atlantic and the Pacific across Canada. They had irrigated and countryfied the Punjab with the help of 40,000 miles of canals, and increased the tonnage of shipping turned round in Ceylon (now Sri Lanka) from 75,000 tons in 1815 to 7 million. Their empire was a huge development agency, the largest ever seen. They had done it largely on a classical education, even though advances in all branches of science were impressive. Games were seen as an essential part of building the character to achieve this. Colonial administrators agreed with headmasters and educationalists that team games taught solidarity, service and duty. Even headmistresses joined in, believing that 'most of the qualities which conduce to the supremacy of our country in so many quarters of the globe are fostered, if not solely developed, by means of games', according to Miss Dove of Wycombe Abbey school. Richard Holt in *Sport and the British* (1989) says that recruiting for service overseas and the cultural importance of athleticism combined to promote the cause of sportsmen. The Sudan, for example, was said to be 'a country of Blacks ruled by Blues', a Blue being the award for representing Oxford or Cambridge University in a sport. Seventy-one of the Sudan's 393 top-grade civil servants were Blues of one sport or another, including Ran Laurie and Jack Wilson, the Cambridge oarsmen who won the Goblets for pairs at Henley in 1938 and the Olympic title in 1948. The Sudan's, according to one of the recruits, was the most overtly sport-orientated service, in which athletic records were taken as an indication of personality, initiative, capacity for judgement and control of subordinates, as well as physical fitness. The ideal recruit was a sportsman with a good second-class degree, but if the candidate was deficient in any respect then it was better to be a poor scholar than a poor sportsman. Even in places where recruiting officers placed more emphasis on academic ability, there was a belief in the notion of 'fair play', which sport, particularly team games, was thought to instil in the British character. Fair play, said a German observer, is untranslatable. It is 'a great conception for in these two words are summed up all that English education and ethics hold most dear . . . Everyone, be he sportsman, soldier, politician, statesman, journalist, employer or employed, finds in these two words guidance and admonishment affecting the whole scope and meaning of his work.' Says Holt: '"Rules" were binding on rich and poor, employer and employed, noble and commoner alike. This became part of a "national tradition" of work and play, sport and politics, through which the British recognized themselves and were recognized by others.'

Points of Departure

For the British abroad, British sport served to enhance the solidarity of their colonial society. Sport provided amusement, but was also a necessity, a means of maintaining morale and shared roots. For example, landowners in the thirteen American colonies aped English gentry and their devotion to horse racing long before independence came. Sport was also valuable in building cultural bridges with local rulers. It encouraged assimilation with the British way of life. It also promoted loyalty to the Crown amongst white emigrants to Canada, South Africa and Australasia, and was particularly important in parts of Southern Africa, where the Boers threatened the Pax Britannica before coming reluctantly under British rule, and in Canada, where there was strong French influence in Quebec. Cricket, despite its division into 'Gentlemen' (amateurs) and 'Players' (professionals) until after the Second World War, became the most universal agent of sporting culture, the cement that bound native peoples and British rulers together more than any other activity. Football was the property of the industrial workers, rugby of the middle class, but cricket was universal. In cricket gentlemen and players played on the same teams even if they used different dressing rooms at Lord's, and in British possessions like India and the Caribbean islands it became a people's game and an expression of nationalism just as much as it inflamed patriotism in England and Australia. Through cricket men with brown and black skins could become honorary Englishmen. The *Toronto Patriot* reminded its readers in the 1830s that 'a cricketer as a matter of opinion detests democracy and is staunch in his allegiance to his king'. Cricket was resonant with the patriotic mission that the English demonstrated at the expense of the minority Celtic nations who made up their united kingdom. It was resonant with high-minded ideals and an aloof superiority abroad. In the person of W. G. Grace it demonstrated another strong English trait, that of getting away with what you could get away with. Grace was an amateur who mostly 'played the game' by his own interpretation of the rules, to his own advantage and that of his pocket.

Meanwhile, back on the water, men were racing boats in many other places. A Long Island crew raced Whitehall of New York in 1811. Ships' crews raced in Sydney Cove, New South Wales, in 1818. The first recognizable club in Barcelona was formed in 1821. In 1827 two Englishmen and a Hungarian rowed from Vienna to Pressburg (now Bratislava), the first rowing in Hungary. In 1830 rowing reached Schleswig Holstein with the formation of the English Rowing Club in Hamburg. In 1832 there was a regatta at Port Jackson (now Sydney) in New South Wales, and reports of disputes between rowing boats in Canton, China. The Canton Regatta Club was founded in 1837. In 1834 came the first Hungarian club, the first American (Castle Garden in New York), the first official regatta in Paris, and watersports in Singapore to celebrate New Year's Day. The first club in Sydney was formed in 1835, a year before Pembroke initiated club rowing in Ireland, setting up shop in Ringsend, near Dublin. In 1836 came Hamburg RC, the first club for Germans, and in 1838 the Société Hâvraise de l'Aviron became the first in France.

The Hobart Regatta started in Van Diemen's Land, soon to be renamed Tasmania, in the same year, a place teeming with oar-powered whale boats. In 1840 there was a regatta in Rio de Janeiro, and the regatta society of Le Hâvre was founded. Women raced in coracles on the Dee at Chester, England. There was pleasure rowing in St Petersburg (later called Petrograd and then Leningrad) in Russia in 1842, and a club in Calcutta in India by 1845. The Arrow Club was formed by Englishmen in St Petersburgh a year later. There was a club at Gothenburg, Sweden, in 1851, the year in which Henley Regatta was granted royal patronage by Albert, Prince Consort to Queen Victoria. The Harvard-Yale race was first held in 1852, the start of inter-collegiate sport in the USA. In 1853 the Rowing-Club de Paris was founded by Frenchmen and Englishmen together. And in 1857 the English were rowing in Buenos Aires in Argentina. A club called the English Crew started rowing in Prague (Bohemia, part of the Austro-Hungarian Empire) in 1860. It later became the English RC. The first race in Table Bay, Cape Province (South Africa), took place in 1861, and Alfred RC was founded in Cape Town. In the same year Canterbury RC was founded in New Zealand and SC Limite in Tuscany, and the *British Rowing Almanack* was first published. Rowing started on the Zürichsee in Switzerland in 1862. In 1863 the first strokes were taken in Vienna (Lia RC), in Victoria, Australia (Ballarat Club), in Turin (Real Societa Canottieri Cerea), in Zürich (See-Club), and in Trieste (SC Triestina). In 1864 rowing reached Denmark through Schleswig Holstein, and an Englishman organized the first regatta at Lake Wendouree in Victoria, Australia. In 1865 English students were involved in starting Frankfurter Ruderverein. In 1866 the Sherwood Foresters regiment won a regatta in Sind (now Karachi, Pakistan).

Tourism by canoe or rowing boat was not a mass activity, but English adventurers undertook lengthy voyages from time to time at home and abroad. In 1852 Robert Mansfield published *The Log of the Water Lily*, an account of a voyage in a coxed four on the rivers Neckar, Maine, Moselle and Rhine. Another cruise was taken in the year of publication, and the third edition in 1873 contained the Saône, Rhône and Danube as well. The Cerea club of Turin celebrated Venice's joining Italy by rowing a four between the two cities on the Po in 1867. Howard Williams kept a diary of his voyage from Oxford to London by way of the Severn and the Bristol Avon

in 1875, accompanied by his two brothers and two other oarsmen.
In 1885 Charles Dickens Jr, son of the celebrated novelist, published
Dickens's Guide to the Thames, which was aimed at boating parties,
and four years later came *Three Men in a Boat*, the classic of tour
rowing by Jerome K. Jerome in which Victorian attitudes and
rowers' postures are scrutinized with a wry sense of humour. It was
also common to read accounts of long-distance tours in the English
and continental press, such as H. A. Gwynne's 'Through the Iron
Gate of the Danube in a Pair-oared Gig' in *Longman's Magazine* in
1895.

Two Languages

For the intrepid Cook's tourist the Continent is the most accessible
first step. In the nineteenth century the adventurous few pulled
themselves across the English Channel, while it was not uncommon
to take a canoe or rowing boat by packet steamer to France or the
Low Countries and start out from the port of arrival. Robert Louis
Stevenson, a Scottish student who was turning himself into a writer,
and his friend Sir Walter Grindlay Simpson set out in 1876, shipping
their respective canoes, *Arethusa* and *Cigarette*, to Antwerp. On a
chill evening they slid into a slipway in the corner of a basin on the
outskirts of Brussels. They were greeted by two 'nice-looking lads
in boating clothes', one of whom took a cigarette out of his mouth
and inquired whether the boats were built by Searle and Son. By
chance the canoeists had found the Royal Sport Nautique.

> They were all very polite, voluble and enthusiastic; and their discourse
> was interlarded with English boating terms, and the names of the English
> boatbuilders and English clubs. I do not know, to my shame, any spot
> in my native land where I should have been so warmly received by the
> same number of people. We were English boating men, and the Belgian
> boating men fell upon our necks.

The club servants washed down their boats and put their sails to
dry, and the members loaned them toiletries and found them an inn
close by. Stevenson, not being a rowing man, was out of his depth
in the three-hour interrogation over dinner about the difference
between the Belgian and the English stroke: *'En Angleterre, vous*

employez des sliding-seats, *n'est-ce pas?*' he was asked. Simpson had at least tried his hand at an oar, and did his best to satisfy his questioners.

'We are all employed in commerce during the day,' said one, 'but in the evening, *voyez vous, nous sommes sérieux.*' To the canoeists' consternation they found that the champion of Belgium was a member of the club and was offering to accompany them on the next leg of their journey. Stevenson and Simpson were intent upon exploring the northern rivers of France – indeed, Stevenson eventually bought a canal barge called *Eleven Thousand Virgins of Cologne*, which never moved, 'rotting in the stream where she was beautiful.' From Antwerp they had paddled off to Boom, where Stevenson's account in *An Inland Voyage* (1878) complains of nondescript food at the Hôtel de la Navigation, 'eaten in the dark cold parlour in the company of three uncommunicative engineer apprentices, a silent bagman, and an empty birdcage'. The voyagers were equipped with an Etna stove which they tried out for lunch when on the Willebroek Canal. They had two eggs, bread and wine, and managed to break one egg while disembarking. Simpson wrapped the smashed egg in newspaper and dropped it into the Etna. Several burned fingers later, they enjoyed a fricasse of egg *à la papier* huddled in a ditch in the rain.

We will leave Stevenson and Simpson here on their travels while we look around Belgium in more comfort. Antwerp, like many seaports, claims rowing and tilting activity in the sixteenth century. In 1844 Robert Newell, a London waterman using an 'extremely light' sculling boat, beat four Belgians in a gig from Ostend to Bruges, a distance of 12 miles, by a margin of a minute a mile. There are references to a club in Ghent in 1846 and a regatta in Antwerp in 1858, but organized rowing began in Belgium in 1860 with the founding of Sport Nautique de la Meuse. Liège held a regatta in the same year, and in 1862 Felicien Rops, who was to find notoriety as an etcher and painter of the erotic, morbid and perverse, founded Club Nautique de Sambre et Meuse at Namur. There were clubs in Brussels, Ostend and Bruges by the time the Belgian federation was set up in 1887. Ostend was the venue of the first eights championship in Belgium in 1888, and the French magazine *L'Aviron*'s correspondent reported: 'I do not exaggerate when I say that a third of the population [total 150,000] is in agitation . . . following training of the crews, comparing records with those of rowers from Brussels and Bruges which are received each evening by telegram . . . Ten thousand Gantois took the Sunday trains for Ostend.' As the rowers embarked he observed King Leopold in the middle of the throng. *L'Aviron* attributed the cause of this activity to close contact with the north coast towns of France. Relations with the English, their neighbours across La Manche, also grew. The Belgians became very strong competitors from 1893 to 1910, winning forty-one European titles from a possible eighty-four, including all the titles in 1897. Two clubs in Ghent, Club Nautique and Sport Nautique, sent combined crews to Henley and won the Grand in 1906 and 1907, the first foreigners to lift the English regatta's blue riband event. Henley Regatta and town joined in a special appeal for the relief of the Belgian war-wounded when the countries were allied in the First World War.

The conflict between French and Flemish speakers was reflected in sport then, as it is now. Until the turn of the century there was no sports reporting in Flemish. Karel de Wijnendaele, a pseudonym for Karel Steyaert who founded and subsequently edited the Flemish sports paper *Stortwereld* in 1912, said: 'Our hard-working people can't even speak their own language properly. How, then, do you expect them to write? Don't forget that our cyclists hail from the working- and small farming-class, where reading is rare.' Stevenson found that the young rowers of the Royal Sport Nautique were all engaged in business pursuits in Brussels, and the names of the clubs betray class differences hidden under those of language. In 1975, after many arguments and misunderstandings based on language, the Belgian rowing federation became the co-ordinator between two leagues, one Flemish and one French, instead of being a federation of clubs. It changed its name as well.

Le Rowingman

And so to France, where boating dates from 1830 when Alphonse Karr, 'the eminent romancer', found that the Seine was the most beautiful river in the world. All Paris took to the river on summer Sundays, *fête* days and holidays, to dabble in the waters and dance at Grenouillère. It was the *belle époque* of boating, when thirty boatbuilders were at work and 10,000 boats at large on the Seine from Le Havre to Rouen and the environs of Paris. In Paris there were races at Neuilly, Suresnes and the pretty village of Asnières, and off the Quai d'Orsay itself. Each Wednesday evening the ferry *Union*, decked out with lights and a grand orchestra and pulled by ten oarsmen, was rowed between the bridges of Louis-Philippe and Saint-Maur accompanied by a flotilla of small boats with multi-coloured lanterns. Entertainment was provided by 'strong men' who took on the marine *yole* crews and could beat them. The sport of rowing burst from the general enthusiasm and enjoyed a decade of anarchy in Paris before the birth of the Rowing-Club de Paris in 1853. Le Havre beat them to it, however, influenced by resident English merchants. The manager of the new Frascati hotel and baths in the port at the mouth of the Seine opened a subscription for rowing prizes in 1838, and Le Havre regatta was an immediate success. Twelve thousand spectators watched racing between thirteen small rowing boats and eight whalers. The Société Havraise de l'Aviron was launched. Competitors from Dieppe and England were present in 1840, the light English gigs unbeatable by French whalers. Gigs had their own event in the following year. In 1843 the Prince and Princess of Joinville and the Duke of Aumale attended on the corvette *Pluton* with *Archimède* and *Napoléon* in attendance. Queen Marie-Christine gave the prizes in 1847. On at least one occasion a sperm whale joined in, dealing a thrashing to a Parisian crew in the Channel. Organized activity spread upstream when the Rouen Regatta Society was founded in 1848.

Throughout the Victorian period, anglomania was abroad in France, in rowing as much as in anything else. Two Parisian amateurs, Messrs Boeringer and Perrin, organized a regatta for different types of boats in 1844. John Arthur of the Rowing-Club brought Thames watermen to Paris in 1858; they won their races with ease, but next year the French accounted better for themselves. A French crew won a race in Rotterdam in 1860. In 1861 the Rowing-Club ordered a boat from Picot of Asnières and racing boat construction was born in France. The Cercle Nautique de France was founded in 1875 and established the first French championship race. In 1879 a four from this club raced a double scull from the Société Nautique de la Marne from Paris to Rouen, 235 kilometres including seven locks, the four's winning time being 21 hours 49 minutes.

There was a proliferation of clubs during the 1880s in several regions of France, and many quickly acquired a social cachet, particularly on the Seine and the Marne. The principal organizer of the Rowing-Club was the Vicomte Châteauvillard, the secretary was John Arthur, and the committee comprised Lord Cowley, Baron Warchter, the Hon. W. Stuart, Count Praslin, F. Ricardo, the Hon. H. Howard and Count Mosbourg. It is not difficult to detect where the influence came from. Rivalry developed between the new clubs with their fancy racing boats and the hoi polloi who messed about from bar to dance hall in hired craft. In *Au Bonheur des Dames* Emile Zola describes a race on the Marne between students and drapers' assistants during which a fight breaks out among their supporters on the river bank competing for the attention of easy women. The Goncourt brothers described boating social climbers disparagingly as 'dish water sailors'. Oarsmen themselves became impatient with the older members of their clubs who were more concerned with holding soirées than getting down to action. Such impatience resulted in Aviron Bayonnais becoming a famous rugby club when a member persuaded his fellow oarsmen to give the game a try in 1897. The Seine and the Marne are a wonderful aquatic playground, looping through Paris, traversing the very centre of the capital, and lapping round the leafy islands where several clubs established their homes. Monet, Pissaro, Renoir, Sisley and Seurat are among those who put *les canotiers* and their world on canvas; lesser-known artists too, notably Ferdinand Gueldry, painted the rowers on the Marne. An oarsman himself, Gueldry brought vivid details to his paintings. While Renoir's *canotiers* take lunch on the terrace of the village café, Gueldry's are rounding a buoy in a close encounter with another crew or driving an eight hell-for-leather in the Seine's equivalent of the Boat Race, an annual fixture between the Rowing-Club and the Société Nautique de la Marne, of which Gueldry and his brother Victor were founder members. Rowing on the Marne has been well served by painters. Felicien Myrbach drew *The Departure for Joinville* for *Paris-Illustré in* August 1887, Marius Heraud captured a fours race in 1885, Charles Bricou's *Le Canotage* of 1911–13 shows Sunday crowds of Parisians embarking in small boats, Martinet's painting of *La Société du Sémaphore* at the end of the century depicts the boathouse of the Club Nautique de Paris alongside the tower supporting the Sémaphore's flagpole. Gueldry paints crews cleaning their boats, skiffs shooting weirs, and a busy Thames lock as evocative in every detail as E. V. Gregory's *Boulter's Lock on Sunday Afternoon*, which preceded it by a year in 1895. Gueldry visited England in the same year when the oldest club on the Marne, Société d'Encouragement du Sport Nautique, competed in the Thames Cup at Henley. The Englishman C. Fenwick, manufacturer of elevators, was in the crew. He lived next door to the club's elegant wooden boathouse on L'Ile des Loups, under the shadow of a tall railway viaduct and a camouflage of trees which engulfed all like a huge hippy mop. Baron de Coubertin was a member here.

While the fanatics, the fashionable and the fancy-free played on the Seine just as they did on the Thames, the peculiarly English notions of the amateur presented themselves in Paris and caused a schism between the clubs. This was essentially part of the struggle between the Union of French Athletic Societies (USFSA) and the National League of Physical Education (LNEP). The former was founded in 1887 by Coubertin to propagate and regulate English sport in France, fuelled by the French upper-class interest in the English education system (see chapter 15) after the disastrous Franco-Prussian war. The League was founded in 1888 to counter the Union and drew support from a large number of prominent republicans, politicians and journalists. It had an explicitly nationalist programme of reviving traditional sports. The Union attacked the grind of *lycée* examinations and captured the appeal of the outdoor life, and schoolboys and graduates voted with their feet. They ran and jumped and rowed and kicked balls about and took to horse racing, and the League was dead by the mid-1890s. Rowing organization had developed regionally in France, and clubs from Paris and the north agreed to ally with the southwest in 1890, the first step to the national federation, which was founded in 1893. But in 1891 Encouragement, Enghien and Cercle opted for the strict English definition of the amateur as adopted by the Coubertin's Union, for they were keen to compete against the English. In 1892 Coubertin for the Union and S. Le Blanc Smith for the ARA signed an agreement in which the Union, although not accepting the ARA exclusion of manual workers, undertook that no French crew competing in England would include an oarsman who fell foul of the ARA's definition. This paved the way for London RC to race Encouragement at Andrésy-Carrières in December. The French dealt them a thrashing.

London's account says: 'The LRC boat was badly damaged during practice and, though repaired, was not fully waterproofed. In the race the crew, still suffering the effects of seasickness on the voyage over, had scant opportunity to demonstrate their true style in a craft which buried its head at every stroke.' But they observed the swivel rowlocks used by the French and adopted them three years later. The French press crowed in victory, claiming that the crew which the *Manchester Guardian* described as 'model' had been humiliated by eight men who were not France's best. London were almost certainly not the best in England either. The schism engendered spirited correspondence, for the three Union clubs had isolated themselves from France's sixty-three other rowing clubs by signing the agreement with the ARA. *L'Aviron* reproduced copious opinion from *The Field* and quoted *Wassersport* of Germany: 'English vanity actually makes the most wonderful pirouettes.' A writer from the provinces questioned the difference between a rich young unemployed man who went rowing in the morning and a poorer young man who went rowing in the evening after work. Why bow to the English and invent a class of professional which did not exist in France? 'We are French, damn it! And I do not see what advantage we will gain by imitating a people of whom we know very little.' One does not need to know history to realize by what method they establish their factitious superiority, he said.

Meanwhile *L'Aviron* was inventing franglais in 1892 by advertising books for the 'Rowingman', including river guides such as Jules Gidé's *From Strasburg to Amsterdam* and M. A. du Orné's *From Limoges to Paimboeuf*. *The Secret of the English Stroke* by Wilhelm Rettig, translated from the German, was available in French. In that year the French federation joined in a congress in Turin which established the Fédération Internationale des Sociétés d'Aviron (FISA). The Union of Amateur Rowers (RAF) was formed and chose the English route, splitting completely with the French federation until the latter agreed to abolish cash prizes in 1899. FISA followed suit. A new definition of an amateur was agreed in 1905 and schism ceased.

Students and Tradition

Chris van der Ploeg began rowing at Nereus in 1935 and remembers bidding for a contract in front of the board of the giant electrical company Philips in the late sixties and finding three European rowing champions facing him. Rowing in the Netherlands is a good example of an activity perpetuating itself by strong loyalty to club and constant regeneration from within, a practice familiar to the English. At Nereus, the Amsterdam University club, Drs Meurer and Marres took time off from their lectures and surgeries during the thirties to coach every day, sometimes twice a day, and young oarsmen like van der Ploeg would be out at 8 a.m. or 7 p.m. or both. Meurer was addressed as 'Doctor' but called 'Pruus' (Prussian) because his manner betrayed a German father. The year's racing programme comprised an 8000-metre time trial on the Amstel, a 3000-metre varsity race in coxed fours over 3000 metres between the five original members of the student federation (Njord, Laga, Triton, Aegir and Nereus), the Hollandia regatta near Leyden, Amsterdam regatta, and the national championships. The last two were held on the Bosbaan course after its completion in 1937. Situated in parkland near the Olympic stadium, it is the world's first architect-designed rowing course and was dug by hand as part of an unemployment relief programme. The premier sculling event, the Holland Bekev, is held in conjunction with Amsterdam regatta. The old clubs hold their own jubilee regattas at regular intervals, nowadays usually combined with another regatta. Van der Ploeg's Nereus crew also competed in Essen, Germany, in 1937–38, sleeping in a skittle alley in the company of New College, Oxford. The New College cox ensured that Hitler's portrait was turned upside down each night before going to sleep.

Dutch rowing developed from two strong influences: yachting as the governing body, and students. During the last twenty years of the nineteenth century racing was organized by clubs forming part of the student corpora, which are old, traditional and selective societies. Accessible to only about 20 per cent of students, the corpora operated what the English call an old boy network after graduation. Many of the student rowing clubs took their names from gods, examples being Njord (Leiden), Triton (Utrecht), Aegir (Groningen),

Argo (Wageningen), Skadi (Rotterdam) and Laga (Delft). English influence was present in these early clubs, and when Nereus won the Thames Cup at Henley in 1895 they became the first club from outside Britain to have their name inscribed on a Henley pot for an eight-oared event. Towards the end of the century attempts were made to introduce professional rowing, but it died quietly, failing to attract backing from a people who do not place bets.

The Dutch rowing federation did not start until 1917. Until then rowing was organized by the Royal Netherlands Yacht Club, which was also responsible for yachting rules. The corpora formed their own federation in 1883 to run the varsity fours race, and also met the non-student clubs once a year under the chairmanship of the yacht club. Student rowing has thus always had a dominant role. All presidents of the national federation have come from one or other of the student clubs. The student federation was given royal patronage after the Second World War, the only Dutch sports body to be so recognized. Many rowers saw war service in Europe or the Far East, and rowing clubs were regarded as safe havens from the occupying Germans' informers. In the 1960s the student clubs detached themselves from the corpora during the social revolution which swept the Western world, as a result opening membership to all students. The student federation grew to include all higher education institutions, but tradition is still passed from generation to generation in the form of ragged blazers which change hands lovingly – the more dishevelled the blazer, the greater the prestige attached to its wearer. In the Netherlands membership of a student rowing club is membership for life, and graduates are expected to acknowledge the good times they enjoyed in student days by lending a hand in organization.

The older among non-student clubs also have strong traditions and considerable success. De Amstel, coached by the German professional Peter Hach and the New Zealander Tom Sullivan, were dominant in racing from 1923 to 1930; De Hoop were also strong at this time. Clubs such as De Hoop and Willem III often combined racing with family outings in fleets of wherries resembling English Thames skiffs. The boats, many of them privately owned, were inriggers equipped for two scullers and a cox; they also had sails and were usually made from mahogany. They are almost extinct, sullied by rival attractions. However, a century after these boats became popular, recreational rowing is once more growing. Thousands participate in long-distance pleasure rowing in clubs across the country, a country where good rowing water abounds.

The club-based Dutch system has brought periods of success internationally, notably 1921–26, 1963–66 and 1968–69. Medals in the Seoul Olympic Games of 1988 and the world championships in Bled in 1989 have been achieved by a national squad system, but even here the Dutch have not moved as far as many other countries. A national squad is put together only during the racing season and there is considerable resistance to the formation of combined crews, although the federation employs a small professional technical staff. It is perhaps not surprising that these achievements have come in sculling events, where there is a long tradition in the non-student clubs. In 1892 J. J. K. Ooms of Neptunus became the first non-British sculler to win the Diamonds at Henley. He was employed in a lowly capacity by a company with connections in the building trade, and suspicion that he may have employed his hands at work led the English to cast doubts upon his amateur status.

Style and Luxury

On a terrace overlooking the Po, hardly ten minutes' walk from the centre of Turin, a long table with a white cloth is laid out for lunch under the trees. A royal feast of salads and pasta is laid out in the club house, hot dishes are available to order, wine is passed back and forth among members and their guests who all sit together. Some arrive up the path from the river's edge supporting sculling boats on their heads. This is a typical day in the summer of 1990 at Cerea, the oldest club in Italy, founded in 1863 and still occupying its original site by the greenish water of the Po. It is small, with about 150 members, men only, and has had its ups and downs. There is a considerable fleet, and in the club hang many embroidered pennants from early regattas. The steward and his family cook and wait at table.

Cerea drew their inspiration from England through business contacts, and started in the heady days when Piedmont's attempt to take over northern Italy resulted in the unification of the whole country by treaty with Garibaldi and the Kingdom of Naples. Turin

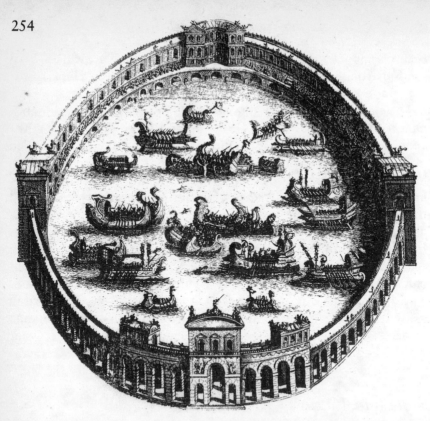

Convicts man the boats in the flooded Coliseum

is capital of Italy's motor industry, and doubled in population to a million during the 1990s, putting some strain on the old style and glory of the Piedmontese capital. There are five clubs along the Po, which, sadly, has become polluted since the industrial expansion. The liveries of hire boats, popular in the 1960s, have gone, as have the pleasure yoles which the clubs once possessed. The gravel business has changed the Po as well, destroying its sandy beaches. Vittorio Suave, an antiquarian bookseller and one of leading lights of Cerea, says that the river was like an autostrada back then. If you hadn't reserved a boat by 10 a.m. you wouldn't get one. There were police in canoes to control the traffic. But attempts to clean the river are bringing back hire boats and reviving rowing. Five clubs share a 5-kilometre stretch inaccessible to motorized craft. The others are Armid, Caprero, Esperia and Fiat, and there is a programme for schools run by the city. Suave and his club run adventurous activities for veterans. They travel to the Head of the River Race in London. In 1975 they rowed there, taking twenty-five days for the 1600 kilometres. In 1973 they repeated the Turin-to-Venice trip that their forebears made in 1867. Suave rows in the Vogalonga in Venice and the Marne marathon. In 1928 a Cerea crew rowed to Venice and then round the Adriatic and Ionian coasts to Rome, 3600 kilometres in fifty-five days.

The thousand members of Firenze are the most privileged people in Florence. They keep their boats in a cellar which burrows into the bank of the Arno under the Uffizi Gallery. Their gymnasium and showers are under *The Adoration of the Magi*, Rembrandt's *Self-Portrait as an Old Man*, Uccello's *Battle of San Romano*. The subterranean club has a bar and television lounge, and rooms for poker and bridge. The furniture is luxurious and the trophies sumptuous, some dating from the time when the club was called Libertas and won the King's Cup for eights seven times. An oar depicts a crew being breezed along by a goddess, all in gold leaf. Outside on the lawn members can take coffee and read the paper, immune from traffic and tourists, with a view of the Ponte Vecchio in one direction and the Ponte alla Grazia in the other. The backdrop is the Pitti Palace, the Bòboli Gardens and the Belvedere. Sculling boats and canoes, traditional and modern, come and go on the Arno, a river which looks innocent but which wrecked the premises along with half the old city in the great flood of 1966.

While money from the state lottery underpins the national rowing team of Italy, administered through the Olympic committee, the card game of bridge underpins the clubs. Typically, they have large bridge rooms, and Aniene, named after a tributary of the Tiber and the oldest club in Rome, is no exception. The original members in 1892 included Victor Emmanuelle III and Queen Margherita. The poet Gabriele d'Annunzio was also an honorary member, and the pretentious nature of Aniene was further illustrated when the club bestowed the title of Honorary Cox on Benito Mussolini. Too much significance should not be read into this, however. The dictator featured in many Italian clubs, and added social cachet in places where it mattered. An original nude by Gustave Courbet adorns Aniene's bar. The photographs in its centenary history reveal four-oared pleasure boats similar to the German *Prunkboot*. Posing and laughter are as much in evidence as rowing. Nine kilometres of river are available for rowing as far as the village of Castelgiubileo. Aniene also offers tennis, swimming and football among its attractions for members, who must pay a joining fee of 10 million lira.

Other Roman clubs, such as Lazio, have similar facilities, as have the rowing clubs of Naples. At La Canottieri Napoli there are burgundy leather couches and gilt-framed sea- and harbour-scapes in the huge marble-floored lounge, flowers by the vase, and sun terraces by the pool which overlooks the Bay of Naples. Round the corner at Porto S. Lucia is CRV Italia whose history documents a long line of parties and visits by Prince Umberto, the Duchess of Aosta, General Diaz, Ingrid Bergman, Queen Federica of Greece, and so on. In 1909 Gordon Bennett presented them with the Lysistrata Cup, and in 1931 the Mussolini Cup appeared. They rowed mostly in yoles and began regular matches against Nice in sailing and rowing in 1903. Since 1946, when the original club, Italia, merged with Naples Sailing Club, rowing has taken a back seat to the yachts moored outside the elegant rooms under the promenade. The Circuolo Nautico Posillipo is another Naples club with a fine collection of artworks. It is also strong in swimming, water polo and sailing. The rowing now mostly takes place on Lake Patria, for the bay is less friendly to modern racing boats than to the heavier yoles.

The motto above the door of Lario Sinigaglia at the very end of Lake Como says 'The art of rowing strengthens the soul'. Lario pride themselves on being a club for ordinary folk. Their building is a handsome one by Giuseppe Mantero, erected in 1932. Founded in 1891, Lario's most famous son is 'The Good Giant' Giuseppe Sinigaglia, winner of the Diamond Sculls at Henley in 1914. His boat hangs on the wall, a very narrow craft in dark mahogany fitted with four-stay outriggers. He came to prominence in 1911 as European champion in the single and in the double, stroked in the latter by his clubmate Teodor Mariani, who was singles champion in 1909. Sinigaglia joined the army in spite of the fact that, as an international sports celebrity, he could probably have avoided military service. In 1916 he was killed fighting against the Germans in the mountains of northeast Italy.

Lake Como is 30 miles long and has at least a dozen clubs situated on it. Throughout the year it is disturbed by a morning wind called the Tivan which blows off the mountains, and an afternoon wind called the Breva which blows in the opposite direction, a natural phenomenon which can cause problems for rowing. An added hazard at Lario are motorboats, hydrofoils and seaplanes which land close to the club. Serious rowing is therefore done at Pusiane where there is less disruption. Another Lake Como club is Mandello del Lario, also known as Moto Guzzi, where the workers of the motorcycle factory of that name climbed to the peak of Italian and European rowing in the 1950s and where a coach first put a cox in the middle of an eight – an experiment that did not catch on, although the Russians tried it in the seventies. Moto Guzzi travelled about on a contraption converted from a motorcycle which conveyed four oarsmen together with their boat.

In the early days of modern rowing in Italy some of the Turin clubs adopted the Venetian style, using *gondolinos* (see chapter 3). Eventually, however, the Italians left stand-up-and-face-the-front rowing to Venice, preferring boats suitable for sea rowing which are still used. The classes of these traditional boats are *canoino* (single scull), *doppio canoino* (double scull), *joletta* (coxed single scull), *doppio pariglia* (coxed double scull), and *jole* (coxed pair, coxed four and eight). However, from before the days of Sinigaglia and Mariani, Italians have had international success in lighter, slimmer shells. They were internationalists in the early days of their rowing, being among the founders of the international rowing federation (see chapter 22) in 1892, together with Switzerland and two of the countries we have visited on this tour, France and Belgium. The Italians have brought style to rowing in the clubhouse as well as in the boat, and they exhibit it even in the 'grunt and sweat' department at Piediluco, the idyllic lake near Terni which since the 1970s has been their national training centre. We will leave them there, for we must take the Viking trail.

THE VIKING TRAIL

FOUR salesmen who traded in building materials founded Norway's first club to row in the modern style. In 1877 they had returned home from England with some outriggers, and they fitted them to boats at Fredriksstad. In the next year Christiania was formed in the capital, followed in 1879 by a club in Bergen which took its rules from Scandia, the Scandinavian club in Hamburg. When the Norwegian federation was born in 1900 two further clubs, Ormsund and Norske Studenters, were neighbours of Christiania in Oslo. The familiar upper-class and mercantile profile was visible in all these clubs, Christiania in particular being associated with the royal family after Norway gained independence from Sweden in 1905.

But Norway already had a strong rowing tradition with proletarian and military roots, and the sport was closely allied with the nationalist movement. Traditional rowing came into conflict with the modern imported developments at least until independence. In the eighteenth century Norway was ruled by the Danes, but was transferred to the Swedish crown after the Napoleonic wars. From 1814 Norwegian national consciousness awoke in a radical constitution which took its ideas from the French Revolution. Constitution Day, 17 May, became an annual date for a secular and nationalistic festival held in most towns during the 1830s and 1840s, celebrated particularly on the West Coast from the Southland to Trondheim, with Bergen as the centre of activity. Rowing was in fishing boats called *faerings*, mostly for two scullers, but four- and six-oared inriggers were also used. Boats varied from region to region and were adapted to local conditions. Prize money was high, in some cases amounting to a fortnight's wages. In Bergen it came from Norway's two best-known cultural personalities of the time, the composer and violinist Ole Bull and the author and agitator Bjørnstjerne Bjørnson. The prize money drew fishermen, sailors, ships' brokers and many other tradesmen to try their hand. Iver Johannessen, a carpenter, and Hans Nielsen, a rope-maker, were champions there in 1850. By the 1870s the upper classes had exclusive clubs with high membership fees for part-time national rowers. Rules and time-keeping made the competitions more formal.

The organizers of Constitution Day were upper middle class; as the century moved on and as conflict with Swedish rule intensified, those of the patriotic-liberal bent gradually obtained the upper hand over officials and conservatives The working classes were included by means of sport, principally rowing, but rifle shooting and skiing also became ideologically acceptable. In 1861 the Central Association for the Spread of Physical Education and the Practice of Arms (Caspera) was formed, a strongly nationalistic body. There were conflicting pressures during the last twenty years of the century. At the same time as the national question became more prominent, the English philosophy of adhering to moral virtues irrespective of aims outside the arena caught on in Norwegian sport. Traditional rowing was dubbed 'national' rowing by the press to distinguish it from English rowing; Caspera furthered the cause of sport as something more than a pastime, promoting it as activity which both improved public health and strengthened the defence of the fatherland through fitness and strength of purpose. Boats made for racing were scorned as being useful only for sport, whereas national boats were multi-purpose and rowing them prepared people for military or strategic tasks. The success of the nationalist movement paradoxically weakened national rowing by reducing its *raison d'être*. In 1892 national rowing dropped money prizes. There was a dispute in 1898 when the Bergen Turnas Association, organizers of a national exhibition of tourism and sport, ruled that nobody over twenty-five could be considered an amateur in national classes, the object being to ban 'professionals' whose presence was thought to discourage participation in the big races. 'The age of twenty-five must be regarded as the absolute peak when the issue is sport pure and simple, like amateur rowing,' they said. The fishing industry read this as an attempt to eliminate their best men and forced the organizers to add an open class for national rowers to their programme. Events were held for both kinds of rowing, but only one of Bergen's six clubs took part in the English variety.

The 17th of May was fading in popularity by the turn of the century and its adherents achieved their main aim of full independence from Sweden in 1905. But national rowing, an important pioneer of sports development in Norway, was to maintain its dominance for a long time. English rowing spread very slowly. English coaches were at work in some places, Christiania having one in 1905 and the Norwegian federation using Mr Follett for their Olympic crew in 1908. The Norwegian federation was founded in 1900. The Nordic federation came along in 1909 and held its first championships for Baltic states in 1910. In the thirties Hannibal Fegh, an importer of English worsted, discovered Fairbairnism as 'the natural way'. He arranged for Fairbairn coaches to visit Norway, and the clubs embraced the new approach to English rowing.

The Western Federation of National Rowing had more members than the Norwegian federation until 1948. Eventually the only difference remaining between the two disciplines was the types of boat used. The suspicion is that, once modern Norway was born and the urge for independence was satisfied, class differences kept them apart for a generation or more. But barriers were coming down, all the same. In the 1948 Olympic Games, Bergen's four were stonemasons.

English Connections

Sailors and fishermen raced one another for centuries on the coast of Sweden, but modern rowing was introduced by John Duff, British consul and businessman, when he founded a club for gymnastics and rowing in Gothenburg in 1851. He began by importing an English wherry from Hamburg. The Scottish industrialist Alexander Keiller and S. A. Hedland, editor of *Handelstidningeno*, were founding members. The Rev. Henrik Ling, father of Swedish sport and one of great prophets of physical education, was a keen oarsman, and Viktor Gustaf Balck, a gymnast with English connections, helped to popularize rowing among gymnasts in Stockholm. The first Swedish regatta was in 1868 at Hälsingborg, and the novelist and poet Viktor Rydberg wrote about regattas in the 1870s. As in many other countries, an explosion of activity occurred in the last twenty years of the century. A further twenty-five clubs were formed by 1900. Races between crews from Stockholm, Copenhagen and Oslo anticipated the formation of the Nordic Rowing Federation. In 1884 there was an inter-country match. Women's clubs were founded for 'style' and 'social' rowing; competitive championships for women did not occur until the 1950s. Swedish rowing did not escape schism over professionalism. In the 1890s the Swedish sports federation wished to include professionals under competition rules, and as a result the rowers broke away in 1904 to form a rowing and canoeing association which divided into two later that year. The English ARA's rules of racing were adopted and regional associations formed, an example being the Rowing Association of the Amateur in Gothenburg in 1906. There was considerable opposition to the sports federation having control over the rowing federation.

In the 1980s competition became popular with companies, outstripping recreational rowing. There is an annual four-oared race from Stockholm to Vaxholm, a distance of almost 13 kilometres, and the 20-kilometre Götaälu River Race in eights between Kungälu and Gothenburg attracts up to forty crews.

Denmark's first modern rowing was undertaken by Germans in the Duchy of Schleswig. After Denmark lost this territory to Prussia in 1864, a merchant by the name of Harald Hansen became hooked on rowing while visiting England. He returned with an inrigger and in 1866 founded Kvik, a club swiftly followed by Copenhagen. Danes themselves started to build racing boats, clubs spread, and by the eighties there were both domestic regattas and fixtures with Norway and Sweden. In 1886 a women's crew appeared in Nykoebing-Falster and had fifty-three outings during the year. The first women's club was Damernes Roklub (1901). Most significant was the introduction of rowing for twelve- to sixteen-year-old boys between 1888 and 1890, making Denmark possibly the first country to cater for youth on a national basis. The social pattern is familiar: students took part, royalty took part in the person of Crown Prince Frederick as a keen member of his student club, and the bourgeoisie took part. The Danes also drew on the legacy of the Vikings: in 1902 a crew completed the round trip from Svendborg to Hamburg in thirteen days, and a tradition of long-distance rowing has developed whereby crews go to sea with pots, pans and tents, and roam the coasts and rivers. During the Second World War many rowers has joined the resistance and several escaped from German-occupied Denmark to Sweden using tour boats.

The Danish federation was founded in 1887 and served as an influential model for the younger Danish sports federation. Denmark was also a founder of the Nordic Rowing Federation which held its first championships in 1910. They now occur every second year for seniors and juniors, the participants being Denmark, Finland, Norway and Sweden, with Iceland as a sleeping partner. Rowing for lightweights was established by 1923 and Denmark has been one of the most successful competitors in this category since it was introduced by the international federation in 1974. Pleasure rowing is popular, and Lake Bagsvaerd near Copenhagen has served as a beautiful, if often wet and windy, venue for five European and world championships.

Between Sweden and Russia

The first modern rowing in Finland took place in Kuopiossa between local crews at Tampere Sportclub. A Swedish-speaking club, Helsingor Roddklub, was founded in 1884, later adopting bilingualism and then becoming Finnish-speaking, so that it is now called Helsingen Soutuklubi. The instigator was Arthur Borgström, who brought a pair of outrigger fours from England. There also seems to have been a Russian influence, sources claiming that Helsinki was introduced to rowing by people from Vyborg.

The name-changes and Russian influence again reflect a political situation, Finland being another Scandinavian country with a long history of occupation by its neighbours. Russia was the dominant power from 1809. The development of a Finnish-language movement resulted in Finnish speakers receiving equal rights in 1863. In 1894 Russian was declared the official language, the year that Helsingor Roddklub trained two crews under the Swedish coach G. Wirström for a regatta in honour of Tsar Alexander III's visit to Helsinki. Officers, academics and shopkeepers made up the crews, and the tsar presented a gold trophy to the winners. The Helsinki polytechnic, university and fire brigade clubs organized the Finnish rowing federation in 1910, and Finland's first win in the Scandinavian championships came in 1913. Finland was the first country to give women the vote, in 1906, but it was not until 1946 that they rowed their first race.

The 1952 Olympics in Helsinki gave rowing a big boost in Finland. Admiral Svante Jundman encouraged company rowing, and sawmills, papermills and shipbuilders became involved, financing their sport by 'social money'. But this changed in the 1970s when workers were given a say in how social money should be spent, and they objected to their employers supporting sportsmen who were virtually full-time. On the other hand, rowing was recognized as complementary to winter sports such as skiing and ice skating, champion cross-country skiers and rowers sharing each other's disciplines. And the taste for taking to the lakes and coastline in boats is far from diminished (see chapter 4). In 1989 two vegetarians, Per-Olof Smeds, a sixty-five-year-old engineer, and Martti Pietilä, a fifty-year-old technician, completed a 5000-kilometre tour round the country in a fixed-seat boat, one pulling and one pushing. They ate only fish and vegetables 'from nature', and lost 40 lb each; the voyage took them almost four months.

Baltic Gateway to the Black Sea

In 1858 the Group of Eight went rowing on the Neva. Messrs Poznanskief, Wilkins, Kvasova, Sitin, Tihanovsky and the brothers V. and D. Fuks, merchants and gentlemen of St Petersburg, established modern rowing in Russia and left behind them the first Russian rowing mystery: who was the eighth man? No matter: in the following year there were forty of them using three boats, *Zabava*, *Seagull* and *Arrow*. Records are sketchy concerning the early days of clubs in this imperial capital set on some forty marshy islands at the gateway to the Baltic, but there are references to the *Arrow* (*Strelka* in Russian) being used for pleasure rowing in the 1840s. An English resident presented a challenge trophy consisting of silver sculls in a leather case to the British colony in 1842; the competition for sculling on the Neva and its tributaries was open only to British residents of St Petersburg. The Crimea War in 1856 in which Britain and Russia were on opposing sides curtailed sport on the Neva for a while, but in 1860 the St Petersburg Yacht Club was formed for sailing and rowing. The club's own volume of history, which covers the period 1860–1910, describes it as the Tsar River Yacht Club. Several later clubs claim ancestry from it, though changes of name confuse the family tree.

The inaugural assembly of the English Arrow Boat Club took place in 1864. The members were in possession of a randan named *Arrow* built by Salter of Oxford and purchased in Putney in that year. The group adopted the articles of Oxford University Boat Club and made some additions, the chief of which was that the committee had to be entirely British and only 10 per cent of the members could be non-British. Members listed in its new rule book for 1864 include Read, Gibson, Wilkins, Todd, Matheson and Saunders. In 1870 three of the four winners engraved on the cup for a four-oared race on the Neva are old boys of Marlborough College in England. This club found a home on Tsar Alexander II's Petroffsky Island. The tsar, anxious to encourage sport to attract the energies of students who were showing a keen interest in 'politics and nihilistic activities', gave them the land under imperial charter, an ironical move because the club's exclusive rules were illegal under the Russian constitution. When, years later, the Russian Home Office declared that the articles did not conform to the law, officials and police agents were silenced when a copy of the charter was proffered. The club built a boathouse in 1856 and developed a haphazard rowing style copied from ferrymen. However, one of their members, T. E. Coulson, won the Henley Grand in 1890 with London RC while completing his commercial education in England. He brought the ideas of the metropolitan London clubs back to St Petersburg, and Arrow were unbeaten for seven years. Other clubs began to copy their methods by infiltration, sending oarsmen to join the club for a few years to learn Coulson's secrets. The anti-constitutional membership restrictions were apparently not enforced, perhaps because the Minister of Justice, Stsheglovitoff, and two senators of the court of appeal were members. In 1901, five years before eights appeared on the Neva, the club moved to the nearby island of Krestoffsky. The new boathouse with all its contents burned down in 1908. In 1914 came a jubilee banquet attended by the British ambassador Sir George Buchanan and his young secretary Eugene Millington-Drake, an Oxford Blue who was to become the man behind rowing in Uruguay. By 1921 the club was in the hands of its Russian members, and in 1923 the Young Communist League took it over and introduced women, as did all clubs in the Soviet Union. Coaching was continued by old members, but, like the blue-white-blue flag with its golden arrow, the portraits of King Edward VII, Queen Alexandra, King George V and Queen Mary came down. Arthur Macpherson, the last foreign president, died in Liubianka Prison in Moscow, and other foreign members were deported to camps in Murmansk. The last president was Maxim Knopmuss, who smuggled the silver sculls trophy and minute books to England when he left Russia with his brother Alfred in 1930. In a letter to *Rowing Magazine* in 1956 he said that he left his copies of Fairbairn and Lehmann's *Complete Oarsman* as a guide for future generations.

Apart from Arrow, there was a student club which still occupies its original site and has been called Burevestnik since the Second World War (known as the Patriotic War in the Soviet Union). The Fortune Club of 1888 lasted until the thirties. Messrs Osetsky and Badsermeister started a Russian rowing society in 1888–89, perhaps the aforementioned Fortune. The St Petersburg Society of 1890 changed its name to Znamia when rowing was revived after the Revolution. Macpherson of Arrow started the Russian Union of Rowing Societies in 1908, and another Neva club called Seagull (Chaika) was started in 1911 by Alexii Stephanov for workers at the power station; it is now called Energy. These clubs found homes on the islands to the north of the city, away from the mainstream of dock and river traffic. They were also helped by N. H. Wilkins from the original Group of Eight, who wrote a book on technique in Russian some time before the secretary of the Moscow River Yacht Club, one B. Wood, published *Rowing and Sculling* in 1889. The latter includes excellent drawings of rowing and sailing boats and swimming techniques, and, curiously, shares a publication year with W. B. Woodgate's book of the same title which was published in London.

St Petersburg was the first Russian city to take up the oar, but there was also an Arrow club in Moscow in 1867. Rivalry in Moscow became intense in 1914 when the director of Moscow Yacht Club told journalists that 'neither we, nor our children, nor our children's children will ever travel to a competition in company with members of Moglivs.' Moglivs was the Moscow Skiing and Watersports Society, against whom the yacht club had arranged a race in eights in 1914. It is not clear whether umbrage was taken before or after this event. Rivalry with Leningrad (formerly St Petersburg) was particularly fierce, focused on the dark hall of the Arrow boathouse presided over by the coach Alex Smirnov. An encounter in 1929 organized by Fizkultura I Sport under the slogan 'Let's go – Soviet Oxford-Cambridge' was an eight-oared race from Kiev Railway Station to Gorky Park on the Moscow River. It was won by Leningrad. The original Moscow boathouse is now used for youth rowing and is situated where the Moscow River joins the Obvodnoy Canal. There is a 2000-metre course ending at the Crimea Bridge, near the British Embassy and the Kremlin, which face each other on opposite sides of the river. On the outskirts of the city is the man-made Olympic basin in Krylatskoe. The European championships were held there in 1973 and the Olympic regatta in 1980. Several other courses are being prepared.

The Revolution ended the foreign influence on Russian rowing. Equipment and boathouses were confiscated, boats and books left behind. Sport was funded by the government and organized according to the principles of the Communist Party through a ministry under whose wing the federations operated. Articles on technique and pieces by Russian 'masters' were published in magazines, but it was not until after the Second World War that serious revival began. In 1957 Shevdov and Shebyev published *Academic Rowing*, academic being the Russian term for Olympic or English or modern rowing. Shevdov was a professor at the Aeronautical Institute in Moscow and Shebyev a chemist. Some of the influence came from Fairbairn, because the first party to visit Henley in 1954 acquired copies of Fairbairn and Gilbert Bourne's *A Textbook of Oarsmanship*. Fairbairn was translated; Bourne was not. After that the coach Igor Demyanov wrote *Technique of Academic Rowing* in 1959 and other books and dissertations followed. In 1967 a teaching manual appeared; its third edition was published in 1987.

Manpower was provided by military and civilian clubs. When the Soviet Union entered the war in 1941 there were twenty-eight clubs in Kiev, Belorussia and other centres as well as Moscow and Leningrad. The service clubs are called Dynamo, students' clubs are called Burevestnik, trade corporation clubs Spartak, labour clubs Trud, and village clubs Kolos. The system broadened after the war, and many places in the Soviet republics have rowing centres similar to the one in Novgorod on Lake Ilmen, which is equipped with a large tank, many boats, and has miles of waterways at its disposal, waterways which brought the Vikings here to set up the northern capital of the Rus.

The international success of the Soviet Union has not been exclusively Russian. The Ukraine, where rowing began in Kiev in 1887, and the Baltic republics, where, for example, the first Lithuanian club was Neptune at Klaipeda in 1885, have been well represented in Soviet teams. Riga in Latvia, Vilnius in Lithuania, and Tallin in Estonia are strong centres. In 1945 there were only three eights in Russia, but revival was helped by the confiscation of all boats and equipment found in German clubs in territory occupied by the Soviet armies, and by reparation payments in the form of boats from Germany. Boats were imported from Pirsch in Berlin for the Olympics in 1952. Now boats for the republics are built at Zintars in Riga and in Samarkand, but the emphasis is on quantity at the expense of quality.

In Leningrad in 1990, Znamia has the oldest surviving building, facing the finish line of a 2000-metre course, on the island of the Primorsky Park of Victory. Today it is crammed with a fleet in poor condition. Next door is a large post-war classical-style building containing an old-fashioned gymnasium, a formal clubroom and offices. Lenin is present by bust. Examination of the boat inventory proves interesting: in 1889 there were nine privately owned coxed doubles among the fleet. Gammerton of England built three boats in 1899, Cyril of London one in 1895, and Brown (or Braun) of Vyburg on the Finnish-Russian border another in 1904. But the next four boats were built at the club by different Russians. The honours board lists regatta entries from 1860 and the club's sculling championship from 1889; the first Russian to win the latter did so in 1912. The number of foreigners who feature in the membership lists is high until the club's first life ceased in the Revolution. The record of the second life is prodigious and impressive. Portraits of fifteen trainers and nineteen Olympic medallists adorn the walls, all of the latter from 1952, 1956 or 1960. Their eight won Henley's Grand Challenge Cup in 1958, and they were European champions in 1961.

Behind these buildings which front the river is a modern training centre containing an enormous gymnasium with twin rowing tanks, each capable of taking eight rowers. The tanks have slides mounted on runners which are mounted on rails and anchored to the wall by means of an elastic rope, so that the seat and its frame simulate the movement of a boat more closely than a conventional structure. Ergometers in the gym are Russian copies of two American-designed and British-manufactured machines which have found their way to Leningrad. Across the path from the gym is a cosy café with colour television and excellent coffee, the only part of this 600-member tennis, canoeing and rowing club that has the appearance of being properly maintained. The rowing clubs generally reflect the neglected and untidy condition of buildings and lack of maintenance in the Russia of the 1990s. If Znamia with its idyllic river setting, large grounds and lofty rooms were anywhere else it would probably be commercially viable as a sports centre. Racks of boats are left open to the severe elements. They are not cared for. Neither are they respected when they are new. Any Russian rower, even very senior officials in the federation, will tell you that the boats turned out at the rate of 1200 a year in Riga are second rate. The national team is supplied with a small fleet of German or Swiss boats.

The Energy club is now a children's rowing centre, its original wooden building housing rest rooms. Nearby is an old, narrow, low workshop for wooden boatbuilding and repair, a structure creaking and rippling with age. The equipment includes a very old Singer sewing machine and a bicycle which looks like a nineteenth-century prototype. At the Physical Training Institute a sculling boat made in England in 1900 hangs on the wall near the boat used by Yury Tukalov to win the Soviet Union's first Olympic gold medal at Helsinki in 1952. The archive since the Second World War is comprehensive and includes large photo albums of Henley visits in the fifties showing the ambience, crowds, tents, buses and everyday scenes that must have been unfamiliar to the photographers. The Dynamo club is part of a huge multi-sport campus, well equipped with rowing tanks and a circular canoe slalom in which a rotating bar pulls canoes round and round. Spartak is housed in a former restaurant, regency-style, again with many boats from the factory at Riga. The Shipbuilding Institute also possesses a boathouse. And navy cadets practise for Navy Day in six-oar *yoles*.

Rowing in the Soviet Union has developed by pulling its own bootstraps. The crews of the Soviets have achieved the highest international honours. They have the ships, they have the men, they have the women, and they have the water. They are tough and proud of their heritage. But they have been prisoners of the legacy of provision by Party. And they have very little money.

18

RHINE AND DANUBE

HAMBURG would have pride of place on any Grand Tour as the gateway to German rowing. It was one of four free ports in the German Confederation, and the English merchants in this powerful Hanseatic League formed the English Rowing Club in 1830. Six years later Cesar Goddefroy started Hamburger Rowing Club with the help of the English club in acquiring their first boat, the *Victoria*. They shared a floating boathouse on the Alster, one of the lakes which the business community helped to create close to the city centre and which serves as a reservoir. There was a regatta between the two clubs that year, and another in 1837 when the English club imported four gigs from London. The German crews were not allowed to talk after the command 'Get ready' had been given, the penalty being either 1 Reichmark or an English shilling. In 1844 these two clubs formed Algermania Alster Club to run regattas, using a triangular course over 4000 metres for double sculls, four-oars, six-oars, gigs and sailors' races. The regattas were run like a big party, open to the public, with amusements other than rowing. Soon professionals were barred along English lines, but members of Algermania wore 'liberation' clothing in black, red and gold during the revolution of 1848. Clubs spread around the Alster and on the Elbe, Favorite Hammonia having a stained-glass panel in their clubhouse showing crests from RC Matilde in 1840 and ten others. Germania, founded in 1853 by eight teenagers at the house of their schoolmaster J. F. F. Kruse, adopted a stylish rowing uniform of blue pea jacket, long white trousers and white shirt, red scarf trimmed with white, and black and white-striped 'Prince Albert' straw hats. Their badge was a double-headed eagle on a black, red and gold band. For some years their rowing success did not match their turnout. By 1878 there was a 2000-metre course with no turns on the Alster.

Meanwhile activity started in Frankfurt with the advent of the Rowing Union in 1865, again with some influence from England via students in Frankfurt and Offenbach. Frankfurter-Germania started in 1869, and the Isle of Main was donated to rowing clubs by the city in 1870. Frankfurter RC went to Putney in 1876 to race against London RC. The Frankfurter oarsmen adopted marine uniform, speech and discipline instead of the English-style hats, ribbons and cravats which were worn farther north. The Rhine and Main club had an eight-oared barge built by Stämpfli of Zürich which carried passengers under a stern canopy; similar *Prunkboot* (literally 'pomp boats') plied the Alster when the clubs attended ceremonies or took their womenfolk out for a spin. A painting in Germania's clubhouse shows two such craft tossing their oars before a large crowd at a landing stage in honour of Crown Prince Friedrich Wilhelm and Crown Princess Victoria in 1877. There is also a photograph of Hamburg's *Prunkboot* carrying nine ladies in their Sunday best in 1895. The Herzog of Nassau presented two Netherlands gigs in 1866, the year of the seven-week war in which Prussia defeated Austria and most of the small German states, paving the way for Bismarck's chancellorship of the North German Confederation a year later which made him master of Central Europe. Victory in the Franco-Prussian War of 1870–71 strengthened German national feeling further. Exercise became popular and many new clubs were founded. By 1876 there were regatta organizations in Berlin, Cologne, Heidelberg, Mannheim and Würzburg. Frankfurt saw its first fixed-seat boats built for racing in 1873, and Carl Leux began building racing boats with sliding seats to English designs in 1878. Two years later there were regattas at Emden, Giessen and Mannheim.

Berlin was the third German centre to get started, this time influenced by British diplomats who went rowing on the Spree. There was pleasure rowing to Breslau, and in 1876 Berlin Ruderverein began to organize regattas, with boats coming from as far afield as Hamburg and Oxford. By 1878 there were five clubs in Berlin following the British lead, and the royal Hohenzollern family soon extended their keen interest in maritime affairs to rowing. The industrialists who were building Bismarck's Reich supported rowing and

took it up themselves, importing English boats and founding clubs
for their workers. The first regatta at Grünau on the Spree was held
in 1880, and in 1883 Kaiser Wilhelm II donated a prize to Berlin
Ruderverein.

The same process was to occur in Bavaria when the Bavarian
royal family took an interest in marine affairs. Royal attention meant
the gathering of the loyal bourgeois, who enjoyed any excuse for a
parade, a centenary or a regatta. After 1900 another influence was
at work. Rowing became a workers' sport when unions and workers'
associations built up sporting and cultural pursuits. The Workers
Sports Association took in those barred from competing as amateurs
by their status as manual workers. The workers' clubs combined
into the Free Rowing League in 1909.

Hamburg (Holstein), Frankfurt (Hessen) and Berlin (Prussia) were
the original main centres in the German states, but rowing quickly
caught on among German speakers everywhere, even though the
British were often involved in the origins. Frankfurt had a regatta
organization in 1865, and Frankfurt and Würzburg clubs founded
the Central German Federation in 1869. Other federations followed:
Berlin (1876), North German Regatta Association (1878) and the
German Rowing Federation in 1883. In 1915 the German Youth
Rowing Association was founded.

On the water, a single sculling championship was held in Frankfurt
in 1882, and there were races over 8, 44 and 56 kilometres in Berlin
in 1890. The earliest reference to a women's club is in 1884, and a
Frauen RC was founded in Berlin in 1901.

Ebb and Flow in Central Europe

The geography of Central Europe was as conducive to rowing as
the German temperament was suited to partaking of it. Given limited
time, the Grand Tourist has difficulty in deciding which flowing
river, which quiet tributary or which secluded lake to paddle to
next, what with the Elbe and the Rhine, the Danube and the Alpine
lakes at his or her disposal. Rowing spread amongst German speakers like a disciplined great escape, an activity suited to an ordered
temperament which offered relief from cities and good fellowship in
the country. Until the internal combustion engine shattered the

silence and ruffled the surface in the affluent years after the Second
World War, toilers at the oar had things much their own way. In
Austria, for example, rowing is the oldest sport, beginning in outriggers on Kaiserwasser near the Empire Bridge in Vienna. The Wiener-
Ruder-Club Lia started in 1863, and one member made outriggers
and fitted them to barges. From 1861 to 1863 rowers built their
own boats and rowed at Greifenstein. Weidner made a few *Flach-
einer* (singles) and an eight named *Alf*. In 1862 there was a six-oar
outrigger from England. Lia claims to be the first sports club in the
Austro-Hungarian Empire and fifth oldest German-speaking club.
(The English club in Prague is in fact older, being founded in 1860.)
There were twenty-two members when it started, taking their name
from the wife of the founder who sewed their first red and white
flag. They built a sailing boat called *Topo* which could be rowed
the Venetian way, and which was faster than steamers at the time.
The Ofener Bootswerft built an inrigger four in 1867 for Lia, but
after that they began to import English boats.

The first regatta on the Traunsee was held in 1864, and the first
race in Vienna in 1868. A year earlier some members of Lia had
broken away and formed the Donauhort Club. In 1875 the Pirat
Club was founded. A four rowed from Vienna to Tulln, a distance
of 35 kilometres on the Danube, in 6 hours 23 minutes, and a double
took seven hours. By 1878 there was an English four with slides in
Vienna, and it is claimed that the paper boat *Alfred-Anna* in 1879
was made in England, although there is no record of English boatbuilders manufacturing American-style paper boats. But somebody
could well have attempted to do so. Another possibility is that the
boat in question was that brought to England by Columbia College
of New York in 1878 for use at Henley. They sold it to First Trinity,
Cambridge. The Austrian boat became a war casualty in 1945.

In 1862 four English butchers who amused themselves on the
Zürichsee by rowing a *yola* imported from England challenged four
Swiss boys to a race. This was the beginning of competitive activity
in Switzerland. Next year the Seeclub was formed. Several others
followed (1869–78), including the Anglo-American BC, Polytechnic
and Nordska. Their names reflect the international pull of Zürich
and its polytechnic where, it is surmised, the English butchers were
studying. The institution drew many students from Scandinavia and
served all of Switzerland until a few years ago, when another tech-

nical institute opened in the French-speaking city of Lausanne. Hence Zürich's club for Scandinavians and Aviron Roman for students from Geneva, which opened its doors to those from other French-speaking areas in 1936. Rowing spread to other university cities and to communities around the lakes, where pleasure rowing was more popular than competition. Championships were first held in 1867. Rowing for juniors was introduced in the 1930s. The Swiss system of military service has always disrupted training because it requires seventeen weeks' basic training at the age of twenty, with a stint at officers' school for many, and each year thereafter two to three weeks are taken up with military service.

The Poles spent the whole of the nineteenth century as subjects of Russia, Prussia or Austria, or combinations of them. Poland was partitioned three times between 1795 and 1918 and again on the eve of the First World War, and the occupying powers opposed any organization which manifested Polishness. In particular, the Saxons, Prussians and Russians persistently denied Poles their nationality and culture. Sports organizations which might have contributed to physical strength and military abilities thus encountered constant opposition. In 1873 the Rowing Circle of University Youth, founded in Warsaw by Konrad Pruszynski, found a way through for Poles by following in the wake of the Warsaw River Yacht Club which was set up by German traders a year earlier. The Circle of Rowing Friendship followed in 1878, becoming the Warsaw Rowing Society (WTW) in 1882. The latter engaged in touring and propaganda on the Vistula and led to the emergence of other Polish clubs. By 1918 there were several clubs in Cracow and Warsaw, including one for women in the latter, and clubs in Plock, Wloclawek, Kalisz, Konin, Czernichow, Lomza, Poznan, Wilno, Kruszwice, Nowy Sacz and Pultusk.

Most Polish clubs were in Russian-controlled areas, but influences in training came from centres in all three occupying powers – St Petersburg, Vienna and Prague, and Hamburg and Berlin. A regatta commission was set up in 1901 to codify rules of racing. Between 1906 and 1914 it organized rowing rallies at Ciechocinko which coincided with assemblies attended by representatives of the clubs. Among other things, the commission introduced compulsory medical tests before regattas in 1904. The most important development was the establishment of the Union of Polish Rowing Associations in 1908.

The WTW was very active in promoting social activities and other sports such as kayaking, boxing, netball, tennis and sailing. Clubs also ran musical groups, choirs, amateur theatricals, concerts and entertainments, participated in local life by cooperating with life guard societies and organizing philanthropic work, lectures and meetings in support of national identity. They also developed an etiquette and staged ceremonial events which marked them out as Polish. Their first pennants were modelled on those of St Petersburg Yacht Club, and in 1884 the WTW was permitted to use the Warsaw coat of arms. Standards were raised on festive occasions, rowers parading in gala uniforms such as dark blue blazers, dark blue or white trousers, black tie or bow tie, and a round cap with a visor. Members addressed each other as 'Friend' (*Drug*). The opening of the season was marked by a church parade in which the club's chaplain and choir performed, followed by the christening of a boat with 'godparents' in attendance. The flag was hoisted and members joined in the Rower's Prayer composed by Wilhelm Troszel, a member of WTW and director of the Warsaw Opera. Formal photographs and a row-past were followed by games and song and dance around town. Many clubs also participated in the annual festival of wreaths which dates back to the sixth century, a harvest festival which included bathing and water games. Elaborate wreaths were floated on the river, and boats were decorated. Clubs used the festival to promote rowing and, sometimes, patriotic fervour in the 1880s when festivities connected with contemporary national events were banned.

During the First World War rowers helped in the Red Cross, in the defence of Warsaw bridges in 1920, and in the collection of funds for the Upper Silesia Plebiscite in 1920–21. During the period of independence until 1939 this extra-mural activity declined while regattas and pleasure rowing increased. The number of clubs trebled, helped by the growth of seventy-five gymnasia clubs for juniors. Before 1918 rowing for under-twenty-one-year-olds was almost non-existent, although some clubs organized activity for juniors through 'circles' at schools. By 1925 there were about 200 boats and nearly 10,000 juniors rowing at school, 5 per cent of the age group. Women also took to the oars, penetrating previously all-male clubs. Here the academic institutions in Warsaw were the pioneers, two women's clubs being formed in 1912. Championships for women began in 1921, and after the Second World War spread to categories other than fours and singles. Despite this newfound freedom and activity, participation generally was in decline by 1939. But touring rallies were popular, eight clubs taking part in a round-Berlin trip in 1934. Three men from Poznan rowed to Le Havre between 14 July and 9 August 1930. After 1945 club life declined and state organization took over, but was less effective than in some of the other socialist countries of Europe.

Until 1918 Czechoslovakia was part of the Austro-Hungarian Empire. The first organized race was held to celebrate the arrival of the railway in Prague in 1845. Rowers from Hamburg took part. But the introduction of modern rowing on the Vltava was once again due to the English business community who formed a club called English Crew. It admitted German and Czech members and changed its name to the English Rowing Club. During the nineteenth and the early part of the twentieth centuries the Czechs struggled to establish a national identity and cultural and political independence from the empire, but were opposed by the sizable minority of Germans in their midst. The authorities opposed the setting up of Czech clubs, but they were outmanoeuvred by Sokol (Falcon), an organization founded in 1862 by Dr M. Tyrs to promote physical activities and Czech nationalism. The basis was gymnastics for the masses using Tyrs's own system of exercises which were influential in European physical education, but Sokol also established its own clubs in other sports, including rowing, which became very popular along the rivers Vltava and Labe (Elbe). Sokol also promoted amateur theatre and festivals, and grew quickly to a million members. Whereas small sports clubs were vulnerable to government pressure, Sokol was in a good position to resist, and rowing thrived under its wing, promoted as a complementary summer activity for ice-skaters. The greatest development was in Prague, where Eisklub zu Prag followed the English Crew in 1868. Prager Ruderklub started in 1870 and merged with Eisklub in 1871 to form a Czech- and German-speaking club of 325 members. Four years later the Czech members broke away, calling themselves the Czech Rowing and Ice-skating Club (CV a BK). There were already two Czech-speaking clubs, one at Vajgar in the south and one in central Bohemia, the

V for Victory at the World Championships, 1986

Kathleen Gorman instructing coxes, Smith College, 1928

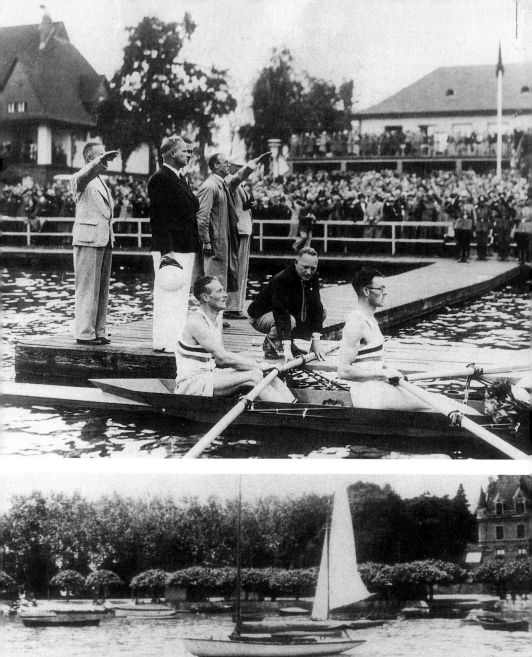

ABOVE: John B. Kelly Jr after coming third at the Olympic Games in Melbourne, 1956

RIGHT: Thomi Keller, president of FISA from 1958 to 1989

OPPOSITE PAGE ABOVE: Jack Beresford and Dick Southwood after winning the gold medal in double sculls at the 1936 Olympic Games

BELOW: Pierre de Coubertin, founder of the modern Olympic Games, rowing on Lac Léman

TOP: The rivals I: The Olympic sculling final at Lake Wendouree in 1956: on the right, the Australian Mackenzie leads the Russian Vyasheslav Ivanov 300 metres before the finish. On the left, Ivanov has moved through Stuart Mackenzie in the next 50 metres to take the gold medal

OPPOSITE BELOW: The rivals II: Jack Beresford Jr (*left*) and John B. Kelly Sr (*right*)

BELOW: The rivals III: Peter-Michael Kolbe (*left*) and Pertti Karppinen (*right*)

ABOVE: Typical whale boat

OPPOSITE ABOVE: Scottish mussel scalp fishermen, 19

BELOW: Greathead's lifeboat, 1803

OPPOSITE BELOW: Trainera from Orio, Spain, 1953

ABOVE: Windy day on the Thames beat   BELOW: Incident at Bolsena

RC Dolni Berkovice. Rowing circles followed these examples in Bohemia and Moravia.

These clubs had a thriving social life. Cycling, track and field, tennis, fencing and football were all part of their activities, as were excursions and fun regattas in which races were interspersed with obstacle courses and entertainments, with fireworks and dancing to complete the day. Ruderklub Regatta organized the first serious regatta in Prague in 1870. A crew called Blesk-Lightning and coxed by the stroke's wife came second in Hamburg after rowing there along the Vltava and Labe/Elbe in eleven days. In 1879 this crew formed RC Blesk in Prague. A double and a six-oar were launched in Prague in 1880, the first Czech-made boats to join those imported. In 1881 a Czech rowing club opened in New York, an indication of migration trends. In 1890 there was a disastrous flood affecting most of the country, and most clubs were left bereft of property. But activity recovered quickly. The Central Association of Rowers from Bohemia was established in 1884 to organize races and encourage Czechs to compete abroad. It affiliated to FISA in 1892, FISA's first year. Eight years later it had to leave FISA under pressure from the Austrian federation which refused to recognize the Bohemian body as having an international role and, in common with the German association, vented its displeasure by boycotting Bohemian regattas. But the Bohemian association persisted in founding new clubs and succeeded in attracting Polish, Italian and Hungarian athletes to visit them. In 1903 an international race under the sponsorship of Emperor Franz Joseph was held, and a year later a rowing manual was published in Czech, a dictionary of terms translated from English and German. The annual race for the Lord Mayor's Eights started in Prague in 1910, its great shield remaining one of the most prestigious trophies. Meanwhile the winner of Czechoslovakia's first sculling championship in 1893, Josef Rossler-Orovsky, busied himself by promoting Czech sport. He imported equipment and founded the Czech Ski Club (1892), the Czech Yacht Club (1893), the sculling circle in Prague (1895), co-founded the Czech Amateur Athletic Union (1897), and was general secretary of the Czech Olympic Committee from 1906 to 1929.

The First World War completely disrupted activity. But the new republic's rowing federation was accepted into FISA in 1920. Around eighty clubs, Czech and German, were active. The Second

World War brought an end to a successful twenty years of international competition, and the revival in 1948 was accompanied by
a complete reorganization of sport along Soviet lines, generously
financed by the state and under the umbrella of large state-owned
industrial enterprises. Three centres of excellence were set up, in
Prague (Bohemia), Brno (Moravia) and Bratislava (Slovakia). This
heralded a thirty-five-year period of highly successful men's and
women's rowing. The coach who did most to make this work was
Vojtech Hveda, one of the founders of army rowing and coach of
the 1960 Olympic double sculling champions Vaclav Kozak and
Pavel Schmidt. At his funeral in 1990 he was described as a 'man
of pithy grain, full of pleasure from life and second father to all his
disciples' by the Czech rowing president O. Maracek. According to
the journalist Vaclav Pacina, he was from the era of gentlemen's
sport, of good fellowship on the water. But the historian Svetla
Hudeokova says that state reorganization inflicted moral damage at
the same time as bestowing material plenty. The elite system provided full medical care, special nutrition, imported drugs, time off
work, equipment, boats, study and foreign travel. But the destruction
of the old-style club life excluded inter-club rivalry while encouraging minimum effort coupled with maximum job tenure. Dissenters
were accused of mistaken ideology. The system of selection regattas
was severely loaded against rowers from ordinary clubs, who were
denied the indoor winter training facilities available to elite athletes.
If they did make it, they were too late to enter the required regattas.
The Prague Spring and Alexander Dubček's aborted reforms of 1968
caused the success of Czech rowing to falter. Of the bronze-medal-
winning eight at the Tokyo Olympics of 1964, all but two were
living abroad after 1968, the best known being Bohumil Janousek,
who became Britain's first professional national coach in 1969. The
gold-medal-winning sculler Schmidt left for Mexico, and later moved
to Switzerland. Janousek's eight reassembled in 1990 to row in the
Lord Mayor's race.

Danube Water

In 1822 Lord Jersey taught Count István Széchenyi to row in England, and on 16 May 1827 the father of Hungarian rowing, together

with his British friends Thomas Hallifax and John Barneby, rowed from Vienna to Pressburg (Bratislava) in 3 hours 52 minutes. In 1830 he rowed from Pest to the Black Sea in the *Juliette* with the English boatbuilder Frank Emmet who in that year fitted a metal outrigger to a boat called *Eagle* and was probably the same Emmet who made the first metal boat. Széchenyi was clearly smitten by rowing for both business and pleasure. A philanthropist and patriot who set out to harness developments which he saw during his travels in Northern Europe to benefit his mountain-locked country bisected by rivers, he founded the first Hungarian club in 1834, the year of his second pull to the Black Sea. This time he was with an American, William Anderson, their object being another survey of the Danube preparatory to the construction of the Iron Gate to aid navigation. A retired British sailor, John Dews, assisted him with the rowing club. Five years later another Englishman, John Paget Thorpe Satchvilleben, described Széchenyi's expertise at feathering his oars in his social, political and economic survey called *Hungary and Transylvania*.

Close by his club, Széchenyi linked the towns of Buda and Pest which face each other across the Danube by a chain bridge, built in the 1840s. It was designed by William Tierney Clark and built by Adam Clark, based on Hammersmith's first chain bridge erected in 1827, under which Széchenyi may have rowed with Lord Jersey. During construction the bridge's Hungarian and English workers formed crews to race against Italian soldiers. Széchenyi, who died in 1860, founded the Hungarian Academy of Sciences in 1825 for the discussion of scientific, political, economic and social ideas, and designed Hungary's railway system as minister of transport. Significant reminders of his activities include 120 books, articles and parliamentary bills. He earned more respect than the aristocratic militants among his contemporaries and was dubbed the Greatest of the Magyars by one of them. In the burgeoning democratization of the 1990s the count is emerging once more as a hero of enlightenment and celebrated as a father of modern Hungary as well as of rowing on its great rivers. The new course at Szeged was named after him in 1989. Széchenyi's family were adventurers and innovators, too. Laszló Siklóssy's history of Hungarian sport (1928) includes a drawing of a Velocipedaquamobile made for his son Ödön by Józsel Keve. It is a contraption like the front wheel of a pennyfarthing

mounted between the hulls of a catamaran with rudder strings running to the rider.

Following Széchenyi's lead, activity spread along the tree-lined
Danube in Budapest, where boathouses and pavilions catered for
large numbers of recreational rowers who could paddle the broad
river and race in the 86-kilometre Szabados Regatta which circum-
navigates a large island. By the turn of the century a 160-kilometre
race from Budapest to Baja was established, and tennis and fencing
were typical activities in the clubs. The club history of Hunnia is a
picture album of bathing, competitive rowing and good times
enjoyed by members drawn from the wealthy and the governing
classes. Many of the rowing terms used in these clubs were in English
because there were no Hungarian equivalents. Geza Krempels
remembers that the National Rowing Club, originally formed by
long-distance adventurers, had all but ceased to go out in boats
when he was recruited in the late thirties. The members were ageing
and content to have parties and play cards. Krempels was a medical
student on a scholarship in Berlin from 1941 to 1942 and returned
home to become singles champion in 1943 while dividing his time
as a paediatrician between the Budapest children's clinic and the
Hungarian air force. The balmy summer of 1943 attracted bombers
from the RAF to the Danube as well as rowers onto the water. The
British pilots would lay mines on the river and the Germans would
then follow to detonate them. 'During the bombings I was afraid,'
Krempels says. 'The most miserable experience was when an old
JU52 flew over my shell. As I rowed, I could see the shadow of this
plane on the water before I could hear the noise of its engine. It was
there to detonate mines, and one oarsperson had been caught in
such an explosion. It wasn't until it flew over and detonated mines
farther downstream that I knew I was safe.' Krempels retreated from
the Soviet armies with the Hungarian officer corps and wound up
in Long Beach, California.

Under post-war communism Hungarian rowing was organized by
the state through factories and institutions, and in the 1990s the
boathouses show the strains of both rival attractions and starved
funds. Nevertheless, there are estimated to be between 2000 and
3000 active recreational rowers and 400–500 competitive ones in
the Budapest area. Istvan Jásdi whose father was the national trainer
after the Second World War, and whose grandfather rowed for

Pannonia, says that club life for the family pumped blood into the veins of rowing in Hungary, and that the sport cannot survive without it. His view is echoed by others in modern Hungary, including officials at the rowing federation. Activity is not confined to Budapest. For example, there is a thriving club on the Tisza at Szeged and two survive in Gyor on the Little Danube. Spartacus started as Győri Csonakazo in 1877, founded by Ernő Nemethy, whose grandson Gyorgy Nemethy is a member. Győri Torna és Evezős, founded in 1897, is now the club of the water authority and has cartoons of ten commandments for rowers on the walls. Both clubs have workshops and employ boatbuilders to repair wooden boats. The latter club has a modern tank and gym and makes moulded plastic boats. The third club, Révay Főreál Iskola, belonged to a large factory until support for its 500 recreational rowers was dropped in 1980. Now the club house is somewhere to play cards, the boats lying idle in their shed.

But the spirit of adventure is not dead in Hungary. In 1987 the 1862 voyage of Istvan Birly and Pällal Rosti from Rotterdam to Pest, accomplished in forty-nine days, was re-enacted. The re-enactment took forty-two days.

Modern rowing spread eastwards into what is now Romania, carried by students returning home from Vienna and Budapest. They started the Society of the Little Boats in Timisoara in 1864. It took the club more than forty years to acquire a boathouse, during the course of which it changed its name to Regata. In 1880 the Gymnastics Society in Arad introduced rowing, and shortly afterwards the Muresul and Regata clubs were rowing on the River Muresul. Until 1916 these cities, not far from Szeged in Hungary, were part of the Austro-Hungarian Empire. Romania, which was originally formed from the uniting of the principalities of Moldavia and Wallachia in 1858, emerged from the First World War a larger place. A national federation started in 1925 and affiliated to the international federation two years later. Originally in Aria, the federation moved to the capital Bucharest in 1936, where there were eleven very active clubs before the outbreak of the Second World War. By this time several other places had taken up the oar, and Francisc Cerhaty, a boilermaker and locomotive riveter, began his rise from single sculling champion in 1928 to a fifty-year career as coach, boatbuilder and umpire. Romanians took part in the European championships for the first time in 1932.

A further adjustment of boundaries took place in 1945 in which Transylvania and the region including Arad and Timisoara, where rowing had proliferated during the thirties, were included in Romania. Sport was also reorganized as part of the social changes which closed down the old club order and introduced a socialist sytem of centralized funding and control. National championships were organized from 1949 on Lake Snagov, only to be forced off the water in 1984 by President Ceauşescu, who wanted the lake for his own use. The championships moved to Yassy, Romania's second city. The federation concentrated exclusively on elite rowing, allowing the recreational and club activities to decline. A national scientific programme of recruitment identified high-calibre athletes, and a thorough training system turned this elite into top-quality international performers. This was particularly the case with the women's team, which emerged as the principal challenge to the Soviet Union and the German Democratic Republic. The three accounted for approximately two thirds of the 131 medals won between 1954 and 1990. The Soviet Union had the lion's share of gold medals until the early 1970s when East Germany took over at the top, and Romania mined the most gold in 1984 when, uniquely among the former European socialist states, it did not boycott the Olympic Games in Los Angeles. The problems surrounding the violent overthrow of Ceauşescu at the end of 1989 and the legacy of his transformation from a comparatively enlightened and principled leader to cruel dictator have given sporting activity a back seat.

At the time of the foundation of the first club in what we now know as Yugoslavia, the northern part encompassing Croatia was the southern border of the increasingly unhappy Austro-Hungarian Empire under the Habsburgs, while Bosnia, Herzegovina and Serbia were under Turkish Ottoman influence. The Rowing and Fishing Association in Zagreb, Croatia, came along in 1872, and in 1883 rowing began on the Adriatic at Zadar with the Circolo Canottieri Damnazia. In 1885 a Croatian club, Jadran, was founded at Zadar. Clubs in Rijeka, Prian, Koper, Pula and Trieste formed the Trieste federation, which became the fifth founding member of FISA in 1892. Clubs followed in Osijek (1907), Ljubliana (1908), Vukovar (1912), Crikvenica (1912) and Split (1914), the latter called Gusar.

In 1912 the Jadran club was trying to start a Croatian federation. The First World War intervened.

The Yugoslavian federation was founded in 1922 and held its first championships at Crikvenica, by which time Croatia-Slavonia had been ceded to Yugoslavia by Hungary, and Austria had lost all claim to areas like Dalmatia and Trieste. In 1930 the lake at Bled entered the rowing calendar with its first international regatta; it has been one of most popular sites for competition ever since. It nestles in the crater of an extinct volcano with a magnificent viewing platform from the terrace of a former monastery on a cliff above the water. Four European and world championships have been held there. The first international regatta after the Second World War took place in 1950 against Austria at Bled. The following year Germany was invited, the first invitation after the war to German oarsmen. Currently there are thirty-seven clubs in Yugoslavia (twenty in Croatia, ten in Serbia, five in Slovenia and two in Macedonia), with 600 active rowers. The republics of Slovenia, where Bled is situated, and Croatia, where there is a superb man-made course at Zagreb, are attempting to loosen the country's federal structure, opposed by their own Serbian minorities and the republic of Serbia. The next rowing Grand Tourist may find different flags and different boundaries in this part of the Balkans, just as he or she may find the Baltic rowing map changed before the century is out.

As the Grand Tourist reaches the Black Sea, a waterway known to the Vikings a thousand years ago when they pulled down the Dneiper, he finds a competitive scene younger than the rest of the Northern and Central European countries glimpsed thus far. In Bulgaria rowing was introduced on fixed seats in 1924 by marine officers influenced by Captain Stefan Zanev's experiences at the Italian naval academy. The first club was Sportni Morski Legioni at Varna on the Black Sea, and the boats were manned by sailors and dock workers. When slides were used for the first time in 1953, the year in which national championships were first held, there were clubs on the coast and on rivers at Varna, Burgas, Widin, Swistoff, Rousse and Plovdiv. Wassil Bojanov, a cox, coach and lecturer at the High School for Sport in Sofia, organized boatbuilding. Bulgarian crews first competed in Europe at Bled in 1956. Kirijak Roupov was in the single, and Bojanov coxed a pair hampered by their heavy boat, but they did not finish last. The cox undertook to educate

more coaches, and in 1957 the Bulgarian championships moved to
a lake at Sofia. Eight-oared boats were introduced a year later. In
1960 Bulgarian women entered the international arena at Grünau,
using boats from the former Pirsch yard in East Berlin, and Levski
Spartak and Trakia Plovdiv became increasingly familiar names on
the European regatta circuit.

The Bulgarian rowing federation started life on its own in 1963
when it separated from the body which supervised canoeing. The
first medals were won in 1967 with second place for the men's
double and third place for the women's quad. Dimitar Janakev and
Theodore Mrankov became Bulgaria's first world champions in the
coxed pairs in 1977, steered by Stefan Stojkov, while Svetla Otzetova
and Zdravka Jordanova became Olympic champions in the double
sculls in 1976, and Stojanka Grujtcheva and Sijka Kelbetcheva in
the pair.

Political turmoil from the Baltic to the Black Sea has already
brought crisis to sport. Since the Second World War countries from
Estonia to Bulgaria have been relatively well-off in terms of resources
for national teams, following the challenge and the lead of the
East Germans. In 1990 they are all actively pursuing other ways of
organizing their politics and their welfare, and the role of sport is
changing too. Different places will doubtless find different solutions,
but the one certainty is that the shift or reduction in resources, at
least for the time being, will contribute to changes in the names
which predominate in the world and Olympic medal tables.

19

SPANISH INQUISITION

PABLO Picasso's canvas of Columbus shows the adventurer on his column gazing seaward through an open window with an iron balcony, arm outstretched to the horizon. Palm fronds reach out for the navigator, a blue-green sea sparkles at his feet, an evening ketchup sunset warms him, the massed balconies of the apartments honour him like the boxes of an opera house. The sailor was not a native of Barcelona, nor did he set out from there for what proved to be the Caribbean. It was Isabella of Castile, ruler of Catalonia, who sponsored his quest for a westward passage to India and sparked a bounty of untold riches for later generations. Five hundred years after Columbus, the Real Club Maritimo looks out on his statue from its terraces and pool, and its restaurant which has a reputation for the fruits of the sea. At one time all you could see from this building were murky warehouses bordering filthy and lumpy harbour water, but once the Olympic flame of 1992 ignited a bonanza of redevelopment, demolition exposed the glory of the elegant nineteenth-century buildings and opened the quays for public pleasure. Columbus stands above all this, but now he must share the limelight with the old customs house and the naval and marine headquarters. The vegetable and fruit warehouses have been moved farther south to the extended port, and the yachts in the marina and the fabulous varnished *yolas* of the Maritimo enjoy less shipping and cleaner water. Tucked behind the customs house on what used to be the waterfront are the old royal ship sheds, now a maritime museum containing a rowers' treat: a full-size reconstruction of the royal *galera* which took part in the battle of Lepanto.

There is mention of a Regatas Club Barcelona as early as 1821, and from time to time races took place near the pilot station. Hulks in the harbour served as a base for clubs. Tarragona, founded in

1878, is the oldest surviving Spanish rowing club, and Maritimo the second; it began life as Club Catalan de Regatas in 1879, after which it had a number of name changes until it emerged in 1913 as Real Club Maritimo de Barcelona. Maritimo is synonymous with the introduction of modern or Olympic or outrigger rowing in Spain. Outriggers were first seen in Barcelona in 1899; championships for *yolas* and the King's Cup started in 1902 with a match between Barcelona and Alicante. The Spanish federation was founded at Maritimo in 1918 and joined the international federation in 1920. In the following year the first championships for outriggers were held and Spain took part in the European championships. Barcelona hosted the championships in 1922. Also in 1922 the clubs in Catalonia banded together to form a regional federation, organizing umpires and coaching commissions before the national body did so.

Canoas were rowed by twelve men and a cox in the Barcelona area until the Second World War. They were similar to the *traineras* of the Cantabrian coast (see chapter 4), fishing boats with fixed seats and usually raced over four laps of a 500-metre course. Regattas were popular among the city folk and the rowers of Maritimo. The crews, however, were not drawn from its exclusive members but from fishermen and the working class. The Club del Mar de Regatas and Maritimo organized the races. Maritimo was a club of high social pretensions, drawing members from the business and commercial worlds. Their travels to London and visits to Maritimo by British merchants brought outriggers to Barcelona, together with knowledge of English rowing. There was also awareness that rowing was all the rage in neighbouring France. The Spanish wanted to compete internationally, and foreign influence was at hand on Spanish soil in the persons of English mining engineers from the Rio Tinto company at Huelva and Aracena in Andalusia.

A group of German Swiss from Zürich brought bodyswing to Barcelona in about 1925. They impressed Luis Omedes, stroke of Spain's 1924 Olympic eight. In the thirties the question being asked on Spanish rivers and coasts was what were the Germans doing to achieve so much success that the Spanish, in their early ventures into international competition, were not. A team was in training for the 1936 Games. It included the sculler Iñaki Sarasura, a farmer and *trainera* oarsman from Orio, who took to the single outrigger only a few weeks before the Games and gained selection after two trial races. He was in Barcelona preparing to go to Berlin when the Civil War broke out, putting paid to any thoughts of the Olympics. The Second World War began as the Civil War ended and, although Spain remained neutral, there was no serious rowing until hostilities in Europe ceased except an Iberian championship with the Portuguese.

After the war vibrations from Germany and Northern Europe were even stronger. Foreign coaches were invited to several coaching conferences and by 1948 Dr Walter Volle from Germany was persuaded to hold several training clinics in Spain. Volle was also a swimming coach, and he overturned the prevalent opinion that rowing and strenuous exercise were dangerous for larger-than-average hearts. Volle said that the man with a large heart should do a lot of training, not a little. Leopoldo Vives of Maritimo was one of the enthusiasts fired by his methods, and he set out to preach the Volle way.

Omedes, who by now owned a factory making venetian blinds and had sons who were rowers, was another who was determined to find a higher place for Spain on the international podium than his own crew had achieved in 1924. When his ideas were not accepted at Maritimo he started a club of his own next to his factory on the River Llobregat and recruited his workers as well as his own sons. He called the club Ruber, derived from the Latin for 'red', and a comment upon the polluted state of the river. This was in 1949, the year in which he also erected a small wooden hut beside the lake at Banyoles north of Barcelona, where he required his crews to spend spartan holidays and weekends eating, sleeping and rowing. His crews had some success in this early example of company-sponsored rowing, one of his sons becoming Spanish sculling champion before he was killed in a motor accident.

In 1967 Omedes, now vice-president of the Spanish federation, turned to France and hired the French national coach Jean Tarcher, who had fallen out with his employer across the border. Tarcher started his working life as a designer of jewellery and graphics, and his sporting career as a fencer at the salon of the Olympic foil champion Edward Gardère, but he was converted to rowing when he saw and admired crews on the Marne. He says that he first saw Fairbairn's influence in the 1920s when watching Australian oarsmen. He rowed for Encouragement in Paris and became

European champion in their eight in 1931. His Sportif des Forces de l'Armée Française won the Grand at Henley in 1956, two years after he became professional coach for the French federation. He coached France's first world champions in the double sculls in 1962. During his French period Tarcher held courses in Algeria and Morocco, two further countries where rowing first had an English accent before French influence prevailed, in Morocco's case before the First World War and in Algeria's before the Second.

In Spain Tarcher was asked to produce a crew for the 1968 Olympics in Mexico. He was given a group of conscript soldiers and sailors and set up camp at Banyoles, where he also coached the local club. Dick Pieper, a German who was in charge of the water skiing at Banyoles, imported the first outrigger eight from his home in Switzerland at the beginning of 1969, and Banyoles's rise to prominence in Spanish rowing began.

Pieper and his friend Pedro Abreu, who was living in Barcelona, became more and more involved as Tarcher and another French coach, Marcel Gracini, produced promising results. They equipped their club with Land Rovers and boats and dreamed of setting up a school where students could live and continue their studies while rowing during term time. Abreu donated his personal library, and in the winter of 1972–73 they rented accommodation and hired teachers, starting what Abreu describes as one of the best schools in Spain during General Franco's dictatorship. 'We probably had the best teachers in Spain. It worked very well at the high school level, not so well at the university level. But the universities were bad anyway.' He was accused of teaching revolution and subverting Spanish youth by the High Court of Public Order, and gaoled for three days. However, the school outlasted Franco, whose death in 1975 set Spain back on the road to democracy. By 1980 there were forty-seven international oarsmen living at Banyoles, in eighteen apartments, taught by eighteen part-time teachers in seven classrooms. Locals hotels fed athletes a calorie-controlled diet prescribed by the rowing centre. Pieper was technical director of the project, and Abreu had plans for a foundation.

On the water Tarcher's juniors reached the finals of the 1975 international championship for juniors in Montreal. The president of the Spanish federation, Fernandez Baqueriza, attended at the expense of Pieper and Abreu, who had by now set their sights on an Olympic medal in 1980. The federation gave them a free hand but no funds. The juniors won a bronze medal in 1976. Then Banyoles hired the Norwegian Thor Nilsen (see chapter 10). As results proliferated, the Spanish federation supported Banyoles more and more, but the Basques and the people from Maritimo were less than enthusiastic. The dominant club of the region and the numerous and powerful northerners who mainly rowed for money in *traineras* had been used to carving up the national honours amongst themselves. The upstart swimming club and its foreign experts challenged their custom and practice.

An Olympic medal may have been the goal, but Pieper and Nilsen rightly judged that the strengths of the Spanish lay in juniors and lightweights. The German Peter Lange was hired to coach lightweights, and Banyoles began to win most things. Nilsen's place became the mecca for anybody who seriously wished to better the East Germans in the international arena. Meanwhile Tarcher, who did not get along with the new regime, was sent by Pieper and Abreu to Seville to start a new club. Soon Seville was sending world champions to the Banyoles scheme, further rocking the smug world controlled by the Basques.

A Banyoles-based lightweight crew won the eights silver medal in 1977 (losing the gold by four hundredths of a second to the British). Antonio Montosa won the lightweight sculling title in 1978. In 1979 the eight won gold. Heavyweight crews were reaching finals too. The eventual target in Moscow was two medals. Spain finished fifth in the quadruple sculls, fourth in the coxed fours, and seventh in the double sculls. After such a momentous build-up, it was a bitter disappointment. But in the same year Juan Antonio Samaranch, who, although a member of Maritimo, had supported Banyoles, was elected to the presidency of the International Olympic Committee. Pieper had another dream. With a Catalan at the top of the Olympic movement, surely Barcelona had an excellent chance of hosting the Games. And surely Banyoles had an excellent chance of staging Barcelona's Olympic regatta. Moving in Olympic circles at the magisterial though boycotted Moscow Games, Pieper floated his idea and stirred the water.

The Sting

On 6 November 1980 Spanish rowing took an abrupt turn at the main news-stand in Geneva, Switzerland. Two strangers with identical dark blue Adidas sports bags were browsing through the magazines. When they departed they were carrying each other's bag. One contained old newspapers; the other contained $2 million in $100 notes bearing non-consecutive numbers. Some hours later a man awoke in a remote wheatfield somewhere near Burgos, close to the main road from Madrid to San Sebastian. He found that he was tied to a tree. It was −7 degrees. He struggled to untie himself, and then realized that he could not stand up. He was drowsy and drugged. He crawled towards the road, but could not get himself up the bank to reach it. He was bitterly cold and cut his legs on the hard ground crawling back to the tree. After some time his family arrived in a car to collect him. He had no shoes and his feet were frost-bitten. He very nearly lost them both. In the car, he remembers, he thought he was dead, tracing his head with his finger, searching for the bullet hole which had killed him.

Forty-six days before this Pedro Abreu had been watching a French talk show on television in his house at Orio, a village in the Basque country, while his mother-in-law went out to feed the family dogs in the garage. When she opened the door she found fourteen or fifteen hooded and armed men from ETA, the Basque separatist organization. Abreu was taken to a farmhouse and incarcerated in a hole 2 metres square which had been dug under the floor. Negotiations for Abreu's ransom began. Letters were delivered to his wife or published in the correspondence columns of *Egin*, the newspaper which ETA used as a mailbox. Abreu marked the days on his prison wall with a pencil given to him with a crossword book. He was allowed one packet of cigarettes a day, a deck of cards and some detective stories. He saw no daylight. His gaolers and questioners were always hooded. The only real comfort was the food, as befits Basque cuisine. But for forty-six days Abreu was convinced his kidnappers would kill him.

The conditions of his release were that he should conduct no further social work or sporting activity in Spain. An educated man of considerable means, Abreu had been supporting disabled fishermen in Orio and had also paid for the land on which the rowing club now stands. When he recovered from his ordeal the chief benefactor of the Banyoles rowing centre told his friend Pieper, who had been working tirelessly on his behalf, 'Dick, I am fed up with Spanish rowing. I am getting out of here. I want to sell all the boats, everything I have.' He wished to take his Basque wife and his two children out of Spain. He stayed for a year, until Switzerland gave him permission to settle there. Several of Abreu's kidnappers were caught and punished. One terrorist was strongly linked to Basque rowing, being a relation of a prominent official in the Basque federation. The owner of the farmhouse was among them, having made a lot of money renting out his property to the terrorists. He was gaoled for less time than Abreu had spent in his hole. The ETA-appointed go-between, who at the time was the deputy mayor of San Sebastian, was arrested later for smuggling foreign currency into Spain.

Nilsen, who had been coaching the Italians on a part-time basis with the agreement of the Spanish, accepted a highly paid job as director of the Italian rowing centre at Piediluco. Banyoles almost slipped back to square one, though Pieper managed to save the boats and equipment, which Abreu had paid for, by persuading the Catalan government to buy them for half of what Abreu asked, a drop from 12 million pesetas to 6 million pesetas. Abreu gave the money to charity. As Pieper says, 'They stole his money and the rest of his material he gave away.' Pieper still works for the club for love, and has orchestrated its rebuilding for the 1992 Olympics. He still maintains the holiday apartment in Banyoles which he shared with Abreu back in the sixties in case he can persuade his friend to come and visit the Olympic regatta on their beloved Catalan lake. The ransom probably went straight from its Adidas bag into a Swiss bank vault.

The Cuban Connection

Cuban rowing has always been close to revolution. The first club was founded in Santiago de Cuba in 1889. Its president was Hermann Michaelson, known as 'Don German', a popular and wealthy president of the chamber of commerce, and a pianist who formed the

Sala Haydn to perform classical German music. He funded a kitchen for the people during the war of independence against Spain, and despite being consul for both Germany and Austro-Hungary, he was detained by the authorities. In 1896 the Spanish governor informed him that rowing was banned because it was suspected that the yachtsmen and fishermen who rowed in the club's boats were running food and arms to the rebels. In 1898 the Spanish lost the three-month Spanish-American war and Cuba became independent. Rowing started again in Santiago in 1901. Havana University produced a martyr in 1929 when Julio Antonio Mella, a founder of the Communist Party, was assassinated in Mexico City. He was a good swimmer, basketball player and oarsman who believed that sport builds character and develops qualities which lead to the creation of a better world.

Jose Antonio Echerarria, an architecture student from Varadero on the north coast, lost his life in Fidel Castro's cause. When he was a schoolboy he competed in a double scull with Orlando Lanza, a plumber employed on Echerarria's father's property. In 1948, although rowing was for the rich and the middle class, Varadero was searching for talent among the lower social orders, 'boys with height, intelligence, running, weight-lifting and discipline,' Lanza, one such recruit, says. When Echerarria went to Havana to study, Lanza carried on rowing and, in 1956, he went to the Olympics in Melbourne, supported by the proceeds of street collections which the rowers themselves had conducted. After that Lanza coached at Varadero for twenty-five years, claiming 252 champions among his pupils.

Regattas were popular with everyone in Cuba, drawing large crowds to the beaches and harbours and often receiving the patronage of presidents. The first regatta in Varadero was held in 1910 between the Varadero club and a six-oar from Halley, a club presumably named after the newly discovered comet. Varadero won the 1200-metre race by 3 feet in 7 minutes 24 seconds. The coast has miles of golden beaches and lush greenery facing a blue horizon which hides Florida, but no vestige of the old club now remains save pictures of its first boathouse in 1910, a sumptuous headquarters in a resort where the well-heeled of both Cuba and America used to play and relax at their holiday mansions. The second clubhouse, a huge wooden building acquired in 1925, fell apart. Lanza is happy to share the secret of one old Varadero legacy, a powerful rowers' punch made up from a can of condensed milk, four egg yolks, half a bottle of white rum added just before drinking, frappé ice, and a sprinkling of grated nutmeg. But now the champions are faded photos between old silverware at the town museum, which has a display devoted to its rowing past and the great heroes of Cuban sport: the boxer Eligio Sardinas, alias Kid Chocolate, the chess master Capablanca, the fencer Ramon Faut, and the baseball player Martin Dihigo.

While Castro's revolution against the dictator Fulgencio Batista was taking root, Pedro Abreu was studying physics, maths and engineering at Havana University. Born in Spain of Cuban parents, Abreu was brought up in Paris before the family returned to Havana before the Second World War. On his father's side he can trace his family back to late seventeenth-century Spain, and on his mother's to Columbus's discovery of Cuba. His grandmother was an expert on primates and built a zoo for them in Havana. In his student days three clubs were prominent in the city – the Biltmore, the Yacht and the Tennis. Like his uncles, Abreu rowed for Tennis. Havana having the worst bus service in the world, his main problem was getting to the club for twice-daily training at 6.30 a.m. and 6.30 p.m. Oarsmen often slept at the club because they could not get home. All the clubs had American college coaches during the summer; Tennis was coached by Tom Bolles from Harvard.

But matters more serious than rowing were afoot. Abreu was on the board of directors of the federation of university students (FEU), which had a long tradition of revolutionary activities. In 1952 a student was killed by Batista's police. Growing disgust led to riots, strikes, pamphleteering, bombings and sabotage. 'It was natural that we should pick up the flag of revolution,' Abreu says. 'We tried to organize through people's home towns, but were not very effective. It never really got off the ground. But we attacked the presidential palace and nearly killed Batista.' After the assassination attempt the students joined up with Castro's 26th of July movement. Abreu was never in the hills with Castro's guerrillas. 'You only graduated to the hills when you were too well known to the police to be of use in the city. It was a sort of notoriety,' he says. With the help of the Popular Socialist Party, which organized a general strike, Castro and the student revolutionaries brought Batista down in 1959. The

Argentinian Che Guevara became military governor of La Cabaña, the fortress gaol where many executions had taken place. Che appointed Abreu inspector of La Cabaña and sent him to Santiago de Cuba to investigate executions there. 'I may have saved a few lives,' he says. Soon, however, he was spending more and more time in New York on family investment business. In the uneasy revolutionary fervour he began to fear for his future, and after the disastrous Bay of Pigs invasion by exiles opposed to Castro in 1961, Abreu flew for the last time from the little-used airport at Varadero. He drifted into a self-imposed exile which eventually led him back to the country of his birth.

Castro himself was not an oarsman, but as president he showed a keen interest and continued the tradition of attending regattas, sometimes to award the Copa Cuba, which the dictator General Menocal first presented to Varadero in 1918. '26th July' was added to the cup's name in 1961. Varadero is now the location of the national training centre which comprises a shed full of boats, a basic dining room serving good wholesome food, and a dormitory. Equipment, some of it made in Cuba, is modern. After 1959 the rowing map changed completely. A new national rowing commission gave opportunities to anyone with talent, at least in theory, to try their hand. Thus club and recreational rowing died, but considerable success has been achieved by the new order in the Pan-American and Central Caribbean Games. Help in the form of coaches and visiting crews was received from the Czechs and the East Germans in the sixties and seventies, and several Cubans saw the inside of the Democratic Republic's sports institute at Leipzig. The first Pan-Am title was that of the quadruple sculls in 1975, and Cubans brought three golds home in 1979. Then, in 1991, they were hosts and won nine gold medals at The José Smith Cornas course near Havana, named after an oarsmen – killed by Batista's police. At the top the results are much better than those achieved by American coaches before the revolution but, like most other things thirty years after Castro's new dawn, rowing is poverty-stricken.

Cuban rowing has two lives, however. Many former Cuban rowers are in Florida, and much of the spirit of pre-revolution rowing is to be found at the sumptuous Miami Rowing Club which they founded.

Xochimilco, a Rower's Garden

The Iberian peninsula has certainly left an indelible mark on the Americas, but so far as rowing is concerned the influences came more from England and Northern Europe than from Spain or Portugal. On our tour we have already met Don German who brought rowing with a purpose to Cuba. In Mexico it was the English, closely followed by the Germans, who first took to the lakes for sport and eventually settled in Xochimilco, a magical place southeast of the mountain-edged bowl which holds Mexico City. The town is old, with narrow streets, crumbling churches and a huge flower market every morning. Its citizens rest under a massive *ahuehuete* tree which has seen many generations come and go. Xochimilco is set alongside a rowers' paradise comprising 500 kilometres of canals, all that is left of Lake Texcoco after centuries of landfill. This maze of waterways is a floating garden: lilac lilies cover the water for ten months of the year, eucalyptus and *huejotes* trees, unique to Xochimilco, line the banks, and farmers bring their flowers and vegetables to market in punts called *trajinera* (or *acalli* in Indian) which they pole along. Someone venturing out in a boat here for the first time could be completely lost in ten minutes as new vistas open round every bend and the lily carpet closes over the channel sliced by the boat. There are big channels and small canals. One has 2500 metres of straight water with room for five lanes; others are too narrow for anything but punts piled high with produce. The Viga canal runs 25 kilometres to the city, stopping just behind the Museum of Anthropology, short of its original terminus. It is no longer used by commercial traffic. Low bridges have severed it. For a long time Xochimilco and its canals have been the principal home of Mexican rowing. Since the Games of 1968 it has also boasted the first rowing course specifically built for an Olympic Games.

Businessmen, most of them British, in banking, insurance, oil or railways, introduced rowing to Mexico on Lake Chalco in about 1888. The site was conveniently close to the Santa Cruz line from Mexico City. The principal organizers were Tomas Lakeside Phillips, a wealthy entrepreneur, and the Rev. Thomas Dod Sherlock, a graduate of Merton College, Oxford, who became chaplain of Christ Church, Mexico, in 1885. Sir Spencer Same Young, the British minister, was also involved. The Lakeside Club was formed officially in 1891, using heavy American sailing boats for rowing. Sherlock donated the boathouse. Its neighbour which shared a birthdate, the Cosmopolitan Club of Mexico, was short-lived. Lakeside held a regatta at Ayotla in May of 1891, but activity also started at Peñén on Lake Texcoco because Chalco was drying up. On 8 December 1892 a regatta picnic was held at Mexicaltcingo on Texcoco which included a 'duck chase' and races in fours, sailing boats and tub pairs, and ended with 'five o'clock tea', games and dancing. Phillips introduced rowers to the Viga Canal and the ancient market town of Xochimilco. Sunday regattas were held there, facilitated by Phillips's financing of a tramway to Xochimilco in 1910. In 1912 an elegant prefabricated wooden boathouse brought from Canada was erected. At the same time the club changed its name to the British Boating Club (BBC). The hand-written incorporation document lists the ambassadors of Britain, the United States and the Tsar of All the Russias as founders, and Porfirio Diaz, Mexico's dictator-president, as patron. Revolution began against Diaz in 1911. He had industrialized Mexico and filled his own pockets by giving concessions to foreigners for almost everything. Brutal suppression of peasants, organized labour and political opposition followed, and long and bloody revolt came from several quarters, including Emeliano Zapata in the south. The BBC was occupied by his men in about 1914, a contemporary photograph showing the members enjoying pipes on their duckboards while guerrillas in sombreros and bandoleros pose behind them.

One source refers to a British versus German race in 1893, but the real foundation of German rowing in Mexico seems to have been in 1909 when a group of boys who had rowed along the Viga Canal formed themselves into the Sportclub Eureka at Xochimilco. A year later Phillips's tramway reached the town, and Eureka changed their name to the German Rowing Society. The founders' first boat came from Hamburg, paid for by the diplomat Baron Hartmann von Richthofen. Regattas against the British began straightaway, and in 1912 Admiral von Hintze attended as an embassy guest. In November of that year the German club won at a regatta at Vera Cruz. In 1913 Prince Adalbert von Preussen became their patron. British and Germans together set up the regatta association of Mexico. The canals became popular for pleasure rowing.

Then the First World War ended meetings between the two clubs until 1923. In 1924 the Club España was founded; in 1925 a crew from Kreuzers Berlin visited the German club; in 1926 systematic training began and the Germans won everything; in 1927 students came to row there. The Club Mexicana started in 1932, the same year as the Germans bought land for their headquarters. The German club, helped by its excellent restaurant, flourished until the German colony found themselves in conflict with the Mexican government when it declared war on Germany in the Second World War.

The picture up to 1939 was one of triangular rivalry between the British, German and Spanish clubs, with a few Mexicans thrown in. But from the time of Obregón's election as president in 1927 and the subsequent legitimization of the Revolutionary Party, nationalization followed, including of oil in 1938. Fortunes fluctuated according to economic and political developments. By this time most of the British in Mexico worked in oil, and their presence diminished, most going just before Mexico declared war on Germany. This caused a further exodus of foreign nationals and the expropriation of German property. But, unlike the Germans and the British, the Spanish were settlers, and so their influence became dominant in Mexican sport. The Club España at Xochimilco is an outpost of a larger establishment in Mexico City. It took up soccer in 1912 after the English introduced the game in 1900 through Pachuca Athletic Club. Women were allowed as members by 1915 when tennis was offered. By 1919 there was a casino and a building large enough to host balls and social gatherings. By 1922 there was a commercial academy to assist Spanish immigrants in finding work. In 1924–25 the club introduced rowing and hired Guillermo Müller to coach it. Its Xochimilco premises stand on a shaded promontory across a canal from the Olympic course, facing the velvety silence of the canals. It has a well-equipped boat shed full of kayaks, Canadian canoes and shells, looked after by José Luis Diaz, and a pool as well as club facilities. Its gardens and showers are spic and span. A hundred or so active rowers among its thousands of members include its former president, nonagenarian Rodrigo Llanos, who takes his boat out each Sunday.

While the Mexican club has long been abandoned, a sad roofless relic amidst beautiful tropical shrubs and trees which run wild in its garden, the German club has risen from its enforced shut-down in

1942 through a series of reincarnations. In 1946 Yucatan moved into the original premises, changed its name to Armonia, and merged with another German-inspired club called Antares in 1951. The name is now Antares; the cultural heritage is obvious as soon as one steps through the door. The large stucco lounge has a fireplace guarded by oars and a heavy metal chandelier. There are crests of German and Mexican clubs. Its lawn is neat, and there are signs of improvement amid the rundown atmosphere. But its premises are still owned by the government.

In the 1950s things generally began to improve. Hugo Enriquez was the first sculler to compete in the United States. 'In Philadelphia I was sculling left over right, while my boat was rigged for right over left. When someone told me I didn't know what the hell he was talking about.' At this time the Spanish and German clubs were strong, while the British were weak. Antares hired a trainer, as did the Spanish club. In 1955 the Pan-American Games regatta was held at Xochimilco. 'Guys who knew how to steer the bend had a boat length's advantage,' Enriquez says. There was the danger of being caught in the reeds. 'Guys like Jack Kelly came down and ran the Games. We all had a lot of fun.' The Spanish club had Giorgio Ballarin from Italy as coach, and they won twelve out of nineteen titles in the national championships. They also went to Cuba to race Varadero in the same year. In 1956 Mexico had its first win abroad, at Royal Canadian Henley.

Lakeside reverted to its old name in 1959, the year in which Antonio Enyedi joined. He arrived from Venezuela having learned to row in his native Zagreb and walked out of Yugoslavia during the war to join the British army in Italy. He encouraged them to add the liberation of Austrian rowing clubs to their tasks. Although the club had first refusal on the land on which its original colonial-style wooden prefab stood, nobody thought to buy it. In 1961 the government expropriated it and turned it into a school, and the old wooden building is no more. The club obtained premises in the twenty-four-bay boathouse at the Gustavo Diaz Orduz Olympic course, named after the president of the time. The Games of 1968 marked a major turning point in Mexican rowing. The new course, the first designed by Thomi Keller, was good, although the high altitude was a problem for athletes. It created new interest in Mexico. The presidential guard, the university and polytechnic and the navy all formed rowing clubs. The Olympics also brought together a band of able administrators and officials from whose experience the sport in the Americas has benefited immensely.

The course, however, suffered from under-use and lack of maintenance once the Olympics were over. It has become a victim of the perpetual problem of Xochimilco, which is that land of the former Lake Texcoco is prone to sink at the rate of 2.5 metres per year. When it was built it was below the level of the surrounding canals. In 1991 the canals had sunk to a lower level than the course, but the boathouses had sunk even farther, so that they are now below the level of the artificial lake. The problem is further complicated because this immense man-made pool sinks faster at its north end than at its south. It has been raised once since the Games, and will probably have to be raised again.

In the nineties there is an ambitious project to develop a nation-wide rowing programme guided by the national coach Oswaldo Borchi and the FISA development coach Ricardo Ibarra. One plan is to build training boats. Borchi and his wife Maggie, who is secretary of the Mexican federation, encourage development outside Mexico City. The Club Corona, for example, an old European rowing club at Tampico, the oil capital, is a wealthy sports club which is being urged to take to the oars again after abandoning them several years ago. There are two clubs on Lake Chapula, and two for students on the Gulf of Mexico at Villa Hermosa. There are several small clubs at the Pacific port of Mazátlan, which dates from Emperor Maximilian's time when machinery was imported there. In Mazátlan clubs come and go, composed of tall, strong fishermen who feed on the fruits of the ocean and enjoy a much better diet than the tortilla and chilli of inlanders. Fishermen are also stronger in the head, according to Borchi. They use coxed four-oar shells, having traditionally used four- or six-oar *feluccas*, fixed-seat boats with two men to a bench.

A Welter in the Delta

Argentina was colonized commercially by the British after the Treaty of Utrecht in 1713. A century later most of the trade and shipping in the united states of the Rio de la Plata (the northern part of

Argentina) was British-owned. From 1821 to 1824 more than a third of the thousand merchant ships entering Buenos Aires were British. A strong British colony developed and created its own entertainment while keeping much to itself. The British introduced horse-racing, rowing, boxing, cricket, football and tennis to Argentina, but did not figure conspicuously in the social life of Buenos Aires. In 1806 there was a Freemasons' lodge and the first game of cricket. In 1811 there were Commercial Rooms, and in 1826 a British Dramatic Society and an English Racing Club had taken root.

The first recorded rowing took place in about 1860 when races were organized by the Boating Society which had a mooring stage on the passenger dock at Buenos Aires. This came to an abrupt end on 3 August 1861 when 'the storm of Santa Rosa' wrecked the pier and smashed the boats. In 1866 *The Standard* reported that Tigre was crowded for a boat race which was cancelled because one participant was in mourning. There are no further references until 1870 when four Englishmen covered the 40 kilometres from Tigre, north of Buenos Aires, to the city's new port in 2 hours 50 minutes. Tigre was developing as an attractive weekend resort on the River Luján, where the well-to-do built second homes, and from where hundreds of miles of rivers and channels meander through the delta of the River Plate. The inaugural regatta of the British-organized River Luján Rowing Club took place at Tigre on 12 February 1871. Scratch crews raced between the *Emilia* and the *Suzanna*, ships moored a mile apart. Duck shooting in fours was included. The Buenos Aires Boat Club, which started life as the Buenos Aires Rowing Club with a boathouse at Barracas al Norte on the Riachuelo in the south of the city, organized the next Tigre regatta in 1873. The captain was the British consul, Ronald Bridgett. President Domingo Sarmiento was among the spectators with the British minister, Lionel Sackville West, who was chairman of the club. At the end of the year *The Standard* published a notice requesting anyone who had a copy of the rules of any boat club to lend them to the committee. Clearly they were feeling their way. They persisted, attracting almost the entire diplomatic corps and representatives of leading families to attend the 1874 regatta by special train. In 1875 there were visiting competitors from Montevideo, Uruguay. In 1882–83 they moved lock, stock and barrel to Tigre. By now they had reverted to their old name of Rowing Club – perhaps 'Boat

Club' had been a misprint – and they erected a three-storey building just across a tree-lined road from the River Tigre, a minute's walk from the terminus of the new electric railway to the centre of Buenos Aires. The building is L-shaped and its clocktower with weathervane and leaded windows would not look amiss on a backwater of the Loire or in the high street of a northern British town. Imposing french windows between double columns open onto a courtyard at the back. Circular crests above the columns show a sailing ship and the visor of a suit of armour. Inside are red tiled floors with white stone walls and high ceilings, and traditional dining furniture. Next door is a swimming pool, and across the courtyard are tennis courts and a long boathouse clad in bougainvillea and ivy over a workshop where craftsmen make and repair boats. Two rail tracks lead from the boathouse across the road and down a slipway: to go rowing in the delta, members simply have to step into their boats, which have been wheeled out by boatmen who place them in the water and prepare oars. There are racing shells, but also hundreds of lovingly maintained pleasure boats with folding riggers and sliding seats, many built on the Thames well before the Second World War.

Tigre holds many treasures, the Buenos Aires RC being modest compared with some. A short walk brings one to more narrow-gauge railway tracks and an astonishing sight behind the trees. The headquarters of the Italian Club at Tigre, built in 1928, is a replica of St Mark's Palace in Venice. In its entrance hall are murals by Enrico Albertazzi celebrating Amerigo Vespucci and St George slaying the dragon, and there is a stained-glass window depicting a Viking ship. The richly carpeted staircase has an ornately carved balustrade. The boathouse has a workshop where Pedro Luis Vicchiola makes sculling boats from wood and fashions plastic training boats out of an Empacher mould.

Facing the confluence of the Tigre and Luján rivers is a huge regency-style building set back from the water and guarded by two enormous palms. The Marina Club is accessible only by boat. The ground-floor committee room contains a piano as well as leather armchairs and a bookcase. A large terrace supported by arches fronts the first-floor dining room and ballroom. The former is austere, darkly panelled and bisected by a large glass cabinet containing dozens of trophies. Red tablecloths add colour. Photographs of Olympic heroes such as the club's coach Alberto Demiddi hang on the walls. The ballroom is also dark and red and heavily baronial. The second and third floors are half-timbered and the building is crowned by a cupola on pillars. Behind it is a gym, a pool, tennis courts, a children's playground and a barbecue area which has jetty access to a small channel. There are about 600 boats, and at the weekend they come and go as scullers depart for the delta and families venture forth for the backwoods. It is a spectacular place with a vista from its lawn as interesting as the view of it is compelling.

Opposite the Marina, across the River Luján is the Tigre Club, which was a breakaway of the old guard of Buenos Aires RC. It occupies a house built in 1856 to which it added a boathouse with a balcony. The club was launched in 1888 at a meeting in the schoolroom of the Scotch [*sic*] church and was for 'British subjects, North American citizens and their sons'. In 1891 two of six boats ordered from London were lost during the voyage, and two more were damaged. The club possessed two inrigger fours, two randans, two skiffs and ten half-rigged double sculls. Maintenance costs of $2400 against an income of $3600 from subscriptions gave a healthy surplus. There were eleven life members and just over 400 subscription members, including two ladies. The boatman was paid $50 per month, insurance of boats and property cost $178.60, and the collector's commission amounted to $95. This item perhaps indicates a common problem with rowing clubs – persuading members to pay up. Staff from the British and American legations were exempt from entrance fees, and Rule 13 (1920 version) said: 'Lady members cannot retain boats, introduce visitors, vote, or make use of the Club boats unaccompanied by one or more male members of the Club.' A hundred years later Tigre has about eighty members who enjoy a snug bar and play slosh, a mixture of billiards, snooker and pool, in an air-conditioned billiard room. The trophies in the office and the leather and rattan-furnished smoking room still effuse a British colonial life style. The magazines are a year old and the bookshelves house bound copies of the *Illustrated London News* for 1914–19 (1916 is missing), plus Roger Fulford's *Votes for Women* and yards of Sherlock Holmes and Hornblower novels. There is a sauna and a defunct pool, and a workshop behind the boat shed, which is crammed full, one of its gems being a 101-year-old triple sculler built by Tom Tagg and Son at Hampton, England, and a Messum boat from Richmond-on-Thames. There is not much sign of rowing activity, but Tigre shared the 1936 Olympic pair with Marina. In the 1970s Margaret and Rudolf Barloschki rowed across the delta to Montevideo in Uruguay, 200 kilometres as the crow flies, and a merchant navy officer, Richie Proven, did the same in 1988.

Argentina RC is housed in a mock-Tudor building betraying its origins as a breakaway from Tigre. Minus the graffiti on its front wall, it could snuggle down as a pub in a village in Buckinghamshire, England. A creeper-covered archway leads to a red and white tiled courtyard, a heavy-beamed dining room with white cloths looks through leaded windows to trees and river bank. By contrast the Swiss Club is a small modern place sporting the coats of arms of the cantons and has a bar run by two ladies of advancing years dispensing drinks as if they occupied centre stage in a soap opera. The Scandinavian Club is a large bungalow beside a creek encircled by an immaculately trimmed hedge. There is a small American club, and a large French one which straddles a road with tennis courts but has little evidence of racing boats. The Teutonia Club became war victims when their Tigre premises were requisitioned for a naval establishment, although the club continued to exist and now has premises deeper into the delta. There are others, including Club Náutico Hacoaj, which began life as Club Náutico Israelita in 1935, partly as a reply to anti-Jewish sentiments reaching Argentina from Europe. In 1936 the name Hacoaj was adopted when a club of that name was burned down by Nazi mobs in Vienna. The Argentine Rowing Association refused to admit the Jewish club, but their crews nevertheless competed in regattas and became Argentine champions in Rio Santiago in 1940. Hacoaj was accepted into the association in 1948, and in 1989 it had 10,000 members enjoying condominiums, football, tennis, basketball and bowls on sites facing each other across the River Tigre, and a pavilion set in a garden alongside the River Samiento. The club also has a large building in central Buenos Aires.

The first eight-oared race took place in 1899 between Tigre and Teutonia. Tigre won by two and a half lengths. Regattas became popular and fashionable, but they no longer take place on the Luján. They have been chased away by the motorboats to the nearby Regulador canal, which has a 2000-metre six-lane course but lacks the cafés, promenade and club terraces of the river. From the old regatta finish where Marina faces the former premises of the Teutonia and the present hacienda-style building of the Club de Regatas Hispano Argentina the river passes the naval museum (where homage is paid to rowing as well as the victims of the 1980s Malvinas/Falklands war with Britain) to the old Tigre Hotel with its splendid covered porch leading from river steps to the casino. Tigre is the pleasure port of the delta, a haven from the bustle of the city, a lung for relaxation beneath jacarandas and planes, *lapacho* and eucalyptus. Rowers used to come here for their holidays, pulling off for fourteen days of camping and cooking on beaches, rowing at night if it was too hot during the day. Many of the islands are occupied by small farmers and weekenders, and the lone sculler passes chalets and jetties and reedbeds in the brown water of the side canals, expecting to meet Ratty and Mole at every turn. Grocery boats ply their produce along the main rivers, and ferries and pleasure cruisers whip up a wash which keeps one's wits about one. As everywhere, messing about in rowing boats is threatened by internal combustion and diesel engines. Occasionally too – about once a generation – Tigre is flooded by the Sudestada, a southeast wind which blows at 100 miles per hour and bottles up the delta water, stopping the outgoing tide until the next one comes in. This destroyed rowing in the city in 1861 and covered the pavements, gardens, tennis courts and backyards of Tigre with a few inches of soft brown mud in 1989.

Mingo Perez and Miguel Gitto make the full range of competition boats from Empacher moulds in a back-street shed and export them to Uruguay, Central America and Mexico. Affording good boats is an acute problem in Latin America, where the distances are vast and the market too small to make prices attractive for manufacturers across the oceans.

Tigre is the most popular rowing centre in Argentina, but there are twenty-five clubs in other places, notably Rosario where there is one started by the English; Mar del Plata on the Atlantic coast; and the 17,000-member Club Mendoza de Regatas near the Andes. In 1893 the Union de Regatas was formed as a governing body by Buenos Aires RC, Tigre and Teutonia. It changed its name to Asociacion Argentina de Remeros Aficionados in 1917.

Continental Drift

Paddling and rowing can be traced back to 1000 BC around the Caribbean and the Pacific coast of South America. But in the era of modern rowing, the Latin world has been insular, its constituent parts isolated from one another and a long way from the mainstreams of Europe and North America. There are signs that the international federation's development programme is changing that by providing technical assistance and encouraging self-help in Central and South America. The countries we have visited – Argentina, Cuba and Mexico – are where most activity is to be found, but they are not the only ones. Brazil is also in the big South American league, and we will complete our Cook's Tour of South America with a visit there, after peeking at the smaller fry.

In Uruguay, for example, Montevideo Rowing Club was founded in 1874, and a survey of British activity in South America in 1878 records that an annual regatta took place on 1 May with Buenos Aires. It also says that there was nothing much happening in Peru at that time, but the Chorrillos Club of Rowing and Shooting was in existence in 1873 and the Club de Regatas Lima in 1875. The latter regards itself as the 'most beautiful rowing club in the South Pacific' and had 18,000 members in 1990. Montevideo was clearly British-influenced, being another battle ground for the commercial interests of European nations. Sir Eugene Millington-Drake, the diplomat whom we met in Russia some time ago, became the grand old man of Uruguayan rowing. Slow development reached a total of thirteen clubs by 1966.

Peru's early rowing was based on challenges between pilot boats and navy crews. Its modern rowing is unusual in that both original clubs have no English influence, all the founders being Peruvian. The only older clubs in South America are Buenos Aires and Montevideo, both of which wrote their rules in English and had English founders. Peru began to compete with Chile in about 1937 and has participated in the South American championships since their inception in 1948. There are seven clubs, one of which, the Italian, is restricted to people of Italian birth or descent, and in a country without rivers and a harsh coastline almost all rowing takes place in Callao, the ocean harbour of Lima. The exception is a 5000-metre irrigation lake to the north of the capital which has ideal conditions, and rowers are allowed limited use, sharing the lake with the government's shrimp-spawning project.

Chile's rowing is also in the harbour. John Trevena, an Englishman who rowed there in the thirties, remembers Valparaíso as resembling Dover with breakwaters projecting into the sea to provide sheltered water. 'It was wonderful to go out at 6 a.m. when it was completely calm and everyone else was asleep, and then go for a huge breakfast in a town café before going to work,' he says. Valparaíso had four clubs in those days, one each for British, Chileans, Germans and Italians. Boats were robust and had greased fixed seats for beginners. There were two regattas each year.

Lake Amatitlán, 30 kilometres from Guatemala City, was the scene of Guatemala's introduction to modern rowing in 1939 when President Ubico brought boats from the United States. Students returning from Europe and America were the main instigators, plus the military academy. There is now a national centre there, and most of the national team, together with much of the funding, comes from the armed forces. There are five centres, three at altitude and two using the ocean. Coaches have been brought in from Argentina. Guatemala is another example of the benefits to be gained from the international federation's encouragement of participation in regional events and development camps. Paraguay, Chile and Puerto Rico send crews to regional championships and Panama and Venezuela have rowing federations.

The Power behind Brazilian Soccer

Brazil has many traditional oar- and sail-powered river and coastal boats, models of which are on show at the maritime museum in Rio de Janeiro. One way of rowing in Porto Alegre is to sit down and face the back but cross the oar handles over so that the left hand pulls stroke side and the right hand pulls bow side. True to form, rowing as recreation and sport seems to have come from the Europeans – but not from the Portuguese who opened up its territory.

The French, British and Italians raced each other at Caju Santa Chitovás in Rio de Janeiro in 1840, watched by the Emperor Pedro II. Clubs were supposedly established on Niteroi, an island in the

Bay of Guanabara, and there are three clubs there today with Indian names – Icaraí, Flumineuse and Gragoatá. But the earliest substantive records identify the Guaiba club at Porto Alegre in 1888 and the Botafogo (Spitfire) in Rio de Janeiro in 1892. Rowing was the first sport to be established in Brazil and has remained the strongest amateur sport into the 1990s. The federation contains nearly ninety clubs from all regions. The largest clubs have tens of thousands of members, Vasco da Gama claiming 150,000. Most are multi-sport, and many run professional soccer teams, which accounts for their considerable wealth. The Flamengo, for example, occupies a site on Lake Rodrigo de Freitas in Rio, five blocks from Ipanema beach and practically under the outstretched arm of Christ the Redeemer, the huge statue which rises from the mist on Mount Corcovado. The club shares the lake with the boathouses of Vasco da Gama and Botafogo, and there is a 2000-metre course which finishes at Flamengo's own slipway and grandstand. The boathouse is large and well equipped, the weights room busy, and the coach constantly available. Behind the stand is a large complex of tennis courts, restaurants and lounges, a gymnasium and Flamengo's soccer stadium. These clubs relocated from their original sites at the beautiful bay of Santa Luzaia when road construction cut them off from the water.

In the south at Porto Alegre, Henrique Lichte, the historian of Brazilian rowing, tends the gardens on the Pavão Island rowing base of Gêmio Náutico União. It was founded as RV Freundschaft in 1906 in an area where German influence is marked. The hundred or so rowing members occupy a promontory where barbecue tables under trees view cranes and warehouses on one bank and woods on the other. An old cannon faces the docklands, enflamed at nightfall by copper footlights of the setting sun. A stunning blue pool amid trees is in the centre of this haven, which has 32 kilometres of smooth Guaiba water on which to row. Three other rowing clubs are on the city shore, Vasco da Gama (Porto Alegre), Gêmio Football, and Guaiba, and there is a 2000-metre course with a stand which runs past them. União has a workshop with modern machinery and a superb boat shed with access to both shores of its island. The restaurant shows paintings of the club's four former clubhouses, traditional structures of the Edwardian form which grew larger as the club grew more portly. The ergometer room has old-fashioned machines, but the tank has a panoramic view of the river. The club has two ferries for access from a quay at a derelict dock; there are two campuses in the city for the other sporting pleasures of the 50,000 family members. In 1989 this was the base for a FISA-run boatbuilding course. Klaus Filter from East Germany, assisted by Oscar Lowe from West Germany, attracted twenty-five boatmen from Brazil, Argentina, Venezuela and Uruguay and spent a month showing them how use a mould. The União staff make boats from cedar obtained from the north of Brazil.

Manaus, capital of the Amazon, has four clubs. There are five, most of them old and traditional, in the northern state of Pará. There are three in Rio Grande do Norte and three in Recife, capital of Pernambuco. São Paulo has eight, and a new 2000-metre course at the university. The Brazilian season lasts from May to December. The federation started in 1897, founded by an idealist from Botafogo called Louiz Caldas, with the help of Comandante Midosi, a marine officer.

Sport in Brazil has been financed by a state lottery since 1971 from which rowing clubs have benefited considerably. During the reign of the sports-loving General Emilio Medici this scheme worked well. But in 1974 General Geysel took over and in 1980 General João Figueiredo was elected. Distribution of the sports lottery was moved from the National Council of Sports to the Ministry of Education, and the proceeds shrank. The new democratic government gave it to the social affairs department.

A Draught of Port

This tour ends with a return to the Iberian peninsula, to Portugal, which shares its language with Brazil. The Portuguese became great seafarers and empire builders, but their rowing culture comes once more from England, rather than from their close neighbours and former antagonists in Spain. Portugal's import came from the heart of the English Orthodox, from Eton College via the Warre family, and from companies engaged in the port wine trade in which the two countries have a long relationship. The River Douro saw two English-owned racing boats before 1866, a ship's gig converted to an inrigged four belonging to Henry Hadrill and William Tait's outrigger double, the latter built on the Thames. The Oporto British

RC was founded in the same year at a gathering at the home of Edward Silva of Silva and Cozens, and an obsession with rowing among the British port families was born which lasted until the club closed in 1955. The club's second meeting dropped 'British' from its title, and so from the beginning it had a considerable percentage of Portuguese members. The first captain was E. Amyas Warre of Silva and Cozens, a relation of Eton's Dr Warre. There were by then two clubs in Lisbon, but they refused to race Oporto. A Lisbonian wrote that it was 'very difficult to get fellows to row against you, for they say Lisbon is sure to be drubbed there being too much of the muff in their competition.' In 1884 Lisbon did race and were beaten. The Oporto club became the Club Naval Portuense in 1879 when King Luiz became president. But before the turn of the century it became a British club again, changing its name to Oporto Boat Club.

At Oporto river picnics became popular, the whole club and most of the British colony embarking in barges towed by a tug to Quinta-das Carvalheiras for races and an ample lunch under the cool of the trees. On the occasion of the Entre-os-Rios picnic boatmen, supervised by the Oporto BC's boathouse keeper Chico, who is described as having waxed moustachios to rival any regimental sergeant major's, rowed the boats to the starting point the night before, and the members spent a nine-hour day drifting back home with the stream, with stopovers to cool off with a glass of vino verde. In 1922 the secretary was Max Graham, an Oxford Blue who installed some kind of tank in his garage for preliminary training and wrote a comprehensive club rowing manual which was published in 1925. Many of the boats were bought second-hand from Eton, and the regatta programmes of the thirties promoted the lore of Gilbert Bourne, the best advocate of orthodoxy as learned at Eton. Attempts were made to revive the club's fortunes after the Second World War, but it suffered from dwindling numbers and eventually died.

Clubs spread in the early part of the twentieth century, the royal family playing a part in Lisbon. A federation was formed in 1920 and Portugal joined the international federation in 1922. In 1948 a Portuguese crew was seen at the Olympics for the first time. Rowing reached Luanda and Lobito in Angola through Portuguese colonists. The long colonial wars in the Congo and Angola severely hindered sport because of the military draft which interrupted training, but since Portugal's withdrawal from Africa and democratization at home there has been an increased presence and improved performance, the latter due in large measure to support from FISA's coaching development programme. It has certainly made more impact than the old Oporto Boat Club. The latter represented a bygone age and a bygone influence. As the Portuguese content themselves with being modern Europeans, we will hop the Atlantic again, this time for the north, where Americans gave an accent all of their own to the art and science of pulling.

20

COAST-TO-COAST AMERICA

PROFESSIONAL oarsmen played a key part in rowing's development in North America, just as they did in the Old Country. For twenty years after the Civil War, which ended in 1865, scullers and crew oarsmen were prominent when few other sports had spawned heroes. Baseball, football, tennis, golf, lacrosse and basketball were unknown. In Boston and New York many were the sons of Irish immigrants, while in the third East Coast centre, the Maritime Provinces of Canada centred on Halifax, Nova Scotia, and St John, New Brunswick, Scots were well represented. Popularity stemmed from a combination of causes. The industrial revolution in the United States rapidly moved the Frontier westwards, particularly after the Civil War, and provided the rail-borne means for the new city dwellers to make use of their leisure time. Commercialism and gambling fanned activity. The last two were also the cause of professional rowing's early decline in America: fraudsters and con-men were on the bank and sometimes in the boats, and their activities brought suspicion on the straight and honourable as well. There were colourful occasions, such as the great match between the Canadian ace of the sliding seat Ned Hanlan and the Union Springs carpenter Charles Courtney in 1879, sponsored by Rochester Hop Bitters (a fraudulent patent medicine). On the morning of the 5-mile, round-the-stake race on Lake Chautauqua for a purse of $6000, Courtney's boat was found sawn in half. He refused to use a borrowed boat, Hanlan rowed over, and the promoter sequestered the purse on the grounds that there had been no race. There were tragedies too, like the rail crash which killed Patsy Reagan on his way home from losing to Mike Davis in a race promoted by the Old Colony Railroad at Silver Lake, which was suspected of being fixed. Nineteen others died and 190 were injured.

Amateur club rowing and college rowing gained great popularity at the same time as professional rowing. But these strands developed separately, the amateurs distancing themselves from the whiff of corruption which surrounded professional activities. When professional rowing went into decline, a decline partly caused by the suspicion of cheating, which frightened off both backers and punters, its demise left rowing with a different evolution from other American sports. Rowing was freer from commercial pressures and able to champion and maintain a unique version of the amateur athlete. At the same time, the get-up-and-go egalitarian society did not allow British-style gradations of occupation to complicate its definition of the amateur. And the benefits of professionalism were not all thrown out with its detritus: many of the better-known professionals such as Courtney, Ten Eyck and Ellis Ward, the latter from a huge family of Hudson River oarsmen, moved into colleges to coach (see chapter 14). In 1867 there were forty-eight races and regattas recorded, and such escapades as pulling two passengers 33 miles round Manhattan Island. The *Oarsman's Manual* listed 237 clubs in 1870, boasting 1676 boats and more than 11,000 oarsmen between them. Their activities, according to Thomas Mendenhall's *A Short History of American Rowing*, were the 'herald of mass entertainment to come'.

Charles A. Peverelly recorded the early developments in America in his *American Pastimes*. The first boat to be fitted with outriggers, a 3-inch extension from the gunwale, was the Carleton crew's *Experiment* at Saint John. The first boat designed and built for racing had the same name and was made by James MacKay at Williamsburg, Long Island, and was fitted with MacKay's iron outriggers, according to Peverelly. But there are rival claims for the *Young Neptune* built by another McKay in Saint John. The earliest recorded race was in 1811 between the Long Island boat *Invincible* and the Manhattan boat *Knickerbocker*. These were derived from the four-oared lapstrake Whitehall ferries which plied New York harbour. The most notable early race was in 1825 between the *American Star*, built by John and William Chambers, who also made the *Invincible*, and the gig *Sudden Death* from the British frigate *Hussar*. The race was from Bedloe's Island to Hoboken and back across the Hudson to the Battery. *American Star* won and was presented to General Lafayette of France, who sent it to Le Havre. In 1971 it was photographed at Lafayette's château, Le Grange. In

1835 *Goddess of Liberty* beat *Devil's Darning Needle* at St Mary's, Georgia. The first regatta was held in St John in about 1836, four-oared pilot gigs, skiffs and double and single sculls being in evidence. By 1844 this burgeoning fixture offered events for eight- and six-oared gigs, whaleboats, wherries, punts and Indian canoes. Harvard began rowing in 1844 in an eight-oared second-hand boat which the class of 1846 named *Oneida*, but Yale were there a year earlier in a second-hand Whitehall which they christened *Pioneer*. In 1845 the *Centipede* was acquired by Yale students, a 42-foot dugout hollowed from a single log cut on the banks of the Susquehanna near Binghamton, New York. Its beam was 2 feet and it was an eight-oar. Harvard and Yale began racing each other in 1852 on Lake Winnepesaukee, thus pioneering intercollegiate rowing and sport. According to Mendenhall, this fixture unwittingly led to a phenomenon unique to the United States: 'In no other country have institutions of higher education had their energies so diverted, their principles so perverted by their evolution into becoming the preparer and providers of entertainment for the society at large.' Mendenhall asserts that Harvard and Yale were typical in this respect, the 1852 race being inspired by commercial interests.

In 1858 Harvard had a six-oar built for them by the St John crew of New Brunswick. It had a yoke in the bow with which to steer, long outriggers and fixed seats, according to Charles W. Elliot, one of the crew, in a letter to his fiancée. Her captain, Benjamin Crowninshield, bought six red silk handkerchiefs for use as head-bands, and that is how Harvard adopted crimson as their colour. So the type of coxless boat which surprised the Europeans in Paris in 1867 (see chapter 15) had been afloat in America for a long time. Harvard and Yale were also pioneers of indoor rowing. The first rowing machines had weights attached to cords and handles, designed for a thousand daily strokes. In 1872–73 Harvard intro-duced a hydraulic machine which gave a semblance of release and recovery. In 1887 Yale moored an old barge in an indoor pool. Harvard's Newell boathouse eventually had a tank equipped with propellors to keep the water moving.

Clubs and regattas spread on a regional basis. The Castle Garden Amateur Boat Clubs Association was founded in 1834 for activity in New York harbour, where the demands of pilot companies pro-duced very fit and fast crews to reach approaching vessels first to secure the pilotage contract. A similar organization existed on the Hudson, and the Schuylkill Navy at Philadelphia was founded in 1858. Detroit Boat Club of 1839 is the oldest survivor, but Peverelly claims that the oldest club was Atalanta in New York, dating from 1848. He rowed for it and was its president in 1852-53. Atalanta was in the Harlem River Association with many other colourfully named clubs such as Nassau, Nonpareil, First Bohemian and Second Bohemian Palisades. There was also the Passaic Amateur RA with a 1½-mile straight five-lane course at Newark, New Jersey. By 1873 there were seventy-four clubs in New York, and rowing in twenty-five states. Industrialization was eventually to drive most of the Harlem River clubs away, but with the damming of the Charles River to create a basin in 1910, the rowing lease in Boston was restored and ensured. Racing changed too, for the clubs' adoption of eights in the 1880s at the expense of smaller boats forced the abandonment of the turn in favour of straight courses or 'straight-aways'. In the college domain the championship at Poughkeepsie attracted thirteen crews abreast in 1875 and 25,000 spectators, the fortunate among them aboard observation trains and yachts, the rest on the bluffs with a view of distant matchsticks.

By the turn of the century professionalism was all but dead except for the world championship, which was to continue well into the twentieth century. The legacy it gave to American rowing, though, was coaching and watermanship. 'A single,' Mendenhall says, 'where the variables are reduced to the boat, the rig, the conditions and the individual oarsman, has always offered the clearest path to effective, powerful and successful rowing.' He quotes a professional describing his task: 'It takes years of patient study and hard work and blade action to attain firm blade "footing" in the water; and until this is secured, no amount of sheer strength will command good speed.' Club rowing went into decline too, partly the victim of its separation from the college programmes. Whereas in England there were usually clubs close to the colleges so that the keen oarsman could continue rowing from school through university to club at several levels of competence, this was rare to impossible in the United States. Also, the college sports programmes, although voluntary, are organized in the same way as the sports which have professional careers open to their graduates. Although students from different classes or years of study can combine, no graduate students are allowed in representative American college sport, which leaves graduates who continue in full-time study nowhere to row. In Britain the contrary is the case: representative sport is open to anyone who is a full-time student before or after taking his or her first degree. In the 1980s, however, there has been a significant expansion in the number of clubs in the United States, and some of the barriers are being broken down. Even in centres with a long tradition of activity, such as Philadelphia and Boston, non-college rowing has been difficult unless one has the means or the connections to row at, say, Vesper in Philadelphia or Union or Riverside in Boston. Not until the foundation of Harbour Boat Club in the 1980s has it been possible for a novice to walk off the street and go rowing in Boston, the breeding ground of great crews and thousand upon thousand of Harvard, MIT, Northeastern and Boston University college oarsmen.

British North America

'Ned Hanlan must be pronounced the Shakespeare, the Napoleon, the Michael Angelo [*sic*], the Bismarck of the Oarsmen. However, he should wash his face before starting a race,' suggested the *Buffalo Courier* after watching the master of the slide against Charles Courtney in 1880. Hanlan was professional champion of Canada, America and England before he won the world title by beating the Australian Ed Trickett on the Thames in London on 15 November 1880. He lost the title to another Australian, Bill Beach, on 16 August 1884 on the Parramatta River in New South Wales and never recovered it in four attempts, two of them against Beach. But Hanlan did for Canada what Trickett had done for Australia: he gave another distant extension of Britain its first world champion. Hanlan was born of Irish parents who squatted on Mugg's Landing on an island in Lake Ontario just offshore from Toronto. John Hanlan was a fisherman who eventually bought a hotel, and the young Ned had a boat as his servant, playmate and means of exploration. When he was five he had a 5-centimetre-thick plank with tapered ends, a fitted seat and outriggers. Born in 1855, he began to compete in 1873 and defeated some well-known scullers in his first year of amateur competition. It was also the year in which the reigning American professional champion, the Nova Scotian George Brown, rowed his last race. In 1874 Hanlan defeated T. Loudon in the Championship of Canada. Loudon had an English boat called *The Duke of Beaufort* which he bought from a sculler called Beasley who was touring Canada; it was an improvement on the *Cigarette*, sculled by Dick Tinning, which was reputed to be the first modern single in Canada. Hanlan purchased *The Duke of Beaufort* and made a spectacularly successful marriage with the sliding seat at a time when sculling and rowing were a runaway first in the affections of sports fans in his vast and diverse country. He also became a great showman who entertained as much as he infuriated the fans.

As in the former coastal British colonies to the south and those on the east coast of Australia, Canadian rowing began with ships' boats and whalers. The Atlantic coast and the Arctic were Canada's first frontier. The first recorded competition was in 1816 in St John's Harbour, Newfoundland. Two years later the 'pond' or Quidi Vidi Lake became the venue for regattas. The garrison and the Royal Navy started competition in Halifax, Nova Scotia, and in 1827 the *Nova Scotian* reported that 'rowing is now permanently incorporated into the frame of our society'. Saint John, New Brunswick, was another centre of enterprise, as Wellington C. Green remembered from his boyhood at the end of the nineteenth century:

Back in the old days the St John fishermen built a boat called a gasperosque [phonetic], built with a bottom board, not a keel. Those boats were built for handling in fast water, and those men made their living rowing. And fast water to row against. They had to know how to handle their oars, and nowhere else in the world do you see oars handled the same as they're handled here, by the old Saint John fishermen, their style of rowing. When I was a small boy with my father when the men-of-war came in, they didn't come to the dock, they anchored out in the stream. There was an English, and a French, and a German, and an American man-of-war in the harbour. They were going to have boat races, so some of the fishermen went out and asked them to give them one of their boats to row in, and they gave them the boat off the English man-of-war. They put it overboard, and they threw the ash oars back on the deck, said they didn't want them, and of course the crew on the man-of-war laughed at them, not using ash oars. They came to Indian Town and they got some 12-foot oars they used up here. Then I think it was Joe Stackhouse who rigged the boat. Joe Stackhouse was a first-class carpenter and contractor. He raised the seats up 4 inches . . . In those boats, the man-of-war boats, the seats were low, and they pulled out from the shoulders. Our seats here in our boats were always rigged up. They were about 4 or 5 inches below the gunwales, so when you lulled, you pulled out from your hips. Well, they started out in the race, and the Saint John fellows came in way ahead, the English crew next. I've heard that afterwards the commander of the man-of-war sent for Joe Stackhouse and asked him why he did those things, why they raised the seats and why they wouldn't use the ash oars. I think Joe got a letter from them saying they'd improved their efficiency fifty per cent.

By 1840 there were inter-provincial races, and the sport spread eastwards along the St Lawrence River and among the French- as well as the English-speakers. Reports appeared in Toronto in 1840, Montreal and Brockville in 1844, and Coburg in 1846. Toronto, capital of the very English province of Ontario and situated amid an abundance of lakes and waterways, was the place where rowing took root as a popular national sport. A club founded in 1848 was the ancestor of both Toronto and Argonaut rowing clubs. By this time competition with Americans had also begun. An eight-oar from St John, New Brunswick, beat an American crew at Boston in 1855 and was called the 'Superior'. The crew took $2000 home. In 1858 the Toronto Shakespeare Club challenged the claim of the Metropolitan Boat Club of Chicago to be the champions of the Great Lakes. The Canadians went to Detroit with a nine-year-old cox, Richard Tinning, to race 5 miles for $5000. The Americans objected to the light cox so the Canadians took an additional passenger on board and won. The cox was probably the Dick Tinning who became amateur sculling champion in the *Cigarette* in 1869.

Canada also achieved crew dominance with the Saint John, New Brunswick, four of George Price, Sam Hutton, Elizah Ross and stroke Robert Fulton at the Paris regatta of 1867 (see chapter 15). In 1868 James Renforth, the English world professional champion, brought a crew from the Tyne to race the Paris crew at Lachine on the St Lawrence, near Montreal. Jimmy Taylor, brother of Matt, the builder of the first keel-less eight, was one of the oarsmen, and he was said to have introduced coxless boats to the Tyne after the example of the Paris crew; indeed, it is claimed that he was the first Englishman to row in a boat and steer it at the same time. The Tynesiders beat the Paris crew at Lachine in bad conditions, and Renforth brought another crew to New Brunswick in the following year. During that race, which took place on the Kennebecasis River

and was won by the Paris crew, Renforth died. The exact cause of
his expiry was never determined, and the Tynesider was mourned
on both sides of the Atlantic. A town in New Brunswick was named
after him, and his funeral practically brought Newcastle-on-Tyne to
a standstill. It was these two crews who provided the most intense
laboratory for testing coxless boats and notions of sliding. The Paris
four were defeated in 1876 by the Fishermen's Crew of Halifax at
the World's Aquatic Carnival in Philadelphia. The Fishermen beat
an English crew in the final over 3 miles in 17 minutes 58 seconds,
but the judge for some reason awarded the English first place. Newspapers were indignant and the English refused to accept the stake,
which still languished in a Philadelphia bank in 1934.

The Canadian Association of Amateur Oarsmen (CAAO), forerunner of the Canadian Amateur Rowing Association, was founded
in 1880, reflecting growing popularity among amateurs and growing
suspicion of professionals. The Australian Bill Beach wrestled the
professional title off Hanlan in 1884 and it remained in Australian
hands until the Canadian Jake Gaudaur won it against James Stan-
bury in 1896. George Towns took it back to Newcastle, New South
Wales, from Gaudaur in 1901, and that was the end of Canada's
professional prowess until Bob Pearce beat the Englishman Ted
Phelps in Toronto in 1933. After he retired at forty-two, Hanlan
coached Ottawa RC and the University of Toronto, and, between
helping his wife Margaret with their six daughters and two sons, he
tried his hand at politics. He represented his island on the Toronto
city council and turned out to be a champion of the disadvantaged
and an outspoken thorn in the side of the complacent. He supported
public works and decent minimum wages for council employees; he
lost his seat in 1900. For eight more years he chewed the fat with
rowers on the waterfront, dying of pneumonia in 1908. Ten thousand paid their respects at his lying-in at St Andrew's Presbyterian
Church, and 155 carriages joined the civic cortege to his burial
service at Necropolis.

Bob Pearce was Australian by birth and won the Olympic title in
1928 and again in 1932, both times under the Australian flag
although he was living in Canada by 1932. Having set out as an
Australian amateur whom the English Henley classified as professional under the manual-labour definition, he became an amateur
in Henley's eyes when his occupation changed from carpenter to

salesman. He won the Diamond Sculls in 1931 representing Leander BC of Hamilton, Ontario. He turned professional after the 1932 Games.

On the amateur side, two men born on the same day needled each other to the top of the Canadian tree. One was Joe Wright Jr, the other Jack Guest. Both were coached by 'Mr Joe' Wright Sr, an all-rounder who was Canadian amateur wrestling champion and heavyweight boxing champion as well as rowing coach at the University of Pennsylvania from 1916 to 1926. He coached his son for the English Henley's Diamonds in 1927. Wright Jr hit the booms in the final when he had a slight lead over R. T. Lee of Worcester College. Next year Guest, also coached by Wright Sr, entered as well. The two met in the second round. Guest hit the piles on his ninth stroke, Wright Jr waited for him, and eventually beat him by half a length. Wright then overturned the previous year's verdict by beating Lee in the final. Both Canadians went on to the Olympics in Amsterdam with Mr Joe, winning the gold medal in the double sculls. Wright Jr was also fifth in the single sculls. In 1929 both entered the Diamonds again, and Wright Jr caught Guest at the line to win their heat by half a length. He lost the final to Gunther of Holland. Guest went home and switched from Argonauts to the Don RC and the coaching of a professional from Henley-on-Thames, Harry Arlett. In 1930 Wright Jr beat the 1924 Olympic champion Jack Beresford in a heat of the Diamonds but lost to the German G. Boetzelen, who in turn lost the final to Guest.

Amateur rowing spread throughout Canada, led by the migrating members of the Argonaut club of Toronto and their offshoot in Winnipeg. The great size of the country meant that for many years regional regatta associations and occasional cross-border links with the United States held more sway than the national body. Argonaut and Winnipeg led several assaults on Henley in England, sometimes encountering emergencies like the sudden stop of the Liverpool-to-London train which was carrying the Winnipeg four and their boat in 1904. The boat was on a flat wagon and had been set on fire by sparks from the engine. Clasper repaired it while the crew visited the Spencer Arms, Tom Sullivan's pub at Putney. They lost the final of the Stewards' to Third Trinity. Lou Scholes of Toronto won the Diamond Sculls after beating the holder, the Australian F. S. Kelly, in the semifinal. Between 1880 and 1900 clubs became established on the West Coast in Vancouver and Victoria, and amateurs spread to the Maritimes. A regatta called Canadian Henley was founded by the CAAO in St Catharine's in the 1880s, later acquiring royal patronage and becoming one of the largest annual meets in North America.

Only Newfoundland kept its distance. It stayed out of the Dominion of Canada until 1948, and stuck to its traditional rowing in coxed sixes with fixed seats on Quidi Vidi Lake. The regatta there has been annual since 1826. The course is 1⅗ miles, and is open to all-comers, from clubs to groups from any occupation or company. The first race for women was held in 1855. In 1866 the Placentia Giants put themselves into the history books by carrying their boat on foot for nearly 60 miles from their village to win the grand challenge race before shouldering the boat home again. The boats were traditional gigs and whaleboats until the 1890s, when lighter shells were constructed adapted from whaleboat lines. Newfoundland rowers did not see modern shells until 1969.

If the 1867 Paris crew personifies the Canadian professional pinnacle, then the University of British Columbia did the same for amateur crew rowing almost a hundred years later. Coached by Frank Read, a hotelier at Vancouver RC, three of them were novices a few months before they won the Olympic title in coxless fours in 1956, a feat their coach described as 'the most phenomenal effort ever made in international athletic competition. At least I don't know of any parallel.' They were lucky to have got to Lake Wendouree in the first place, because they were spares for Read's eight. The latter took silver at the same Games behind the Americans, having first made Canadian headlines by crushing the Leningrad crew Krasnoe Znamia in the semifinal of the Grand at Henley, England. They lost to the University of Pennsylvania in the final but came home to a heroes' welcome, having shifted the centre of gravity of Canadian rowing from Toronto to the West Coast. The eight were a combination from club and university whom Read trained at Vancouver RC, a club established by railway engineers who brought the Canadian Pacific to the Coal Harbour anchorage on the waterfront of the city which they made possible. The squad of sixteen lived at the club, rowed from five to 6.30 every morning, took a second outing of the same duration in the evening after working on construction sites, and went to bed at nine. At weekends they undertook 35-mile rows, and their training on the lumpy water of the Coal Harbour, where the Pococks had first set up shop and where driftwood and junk joined small boats and shipping, necessitated keeping their blades feathered until a split second before taking the next stroke. This became the Read characteristic, remarked upon by the Russians at Henley and the world's press. While Karl Adam was turning the world upside down in Germany, Read was preaching maximum effort and maximum cohesion at dawn and dusk in Vancouver. 'All of us,' he said, 'have more courage and more capacity for understanding and developing than we ever call upon. By demanding the supreme effort from these boys, I believe they will discover these latent forces.' One of his crews had seven first-class degrees on board. Rowing, he said, is a philosophy about giving something later. It is a matter of education, of persuading parents that it is worthwhile.

Read came out of retirement in 1964 for the Tokyo Olympics, and his eight, who included the golden four of Archie McKinnon, Lorne Loomer, Walter d'Hondt and stroke Don Arnold, came second behind Adam's Ratzeburgers. The story of the Tokyo regatta, though, belongs to George Hungerford and Roger Jackson. They were Canada's spare men, Hungerford having been dropped from the eight because he was suffering from mononucleosis, from which he had not fully recovered when he reached Japan. Working out together, Hungerford and Jackson borrowed the University of Washington's boat which had won the 1956 Olympics and entered the coxless pairs. Perhaps helped by drawing a lane with some shelter from the rough conditions, they won, becoming Canada's only champions of the 1964 Olympics in any sport. They were such an afterthought that no Canadian journalists were there to see them do it. They celebrated by drinking seven Cokes apiece.

After Vancouver's exploits in the fifties there was a lull on the international scene, but a new development was taking place round St Catharine's. A wine grower and filling station proprietor, Neil Campbell, took charge of a programme at Ridley College which brought his powerful junior eights five wins in the Princess Elizabeth Cup at the English Henley between 1970 and 1979 and laid the basis for Canada's gold medal in the Olympic eights in 1984. Women's rowing rose also, providing hard competition for the Americans and the Europeans in the seventies.

Gales Ferry

It is good to think that, way back in 1923, young Ben Spock, yet to become the most famous baby doctor in the world, went to Gales Ferry in Connecticut to escape from his mother's apron strings. A gangly youth who was a high-jumper, he had found sanity, sanctuary and stature in the crew programme at Yale, which had just been taken over by Ed Leader from Washington. Fame came to Spock a year later when the Varsity went to Paris with Leader and won the Olympics. All Spock cared about then was winning. He gave up pulling and became a paediatrician, publishing the first edition of his world best-seller on tips for mothers in 1946. In the sixties he turned his attention to fighting the battle against warmongers and nuclear weapons. Sixty-three years later, Gales Ferry, a miniature clapboard campus half a mile down a leafy country road from Harvard's quarters at Red Top, has changed little since Spock's day. The elaborate coaches' house burned down in the 1970s and was replaced by a house for Billy Stowe, former coach of the Coast Guard Academy which lies downriver on the opposite side of the Thames (this Thames is pronounced with a soft 'th' and rhymes with flames). Yale's crews go there for three weeks each year before their race with Harvard to live in spartan dormitories, play vicious games of croquet, watch videos of Yale winning, and indulge in a vigorous cycle of rowing, eating and sleeping. 'If the rowing's not right, life's not right,' one man commented. A Peanuts cartoon on the door of the coaches' reserve beer store says: 'It doesn't matter if you win or lose – until you lose.' A coxswain's tee-shirt says: 'I row, therefore I am.'

Gales Ferry was a good place to be a fly on the wall in 1986. The lapstrake wall of the tiny guest room bore the legend 'Bless this Mess'. Tony Johnson the coach, Rob Mullen the manager, and freshman coach Jamie Gordon squatted in the same house, which has the only pay phone on the campus and a view of the Gales Ferry power station across the river. One old Yalee said that in his day it helped to pass the waiting, counting the trucks in and out, watching the lights twinkle. Living above the boat shed were the rigger, Jerry Romano, for forty years the nursemaid, butt of jokes and chastiser of men; Skip, the launch driver and handyman; and George Pew, guru and guiding hand of the Yale Crew Association. Trainers and Old Yalees came and went, like the historian Tom Mendenhall. Before the wind gets up and the sinister submarines from their base downstream break the surface of the course, the shells go afloat. Breakfast follows at ten in a dining room lined with alumni portraits. Newcomers to dinner must introduce themselves by singing their prep school song. Next door staff and coaches eat around a large oval table, read the *Boston Globe* and the *New York Times* and do not talk much. In the crews' rest and recreation room there is ping-pong and heavy rock, and shelves of books which seemingly came with the founders, including a novel by Rosalind Lehmann who, probably unknown to the oarsmen, is the daughter of Rudie Lehmann, the English coach, who courted her mother at Radcliffe when he coached Harvard at the end of the nineteenth century. The crews go out again in the evening, when the wind dies. Sometimes there are entertainments at dinner.

Gales Ferry is presided over by a Yale character called Ball and Mallet, a mystery to an outsider. It is the haven before the storm in Gatsby country. Surely the Glee Club, which way back in the mists of time raised money for Yale crews in New Haven, will appear one evening to sing

> Now comrades, raise the strain,
> And let no man refrain,
> Though he may not quite attain
> To the tune;
> While the insects phosphorescent
> In the ripples shine incessant,
> And above us beams the crescent
> Of the moon.

In the showers and toilets, which are palatial thanks to the generosity of Yale's 1956 Olympic gold-medal crew, the trappings of a classical education live on. Each stall and cubicle has a legend to a member of the class of '56 freshman crew. For example, '*Non magna loquinior facimus*' for Reed Rubin ('We don't just talk of big things, we do them'), or '*Pars magna cervisia eius fuit*' for Donald Beer ('Beer was a great part of it'). Charlie Grimes's says '*Post me omnia apidus vorat aequore vertex*' ('After me the rapid whirlpool consumed everything in the water'). Grimes, 6 feet 7 inches and over 200 lb, is known as Maximus.

Down at Red Top there is more space but the same 'settler' feel about the place. Harvard's coaches, Harry Parker and Ted Washburn, doze in the afternoon, unshaven. Outside the Varsity crew's dormitory is a bamboo cross saying 'RIP Yale'. The view looks towards the sub base and the start of the course. In a darkened room the lettermen watch a horror movie, and the lobby is lined with cartoons featuring Red Top Rosie, a buxom mermaid set to ensnare the Elis, as Yale men are known. To an illicit visitor from the Yale camp there is a sinister air, even though the men are doing nothing more than those at Gales Ferry – eating, sleeping and rowing. Two days before the race the protagonists do not feel like talking to one another.

At Gales Ferry Johnson grows quieter and more nervous, while his two small daughters charm the company and manfully tackle oarsmen's meals. The '56 crew are holding a reunion at the nearby Sheraton Hotel in Norwich. Eight are present, plus their coach Jim Raschmidt. After consuming huge steaks and baked potatoes and stuffed chicken they are regaled by their No. 6, the surgeon Caldwell Esselstyn, from a prepared text. Get your cholesterol level down to below 150, Esselstyn says very seriously indeed, because nobody has ever keeled over with a coronary with a score of less than 150. My profession, he says, has failed to tackle the Western disease despite all its bypassing, and I love you all. Grimes, the No. 5, reflects on his life style and describes it as 'practising law on Wednesdays'.

On race day it rains hard; when it rains it pours. The sub base is smudged to bulbous smears in grey mist. Harvard achieves a clean sweep on the Thames, winning the veterans, the freshmen (2 miles), the Junior Varsity (3 miles) and the Varsity (4 miles) races. The last is a superb tussle in which the Crimsons do not achieve clear water for 3 miles. At Red Top spectators huddle under a tent, Harvard and Yale folk together, with champagne and picnics. They hardly see a thing. Long gone are the days when the course was lined with gigantic steam yachts packed with half the society of New England, when navy ships were dressed overall, when spectator trains thundered along the bank, and when the programme was as thick and fashionable as *Vogue*.

Back at Gales Ferry, the home truth of Peanuts takes its toll. But instead of blubbing and slinking off to the nearest bar, the Yale crews dress in collars and ties and dine splendidly together. They present sunglasses to coach Gordon, 'the man who needs everything', and give binoculars to Johnson, who courageously stands up and pays them his respects. So does George Pew on behalf of the alumni. Maybe the suffering of defeat is not hard enough, but what is impressive is the old-fashioned sportsmanship and confidence and humour of these men. Even the names of the Varsity crew make a statement about American society: imagine the ethnic origins of a boat which includes Wilmerding, Werling, Kraczkowsky, Nordell, Barnett, Meyer, Donnelly, von der Schulenburg and Pirozzolo. They link arms and sing the Yale song, an antique song of a bygone age, but they make it sound modern. At seven the next morning they meet in the Blue Room to elect a new captain. There are five candidates and four polls to arrive at a winner. The ballot box is an old shoe and the result is announced by the breaking of a champagne glass. It was ever thus.

East Coast and West Coast

The Montlake Cut which links Lake Union with Lake Washington in Seattle is the venue for the Opening Day Regatta on the first Saturday of May. It was started by Seattle Yacht Club in 1919 as a parade of blue-blazered, white-trousered yachties to usher in the boating season. The University of Washington boathouse, named after Hiram Conibear and home of the Huskies, is nearby on a cut; the canal is a four-lane channel in a gorge with an iron swing bridge across it, and is extended to 2000 metres by booms stretching out into the waters of Lake Washington with its backdrop of snow-capped Mount Rainier. Hundreds of small boats, loaded with revellers and six-packs, moor alongside the booms, and after rowing races herald the new season, craft of every description from old tubs to fire boats and tugs pass through the cut to reclaim their lake. Until the seventies, university crews had the rowing much to themselves, but along came Lake Washington Rowing Club as a regional national team base for aspiring internationals. Then the ladies of the yacht club, many of them mothers of people involved in crew, showed an interest in pulling oars. One early March morning in

1982 Dick Erickson, the Huskies coach, agreed to take a dozen
yacht club women out for some elementary instruction, and Dick's
Chicks were born – christened thus by the university campus car
park attendants, who did not know what to make of this development in athletic enterprise. The women of other yacht clubs followed. Then rowers turned up from Vancouver in British Columbia
and from Portland, Oregon, and the vast yachting community of the
Puget Sound was drawn into rowing for fun. This was a spontaneous
phenomenon, but was also symptomatic of what was happening in
the United States in recreational rowing. While demand for rowing
by college veterans grew, resulting in the revival of old and the
foundation of new clubs, sculling became the thinking person's jogging in places where there was quiet water and a temperate climate.
Manufacturing recreational shells boomed, the most famous being
the Alden Ocean shells, which are only one of many examples.
Membership of the United States Rowing Association, successor
to the National Association of American Oarsmen (NAAO) and
publisher of *American Rowing*, which changed its name from *The
Oarsman*, soared from perhaps 12,000 to more than 25,000 in five
years by 1989. Crew became the favourite vanity for the young
thrusting brokers of Wall Street; rowing-motif designer sweaters and
tee-shirts could be seen in the windows of Fifth Avenue, and self-
powered boating boomed together with a burgeoning interest in
wooden boats.

Seattle did not stop with Dick's Chicks: pretty soon a group of
physicians took up the oar (Dick's Docs), and then a group of traffic
cops (Dick's Dicks), and soon Erickson could not cope with the
demand. Opening Day found a real estate company as sponsor in
1989 and started an international event, inviting Italian and New
Zealand crews. Stan Pocock, son of George, was there among the
gala crowd, a chip off the old block. He had qualified as an engineer
from the University of Washington but went by choice into his
father's business and coached the college crews on Lake Washington.
In retirement he does his bit at the Lake Washington club along
with Frank Cunningham, stroke of the Harvard crew who won a
famous victory against Penn and Navy in 1947 with half the US
fleet giving chase (see chapter 14). Spend an hour in the coffee shop
with these two and you will learn more about rowing than posing

at the Montlake Cut on Opening Day. But Opening Day is a gala, as American as blueberry pie, and Americans are good at galas.

Another great West Coast gala is the San Diego Classic on Mission Bay, which started in 1973 as an intercollegiate event and has since grown into an international affair which includes a round of the international federation's World Cup. Rowing began in San Diego in 1888 with the San Diego RC, which was followed by the women's club Zlac in 1892. San Diego State University began its athletics programme with rowing for women in the late nineteenth century, and the San Diego Yacht Club also became involved in rowing. Commercial activity in the harbour after the Second World War forced the clubs to move to Mission Bay Park, especially developed for aquatic sport. The Classic has been a success from its first day and attracts more than 30,000 spectators along the sandy Crown Point Shores in April to watch an eighty-race programme over two days.

The East Coast has its eqivalent galas, but in a different climate. There are the three great college regattas, the Intercollegiate Rowing Association at Syracuse (formerly the Poughkeepsie race), the Eastern Sprints at Worcester in Massachusetts, and the Dad Vail Regatta, which is for schools with small rowing programmes. The biggest gala of all is the Head of the Charles at Boston. This is an autumnal time trial run in divisions which are sent off at half hourly intervals from morning to late afternoon, while a great picnic takes place along both banks. Families eat feasts from the trunks of their cars, hot-dog and tee-shirt stalls do brisk business, jugglers and fire-eaters provide cabaret, and boathouses and bridges are thronged with spectators. The lawn of Cambridge Boat Club is a popular vantage point with a view of a bridge which has claimed many inexperienced coxes and created a lot of work for the shell repair men. It is here that the Kellys used to gather to watch Jack Jr win the masters sculling title or help Vesper to another honour. The Kelly family have been synonymous with Philadelphia rowing since John B. Kelly Sr won the Olympic sculling title in 1920 just after his entry for Henley Regatta was refused on the grounds, it was alleged, that this one-time bricklayer could not be an amateur. It is said that Kelly sent his green cap to King George V after beating the Diamonds winner Jack Beresford Jr at the Olympics as a comment on the Henley stewards' attitude towards manual workers. Kelly was an

apprentice bricklayer before volunteering for the Ambulance Corps
in France. While there he kept himself supremely fit and planned
races against scullers he admired, and in 1919 he won the national
title. Kelly's own version of his Henley rejection is that three days
before he was due to sail for England he received a cable reading:
'Entry rejected. Letter follows.' Years later he wrote: 'I remember
reading that cable over and over, and seeing the tears drop on the
paper, and realizing that all my castles were tumbling down about
my ears.' He never received the letter. Later, the Henley stewards
said that it would have been sent to the NAAO, which had to
vet the American entries. But there is no trace of it in Henley's
correspondence book. Kelly wrote that he assumed the reason to be
'the old rule that a man who worked with his hands could not
compete . . . As I looked through the tears, I felt that my grandfather,
who really hated the English, was right and all the disappointment
that I felt was turned into bitterness towards the English.' Henley's
minutes for 20 June 1920 say that he was barred on two grounds,
the first that their 1906 ban on future Vesper entries was still on
the books, the second that 'Mr Kelly was not qualified under Rule
I(c) of the General Rules (manual labour).' There was a great stir in
the press. For many years after, while he was building his business
and much of Philadelphia, Kelly exploited Henley's judgement that
he was not a gentleman to his own advantage. In 1920 he also won
the Olympic doubles title with his cousin Jack Costello, and they
repeated their triumph four years later. Kelly, for long a great friend
of his rival Beresford, avenged his treatment by the stewards by
coaching his son to two wins in the Diamonds in 1947 and 1949.
Jack Jr became a famous Olympian and his sister Grace, one of
three daughters, became a film star and then princess of Monaco.
Grace often repeated the story of her father's rejection, but nevertheless the wounds were finally healed in 1981 when she came to Henley
to give away the prizes. The Kellys of County Mayo and Philadelphia
and the Rainiers of Monaco accompanied her in force. Grace died
in a motoring accident in 1982, and Jack Jr died while jogging in
1985. He was American singles champion eight times, Canadian
champion six times, European champion, Pan-Am champion, and
won an Olympic bronze in 1956, the third of his four Olympic
regattas. He was also a great swimmer and a tireless worker for
sport, serving as vice-president of the US Olympic Committee. He

almost ran for mayor once, but was tripped up by internal Democratic Party wrangling and rumour of scandal. Jack Seitz, from his veteran Vesper crew, remembered him in *Rowing USA* and took issue with the medical examiner who said he had a bad heart: 'John Brendan Kelly Jr did not have a bad heart; his heart was as good as God ever made. I would agree that he had an enlarged heart for in it there was room enough for Philadelphians, immigrants, Americans, Chinese, royalty, bricklayers, politicians, honest citizens, athletes, handicapped kids, and all the rest among humankind.'

The Painter and the Schuylkill Navy

Rowing on the Schuylkill boasts a continuity and distinction which no other place can match, thanks to the determination to dig half a century's silt out of the river and a readiness to adapt to the many changes which have overtaken the sport. This is the assessment of the historian Thomas Mendenhall. The Fairmount dam was built in 1822 and contributed to the silting up of the river by anthracite which was mined upstream, but Fairmount Park straddled the waterway and made it a popular place for recreation. The Eakins family were one such to take advantage of it. Benjamin Eakins was a writing master who lived near the Schuylkill in Mount Vernon Street. He and his wife and children, especially his son Thomas, enjoyed getting out in boats. This was before and during the Civil War when English ideas of education, healthy body and healthy mind became the vogue in America, particularly in the Quaker City blessed with a fine environment and an appreciation of the democratic aspects of society which in their eyes had the edge over England. Thomas went rowing and sculling with his masters and schoolmates from Central High School, including the school's professor of chemistry Dr B. Howard Rand and Max Schmitt, who became the first amateur champion of the Schuylkill in 1867. Eakins was to become one of America's greatest painters and the best chronicler of rowing on canvas. Born in 1844, he studied drawing at Philadelphia's Academy of Fine Arts and anatomy and surgery at the Jefferson Medical College. Then in 1866 he enrolled at the Ecole de Beaux Arts in Paris and lived in the French capital for four years, studying under the foremost academician Jean Louis Gérôme. Before returning to spend the rest of his life in Philadelphia he went to Spain and studied Velasquez and Ribera. His letters from Paris reveal a good knowledge of rowing, although they do not mention rowing in France even though he was there at the time of Paris's exhibition and international regatta in 1867.

Eakins seems to have been a member of Undine Barge Club or of his friend Schmitt's club, the Pennsylvania Barge, or possibly of both. Barge clubs were originally so named because they possessed large boats which enabled the oarsmen's girlfriends or wives to sit beside them and be rowed up river to the clubs' summer houses or picnic spots. When he returned from Paris in 1870 Eakins began a series of rowing paintings which were to be his debut as an artist and were to keep him occupied for the best part of four years. He portrayed his friends John and Barney Biglin, who were New York professionals, and Schmitt, now a champion sculler. Schmitt's title came as a result of the Schuylkill Navy's new commodore Charles Vezin's declaration that Philadelphia 'would make a bold struggle for boating supremacy in our country'. The subsequent regattas drew large crowds and notice by newspapers outside Philadelphia. Eakins saw his friend win again in 1870, receiving a championship belt and a pair of silver-mounted sculls and a lot of publicity. His rivals fouled each other twice before the race had reached the turn. Eakins made meticulous studies of the mechanics and dimensions of rowing and rowers for his pictures, combining his knowledge of anatomy with that of rowing and illuminating both with his particular attention to light, shade and perspective. His masterpiece of Schmitt is *The Champion Single Sculls*, later called *Max Schmitt in a Single Scull*, and now hangs in the Metropolitan Museum of Art. It celebrates a particular victory by giving Schmitt centre stage near Turtle Rock, the start and finish of the 3-mile amateur course. Slim of physique, he looks around in the cockpit of *Josie*, his drifting 33-foot 13-inch wide 40-lb boat built by Judge Elliott of Long Island. It is about half past five in the afternoon, time to wind down after a twenty-two minute race which had been scheduled for five o'clock. Under the second lattice railway bridge which closes off the bend in the river is a steamboat, and before the first bridge is a heavy double-sculling barge crewed by men in Quaker dress, possibly from the club of that name. There are four tiny conquered scullers in the background, while in the middle ground is the artist himself, a

MAX KLETTERER IN A SINGLE SCULL

"You're <u>drifting</u> again, Mr. Kletterer!"

recreational sculler who has just passed our hero and is intent on his task. Captured on canvas are two young men one of whom is intent on competition and the other on recreation, but who share physical exercise, mental judgement and moral discipline. Eakins painted pairs and fours as well, including *The Biglin Brothers Turning the Stake* which catches Barney backing down while John pulls. This festive occasion took place in 1872, and featured the first pair-oared race in America. The sliding seat was in its infancy; the painter does not reveal whether the boats he depicts have slides or not. According to Mendenhall's detective work, there was room for a short slide in the boat, but the position of the rowers' knees is not conclusive. Maybe the Schuylkill boats of this period had the 'buckskin and butter' slide seats which were only half a step towards the real thing. The period was certainly an exciting one: in 1871 the Ward coxless-four crew achieved 4 miles round the turn at Saratoga in 24 minutes 40 seconds, though one correspondent alleged that the course was slightly short. One of Eakins's biographers says that the history of rowing itself provides a metaphor for what the painter saw. Just as boats were refined and loners subjected themselves to the self-discipline of the single, so Eakins himself, metaphorically, was to be a single sculler all his life. He ceased painting rowing in 1874 although sailing and boxing later figured as subjects. He seems to have given up when his contemporary heroes stopped trying to remain champions. They felt the age when the body goes sour on training: 'On some fine sunny day Biglin will realize . . . the sensations and discouragements of the proverbial stern chase,' *Aquatic Monthly* said in 1872. Eakins's rowing paintings fed a national appetite which the illustrated papers satisfied by pursuing an English lead. While the Schuylkill painter was learning his trade in France, Currier and Ives published the first of their prints, *James Hammill and Walter Brown, in their Great Five Mile Rowing Match for $4,000 and the Championship of America*, a double portrait and celebration, even though the match, itself a replay because of a foul, ended in another foul. Portraits of sportsmen in their street clothes or racing gear were also popular, the oarsman-photographer John O'Neill of New York making a reputation for himself in this line. *Harper's Monthly*'s exhaustive account of the 1869 Oxford versus Harvard four-oared match at Putney – the first time an American sports team had ventured abroad – included nine prints of the Oxford and Cambridge Boat Race and several others of prominent professional scullers and amateur crews.

Zlac and Title IX

Once upon a time Zulette and Lena and Agnes and Caroline went rowing in a whaler on San Diego Bay. Finding that it was good, they formed a club and named it Zlac, after themselves. That was in 1892, and the leading light was Lena Polhamus, a zoology teacher who set an energetically feminist tone as far as rowing and civil rights were concerned. Before long they had four eight-oared barges, letting them down to the water from the boathouse by a rope hoist and following down the rope themselves. They were given a wide berth by many young men and rowers in San Diego, but they received encouragement from the men of Excelsior Rowing and Swimming

Club. In 1930 they moved to Mission Bay with the other clubs in San Diego. Zlac has remained an exclusively women's club, a rare institution in a predominantly man's world. Membership was originally for white Christian women and is by invitation only. Jan Palchikoff's *The Development of Women's Rowing in the United States* says that by 1915 there were twenty-two 'afternoon tea' type crews in San Diego, of which Zlac is the sole survivor. Competition was never far from the interests of the members there, and in the mid-sixties the club purchased racing shells. By 1968 there were weekly workouts.

A twentieth-century pioneer of women's rowing was the 'Enjoy Your Lake' campaign in Oakland, northern California, where the city's recreation department began a public programme based on two municipal boathouses on Lake Merrit. But ten-women crews with coxes and pilots pre-date this, organized by the Oakland Women's Rowing Club for inter-district races on the bay at San Francisco from 1900. On the East Coast the tradition is more refined. At Wellesley College singing ability was much more important than rowing technique or fitness as a criterion for crew selection. To judge from some of the disputes which have surrounded the make-up of crews, it might be that the college's founder, Henry Fowle Durrant, and its director of physical training, Lucille Eaton 'Miss Gym' Hill, discovered something that others might envy. But no; rowing was not for competition until 1970, previewed in 1966 when the first race for the women of Wellesley took place against their neighbours, the Massachussetts Institute of Technology. An annual tradition called Float Night was responsible for the singing on Lake Waban. The crews would drift out on the lake of a summer evening and serenade the campus from their specially built heavy boats in which they sat two to a bench. Float Night was a formal occasion. The boats paraded and formed a star, while a brass band played and fireworks enthralled guests. This continued until the Second World War. Lighter eight-oared sliding-seat boats came into use in 1892 and 'scientific oarsmanship' was introduced by Miss Gym, who also replaced singing by general physical fitness as the basis for crew selection a year later. But the programme was designed for health, not competition. Miss Hill taught the 'English pleasure paddle' and identified improvement of figure and bearing among the benefits. Skill and grace were her ingredients of health, and in 1893 a study of chest girth, lung capacity, chest and back strength, chest depth and shoulder breadth at Wellesley proved rowing to be as beneficial as 'conventional gymnastic exercise'. Sweets, caffeine, iced beverages and snacks between meals were banned at this time. The regime of health, discipline and technical skill laid down by Miss Hill's department continued for many years, and similar programmes were to be found at a few other colleges, such as Smith. In 1922 Wellesley crews were judged for both slow and racing form as well as speed; form was dropped in 1964. After all the boats were wrecked by the collapse of an ice-laden roof in 1962, rowing was revived with a new fleet, still constructed with safety in mind to a shorter, wider and heavier design than the shells used by competition rowers.

There were women rowing at Cornell in 1897 and at the University of Washington in 1904. Three years late Hiram Conibear took over the latter programme and introduced an element of competition. The authorities suspended the programme in 1910 but soon reinstated it, and the Pocock brothers' sister Lucy, an accomplished sculler, became one of the coaches. When the First World War brought the programme to a temporary close, 160 women were on it. The Schuylkill largely escaped the attention of competitive women until 1938, when seventeen wives and girlfriends of men in Philadelphia clubs formed the Philadelphia Girls' Rowing Club. Ernestine Bayer, a founder member who was a participant in the 1989 tour of the Merrimack and Concord rivers to commemorate the brothers Thoreau's exploration of those waters 150 years before, recalled that some of the men disapproved of the women's competitive activity at first, and the club had an uphill struggle. For thirty years they had only themselves to compete against, until in 1965 they met Florida Southern.

Palchikoff identifies four factors which led to a rapid increase in women's rowing in the 1970s. The first three had a worldwide effect. First, the inclusion of women's events in the Olympic Games, approved by the IOC in 1972 and seen for the first time in 1976 in Montreal, caused governments and national Olympic committees to support more activity. Secondly, the women's liberation movement broke down genuflection to the view of rowing as unfeminine and made feminity unfashionable. Thirdly, the emergence of athletic superstars in gymnastics, on the tennis court and on the track brought women's competitive sport into the limelight. The fourth factor was peculiarly American, and was brought vividly to public attention by the Yale women's crew in March 1976 when, led by Chris Ernst, an Olympic team member, they stripped in the office of the university's athletics director to reveal the words 'Title IX' painted on their chests and backs. Title IX is a clause of the US Equal Education Amendment passed in 1972 which requires equal funding for men's and women's sport in schools receiving aid from the federal government. It gave women legal backing for their demands for more athletic opportunities. Faced with the gooseflesh exposed in the director's office and in the *New York Times*, Yale quickly agreed to build permanent showers for women at their boathouse. The oarswomen's statement read: 'These are the bodies Yale is exploiting. On a day like today, the ice freezes on this skin. Then we sit for half an hour as the ice melts and soaks through to meet the sweat that is soaking us from the inside.'

Women rowers were on the move on campuses before the IOC decision and the coming of Title IX. The National Women's Rowing Association was formed in 1962 and suffered some obstruction and obfuscation from the NAAO. It was born out of pressure from both East and West coasts for more competition, and Ted Nash, who coached women as well as men and who became their first president, was told by an official as he boarded the plane to go to the Rome Olympics in 1960 that if he did not 'give up this crap about women rowing' he would be thrown off the US team. The NWRA was dissolved in 1989 when it brought pressure to bear on the restructuring of the United States Rowing Association, successor to the NAAO. On the campuses, Washington were rowing by 1969, UCLA by 1970, Princeton by 1971, and Yale, Wisconsin and California State at Long Beach by 1972. Some of these programmes grew out of women's campus organizations called Shell and Oar which originated as social support groups for men's crews, cooking their breakfasts and arranging parties. Shell and Oar came from a tradition of ladies' days in American clubs, but in the sixties they decided to go rowing too. Then they became serious, and when the IOC's inclusion of women's events came along, the US Olympic Committee established the United States Women's Olympic Rowing Committee in 1973. That year Joan Lind became the first American to reach a final in the European championships. Internationally, women in

Europe were rising to the challenges set by men. Women were the
first to benefit from interval training, introduced to rowing by Gerda
Stöck at Hamburg in the fifties. The Olympics were a spur from
1976, particularly so for the socialist countries which had a head
start which they maintained into the 1990s. But others went after
them. Americans in particular did not allow them to have things
all their own way, the first US medal coming at the 1975 world
championships with second place for their eight. By the eighties
women made up 40 per cent of the membership of the USRA.

Unfair Sex

There is no question but that rowing has been a predominantly male
sport for all of its history, and a predominantly male chauvinistic
sport in many places for much of its history. In the motherland there
have been some spectacular feats by women, such as the nineteenth-
century fisherwomen's crew, skippered by Anne Glanville, who
rowed a pilot gig from the Tamar River in Cornwall across the
Channel to Le Havre and won a regatta there. Such achievements
seem to have been rare; although there are occasional references to
the prowess of nineteenth-century oarswomen, documentation is
hard to come by. Most women were confined, or preferred to be
confined, to the decorous role so loved by their menfolk.

The Germans in particular were keen on chauvinistic aesthetics
of bodice and stocking for their female wander-rowers, at the same
time as strength and fitness were gaining ground as essential aims
for future mothers of the Fatherland. The earliest German women's
club was based in Friedrichshagener, drawing its membership from
the middle classes. In 1900 it charged 20 marks to join and 2 marks
a month subscription at a time when the average weekly wage was
11.36 marks. Men were against women competing, but saw style
and pleasure rowing as fitting for German womanhood, just as
qualities of leadership were seen as correct for manhood. In the early
days women rowed well-corseted in long summer dresses and cotton
gloves. The 'tying skirt' was introduced later for slides. Then came
the sailor look. No woman was seen without long stockings in the
boats. But for a long time men set the norm which prevented changes
in women's clothing, according to the centenary history of the

German federation. It was said that a 'light obstacle to the legs is no hindrance to fresh air' and that 'with the unstockinged leg we no longer see the line but only the leg, the leg in all its naked fleshliness'. No matter that long stockings prevented the airing of the pores. However, the *Trikot*, a knitted cotton garment which clings, was favoured for women with good figures, so the preference for charm over moral scruples was shown up in its fleshly nakedness.

All this changed gradually after the First World War. Women were the carriers of the coming generation after the German loss of face. Beauty was seen as part of health, sport as essential for a fit workforce, and strong women as guarantors of a healthy future. But the aim of sport came to be regarded as gracefulness and beauty for the delight of men, emphasizing skill rather than strength. Furthermore, rowing's reputation was threatened by the notion of women competing. Dr Oswald Gerloff pointed to the different physical characteristics of men and women, saying that muscle development was bad for childbirth. He encouraged activeness for men, passiveness for women. O. Herms wrote: 'The man looks for definite qualities in a girl . . . the purer and more feminine are the female qualities in a girl, the more will he be attracted to her. The woman loves the heroic qualities in man . . . For ladies, style rowing is the basis for developing their charm.'

These views were fairly representative in rowing as in other sports. There were rules for style rowing, and the aesthetic impression of the crew counted. Wander or pleasure rowing became very popular with women, but style performance did not generate a following. The demand for competition, introduced by Berlin High School in 1927, grew. By 1930 the German federation allowed all women's clubs to join.

If the philosophy and motives were not always the same in other countries, attitudes were often similar, as is seen above when considering the American experience at Zlac and Wellesley. To read Margaret Bisland in the American magazine *Outing* in 1889 you would think that half the women of England and New York were working out for poise and posture, inspired by Queen Bess, who 'lent her royal countenance to a university regatta'. Where Bisland uncovered this latter piece of intelligence nobody knows. She also claimed that American girls learned to row at numerous rowing schools in New York, but provides no further details. In Britain women were found to be rowing in only a handful of places before the First World War. An article in *Overland Monthly* by Harold Montague Spark describes the octuple of Dr Furnivall and his women's sculling club in Hammersmith (1895), where members were drawn from all classes and where social work went hand in hand with rowing. Slum children were rowed upriver for tea and buns, and the club members had evenings of games and singing, needlework and letter writing. According to Spark, discussion of the 'doings of the shrieking sisterhood', as the Suffragettes were called, was banned. This seems a little out of character for Furnivall, the muscular Christian leader and scourge of the Amateur Rowing Association's exclusion of manual workers as amateurs.

Although there were facilities for women students at Oxford and Cambridge before 1900, these universities did not yet admit women as full members nor allow them to take degrees like Britain's other fourteen universities of the time. From 1884 the women of Somerville College, Oxford, were allowed on the upper Cherwell, tributary of the Isis where the men's crews roamed, but only at times of day when male students were unlikely to be encountered. Boating was nevertheless popular, more than half the college's girls being members of the boating society by 1898. There was a boating club at Newnham, Cambridge, by 1891. Other women's halls followed, several of them enthusiastically. St Hilda's (Oxford) students used elastic bands to prevent their skirts becoming entangled in the sliding seats of their four. St Hilda's was the first women's college to have an eight, but they used it only on a secluded part of the river to 'avoid undesirable attention'. At Girton in Cambridge proficiency tests in rowing and swimming were required before girls were allowed on the river, which was regarded as dangerous; rowing was 'not a strenuous thing at all' and involved no competition. The Newnhamites went for properly chaperoned paddles to upriver inns for tea. The Ladies' Boat Race between Oxford and Cambridge was first held over half a mile in 1927, but this was a style contest. The present series began in 1975 and is a 2000-metre race held on the Henley course.

In London University's women's colleges, meanwhile, competition developed abreast with pleasure rowing. Bedford College began hiring boats on Regent's Park lake in 1892 and by 1914 230 of its 400 students were rowing and sculling, skiffing and canoeing.

Westfield and the co-ed University College also used Regent's Park; King's tried to use the Serpentine in Hyde Park but did not have many takers; and Royal Holloway at Egham (now merged with Bedford and co-ed like the rest) took to the Thames. King's also rowed from Dr Furnivall's Ladies' Sculling Club. Discussions concerning a university association were held in 1906, and in 1912 the London United Colleges Women's Boat Club was founded, a branch of the university's Athletic Union.

Enhanced interest and changing attitudes in the twenties changed clothing too. For example, Weybridge Ladies in England gave up stockings in about 1925 and hoisted their shorts a little above the knee: 'Suspenders were very uncomfortable for sitting on,' said Eleanor Lester, who suffered this form of torture. They also had short-sleeved tunics with V-necks. Bolder colours and emblems became the vogue. The English clubs seem to have been further advanced at this time than, for example, South Australia's women who in 1922 were racing in square-necked dark gym dresses edged in white, black stockings and wide-brimmed hats.

The introduction of women's events in the European championships in 1954 was the most positive encouragement to competition. The French and the Danes organized women's regattas as curtain-raisers to the men's European championships in the two previous years. In 1976 women competed at the Olympics for the first time, and this had the effect of giving their rowing equal status with men's in a few countries, notably Romania and others of the former socialist states of Eastern Europe. Women have made great strides in other countries as well.

But old attitudes die hard, and in most places it has been a struggle for women to be taken seriously. Two of England's largest and most influential clubs, Leander and London, are still exclusive to men. Sydney RC still resists the membership of women, though the whispered opinion of a committee member in 1990 that women's inclusion was inevitable before long could probably be echoed in other male-only centres. The fact is that men's clubs which fall on hard times have often solved their problems by becoming mixed. In England there were forty-one mixed clubs in 1969, not all of which permitted women to row competitively, and 157 by 1979. The backwoodsmen are fewer and quieter than they used to be. But time now to travel to backwoods on the other side of the globe.

21

PACIFIC APPROACHES

IN the 1990s it is taking a liberty to include Southern Africa in a tour of the East, but before de Lesseps dug the Suez Canal, the shortest sea route from Europe to the subcontinent of India and the Far East was via the Cape of Good Hope, a landmark which signalled passage from South Atlantic to Indian Ocean. Posh people who could afford to do so sailed portside-out-starboard-home, buying protection from the sun. The southern part of the dark continent was particularly attractive to Europeans; Boers and British settled to farm, extract gold and fight. The British, of course, went rowing as well. Two months after the Victoria Falls Bridge was completed in 1905, the first regatta was held on the Zambesi. Otto Beit presented the Zambezi Challenge Cup. Crews came from Kafue, Kalomo, Port Elizabeth, Cape Town and East London. Bulawayo withdrew. In 1907 Zambezi Boat Club was formed at Livingstone (Northern Rhodesia, now Zambia); it seems to have been an amalgamation of several small clubs. In 1908 a railway was constructed which linked town and club.

At the 1910 regatta various sponsors, including the railway company and the London newspaper *News of the World*, backed a world championship match for a £1000 purse on the Zambesi between Dick Arnst of New Zealand and Ernie Barry of England. The race was about 4 miles on a 2-mile stretch between Loando or Long Island and the Northern Rhodesian bank, so there was either a turn or a course round the island. The river was a difficult proposition, as the writer of *Sport in Southern Rhodesia* pointed out: 'The currents varied from day to day, and at certain points the shortest course was not always the quickest. Wind was also most trying, and the hot African sun prevented most of the crews from exerting themselves as in milder climes.' Dense tropical vegetation reached to the water's edge. And there were, of course, crocodiles. The occasion was enhanced by other races, but the tentacles of the amateur definition reached even this quiet tropical backwater. An Australian journalist recognized W. P. T. Hancock as having once taken part in a professional cycle race in Melbourne, and Hancock was unable to produce proof that he had regained his amateur status. The committee ruled him out and Southern Rhodesia were without a bow. The British South Africa Police came to the rescue by sending H. A. Knott up from Marandellas as a substitute. However, policeman Knott proved not to pull his weight and Lark, bearing all the work on bowside, collapsed, leaving the crew last in the Zambezi Challenge Cup. A small crowd of New Zealanders had assembled to witness their countryman beat Barry in the championship race, plus cinematograph operators especially sent from Johannesburg and from England by the Warwick Company. Special trains brought crowds from Bulawayo and the south. But the race was an anticlimax. Both men stopped after 3 miles, overcome by heat. Arnst recovered sufficiently to paddle home the winner. Barry said it was the hardest race of his career. What nobody realized at the time was the effect of such exertion in a high temperature and at approximately 2000 feet above sea level. It is possible that the men were affected by being at a higher altitude than they were accustomed to. A few months later, Barry reversed the result on the Thames at Putney.

The first competitive rowing was along the coast in the Cape Colony, and the earliest club was Civil Service RC in 1861 at Cape Town. Other clubs followed there, and were imitated in Durban (1874), Buffalo (1875), East London (1879), Zwartkops (Port Elizabeth), Port Alfred and Port Shepstone. The Grand Challenge trophy at Buffalo regatta (1879) is solid silver and was valued at £200,000 in 1991. In Durban the first boathouse was built on the beach – a good place to catch stranded shrimps when the tide went down. At low tide crews had to walk their heavy boats a considerable distance to get afloat until somebody fitted up a trolley. It was fierce water too. The *Natal Mercury* reported that the club's diamond jubilee regatta was 'literally swept off the angry surface of the Bay by one of the worst South Westerly Busters for years'. In 1919 the Australian army crew called at Durban on their way home from winning the King's Cup at the Henley Peace Regatta. Twenty-three of

Durban's fifty active members had gone to the war in German East Africa or Europe.

Clubs were in evidence at Bloemfontein and Kroonstad in the Transvaal early in the twentieth century, and Wemmer Pan became the best known outside South Africa through its production of internationals. University rowing in South Africa began in 1925 at Witwatersrand, and in 1932 Alan Youell competed in the Olympic sculls, the first time that the Springboks were represented in rowing. Eight-oared rowing was introduced by Durban in 1938, and ten years later the first South African club to compete at Henley, Victoria Lake, won the Wyfold. In 1964 Ratzeburg of Germany paid Durban a visit, and by 1986 Kurt Hipper, a former Ratzeburg oarsman, was president of the South Africa Amateur Rowing Union (SAARU), which had been founded in 1897. Ratzeburg's influence led to a national squad system being set up in 1968 under the name of Trident. But South Africa was excluded from the Olympics from 1964 because of the racist policies of its government. From 1968 there was an understanding with FISA that no crews be entered in FISA events, and in 1986 Henley requested that no more entries be sent. By such means, and by doing its best to be non-racist and to introduce some schools programmes in Soweto, SAARU found enough support in FISA to resist expulsion from the international federation.

Rowing in present-day Zimbabwe was started by a university lecturer, Dick Christie, in 1952. At that time Zimbabwe was Southern Rhodesia and Zambia was Northern Rhodesia, and the latter decided to celebrate the centenary of the birth of Cecil Rhodes with a regatta above the Victoria Falls. Christie founded a club called Hunyani, named after the river on which they rowed at Salisbury (now Harare), to take part. The Rhodes regatta was a success, two-abreast racing taking place for four days with as much reproduction of Henley as possible. Eventually the governor of Northern Rhodesia, Sir Ivor Benson, stroked a crew containing the administrator general, the curator of the Livingstone Museum, and Christie, and to the accompaniment of a military band playing 'Life on the Ocean Wave' they hit a buoy and sank in dignified fashion, the governor going down last. Hunyani became established on a beautiful lake at Mazoe (now Mazowe), 1600 feet above sea level and surrounded by hills and bush. Others took up rowing, including the police. The

1970 declaration of independence by the whites in Southern Rhodesia brought boycott and strife and disrupted rowing for some time. Equipment was impossible to get and contact with clubs in Zambia and the Copper Belt was lost until the new state of Zimbabwe was formed. The rowing federation was elected to FISA in 1981.

Portside Out

The next stop is what the British called the Subcontinent, the Jewel in the Crown of the British Empire and an important nineteenth-century staging post for trade and communication with places whose shores are lapped by Pacific waves. In the 1860s Mrs Daniell was coxing on the Hooghly, 'her extraordinary height enabling her to look clear over the head of the bow oar in an eight' and spot the clipper ships, the pride of the merchant fleet, moving in and out of Calcutta's docks. Oars served the British and the maharajahs long before sport came to Bengal. Writing in the 1880s, W. H. Carey describes 'the principal conveyance for officers and others proceeding to the north-west provinces' before steam to be the *badjera* or *budgerow*, 'a heavy boat, of the usual spoon shape below and at the stern; but at the stem or head it was shaped like an English boat, and not infrequently there was a figurehead, a hideous attempt at a European, with a black hat, a bright blue coat, and a yellow waistcoat.' In 1781 hiring such a craft cost between 2 and 8 rupees a day depending on the number of oarsmen employed. The first mention of a regatta on the Hooghly is in 1814, but the rowing club did not come along until 1858 when anxieties were dying down after the Indian Mutiny. A mud-walled and thatch-roofed boathouse was built on Chandpal Gat. Boats were brought by clippers from Hong Kong and Canton, and several founding members were associated with London Rowing Club. The cyclone of 1864 wrecked everything, depositing pieces of boat under the columns of the town hall, which is a considerable distance from the river. The Hooghly is dangerous and unpredictable, brown and wide, subject to tidal waves, and crowded. New boats, including an eight in 1866, were imported from China and England. The club had to move from its new site because it was in the way of the fort's guns, but it was helped by the adjutant at the fort, a keen oarsman, who recruited officers to row with businessmen and government officials. It goes without saying that Calcutta RC was very well connected from its inception. Its list of presidents includes viceroys of India and governors of Bengal, and it was strictly racialist, that is, for whites only. From 1870 to 1874 Charles Norman was a stalwart who brought a sculling boat fitted with a sliding seat from England, a contraption which he claimed to have invented. In the mid-seventies the East Indian Railway employees were rowing on the Hooghly at Howrah BC, and crews began to visit Calcutta from distant Madras, Poona, Lucknow and Bombay, the west coast 'Gateway to India'. The regatta course was moved 17 miles upstream to the military base of Barrackpore. In 1878 Colombo came from Ceylon (now Sri Lanka) to win the Hooghly Cup. They were coached by a London man, J. M. Boustead.

In 1885 an eight was swamped and a member drowned, and soon after this the river was abandoned in favour of a canal, now filled in, called the Long Tank at Eden Gardens. New premises were found, and then in 1897 rowing moved to Kidderpore Docks where three-abreast racing could take place. During the floods of 1900, by which time Calcutta RC was using shell fours, a crew rowed right down Theatre Road (later renamed Shakespeare Road). In 1901 the club affiliated to the Amateur Rowing Association in London. In 1906 dock developments caused it to move yet again. It found another canal, muddy and not very suitable, and interest waned. In 1914 its Strand Road clubhouse became the headquarters of the volunteers for the defence of the port. In 1929 Calcutta made its last move, this time to Dhakuria, a man-made lake controlled by the Calcutta Improvement Trust, where it shares the quiet green water with three other clubs.

Among the founders of the Lake Club in 1932 was Sir Biren Mookerjee, the Maharajah of Coochbehar, and the nationalist leader J. M. Sengupta. Mookerjee coxed at Cambridge while he was a student there, but was barred from Calcutta RC because he was Indian. These men knew the rules of the British game; having sounded out the impossibility of joining Calcutta, they formed their own club for Indians – including ladies who began rowing in 1934 – and the Mookerjee family firm of steel and railway contractors erected a handsome boathouse next door to the 'British' club. A unique feature is a 5-foot square revolving speaker made of concrete and capable of broadcasting music to the club's gardens or beaming the instructions of an irate coach halfway across the lake. The club's Chinese carpenter, Chung Wong Suiking, is an expert boatbuilder, and the coach Ashok Mehta has established a programme making wooden training boats and plastic singles from moulds supplied by Empacher. The Lake Club has an active social and rowing life and its membership is mainly Bengali. Meanwhile Calcutta RC remained a British club until 1969 when the first Indian member was elected. Although it is now the most cosmopolitan club at Dhakuria, it retains some of the British trappings, including a unique mechanical *bankha* or fan, designed by a member, in its changing room. Rowing takes place in the early morning and members take breakfast on their immaculate lawn. The third club is the University which began rowing in 1926 on a canal to the north of the city before moving to the lake. The fourth is Bengal RC, formerly Marwaris RC (1929), which draws its membership from the wealthy Rajastani business community. It runs a rowing programme for local youth.

Madras in the southern state of Tamil Nadu is strung along the ocean behind golden beaches. It was the first settlement of the East India Company and was the British headquarters before influence was extended north to the tea- and coffee-growing areas and iron and coal fields round the Bay of Bengal. Madras still wears its Britishness in its enormous Fort George and its Victorian university buildings, and the suburbs, which used to be bachelor quarters for foreign companies and civil servants, retain their ambience for wealthy Indians. Here beside the River Adyar can be found the Madras Club, formerly a pleasure dome for the manager of the East India Company and now an exclusively Indian bolt hole for tennis, swimming, billiards and balls. Next door is the rowing club, founded in 1867 and moving to this site in 1892. It serves breakfast at dawn while students take to the polluted river in fours and singles, their boats carried to the pontoon by the club's lascars (the name comes from seamen). It is a lovely example of bungalow architecture, baskets of flowers and creepers adorning its façade and verandah and hiding the gym and workshop. Part of the bar is air-conditioned, part has ceiling fans, and there is a handsome bust of Budda, head lascar from 1911 to 1964, by a former captain. Wood engraved honours boards abound, and the bar and tables are marble. The kitchen serves Chinese and Indian menus. The club's roots were in business houses which founded the Merchants' and Bankers' regatta in 1900, an occasion which had plenty of fun events such as Blind Man's Buff and Damsel in Distress to keep the family entertained. In the 1990s games are confined to the lawns and aimed at the 600 members' children, the water being too polluted for fooling about in boats. The club has 3 kilometres of rowing to the mouth of the river, but its mileage upstream has been curtailed by a new low bridge. A scheme to clean and restore the level of the river has been shelved because the authorities have no money with which to implement it.

Like Calcutta, Madras BC began to Indianize itself after independence in 1947. The first Indian name appeared on the committee in 1964 and by 1970 only one English name was left. The club has continued to bow to the people who matter – in 1971 invitations to its regatta were sent to the consul general of the USSR, the consul for Ceylon, the president of the Royal Yacht Club, the inspector general of Police, and the resident officer of the Indian Navy.

By studying the objects on the walls of these clubs and by half-closing one's eyes in the bar or on the lawn, it is possible to discern vestiges of the pre-Victorian Britons' ideas of how they should attempt to mould this land in their own image. Lord Macaulay's Minute on Education in 1835 said that Britain would create 'a class of persons Indian in blood and colour but English in taste, in opinions, in morals, and in intellect'. When the clubs were British they were isolated from home and far distant from each other. They had a tendency to forge associations with London while looking east for rowing contact. There were annual or occasional fixtures between, for example, Madras and Colombo or Calcutta and Rangoon, Burma, where Professor Arthur Eggar introduced rowing to his students after the First World War. A graduate of Trinity College, Cambridge, Eggar published a book entitled *Rowing and Sculling* in 1914 in which he states that 'the style which is outlined in this treatise has been proved to be good enough to carry a raw crew to victory, after ten days' training, against a crew of the most experienced Orthodox oarsmen'. The proof was at the 1913 Monsoon Regatta in Rangoon when a scratch four from the 1st Battalion of the Royal Munster Fusiliers, coached and coxed by Eggar, beat the Ancient Mariners, former Cambridge oarsmen, by a quarter of a length.

In 1933 the ARA of the East was formed after an all-India regatta at Poona (now Pune), and regattas rotated between the Royal Connaught BC at Poona and Calcutta, Madras, Colombo, Karachi and Rangoon. The Bombay Gymkhana Club was a founding member, but the great west-coast port of Bombay has not featured in rowing. In 1976 the state rowing associations of West Bengal (Calcutta), Tamil Nadu (Madras) and Maharastra (Pune) formed the Rowing Federation of India, and there were about fifteen states affiliated by 1990. Much of the influence has come from the army at Pune, but there is also rowing through universities, railway companies and industry. In 1981–82 India and Japan set up the Asian Rowing Federation to take in countries in the Far Eastern ARA as well as states formed after the 1947 independence and partition of India, such as Pakistan, Bangladesh and Sri Lanka. India hosted the Asian Games in 1982 and included rowing on the grounds that it was a founding Olympic sport. The British Council supplied a British coach and six countries took part. The first Asian championships followed in 1985; they are held every two years. In 1989 they were in Chandigar, in the Punjab, where the lake was extended by 500 metres in three months, dug out by hand

A rowing centre has been set up in Kerala on the southwest coast where waterways abound and where traditional snake boats take part in festivals. India has had help from FISA programmes through Olympic Solidarity and from Britain and the USSR in the form of cultural aid. The problems for rowing are familiar ones, magnified in such a large and poor country. For example, in 1990 the Asian Games dropped coxes from fours. 'We don't have the money to do this,' Borun Chanda, secretary of the federation, says. 'We need coxed boats because the cox can coach. We don't have coaching boats.' He says that transport of boats to championships is too expensive. Hosts should provide boats and take the opportunity to expand their own fleet by so doing.

Silk Road and the Party

'The river succours and impedes native and foreigner alike; it limits and it enables, it isolates and it joins. It is the highway of commerce and it is a danger and a nuisance. Children fall off fragile native craft; drunken sailors topple from the decks of the Company's chequered ships.' The company is the East India and the river, which 'at its mouth stains the clear blue sea yellow-brown, the colour of tea as drunk in London', is the Pearl River or Wang-Po as described in Timothy Mo's *An Insular Possession*. In 1833 the anchorage at Whampoa Island was two hours' rowing in a gig from the old walled city of Canton and its adjacent foreign 'factories', and Mo describes the river life to be seen on the way:

> Awkward barges, full of salt or coal. Graceful mandarin boats which skim the river like so many dragonflies, with gaudy shields between their oars and dragon's eyes painted on the bow. Flat, comfortable house-boats. Lean suspicious craft with their decks full of staring cut-throats. Rope-drawn ferries, glorified rafts these, noisome with livestock, which cut across the grain of the river's traffic, one whole mile.

On 27 April 1837 the *Canton Monitor* reported that a watery battle commenced at two o'clock:

> The contestants, the flower of our foreign youth, stretched their limbs and loosened their sinews on the bank or lay in postures of graceful repose, while their cliques exhorted and encouraged them the while, chafed their muscles, or offered a refreshment to bring the blood tingling and coursing to the surface, while the 'generals' paced about and about the glistering, sharp-prowed craft, attentive to the minutest repair or adjustment which might give their champions the necessary advantage of even inches gained.

Perhaps this was the first regatta in Canton; at any rate, it was held in the year that the British and Americans who worked in the *hongs* or factories formed Canton Regatta Club. 'Conquerors in the first six races were champions of the houses of Russell & Co., Meridian & Co., Dent, Innes, Jardine & Matheson, and Bevan & Co.' – the first two named being American companies. The factories were not manufactures but were engaged in import and export of tea, silk and a myriad of necessities and exotica, including – some of them – opium, which was officially illegal and soon to be the cause of war between the mandarins and Britain. The foreign businessmen lived above their *hongs* and were not allowed into the old walled city. Nor were women allowed to accompany them during their stay. So the men sought pleasure on the river and took their leave after the northeast monsoon in the old Portuguese settlement of

Macao, 80 miles downstream, where society could be found, and restrictions could not. There were scores of wherries and gigs in Canton, and the energetic sometimes made the journey to Macao by skiff.

The development of racing alarmed the Chinese merchants who acted as guardians of the *hongs*, as well as their trading partners. Apart from the fact that an old decree forbade personal rowing, they implored the foreigners to abandon the idea on grounds of safety: 'We have heard of the intention of our respected elder brother and other chinte-le-mun [pidgin English for "gentlemen"] to race boats on the river . . . the chances of contact are many, so are accidents, even to the breaking of one another's boats.' They were under the impression that foreigners were about to take up the *tow-sam-pan*, a Chinese term for competing with boats which entailed battles with oars and boathooks – not unlike, perhaps, the sort of behaviour at Durham Regatta in those days (see chapter 15). In the event the Chinese took a great interest, helping to clear a course and keep intruders off it, and the first race of the club was between a six-oar *The Not So Green*, manned by the Swedish factory, and an English boat.

Trade in opium was carried on by gentleman's agreement. It was highly organized, sales being cash-only by brokers and orders being sent down to the anchorage in Whampoa by 'scrambling dragons' or 'fast crabs', known to the foreigners as smug boats. They were long and beamy and propelled by a crew of seventy oarsman assisted by rattan and bamboo sails. They were armed with a large gun on the bows, and were brightly varnished to distinguish them from government cruisers, which were painted black and red. The morality of the lucrative trade led to dispute within the foreign community and trouble between the Chinese and the British. In 1841 British troops on the heights to the north of the city walls refrained from attack when the Chinese paid a ransom of $6,000,000 to save their town. One result of the Opium Wars was the temporary closure of Canton as an international trading centre and the lease of a barren rocky island called Hong Kong to the British. They found a wonderful anchorage there and named it Victoria after their young queen. Along with the *hongs* and the English newspapers, Canton Rowing Club, as it was then known, moved to the new centre. It was established there by 1849 and changed its name to Victoria Regatta Club.

On 14 February 1845 the Royal Navy put on a regatta in Hong Kong, and all the beauty and fashion of the fledgling colony came aboard HMS *Agincourt*, 'about forty ladies and four times as many men,' Edward Hodges Cree, a naval surgeon, wrote in his diary. 'In the first race our cutter pulled over the course, as none of the others would venture to compete with her. The race which excited most interest was one pulled by officers.' Purses of dollars and silver cups were distributed on the poop of the *Agincourt*, dinner was served on the main deck, and there was dancing until 2 a.m. on the quarter-deck, which was 'decorated with the flags of all nations, chandeliers of bayonets, variegated lamps, transparencies, and flowers'. Cree spent his time in Hong Kong chasing girls, of whom there were not enough to go round. 'Wed. 19th: Went to see my fair little patient, Alice Hickson, who is indisposed. Ladies are so scarce and doctors so plentiful, that each lady has her own doctor exclusively.' Cree recorded his adventures with the Navy in the Far East, India, the Baltic and the Balkans in charming watercolours, and his painting of the regatta shows HMS *Agincourt*, *Iris* and *Vixen* and a fleet of multi-oared cutters going for dollars.

The old Canton club still exists. It is known as Victoria Recreation Club and moved from its original Hong Kong site on the waterfront to the seclusion of Deep Water Bay. It changed 'rowing' to 'recreation' in the 1890s when swimming, billiards and track and field were added to its activities. Its past link with Macao is reflected in the many Portuguese names among the membership. Rowing also revived in Canton when trade resumed in the 1850s. A new boat-house was built in 1907 on Shameen Island, where the British and French communities then lived and traded. Bertie Rasmussen revived rowing at Shameen when he was sent there in 1928 to manage the Russell *hong*. A Dane who was taken to Hong Kong when he was two and learned to row at the Victoria and at the Royal Hong Kong Yacht Club, Rasmussen became captain and recruited British civil servants and police cadets who were sent to Canton to learn Chinese as part of their training for work in British Far Eastern possessions. There was also a foreign community of about 500 on Shameen who enjoyed the rival attractions of the Canton Club and the Lawn Tennis Club. There was no contact with the Chinese except for business purposes. 'We were very racist then,' Rasmussen, who was also the honorary Swedish consul, says. 'Not like now.' His wife Norma used to cycle around Canton, which was thought very odd behaviour by Europeans and Chinese alike. The last regatta in Canton was a year before the Japanese invasion, a gala affair with the RHKYC as guests and a finishing line marked by British and French gunboats. The Rasmussens and their baby were trapped by the Japanese in 1938 and given three hours to clear out of their house. The French *hong* gave them an empty building and they sat out the occupation on Shameen, selling possessions to feed themselves. The boats were taken to Hong Kong in 1946, when the Victoria revived and started rowing again. It was Rasmussen who re-started it and designed its boathouse at Deep Water Bay. More boats arrived from Shanghai a few years later when the Communists took over there and brought another old club with a distinguished history in China to an end.

Shanghai on the Yangtze was opened to foreign trade in 1842 under the Treaty of Nanking, the year after Hong Kong was leased to the British. The first regatta took place in 1849, and sport and recreation clubs were established as the foreign community, particularly the British, grew in size and influence in the city. The rowing club started in 1863, born of the Shanghai Regatta Club of 1859, with an English captain and an American secretary. The editor of the *North China Daily News*, who had rowed in the Boat Race, wrote in 1893:

> In the older days, when the suburbs now covered with villas and gardens were still paddy-fields . . . the rowing man could leave his desk an hour before dusk, run down to the boathouse — for rowing men used to run in those days, carriages of any kind being very rare — have his exercise for the day, and be back at his desk within little more than an hour.

The climate allowed rowing for nine months of the year, so it became Shanghai's pre-eminent sport. Rowing started on Soochow Creek, one of the hazards of which was stern-wheeler passenger boats propelled by up to a dozen men treadmilling on the paddles of the wheel. The service to Soochow took forty-eight hours, and the skipper used a conch shell at every bend to warn other traffic of their approach. The club held spring and autumn regattas with racing between the merchant houses, international races between those of different ethnic origins (i.e. European or American, those most prominent among the eights being England, Scotland, Ireland and Germany), and often races between visiting merchant and British naval ships. The town or the British navy band played, and considerable numbers of Chinese turned out to watch the 'sampan pidgin'. In 1871 there was a remarkable incident when the Scottish crew in the international eights carried 28 lb of lead shot on stroke side to balance their side-seated boat because the No 5. weighted 186 lb and the No 4. only 140 lb. They won. In 1878 five boats competed for the Merchant Vessels' Gigs' Race, including crews from the famous tea clippers *Cutty Sark* (now at Greenwich, England) and *Thermopylae*. There are early references to 'opium ship' six-oared gigs, and in 1900 a British admiral forbade his men to compete in the men-o'-war races 'since a free fight might ensue afterwards'. There was difficulty at regattas both with weather, stray junks and vessels swinging at anchor, and in 1885 a decline in popularity was blamed on tennis, a new craze considered an effeminate game by the club's chairman. But five years later recruiting to the manly sport of rowing revived. In 1896 the river was used for regattas instead of the creek, and then in 1906 the club found a quiet inland waterway, the Tsinyangkong, which they christened Henli. The chief engineer of the Nanking-Shanghai railway discovered it while building his line. N. M. W. Harris's club history describes the pictography of the Chinese name as conjuring an image of lush green banks and a creek that sparkles with the glitter of radiant sunbeams, and Duncan Glass conjured the name in Chinese characters to mean 'abounding prosperity' to foster the idea of a Chinese Henley. The police tried to stop the first regatta to be held there, but their gunboats were bought off with 'Algerian cigarettes and Hongkew whiskey'. Thousands of Chinese turned out to watch Father Neptune open the proceedings, followed by eights rowing and sampans sailing. The move to Henli had the effect of putting more emphasis on competitive rowing and less on pleasure rowing, but it also brought about a new challenge: to set record times for rowing from the club to Henli, a distance of 46 miles, first tried in 1915. The record was 7 hours 30 minutes (1931), and then 5 hours 24 minutes (1937) for a shortened course of 37½ miles.

In 1937 the club was embroiled in the heat of war when the Japanese navy attacked Shanghai. The boats were moved to the cricket club for safe keeping, but its motor launch was destroyed by a shell. When the club reopened Japanese planes were in the habit of 'laying eggs' on the North Station, and some oarsmen thought it politic to wear tin hats and adhere to the maxim 'eyes in the boat'. The club survived this incident, and survived in some form until the Communist takeover in 1948, when many of the boats were brought to Hong Kong and shared between the RHKYC and the Victoria Recreation Club.

Another Englishman Abroad

A feature of rowing in the Far East was inter-port contests, held intermittently in a number of places. The first was in Nagasake, Japan, in 1875, with events in fours and sixes with sliding seats, plus naval cutters and yachts. Rowing in Japan began in Yokohama when resident Englishmen formed a barge club in 1866 'with several boats with sliding seats they had brought from England'. This is the earliest claim of sliding seats in the Far East, but is unlikely to be accurate. In 1869 the club became Yokohama Amateur Rowing Club and raced against Royal Navy cutters. Again the sliding seat claim is made, and again it is unlikely. Then South College, the predecessor of Tokyo Imperial University, bought some lifeboats from a foreign whaler in the 1870s – accounts vary from 1874 to 1879 – and used them for pleasure on the Sumida River at cherry blossom time. At about the same time students began to row on the sea and rivers around Osaka, and then on the freshwater Lake Biwa and the canals at Kyoto when their university was relocated there. Two forces combined to promote rowing in Japan: the drive to establish an imperial navy brought the Meiji emperor to a cutter race in 1883 (the sixteenth year of the Meiji – conversion from Japanese to Western calendar may account for some discrepancies in rowing dates). In the same year the first race between the Imperial University and Tokyo Shihan Gakko (now Tsukuba University), won by Gakko using a light boat specially bought for the event, signalled a growing interest among students. Imperial's use of a heavy whaler probably prompted Frederick William Strange, a mysterious and lugubrious-looking English teacher at the Imperial University, to supervise the building of some six-oars in 1884 and to

introduce inter-faculty races. Strange was very influential in introducing modern sports to Japan. He arrived there in 1875 to teach
English and was reputed to be an old Etonian, but Eton has no
record of him, and their archivist has failed to find any reference to
him at the other leading schools of the day or at Oxford or Cambridge. He died at the age of thirty-six in 1889.

   Whoever Strange was, he left his mark on Japanese rowing. In
1885 he challenged Yokohama to a race over 1000 metres in front
of the Grand Hotel. His students were badly beaten on a very rough
day and after only a short training period on slides. It was students
who grasped the oar and established a strong tradition of rowing.
The Hitotsubashi versus Tokyo boat race began in 1887–88, and
the Keio versus Waseda race in 1905. Seven leading student clubs
founded the Japan Amateur Rowing Association in 1920 and the
first inter-colleges regatta was also held in that year; this developed
into the national championships. A coxed four and a sculler were
sent to the Olympic Games in 1928, and an eight to Berlin in 1936.
On the way the latter caused a sensation in England by winning the
Grand Challenge Cup at Marlow regatta at an extremely high rate
of striking. But at Henley, after beating Quintin BC, they were
eliminated by the eventual Grand winners, Zürich.

From Singapore to Saigon

Twelve inter-port regattas took place between 1875 and 1929
involving Shanghai, Tientsin, Hong Kong, Kobe, Yokohama, Nagasaki and Ningpo, with Shanghai heading the overall table of wins
and Kobe the table of wins per entry. Another series of inter-ports
began in 1927 when the Royal Singapore Yacht Club raced Malacca.
The latter club died young, but BS Hollandia of Batavia (now Jak-
arta, Indonesia) and Miri BC of British North Borneo (now in
Brunei) joined the RSYC in regattas. This tradition was revived after
the Second World War in Southeast Asia, though at this time rowing
had disappeared in China, while social contact with Japan was
shunned for some time. In 1951 RSYC invited the Royal Hong Kong
YC, Miri Belait and the Club Nautique de Saigon to a regatta at
which the Hong Kong sculler Thomi Keller won the sculls; a second

regatta was held in the same year in Saigon. From this was born the Far Eastern Amateur Rowing Association in 1953.

Singapore Rowing Club was founded in 1879. One of its founders was an employee of the Peninsular and Oriental Steam Navigation Co. and he arranged for a ship to bring the first boat from Hong Kong. Pollution of the Singapore River forced the club to amalgamate with Singapore's new yacht club in 1921. The club lost most of its property during the Japanese occupation in the Second World War, but after the war participated in inter-port regattas until 1964, when it had to move again because of port development. During this period, however, crews were relatively strong and competition was available in other parts of the Malay peninsula because of the presence of British forces. Army, Navy and Air Force all rowed, but none so far as the RAF. Clubs at RAF Seletar and RAF Changi practised in the Straits of Johore before flying by Shackleton to Hong Kong, Ceylon and Australia for regattas. All ranks joined in the crews. (The RAF were strong in Britain also during this period, having around twenty-five clubs attached to their bases and forming the nucleus of crews from Barn Cottage and Molesey who were making international waves.) Charity work was undertaken as well: Squadron Leader David Packman and Sergeant Jim Andrews sculled round Singapore Island in 1970 to raise money for the Red Cross children's home. The withdrawal of British forces during the seventies left rowing struggling again in Singapore, and the arrival of the North Vietnamese in Saigon did not help the cause there.

Ian Purslow rowed and coached in Saigon, where the club was situated about 200 metres upstream of the commercial docks on the Saigon River. The rowing membership was mostly French and numbered about sixty when Purslow arrived in 1953. They shared large premises with a larger social membership attracted by the club's renowned cuisine, its cool verandah, and annexe a few miles upstream, where rowing only took place when security was assured. The Viet Minh guerrillas (later the Viet Cong) were sometimes within shooting distance on the opposite bank. Saigon crews occasionally raced against Phnom Penh in Cambodia, and Purslow, who worked for a bank, went rowing at the Club Nautique d'Hanoi and attempted to re-start rowing at Haiphong, also in the north of the country, where activity had fizzled out as French forces moved on. In the sixties the club at Saigon was still a gourmet's paradise remembered by reporters covering the war and by Billy Stowe, who arrived in the South Vietnamese capital in 1963 as an ensign in the US Navy to run the American officers' club. On his first evening he was in the bar of a hotel looking out over the city when he saw a rowing shell gliding up the river at sunset. He followed it, and became the only occidental to row at the club during his year there. 'I would go down at lunch time and for about 70 cents be served a tray of "oars" d'oeuvres and a litre of Larou beer on the sun deck, then cold lobster tail and fresh mayonnais, then steak and fruit. It served the best food in Vietnam and was largely a dining club.' Stowe once entertained the entire rowing membership to dinner at the officers' club for $100. CN Saigon had 'lapstrake *bateaux*, French built, fours, pairs, and singles, and you could row 6 or 7 miles up river to the club's weekend barbecue place where there was water skiing and such like.' Stowe spoke only English and was in a crew who included an alcoholic French lady cox and a Pakistani. They had a Vietnamese coach called Jo Hi who instructed in Vietnamese, after which the bow man translated into French, and somebody else into English. Stowe later represented the United States and become coach to the US Coast Guard Academy, but in Saigon he found 'rowing as it should be . . . coolies put the boats in and out of the water and scrubbed them down. You had to wear whites to practise.' The last inter-port regatta to be held in Saigon was in 1974, just before the Viet Cong took control of the city.

In the 1990s it is difficult to know whether rowing is dead, dormant or alive in some of these places. There are occasional references to it in Thailand; Rangoon University's club was going strong in 1957 when its founder Sir Arthur Eggar, the old-Etonian law professor, flew out from retirement in England to attend the annual regatta on the Inya Lakes. Colombo thrives in Sri Lanka. Miri Belait, actually at Kuala Belait, is part of the Panaga Club of the Brunei Shell company, where Dutch and British employees row. There are murmurings of activity in Indonesia and Malaysia. Japan has come in from the cold. Taiwan (formerly Formosa, inhabited by the rump of the nationalist Chinese) and both North and South Korea have joined the FISA family, and Hong Kong has made determined strides with the development of a 2000-metre course at Sha Tin in the New Territories and a programme at the Hong Kong Institute for Sport alongside it. But the spectacular revival story of

Asia belongs to China, which first sent a crew to a world championship in 1975 as a preliminary to becoming the power in the region,
and reached Olympic gold in Seoul in 1988. We will visit China
again before our last port of call in the East on this great Cook's
Tour of rowing – Australasia, a continent enjoying close ties with
the mother country of rowing and, increasingly, with Asian neighbours on the Pacific rim.

Star Lake

In 1954 the Chinese revived rowing at Shanghai using equipment
left behind at the rowing club. Five years later some twenty-five
provinces were rowing and coaches were being educated by a programme set up by the Polish coach Roger Verey who was in China
in 1957. A year previously a three-city match had been staged
between Harbin, Hangchou and Shanghai for which Harbin had
received assistance from the USSR. Before the cultural revolution
stopped everything from 1966 to 1972, triangular contests were held
between China, North Korea and Cambodia. Rowing re-awoke in
the seventies, and the eighties have seen a trickle of foreign coaches
passing through seminars in China, including Bob Janousek from
Britain and Joachim Ehrig from West Germany. Fifteen-year-olds
are recruited by an East European-style selection programme, and a
high profile has been achieved through exposure at China's National
Games. There are at least seven big centres apart from the national
team training quarters at Beijing and Zhao Qing, and several other
places where racing boats are to be found. Liu Aijie, China's technical director, gives himself eye strain translating coaching manuals
into Chinese. 'We have to find our own way,' he says.

The Chinese rowers at Star Lake, the summer training water at
Zhao Qing, lead a spartan life. They live four to a room above the
boat shed, sleeping on iron bunks with thin mattresses. The gym is
a lean-to with no modern equipment, old mattresses serving to soften
the landings of the weights. Meals are plain and wholesome, a
bucket of rice and meat and vegetables or fish from the lake followed
by pears, twice a day. The water is good, the mountain scenery
restful, and the facility is spacious, but the furnishing sparse. The
dining room is brightened only by an ornamental mirror and paper

streamers. It is a stark contrast to the Party guest house or the hotels nearby, the latter a series of pavilions stepped up the lush hillsides and packed with tempting duty frees for holidaymakers from Hong Kong. The athletes express little of that air of a certain future which East German athletes used to radiate. The nearest thing to a secret weapon for achieving world dominance at Star Lake is a plentiful supply of Jianlibao, an orange and honey drink, developed by the Guangdong Sports Science Research Institute, which keeps fresh without refrigeration. This is just as well, because there is no refrigerator at the rowing centre. There is no laundry either; the staff wash the bedding in the lake.

China's achievement is impressive, given the relative isolation of Liu Aijie and his colleagues. They are fully aware that the only thing their paymasters understand is medals, while their athletes increasingly have other things on their minds. Coaches voice the same frustration as their colleagues in the sporting minnow countries around them. Chris Perry, who runs Hong Kong's programme, says that Cantonese youth are physically lazy and always choose to pursue dollars when given the option of reserving some leisure time for sport. Aijie says the same thing: 'They know they must get an education to get on, and they are reluctant to give the amount of time to rowing that we would like.' You hear the same sentiment in Singapore and in India. The rich and the poor athletes of the East, whether they live under a post-imperial or state-promoted sporting system, speak with the same voice. They do not share the Western willingness to delay pecuniary and career advancement.

Heroes for a New Nation

'The victory of Trickett over Sadler will have done more to make these colonies known throughout the old world than all the lectures given and statistics published during the last twenty years,' said *The Advertiser* in Melbourne on 9 August 1876. Ed Trickett of Sydney had gone to England to take on the world professional sculling champion Joe Sadler and beaten him by four lengths to become Australia's first world champion. He returned to a hero's welcome at Circular Quay.

Rowing was illegal in Britain's early penal colony of New South

Wales. The British authorities and the mighty East India Company, which had a monopoly of Britain's trade in the East, were both determined that convicts should neither have the opportunity to escape by boat nor to learn seafaring ability. So building craft of any sort for the use of private individuals was forbidden in 1788 at the settlement in Botany Bay. The ban was renewed ten years later, and in 1791 permission had to be requested to build any boat longer than 14 feet. Before long, however, the desire of the governors of the rapidly growing colonies to reduce their economic dependence on distant Britain made the regulations untenable. The southern ocean was full of seals with valuable fur and whales with valuable fat, and the new South Waleans went after them.

A 'compulsory resident' called Brennan was said to be the first sculling champion, possibly in 1805, clear evidence that attempts to keep potential escapees out of boats did not work for long. The first recorded race was in 1818 between four-man gigs from the ships *Batavia*, *Guildford* and *Minerva*, arranged by Captain John Piper. It was from Bradleys Head to Sydney Cove, and Piper, who was in the winning crew, arranged races until 1824, many accompanied by side wagers. In 1819 his crew met one from the American ship *General Gates*, the first international race. In 1820 Van Diemen's Land (Tasmania) saw its first race, and from 1827 whaleboat regattas were established there. Whaleboats were familiar in other Tasmanian ports, racing on the Tamar at Launceston, on the Mersey at Devonport, on the Huon River and the Upper Derwent. In 1833 Sydney and Hobart contested in whalers, the first intercolonial match.

Naturally, settlement of Europeans in Australia took place round anchorages and along rivers. Once more the rowing boat was an essential tool of communication, carting farmers' produce to market, transporting children to school, and taking families on shopping expeditions. Racing and betting took a particular grip around Sydney Harbour and on the up-country rivers which wound into farming country and the world of country fairs, where roads were rudimentary and travel to towns might take weeks. Henry Searle, the 'Clarence Comet', lived on Esk Island in the Clarence River and rowed his siblings the 7-mile round trip to school. George Towns, who like Searle became world champion, often took farm produce 4 miles from Dempsey Island to Newcastle. Butchers delivered by boat and had boats named after them, and rivers like the Parramatta, Hunter and Hawkesberry, Richmond and Shoalhaven had plentiful oarpowered traffic. The climate, too, was conducive to competition, being suitable for rowing the year round. Rivers and harbours were a breeding ground for scullers, and arrivals from England in the late 1850s brought the latest ideas with them, including, it is said, the outrigger, which was introduced to the continent by James Edwards. Prize money was readily available and grew to £500 a side for a world championship race by the 1880s. According to the *Brisbane Courier* in 1888 the activity drew support from all sections of the community, the 'brown-bearded bushman' as well as the 'merchant and clerk, the labourer and the fair sex'. It was much less tarnished with the whiff of corruption than was the case in Britain or the United States, which possibly accounted for the large number of Australian victories in the world championship during the period around the turn of the century – twenty-two years between 1876 and 1907 shared by seven Australians. Many were brought up on quarrying and tree-felling and they were granted heroic status by their press and public. In 1939 the *Sydney Morning Herald* looked back at Gladesville, a waterside suburb of Sydney:

> Stalking with their trainers through the little town . . . they were like Kingsley's Gladiators stalking through the degenerate Romans. Elias Laycock could eat a dozen eggs for breakfast; Maclean, an axe-man from the northern rivers, could take an axe in either hand, and fell any tree without stopping for rest; Searle had an extra rib on either side of his body, or so his opponents implicitly believed.

Nehemiah Bartley caught the mood in his reminiscences of life in Australia and Polynesia in 1892. Against footballers and cricketers with their mates around them and boxers who are allowed breathing spaces, the man in the outrigger is in it alone:

> No ministering angel with sponges, or lemons, may *tend* him, during these 1,200 strictly consecutive seconds of supreme and relentless struggle, nearly every one of which brings out a tremendous spring and effort, of arm and thigh, of back and loin; 800 strokes per man in each race, and each stroke calling hard on every muscle in the body.

Trickett and those who came after were the foundation stone in the Australian measurement of character and nationhood through sport, though not without blemishes. In 1888 the Clarence Comet came into bad odour with his manager Neil Matterson and the public for obstructing Bill Beach, who had retired as world champion in the previous year after defending the title successfully six times. The incident occurred in a race at Brisbane's aquatic carnival at Breakfast Creek. Searle had won the world title little more than a month before. Less than a year later he was dead, succumbing to typhoid in Melbourne on his return journey from England after defeating William O'Connor. His death brought flags to half mast in the six colonies and restored him to public favour. Between the achievements of Trickett and Searle, Beach sharpened the pencils of the purple-prose writers and reached the pantheon by defeating the great Canadian Hanlan four times. After the first, the *Sydney Morning Herald* said: 'Ship after ship takes up the cheering. Wave upon wave, the ever-gathering volume of sound rolls on! There are a hundred thousand throats straining. There is a roar as the nation rejoices.' The win made amends for the loss of Trickett's title four years earlier, when the paper remembered 'how Sydney kept awake all one night awaiting the arrival of a certain telegram, which, coming, sent a sigh and a shudder through the city such as might follow on the loss of some object long cherished and dearly beloved.' Professional sculling lasted longer in Australia than anywhere else before it fizzled out in the 1950s after a post-war revival failed to arouse public interest. Crowds began to decline soon after the death of Searle, even though Australians continued to do well for some years. Scott Bennett, Searle's biographer, attributes the decline to an economic and betting slump, suspicions of cheating and rival spectator attractions. World championship races in Australia were infrequent, and little happened in between.

The public response to professionals may have reflected a straightforward nationalism, but the amateur world was more complex. Here six colonies, some of them beginning life as penal settlements and some as new homes for settlers, each put their own interpretation on the amateur. Tasmania, for example, took a similar view to its southern neighbour New Zealand, that cash prizes were acceptable as long as the proceeds went to the club and not the individual. The strongest colonies were at odds, New South Wales (Sydney) adopting the English ARA's line that manual workers were barred, while Victoria (Melbourne) preferred their inclusion. This caused

much debate and disagreement and, from the inception of the inter-
colonial eight-oared races in 1878 until the First World War, also
involved South Australia, Western Australia and Queensland. In
1888 the possibility of sending a representative crew to England
arose, and so a way was sought to comply with English rules while
cooperating under Australian codes.

But in 1888 Victoria included two saddlers in their trial crew for
the trip (which never came off) and New South Wales objected. This
began a series of tortured arguments over manual workers, cash
prizes, the status of cash-prize winners in other athletic sports, the
question of whether sailing was an athletic sport (NSW wanted to
exclude sailing from a ban because many of their members sailed
for cash prizes, so they maintained that sailing did not require real
physical exertion), the inability to control or monitor rowing far
away from the city clubs of Sydney and Melbourne, states' rights
and self-determination versus federalism and, of course, social class,
which had been transported to Australia along with the convicts,
the Navy, economic aid and a culture which enveloped indigenous
Aboriginee society quickly and thoroughly. The Victorian association's definition of trophies, which included jewellery, cutlery,
bicycles, walking sticks and musical instruments as well as boats,
oars and sculls, led to dispute over when a trophy became a cash –
that is, a saleable – prize. The differences over the amateur definition
led to the North Coast Rowing Association being set up in Grafton
in 1899 to align some New South Wales clubs with Victoria's definition. New South Wales dropped the manual clause in 1903. The
rest of the arguments were not so much settled as glossed over while
racing continued until the disruption of the First World War. Like
the ARA in England, the colonial associations did not really possess
the power to enforce their rules.

In 1912, however, a crew from Sydney RC overcame objections
to the status of Hauenstein, a policeman, and won the Grand at
Henley before taking part in the Olympics in Stockholm.

Umbilical Chords

The Referee, a Sydney weekly sports paper, informed its readers of
the exploits of oarsmen throughout the First World War. On 24 May

1916 it printed extracts from a letter from Lieutenant Wentworth of Leichhardt Rowing Club, sent from a troopship, giving news of Sydney oarsmen whom he had met in Egypt, in the Peninsula and in England. 'Kind regards to all at the shed,' he concluded, 'and hoping for a row in 1917.' Progress of the Empire's call to arms was monitored in detail, with long lists of men overseas. Alongside reports of Leichhardt and District Ladies' Sculling Club races was the news that Toowong Rowing Club had sent 70 per cent of its men to the front, Brisbane more than half, and Commercial two thirds. On 12 July the paper reported that the King's third son, Henry, had taken up rowing at Eton, that J. Goswell of Enterprise RC had encountered eighteen oarsmen on board his troopship all intent on visiting Thames clubs during their training in England, and gave results of a regatta at Putney for blinded soldiers. On 9 August Guiseppe Sinigaglia, the Italian winner of the Diamond Sculls, was reported killed in action. Another Diamonds winner, the Australian Lieutenant F. S. Kelly, was awarded the Distinguished Service Order for his part in the evacuation of the Gallipoli trenches. Sadly this was followed by news in September that he had been killed in France, and there was glowing tribute to this Australian Oxford scholar from Rudie Lehmann reprinted from the London paper *The Field*:

> There never was a sculler who had achieved a more perfect counterpoise between the two sides of his body, and the consequence was that not an ounce of his great strength was wasted . . . In music he had shown high promise of brilliant success as a pianist and composer. He seemed to exercise over the piano something of the same mastery with which he controlled a sculling boat.

Captain Keith Heritage from Sydney's Grand eight of 1912 was awarded the Military Cross for carrying a wounded man on his back when leading a raid on the German lines which resulted in twenty dead Germans and four captured. Ed Trickett, the former world professional champion, was an envoy of the Salvation Army responsible for raising funds for social and missionary work. He reported thirty-six fully equipped Red Cross motors at work in France and Belgium. From Canada came the news that the Argonaut Rowing Club 'is swept clear of scullers and oarsmen' by the Canadian Expeditionary Force. On 6 December *The Referee* reported the death of Trickett from injuries sustained when the sides of a well which he was helping to dig on his son's farm fell in on him. That month Copenhagen Rowing Club's sculling championships were held on the Thames, both contestants being in the forces in England. J. Oakford won his appeal against disqualification as an amateur by the Tasmanian Rowing Association for competing for cash in a chopping contest at a regatta. In January 1917 Yale moved to their new water on the Housatonic River, reported *The Referee*, under their English coach Guy Nickalls, while their second freshman crew had a shock at New Haven when their cox misjudged a low bridge and seven men struck their heads against the arch. Canadian Ned Hanlan's son, Captain Edward Hanlan, was killed in an aeroplane accident. Australian military men beat English military men in an eight-oared race from Putney to Hammersmith. *The Referee* heard from the English world champion Ernie Barry, wounded near Ypres: 'What a lot of good boys have left us through this war . . . Without fighting, the surrounding conditions are enough to kill anyone . . . Poor Bill Albany was killed when, after being badly wounded, he tried to bring back a wounded officer.' Not long after, Barry was sculling on the Thames when he suffered the cramps and capsized, but fortunately someone was at hand to rescue him. Before 1918 was out the war with Germany was over. On 21 December there was a regatta for blinded soldiers at Mosman Bay, Sydney.

The Wizards of Oz

Australian rowing kept much to itself between the world wars except for Bob Pearce's exploits in winning two Olympic sculling titles (1928 and 1932). The teachings of Australia's most famous rowing son, Steve Fairbairn, began to take a hold in the early thirties, more and more crews rejecting Orthodox rowing. In 1934 the centenary celebrations of the state of Victoria included a Henley-style regatta and brought London Rowing Club and the University of California to the Yarra at Melbourne. The third British Empire Games (now the Commonwealth Games) were held in Sydney in 1938, and in the following year a new sculling champion emerged at the Police club in Sydney, Merv Wood. Nine years later Wood travelled to England and took the sculling titles at Marlow, Henley and the

Olympic Games, the latter in a blinding hailstorm on the Henley course against the Uruguayan, Risso, and the American, Kelly. Two years later he was Empire Games champion at Karapiro, New Zealand, and doubles champion with another policeman, Murray Riley. Wood also established a record on the Yarra and went to Philadelphia to 'defend' the Philadelphia Challenge Cup, which the Americans regarded as the premier sculling trophy, against both Kelly and Rowe of Britain. In 1952 he won the Diamonds again and, troubled by an old wrist injury, came second to the Soviet sculler Tukalov at Helsinki in the Olympics. In the 1954 Empire Games in Vancouver he was in the winning coxed four and won the double sculls with Riley. Then in 1956 Wood was beaten for the Olympic nomination by a young sculler from the Mosman club called Stuart Mackenzie. Mackenzie took the silver medal in the Melbourne Olympics, beaten by the Russian Ivanov, but he went on to win the Diamond Sculls a record six times, including two victories over Ivanov. This was one of the great sculling duals; as Beresford and Kelly Sr stalked each other for a number of years, so did Ivanov and Mackenzie, even playing chess together to learn each other's approaches. Mackenzie had something of the charisma of the Canadian Hanlan nearly ninety years earlier; a chicken-sexer by trade, he was a charmer, a practical joker, and a showman who could pull a crowd. He enjoyed ridiculing and challenging establishment figures on both sides of the world, and became a master of psychological warfare against opponents by such tactics as showing them how extraordinarily long his arms were before going out to race, or lining up vitamin pill boxes on the breakfast table to sow suspicion of a secret performance elixir. He once stopped in a Henley final to raise his hat to the crowd, behaviour which the English frowned upon while flocking to watch him race in the hope that he would do something outrageous. He was eventually embroiled in controversy by attempting to influence selection of an Oxford crew for pecuniary gain while a member of the coaching team, and was later an unsuccessful coach at Columbia University in New York. Wood too has not escaped controversy in his life, having his job as chief policeman of New South Wales cut short after his sculling partner Riley earned himself a criminal record in the murky world of high finance. During their prime years, though, these men were champion characters as well as performers, and Mackenzie would take first prize as rowing

Entertainer of the Century by several lengths. The next great sculling duel to emerge, that between the Finn, Pertti Karppinen, and the German, Peter-Michael Kolbe, was longer and more epic but much less colourful.

Professional sculling persisted in the Sydney area until the 1950s. The Federation of Professional Sculling held its meetings at Sydney RC, one of the bastions of amateurism. But interest and prize money was hard to sustain. Wood refused offers to turn professional. Several 'country' clubs abandoned professional status and adopted the amateur code. Evans Fischer from the Clarence River defeated Evans Paddon three times for the world title before the latter retired in 1957, and Fischer was never challenged again. He was left as the undefeated champion of the world.

At the End of the World

A member of the Queen's Drive club of Otago, New Zealand, painted a red stripe on a piece of tin shaped like a rooster to celebrate their winning the coxed fours title for the third successive year in 1897. Before the race it had been blue and white, the colours of their rivals Port Chalmers, and nailed up in a prominent place to signify the 'cock of the walk'. It came to be known as the 'Boss Rooster', and a crazy tradition was born. Each year the club holding the title must take the Boss Rooster to the championship venue. New winners must paint the trophy in their own colours within an hour of their achievement. The Rooster had twenty-four coats by 1938, when a poultry farmer in the winning crew noticed that the comb had been fixed on back to front. It was stripped for surgery: the comb is now the right way round and the layers of paint increase with the years.

New Zealand rowing began in harbours in the shape of challenge matches among the boats of the whaling fleet at least as far back as the mid-nineteenth century. Whalers were rowed by five men and steered by a coxswain with a long sweep oar; they raced round a stake over 3 miles. Women's crews raced over 1 mile. The latter wore bodices and long skirts, with boaters and scarfs sporting their club colours. Landlubbers joined in these races and began to build their own boats in pursuit of considerable stake money. They eventually turned their attention to making English-type skiffs and racing craft when modern rowing spread through the islands, although imported English boats were preferred for racing. Modern rowing began at Christchurch with Canterbury Rowing Club in 1861. Several men of the cloth from England were among its founders. Six members were soon in trouble with the magistrates for bathing in a public place without proper costumes in the presence of boats which contained ladies. Naturally controversy over the definition of an amateur did not leave this remote British settlement untouched. Early regattas included professionals and amateurs, until the New Zealand Amateur Rowing Association came into existence in 1887 and required all clubs to join up if they wished to take part in national championships or to represent their country. Anomalies continued. For example, Jack McGrath, aged twenty-one, clubbed together with friends to buy a four built by Edwards of Melbourne. They borrowed a shed, called themselves Dunedin RC, and set out to win money. In 1890 the South Seas Exhibition in Dunedin offered 100 guineas for winning the fours in their regatta. Two Australians struck a deal with McGrath to join the crew. They were Neil Matterson, beaten in Australia for the world professional championship and in England for the English championship, and one Stephenson, who was holder of the New Zealand title. McGrath's crew duly won, and McGrath bought Matterson's sculling boat and joined Otago RC, which he had not been able to afford before. He thus became an amateur overnight. In 1896 New Zealand's champion amateur four were refused entry at an Australian regatta because two of them were fishermen. There were some notable professional scullers in New Zealand including Billy Webb who won the world title in 1907, retained it in 1908, and lost it to Dick Arnst in the same year. People in his home town of Wanganui seriously proposed to rename the place Webbanui after their favourite son's successes. Arnst, a New Zealander who won the NZ Wheel Race for cycling in 1903 and then the Sydney Thousand (pounds, not miles), and whom the Australians claim as one of their own, retained the title against four challengers up to 1911, including one from Webb. Then in 1921 these two had another go, Arnst winning again. George Welch, like Tom Sullivan, who was to become a famous coach in Germany, was a Kiwi who challenged for the world title but never won it.

In 1928 the NZARA purchased a dozen eights from England and sent two to each of the main rowing centres, thus establishing eight-oared rowing for men and sowing the seeds which brought spectacular success in the seventies when Rusty Robertson ran a national squad from Christchurch with the sponsorship of a tobacco company. His eights won the Olympic title in 1972, earning him the title '24-Carat Rusty', and medals from 1974 to 1976. It was a golden age which began with a win in the North American championships in 1967, led by Robertson from the tiny club of Oamaru, where they did not have an eight. Robertson became a part-time carpenter while coaching the New Zealanders, the latter job taking a toll of his career and his marriage. He eventually took his talents to New South Wales, a move which brought him further success and another marriage. Harry Mahon from the Waikato club took up the national mantle and his international medal tally includes world titles for the eight in 1982 and 1983. Mahon then combined the job with that of director of coaching for Switzerland. Running programmes in two countries which enjoy summers at opposite times of the year allows him to coach, live and work perpetually in the competition season.

New Zealand's first success in eights was in 1919 when the army trained at Putney in England while waiting for demobilization and won the Paris Peace regatta, which was presided over by General Pershing. An American military band played as they beat the United States, France and Newfoundland. The forces were in rowing action in the Second World War too, this time in Egypt, where head races in eights, fours, pairs and singles were held on the Nile with the cooperation of Egyptian clubs. The trophy now known as the Maadi Cup for the NZ Secondary School Association's regatta was presented by Dr Youssef Bahgat, the Egyptian singles champion.

Starboard Home

Lake Karapiro, scene of the world championships in 1978, seems a fitting place to end this Cook's Tour. There, 35,000 spectators roared the young Kiwi eight to a bronze medal at the rowing centre which the oarsmen had helped to build. A portrait of their predecessors, the Olympic champions of 1972, adorned a million cans of

Leopard lager on sale nationwide. There, for a week or two, rowing rivalled a national election campaign for television coverage, and filled screens with drama. A tiny rowing community had brought its sport into its own backyard and thrilled its kinfolk with its achievements. New Zealand, settled by pioneers from Britain, is about as far away as one can get from the motherland of modern rowing whence we set out, yet it maintains some of the strongest cultural links with the Old Country. We sailed the sea route via prime places of British interest such as South Africa, India, Hong Kong and the old convict settlements in Australia. Let us return starboard home through Suez, pausing to view the Nile Boat Race at Luxor, where clubs such as Harvard or Yale, Oxford or Cambridge, Leander or Trinity Dublin, Brussels or Paris do battle with the Egyptian police and universities, and to take a juice and a coffee on the deck of, say, the Arab Contractors barge in Cairo to marvel at the dhows, dilapidated ferries, and peace in the centre of a chaotic, bustling city. And so to the Mediterranean, where Phoenicians and Persians, Egyptians, Venetians, Turks, Carthaginians, Greeks and Romans plied the oar in pursuit of conquest and riches, mercy and justice. To them the oar was a tool and a means to various ends. To the men who reconstructed the Athenian trireme with whom we set out in this book, the oarpowered warship safeguarded the future of Western civilization and culture when it defeated the Persians at Salamis. Reflect on that when you see *Olympias* testing her speed off Poros, or a *sandolo* on the Grand Canal, or a Maltese fancy boat in Valetta harbour, or a *yola* off Gibraltar, or a *trainera* racing for San Sebastian, or a pilot gig off the Scilly Isles. If you are really lucky, you will share the poet John Masefield's vision before this voyage docks in Mecca-upon-Thames:

> Quinquireme of Nineveh from distant Ophir
> Rowing home to haven in sunny Palestine,
> With a cargo of ivory,
> And apes and peacocks,
> Sandalwood, cedarwood, and sweet white wine.

PART FIVE

FISA FAMILY

22

COUBERTIN TO KELLER

IT is accepted by the Fédération Internationale des Sociétés d'Aviron, the international rowing federation (FISA), that it was founded on 25 June 1892 at a congress in Turin, and that the first European championships – the main reason for the establishment of the federation – were held on Lake Orta in northern Italy in 1893. But the Belgians dispute this, claiming to have organized the first European championship on the Terneuzen Canal at Cluysen-Terdonck on 21 September 1890, when three scullers from an entry of five in outriggers raced 2800 metres. All the competitors except Charles Hahn of Strasbourg were Belgian, and the race was won by Edouard Lescrauwaet of Sport Nautique de Bruges in 12 minutes 8 seconds, with Hahn second. On 13 September 1891 Lescrauwaet won the second championship, with Hahn in third place. Two months earlier a congress had been held in Brussels, called by the Belgian federation to discuss a European entente. It was attended by representatives from clubs or federations in the Netherlands, France, Switzerland and Italy, and the Trieste federation from Austria and the Royal Regatas Club of Barcelona sent messages of assent. This congress drew up a list of proposals, and a further congress was called in Turin in 1892 which refined and approved them. The founders were Belgium, France, Italy and Switzerland. A representative from Trieste was present who said he could not engage formally until he received recognition from the Austrian government. Alsace-Lorraine was also represented. The Spanish club sent notice that it would adhere to the decisions of the congress. The Amateur Rowing Association sent its apologies and its good wishes, and the German federation did the same. Proceedings were covered at length in *L'Aviron*, the editor of which, P. V. Stock, was a leading advocate of the international federation.

The vexed question of the amateur was the first issue to be settled on the establishment of FISA. Perhaps it was fortunate that the ARA showed no interest, because the fledgling English association, founded ten years earlier, was struggling in a quagmire largely of its own making (see chapter 15). The Turin definition stated that 'all rowers who are considered amateurs in their own countries will be considered amateurs for international purposes too.' Rule II defined those not admitted as amateurs as 'professional rowers, sailors, watermen, ferrymen, professional fishermen, professional boatbuilders, boatmen, paid coaches, rowers who compete for wagers'. Also excluded were rowers who had competed against any of the above, and anyone barred or struck off by an affiliated federation and reported to FISA. They also tackled the question of cash prizes, deciding that if a regatta offered such, they should only be awarded to the clubs to which the winning crews belonged. They applied the same principle to travelling expenses. They also insisted that winning clubs could ask for cash prizes to be replaced by *objets d'art* or the equivalent value in racing equipment, the latter taking the form of vouchers for equipment by a stated manufacturer. Clubs whose rules did not permit them to receive cash prizes were obliged to opt for one of these substitutes. The cash-prize rules were instigated by the Italians. It was a delicate topic in, for example, France, where clubs were mindful of not offending municipal and private donors at regattas, some of whom were generous in their support, and where clubs were split as to the ethics of cash prizes, some prominent ones – including Coubertin's – following the ARA's line. Count Villanova, president of the Royal Rowing Club of Italy, produced a thoughtful paper pointing out that one attraction of permitting racing equipment as prizes was that it encouraged clubs, sailing as well as rowing, to develop by providing them with new means to enable them to compete for other prizes. 'Consequently, you might draw the logical conclusion that there is nothing professional or lucrative in this,' Villanova said.

One thing which confirms us in this opinion is the fact that the London Rowing Club, one of the founders of the puritanical Amateur Rowing Association, holds an annual race for its junior members, and the prize is a racing skiff to be ordered from the boat manufacturer Clasper's. Therefore, there is no possible danger that the material prize for the race might be considered a cash prize in accordance with the English code.

He went on to place the English code in a continental context:

The spirit of such a code is the constant preoccupation with keeping out all that is professional and preventing it from infiltrating the world of amateurs. Now that may be justified by English tradition. Professionals can survive there because they are fed by the large cash prizes which the passion for the sport commands, and which enable those who win them to live on them and even make a profit. However, such concerns have no place on the Continent, where clubs can scarcely find the means to send their teams to a few regattas. We believe we are right in saying that, on the Continent, there are no professionals in the English sense, for the simple reason that the passion for rowing is not so advanced as to produce rowers such as Hanlan, Beach, Searle, O'Connor etc. etc. and to crown them with laurels and pounds sterling. Another point of the English code is its complete opposition to our ideas of the definition of an amateur, and that is the absolute exclusion of the working classes, i.e. of all those who earn their living by a manual trade. We feel such exclusion is unjust and inappropriate. Rowing, as a sport, is highly beneficial physically. Therefore it should be open to all those who wish to participate for exercise purposes, not just to the privileged classes. However, we are of course all agreed on one point, i.e. the exclusion of the profit motive, and we shall direct all our efforts towards this noble aim. But let the poor as well as the rich, the workman as well as the graduate have the same *a priori* right to be considered amateurs. Let those who violate the rules be severely punished, but let us not set up the kind of caste divisions which common sense and the liberal laws of our countries should rule out automatically.

FISA expressed the intention of promoting the formation of national federations and of drawing up a code of conduct for championship regattas, and of not interfering in the internal affairs of its member federations. Under its auspices the first European championships were held on Lake Orta, Italy, in September 1893 for single sculls, coxed fours and eights, with each country being restricted to one entry per event. Lescrauwaet won the sculls, so the Belgian is indisputably the first European champion whichever regatta one adopts as the first. By adopting the Italian proposals regarding prizes and resisting making class an issue, FISA avoided many of the difficulties which the British had got themselves into. Nevertheless, growth was slow. Austria, the Austria of the Austro-Hungarian Empire, said that it adhered to the ARA's definition of an amateur but Trieste's claim to being a founding member did not find its approval. Nor did Bohemia's affiliation in 1892; it was forced to withdraw eight years later by the Austrians. Austria-Hungary itself did not join until the German federation did so in 1913, having stood firm on not recognizing Alsace-Lorraine as a representative federation. Russia and the Netherlands also came in then. The interregnum of the First World War resulted in Germany, Austria and Russia being barred or leaving, but a further sixteen countries joined between the wars. Germany was readmitted in 1934. Most were from Europe, but the new entry included Argentina (1928), Brazil (1931) and Uruguay (1932), as well as Egypt (1925) and Turkey (1931). The most significant among them was the United States (1929). The Americans sent an eight to Liège in 1931 and won the European title, and were the only English speakers to show any interest in FISA until after the Second World War, when both English associations (the ARA and the National ARA, shortly to merge) joined in 1947 in time for the Olympic regatta of 1948 at Henley. Australia also joined in 1947, Canada, Ireland and South Africa in 1948, and New Zealand in 1952. Thus the two power blocs of rowing – the English-speakers and the Western and Central Europeans – who until this time seldom encountered each other outside the four-yearly Olympic Games, began to intermingle. They were soon to be challenged by a third, new, bloc from Eastern Europe. Austria joined again in 1947. The Soviet Union, having stayed away from the Olympic movement after the Revolution, entered the Games in 1952 and joined FISA in the same year. Hungary (1921), Poland (1924) and Romania (1927) were already members. Bulgaria came along in 1955, and the German Democratic Republic gained membership in 1956, although it was unable to enter crews at championships until 1966 (see chapter 11). Federal Germany had been readmitted in 1951. It is said that FISA would not allow the Germans to return until the Dutch invited a German club to take part in a regatta as the sign that war wounds were healing. The twenty years between 1948 and 1968 increased South and Central America's presence by bringing in Cuba, Chile, Peru, Paraguay, Guatemala and Equador. The Mediterranean countries of Algeria, Israel and Morocco joined in the same period. North Korea became a member in 1969. The most important new member during the seventies was China, an awakening giant of rowing. Other appearances in the seventies were Libya (1971), Nigeria (1976), India and Pakistan (1979). In the eighties, half the newcomers came from the East – Hong Kong, Sri Lanka, Taipei, Indonesia, Singapore and the Philippines – and Tunisia, Gibraltar and Cyprus joined the Mediterranean contingent. (The Chronology gives an alphabetical list of the FISA members and the dates when they joined.)

Thus, in terms of membership, FISA encompassed all the large rowing countries by the time that Thomi Keller took over the presidency in 1958. Travelling habits were changing as pre-war isolationist thinking declined. Britain was no longer isolated from the Continent, but as the British Empire creaked towards self-determination and transformed itself into a multiracial club called the Commonwealth, its Empire Games, which had brought the 'white' British together from time to time since 1930, became further distanced from the mainstream of rowing. The United States was much closer to Western Europe in both travelling time and relationships than most of the Commonwealth nations. Both American and British spectacles had been almost exclusively Olympic-tinged until the Second World War. Both countries were now faced with much more powerful opposition there and in the annual European championships from the Soviet Union and Germany, in the latter's case first from the West but increasingly from the East. The Western European countries, with the exception of Federal Germany, were also relatively weak compared with their Eastern neighbours. In addition, the general atmosphere between Eastern Europe and the West was frosty, the Cold War being at its bitter height. As the Russian bear squared up to the American eagle and its Western European friends, old ideas of sportsmanship and fair play came under increasing strain from the forces of politics and propaganda, commercialism and publicity. Chance put Keller into the chair at a time when survival, let alone expansion, of the sport and the future shape of competitive and amateur rowing required some hard decisions.

Thomi, the Athletes' Champion

When Thomas Keller was elected president of FISA in 1958 he became leader of a small gentlemen's club. When he died in office in 1989, he was head of a worldwide family. This was a towering achievement, and its effect was felt far beyond the founding Olympic sport which he headed. Keller, the little-known and frustrated Olympic oarsman, became Thomi, the athletes' friend. When power politics came into sport, Thomi gave the performers a voice. For a man who had presence and effused effortless success, an early disappointment and a decision to stay close to the interests of the competitor were to shape his thinking and deal a blow in favour of athletes' self-respect. First, the boycott of the 1956 Olympic Games by Switzerland deprived Keller of representing his country in Melbourne, where he would almost certainly have won a medal. This made Keller realize that if sport was going to be saved from ruination by politicians, then sportsmen and women would have to take charge of their destiny and resist politicians. Secondly, when Avery Brundage of the International Olympic Committee was trying to coax Keller to succeed him as president, Keller refused the necessary preliminary step of taking the proffered seat on the IOC. This was in 1969, when his friend Mark Hodler of the international ski federation occupied one of the Swiss seats. The IOC's loss was rowing's gain. From his reply to Brundage's entreaty on 7 February 1969 Keller was clearly tempted: 'The tasks and opportunities to serve our ideals would tempt me very much as I realize the enormous possibilities it offers to influence the future development of sport in general and its role in our society. For good order's sake I would like to mention that my financial and business position would permit me to serve in such a capacity.' But he never made the move.

By the time Brundage dangled the presidency before him, Keller had already made up his mind to steer a different course in the Olympic movement. He had founded the General Assembly of International Sports Federations (GAISF) to give sports themselves a voice. He knew that he had to choose sides, and he knew whose side he was on. He wrote to Brundage:

I am convinced that it is not correct or advisable at the same time to be a member of the IOC and to hold the presidency of an international sports federation. At the present moment I could hardly leave my position in the international rowing federation as there is still a lot of work to do. I also intend to choose myself a successor and train him for the job . . . Besides, it is quite possible that [this] coming May I shall be elected as president of GAISF for a period of two years.

His mark would be made outside the IOC by giving FISA and the other sports federations their forum in the movement. Besides, Keller probably realized that if he had been elected to the IOC instead of Raymond Gafner, there is no guarantee that, as Brundage's nominee, he would have reached its presidency. Brundage had become unpopular during the last years of his long reign. In addition there were many besides Brundage who resented the creation of GAISF as a challenge to the IOC's authority. The Irish peer Lord Killanin, an oarsman while at Eton, who had been asked to stand against Brundage in 1967, refused to do so until some provision was made to pay the president's expenses. When this was forthcoming in 1971 he put himself forward, but was handicapped because he was by then Brundage's candidate for the presidency. Two others stood against him unsuccessfully, and he succeeded Brundage in 1972. Meanwhile both rowing and GAISF continued to benefit from an able, enthusiastic and humane leader.

To reach a position of being head-hunted by the most powerful man in world sport, Keller had a thorough grounding in sport himself. He was born on 24 December 1924 and was first attracted to rowing when he was taken to the Olympic regatta in Berlin in 1936. From 1940 to 1947 he rowed at Grasshopper, Zürich, in fours and eights. In 1947 he represented Switzerland in cross-country skiing and ski jumping at the Academic World Games (later to become the Universiade). In 1950, the year in which he graduated in chemical engineering from the Swiss Federal Technical Institute (the Polytechnic) in Zürich, he became single sculling champion and took the bronze medal at the European championships. He joined the family company of Eduard Keller at the age of twenty-five, with military service behind him and with a talent for shooting. He was an expert motorcyclist in the army and formed part of Winston Churchill's escort when the British leader visited Switzerland. From 1951 to 1954 he was in Manila, where he became captain of Manila Boat Club, and also rowed for the Royal Hong Kong Yacht Club. Ian Purslow, his predecessor as Manila captain, remembers his arrival with his wife Dorry: 'I envied him when he told me about the regattas he competed in, with his sculling boat *Pourquoi Pas* fixed to the roof of his car while he toured Europe.' *Pourquoi Pas* travelled to Manila with the Kellers. Many years later in London the Amateur Rowing Association invited Purslow, now the president of Bristol Ariel RC, to a lunch on the occasion of a presentation to Keller. He was agreeably surprised when his Philippines aquaintance remembered him after thirty years and introduced him to some of the ARA dignitaries who were very standoffish, 'a fact about which he was very much aware and wryly commented to me about.'

On returning home in 1954 Keller became a board member of Eduard Keller, and continued rowing. He had acquired a taste for chilli-hot food and could cook a mean chicken curry, and in later life was never without the silver pepper mill given to him by Dorry in his pocket. His sculling partner Hans Frohofer became his friend. 'When we were rowing we were partners, afterwards we were friends. That's an important difference,' says the lecturer from the Polytechnic. 'I accepted him all the time as the leader. He always beat me in races. I was a fast starter but he always came through and I couldn't raise enough breath to stop him. Thomi was also first in the Melbourne Club competitions.' The Melbourne Club is made up of the Swiss athletes, journalists and aircraft crew who never went to the Olympics in Australia because of the aborted boycott. Ironically, the neutral Swiss invented the sports boycott by refusing to send a team in 1956 because they objected to the Soviet invasion of Hungary. However, when it became apparent that the Hungarians themselves were going to Melbourne to take on the Russians, the Swiss realized that the boycott was senseless and gave permission for federations to make up their own minds. Their shooters and gymnasts decided not to go, but the rest packed their bags. Unfortunately they were then unable to fly because the Red Cross had chartered every aircraft available to deal with the Suez Crisis. *Encore*, the Keller double, spent the Olympics idly. The shooters and gymnasts were not invited to join the Melbourne Club, which holds an annual reunion and sports day.

Keller and Frohofer were part of a powerful squad from Grasshopper and See-Club, half a dozen men who chased each other and made up different combinations for the honours. In 1955 Keller with Hanruedi Vollmer lost the final of the Double Sculls at Henley to a Burevestnik crew of Zhilin and Emchuk by half a length. In 1956 he won the Swiss championships with Frohofer. He was ill during the European championships, but nevertheless came fourth, partnered by Erich Schriever, and it was with Schriever that he was selected for the Melbourne Olympics. In 1957 Frohofer and Keller retained their national title after only ten days' training, and came fourth in the European championships. When he was elected president of FISA in 1958 Keller's only experience of office was in Manila. He was still an active oarsman, and was precipitated to the leadership of FISA prematurely when Gaston Mullegg, who had marked him out as a successor some time hence, was killed when he crashed his plane. Keller took soundings before he stood. When Eric Holford wrote to him on 7 October to say that he had found a wonderful course in Honolulu, Thomi replied that 'the fight for the presidency of the FISA is going on merrily and I enjoy watching developments. Things do not seem to look too bad as far as my candidacy is concerned.' He found support from his former coach Hans Walther, the FISA secretary Charles Riolo, and the president of the German federation, Walter Wülfing. He was thirty-three.

The first thing that Keller set out to do was improve the standard of umpiring at regattas. The umpires' commission was the first commission that FISA set up. Members of the council were forbidden to officiate. When the commission improved the theoretical and practical examinations for a FISA umpire's licence, member federations took up the cause. Another campaign was the improvement of regatta organization on the principle of putting the oarsmen first. Besides Walther and Wülfing, Keller's first helpmates were the Belgian vice-president Jacques Spreux, the Dane F. Aa. Hansen and Louis Patricot, the president of the French federation, who had been badly smashed up in the plane crash that killed Mullegg. (Patricot had to be fitted with artificial joints, and Chris van der Ploeg, another FISA official, remembers stopping at a petrol station with him to lubricate them.) The first big technical development was the system of lane marking introduced in the Rome Olympics of 1960, known as the Albano system after the lake on which the regatta was held. Submerged wires are laid along the course and buoys floated above them, with yellow and black lane markers at the start as a visual aid to crews. By this means the whole 2000 metres is separated into lanes, leaving no argument about whether a crew has taken somebody else's water. In 1961 Keller proposed a thorough overhaul of the racing procedure which was still based partly on the Laws of Boat Racing drawn up in 1872, before FISA was founded.

The first real test of FISA's authority came in 1961 when the European championships were held in Prague. At that time the host country Czechoslovakia was a member of the Warsaw Pact and, as a socialist state of Eastern Europe, was embroiled in the Cold War. The Czechs refused an entry visa to George Justicz, a British competitor with a British passport who had left Czechoslovakia after the war. Justicz went to see the ambassador to no avail. The secretary of the ARA, Freddie Page, contacted Keller, who sent a cable to Prague threatening to move the championships, due to begin in about three weeks, to Duisburg in Germany unless the authorities issued Justicz with a visa and a guarantee of safety. The visa came within days, and Justicz heard later that the ambassador had been reprimanded. Then there was flag trouble. At this time the Federal and Democratic republics of Germany rowed internationally as one country, using a special tricolour with the Olympic rings added to it. The Czechs hoisted the Democratic Republic flag as they prepared for the European rowing championships, thinking that they could 'go sledge riding' with Thomi. But they had to think again. He demanded that the flag be changed and that Justicz be treated the same as everyone else. When they refused, he threatened to call off the championship an hour before the opening ceremony. The hosts relented, and Justicz won a silver medal in an event close to Thomi's heart, the double sculls.

By the early sixties a new FISA logo was designed by Hans Ruedi Scheller, a European rowing champion. It replaced one which depicted a big-chested female athlete and was used first on medals made by the Huguening company. Scheller's motif of five oars (described by some as five bottles) was based on the 'five continents' theme of the Olympic five-ring symbol, and the same colour sequence was adopted when it replaced FISA's old blue and white logo. FISA had thus changed its image before a test more severe than that posed by the Czechs arose. The German Democratic Republic mounted pressure to gain membership in its own right. It was clear that this would be inevitable sooner or later, and so FISA under Keller's leadership took an important step in depoliticizing itself at the same time. At the congress of 1965 the council's proposal that flags and anthems be supressed at championships was accepted by forty-six votes with four abstentions, and the same number of votes then admitted the two German federations to row in the 1966 championships. A magesterial fanfare, specially commissioned from Paul Burckhardt, composer of 'O Mein Papa', was substituted for national anthems, and national flags were dropped from medal ceremonies. Given the subsequent dominance of gold medals by the Democratic Republic and the Soviet Union, this saved regatta-goers from much repetition and monotony, but it was not a popular move in all quarters despite the size of the vote in its favour. Many countries were proud to have their anthems played even if there was no internal pressure to do so. Time and again the Eastern Europeans tried to persuade congress to reverse this decision. Eventually it seemed that even they were doing so as a ritual, at the behest of their political bosses. When the vote was taken in 1986, it was clear from an analysis of the voting figures that not only had support for flags and anthems fallen away, but that at least one socialist country had taken advantage of the secret ballot to vote against them.

This stood Keller and FISA in good stead when it came to the issue of South Africa. During the worldwide boycott of South African sport, brought about by that government's discriminatory racial policies, the South African Amateur Rowing Union remained a member of the international body. There was a gentleman's agreement that the South Africans would uphold the principles of FISA but not enter crews in FISA championship events. This turned out to be a wise decision, one which all parties could live with, and one which will ease SAARU's quick return to international competition now that the IOC, satisfied that the apartheid system is crushed, has removed its ban on South Africa's participation in the 1992 Olympic Games. The only problem concerning the gentleman's agreement arose on the fringes of FISA in 1973, when the Soviet Union brought pressure on Nottinghamshire International Regatta and Henley Royal Regatta in Britain to disallow South African entries, and both gave way. The former was run under FISA rules and the latter is recognized as a FISA regatta although it runs under its own rules.

Keller found support among rowers and his member federations because his principles were clear from the moment he took office. He separated politics from sports events, and he developed facilities for sportsmen by always asking: What is the best for the athlete?

He learned his business from the bottom up. The autocracy which
he sometimes displayed was backed by a knowledge of every techni-
cality of the construction of a course or the running of a race. He
was not a man to be bluffed by science.

Before world championships and Olympic regattas he would
spend one or two days at the course checking every detail, and
organizing committees would quake at the thought of being caught
out by omissions or for not following the FISA 'cookbook' to the
letter. Meanwhile, FISA's annual programme grew: world championships were held every fourth year from 1964 and became annual
in 1974, when European championships were dropped; the women's
European championships joined up with the men's during the fifties;
women were included in the world championships from 1974 and
admitted to the Olympic Games regatta in 1976. (The IOC session
which admitted women may have been assisted in their decision by
the presence of two blonde female athletes dressed for the occasion
in cut-down jeans. Keller diplomatically included them in his dele-
gation to demonstrate that women rowers were not Amazons.)
Championships for lightweights started in 1975 (women in 1985)
and juniors appeared in 1970 (women in 1983); regattas for under-
23s were introduced. The veterans or masters meetings became the
largest regattas in the world, and international tours were started
for pleasure rowing. All these developments required many people
to run them. As more courses became available and events grew in
number, a growing band of able men and women were drawn mainly
from the ranks of former competitors to man the FISA commissions,
to run coaching programmes, to represent far-flung parts of the
world, and to run regattas.

This was achieved partly by Keller's great ability to make ties
throughout the world. A man of few personal possessions, he lived
out of a suitcase for much of his time, often declaring that he would
reduce his activity but continuing to fly from meeting to meeting.
He was seldom in his seventh-floor office at Eduard Keller with its
view over the rooftops of central Zürich. He always checked rowing
courses long before their designated regattas were due to be held.
He listened to others and built an enormous knowledge of people
close to rowing. He was as often to be found in the back of a small
boathouse as fronting a ceremony or making a speech. The former
was where he preferred to be, among the competitors. It is note-

worthy that in a sport which is so sparse, far-flung and localized, there were few places where nobody knew the name of Thomi Keller when he was FISA's president.

Keller at Nottingham and Henley

The standards that Thomi Keller expected permeated the sport which he headed. It was impossible to organize a championship without reference, consciously or unconsciously, to what Thomi would say or think or how he would react to a proposal or an arrangement. This was the case even with efficient and experienced organizers, such as those of the world championships in Nottingham in 1986 who were in the position of enjoying Thomi's trust to get on with the job in the manner in which FISA would expect. Many of them had cut their teeth in a previous world championship in 1975. In spite of this, however, there were few meetings in the two years before the championships at which the name of Keller did not come up, as the author, being a member of the committee, can testify. The danger was that by leaving nothing to chance the committee would leave the FISA president with time on his hands and the temptation to meddle with carefully laid plans.

Keller was sharp in his observations and sometimes deliberately outspoken. His style, especially on the first day of an event, was to provoke confrontation to establish his authority. He was a good confrontationalist when the situation required it, but he was also good-humoured and found time to chat to anybody. Nottingham ran true to form, but in the event the only disagreement with FISA concerned the effect of a weather forecast on the conditions for repechage day. At the team managers' meeting which follows each day's racing Keller decided to bring next morning's programme forward by several hours. The organizing committee's weather forecast from the local Air Force station indicated that this would be unnecessary, but the committee accepted the decision without demur because it was made in the interests of the athletes. A risk was removed and the army of officials was in place by 7 a.m. the following morning (seventy officials are required to stage a championship race). Only the television broadcasters failed to get up early.

Ironically, the Air Force's forecast was proved right, but the interests of the athletes had been put before the interests of television publicity.

Keller inspected the course a couple of days before rowing began, and he chaired a long and harassed FISA congress in which both the question of flags and anthems and the question of South Africa's membership arose, the *status quo* prevailing in both cases. Nobody ever read a newspaper during a congress with Keller in the chair. He reprimanded officials if they were wrong, kept delegates to the point, and was deft with procedures. In the words of his son Dominik, he could 'tell people where hell and heaven was'. He agitated from a position of strength, and he could be just as effective using charm and humour, and in a choice of several languages.

On this occasion he gave particular attention to statements for the press concerning the South African question, a potent one in the light of the Commonwealth Games, which had just closed in Edinburgh, having been boycotted because of breaches in the Gleneagles Agreement concerning sporting ties with South Africa, and the Olympics, due in Seoul two years hence, which was under threat of boycott. During the regatta he followed racing on the course, attended the usual managers' and jury meetings, and took the chair at the athletes' meeting which he had introduced some years before as a feature of championship regattas to allow competitors their say about their sport and its governing body. He was sent up mercilessly in the press centre's daily news-sheet, and he shared the jokes. He talked to the press, attended a round of official functions including a reception for Princess Anne, who was later to become a member of the IOC. He was cheered to the rafters at the roisterous workers' dinner where he expressed profuse thanks to the 400 volunteers and paid tribute to their chairman, Peter Coni, whose heart attack a week before the opening ceremony had kept him away from most functions. Keller gave away most of the medals and greeted most of the winners by their first names. No anthems were played except FISA's until 'God Save the Queen' at the closing ceremony; no flag except FISA's was raised and lowered.

Another side of Thomi's character was seen at another British occasion – Henley Royal Regatta, where he was made a steward in 1976. The stewards are a self-perpetuating oligarchy. They are in full control of the regatta, are elected for life, and have a management committee and a permanent staff for day-to-day affairs. There are approximately fifty of them, listed in their programme in order of seniority, i.e. length of service. Assisted by a large number of volunteers, they all have jobs to do at the regatta, fitness permitting, from marshalling in the trailer park to umpiring and timekeeping. They are all men. New boys begin, as Thomi once remarked, by 'cleaning the lavatories', and this was metaphorically the case with the president of FISA just as with everyone else. Thomi was promoted to umpire in 1985, a job in which he shared a launch with Coni, his friend and the chairman of the management committee. One of Coni's aims when he became chairman was, in company with the eternal problem of giving a group of men elected for life a more youthful profile, to improve the standard of umpiring, and this he did gradually by retiring umpires who did not possess a FISA licence and replacing them with those who did. Thomi quietly and efficiently got on with his job, happy to be part of a team and never expecting (or receiving) treatment different from anyone else because he was president of FISA. He only summoned his steward's authority on the rare occasion that required it. During the eighties, for example, when the regatta was in danger of being swamped by commercial hangers-on who were profiting on its back, he delayed the start of a race while a helicopter landed in a nearby field to deliver more sponsored guests to a private enclosure. Apart from the noise, which rendered maximum decibels of the Swiss-German voice and its megaphone ineffective, the rotorblade sent a whirlwind of grass-cuttings over crews, spectators and umpire's launch. Thomi waited until conditions returned to some hint of regattas long ago, when the dropping of a pin could be heard before the terrifying moment when the crews left the hands of the stake-boat boys in a swoosh of blades. Then he picked up his two-way radio, contacted the regatta control, gave the number of the helicopter, said 'have it shot down' just loud enough for the crews awaiting his word to hear, and started the race in a considerably calmed atmosphere. After the regatta Coni, himself a lawyer, threatened all the commercial interests with the letter as well as the spirit of the law: if you do not behave yourselves and respect the sportsmen who provide the entertainment in front of which you parade your guests and line your pockets, he effectively told them, you will kill the goose that lays the golden eggs. The stewards will call off the regatta. Next year there were no helicopters; bands on steamers stopped playing just before the start and the finish. An atmosphere of peace, if not tranquillity, returned. For Keller Henley was a place of relaxation, where good fellowship was to be found in the boat tents and in the home where he stayed, that of his fellow steward Alan Burrough, right opposite the finish line. And on the most exclusive lawn of British sport, that of the stewards themselves in a hidden corner of their enclosure, he could have discussions ranging widely over rowing with his guests, such as the planning of this book, much of which was outlined between his bouts of umpiring.

Olympian Keller

When the Olympic Games held a congress at Varna, Bulgaria, in 1973 Keller nailed his colours to the mast.

> The Olympic Games have grown from a modest sporting event into a gigantic undertaking and this has led to a fundamental change in their character. The principles of the original Olympic rules were that the object of the reintroduction of the Games was not primarily to give competitors the opportunity to win medals, nor to break records. The Games were not principally to entertain the public, nor were they to provide athletes with a means to furthering their professional careers, nor were they to provide the opportunity to prove the superiority of one political system over another.

The original basic principles of Coubertin had been overtaken by events, principles rendered pointless by both the changed role of sport in modern industrial society and the success of the Games. Recognizing that winning medals now counted above all else and that Olympic medals often acted as a springboard to a career with material gain, Keller went on to lambast Rule 26 which limited an athlete to thirty – or in certain cases sixty – days of full-time preparation in a year.

> Everyone interested in sport knows that entries for the Olympic Games have largely become an open exhibition of lying quite incompatible with the ethics of sport and the spirit of Baron de Coubertin . . . The IOC attempts to support the fiction of amateur games with the help of Rule 26, although it is fully aware that most national Olympic committees

and sports federations are primarily concerned to ensure that these conditions are circumvented as discreetly as possible, in order to be able to nominate their best athletes for the Games.

It was high time the IOC recognized that the changes in sport and society since 1896 were irreversible, and it should act accordingly. There was no definition of what physical and mental performance was required to make a sport recognizable by the IOC. Keller roundly attacked the ceremonial aspects of the Games, pointing out that the ceremony of hymn, anthems, parade, speeches, flights of doves, flame and flag ceremonies, with its roots in Coubertin's notions of the religious connotations of the original Greek Games, was being extended by folk displays, entertainment of political dignitaries and the 'gratification of human vanity'. The athletes' parade was turning into a fashion show, and they were expected to be on their feet in the stadium for far too long.

For me, Keller said, the objectives should be the development of mental and physical health in the young through competitive sport and its maintenance as a leisure activity. The responsibility of sports federations in pursuing these ends is to establish rules of competition, requirements of equipment and sites, the division of athletes into categories (age, sex, weight, performance level), the definition of amateur status, medical care for athletes, organization of championships, supervision of international competitions, fostering development, and co-ordination of member federations. 'These . . . do not exist in the Olympic movement,' he told his audience. Coubertin's laudable aims have been lost in euphoria. Keller also attacked the hierarchy of sport:

> An administrative career in sport is often misused to satisfy personal vanity. To my mind it should above all be the fulfilment of an obligation to youth. Everyone holding a responsible position in sport should have a thorough knowledge of it . . . It is not enough to have been a competitor oneself . . . It is not enough to watch competitive events from the stand. There must be personal contact with athletes on the training field.

He recognized the dangers of gigantism on the Olympic balance sheet, and outlined the alternative routes that the IOC could take. It could either ally itself with 'modern competitive sport' and face the consequences, or limit its Games to genuine amateurs as Coubertin had originally intended. Keller did not choose, only pointing out the disaster which would befall the Games if doing nothing prevailed. 'All over the world,' he said, 'people are tired of the insincerity, the excessive cost and the ceremony which accompany the Games. Their huge success in this century is no guarantee for the future.' The federations stand ready to cooperate, but, he said, they expect to be treated as partners by the IOC.

Three years earlier, in 1970, he had pointed out to members of the IOC that their rule book gave the same amount of space to the question of candidate cities' facilities for participating sports as the clause which read: 'At the session when the invitation and the questionnaire are discussed, cocktail parties, receptions, etc., must not be arranged by the inviting city before the allocation of the Games.' Although considerable progress had been made by 1981, Keller was still arguing for the revision of Rule 26 at the Baden-Baden congress and demanding immediate action on the control of doping.

Keller's Gamesmanship

In FISA, as we have seen, difficult decisions were made early in Keller's presidency which set the tone for much that was to follow. His policy of getting close to rowing people in different countries paid off. The British thought of him as one of their own when they saw him at Henley; he was also close to the East Germans, understanding how their society worked and therefore able to tell their president, Wilfried Hofmann, that FISA was about rowing and not about politics, an attitude which the Democratic Republic respected from the time it joined until the time it disappeared. Hofmann later became chairman of FISA's junior commission, and others of his countrymen were also involved, notably Klaus Filter on the materials commission, Theo Körner on the competitive rowing commission, and Helmut Pohlentz on the medical commission. The Russians too liked Keller, recognizing that he could play their game, over vodka and Georgian cognac if necessary. They presented him with two dogs during the course of his presidency. Knowing that his members supported him, he was able to influence Olympic organizing committees, as in the case of Munich in 1972 when the rowing course was planned to end within the municipal boundaries of

Dachau. The Polish army officer Jerzy Borkovski, who was a member of the FISA council, said that he had been in Dachau before, 'nearly in the oven'. The course was moved a few hundred metres out of Dachau. Others who served with Keller were the Argentine Gaston Walbaum who, while living in Paris, became FISA's first continental representative for South America; Christopher Davidge of Britain became the expert on course installations; Horace 'Davy' Davenport made the Americans active in FISA; the vice-presidents Chris van der Ploeg from Holland and Yevgeny Kabanov from the USSR became trusted lieutenants. David Cazes, a brilliant multilinguist from Britain who took charge of translation, was never far from Thomi. Don Rowlands of New Zealand became his eyes and ears in the southern hemisphere; Pablo Span of Mexico fulfilled a similar role in North America. Thor Nilsen came to play a highly influential role and, latterly, Mike Sweeney of Britain took over responsibility for controlling regattas from Davidge. Indeed, the list of Keller's collaborators is a long one, too long to complete here.

FISA's horizons were widened considerably during Keller's presidency. Fifteen years into office, he outlined his thoughts on where rowing should be going at the 1973 congress in Lucerne:

> The structure of rowing today is like an obelisk with a high point and a narrow base. It is our duty to see to it that it again becomes a pyramid. We were and still are proud that competitive rowing belongs to the most exacting forms of sport. Our task is to show that rowing is also an ideal physical activity in the open air. We must find additional forms of competition which emphasize pleasure and good fellowship. We must convince more people of the beauties and delights of pleasure rowing and simple outings with friends . . . Nature conservation is of the utmost importance to us. Fortunately the use of motorboats on lakes and rivers is being increasingly limited.

He concluded that new boats which did not involve advanced techniques of construction were required, at moderate cost. He supported veteran rowing but did not wish it to turn into another high performance category of sport. He supported the development of lightweight rowing. He became increasingly cost-conscious, eventually leading FISA to ban sliding riggers after the 1983 world championships because, although the boat may go faster, 'we are opening a door to spending money for nothing.' He realized that

FISA Family

392

this development was easy to apply to the single boat, but adapting it to larger boats was fraught with difficulties.

The decisions of principle taken by Keller early in his reign at FISA were also to stand him in good stead – maybe to lead him – to become a champion of the athlete and the athlete's interests when the Olympic Games began to run into trouble in the 1970s. After the somewhat improvised Games of 1948, hastily arranged after the Second World War, the quadrennial meeting changed its nature as it grew. As more sports were admitted it became increasingly difficult to adhere to the informality of the 'village'; as more countries joined in, greater weight was placed on taking part and winning medals for political as well as sporting reasons. In 1956 the word 'boycott' entered the Olympic dictionary; by 1968 black athletes from the United States had introduced the black power salute from the medal winners' podium (and were disciplined for it, unlike those who saluted Hitler in 1936), and television was adding up medals in tables almost before athletes had caught their breath; in that year also the Mexican government, hosts of the Games, brutally suppressed student dissidents by shooting them dead just before the Games opened; 1972 saw Black September terrorists wreck the Israelis' participation, and the sport went on almost without a break; by 1976 the Games had become an enormous financial burden on the host city, in this case Montreal. Boycotts reduced entries in the 1976, the 1980 and the 1984 Games, but paradoxically the Olympics gained in prestige through this period, one of the effects being that the American television networks were prepared to pay millions of dollars to secure broadcasting rights. In the seventies and eighties commercialism involving sponsorship, advertising and television contracts moved into sport in a big way, particularly in motor racing, tennis and soccer, and the Games ran with the trend. Sponsorship and television provided a way out of financial crisis, manifest at the 'Hollywood Olympics' of Los Angeles where the combination of a huge market in the host country and Californian pizzazz put the organizing committee's balance sheet into profit. The television contract had been signed by Killanin, but by now the Olympics had acquired a new breed of top brass, the 'Latino mafia', who were guiding the Games into an area which people like Keller regarded as both dangerous and vulnerable. One effect was that the pressure to include sports which were not traditionally Olympic ones but were attractive to television was increased, so that highly developed professional sports like tennis and theatrical experiences like synchronized swimming muscled in. At the same time sports which had never become – or in rowing's case, were no longer – professional and which did not have high television appeal became vulnerable as well as dependent on their Olympic status to sustain themselves. The bulk of income for sports like rowing, which have low spectator appeal and therefore less attraction for sponsors, comes from their share of the Olympic television contract. Keller argued for equal shares among sports, and worried that the Olympic bubble would burst, that the sponsorship boom from shoes to television advertising would, in the long run, stretch sport beyond its means. He therefore devoted much energy to applying the footbrake to the financial panacea advocated by the Latino mafia led by Juan Antonio Samaranch, member of Real Club Maritimo and General Franco's ambassador to the USSR, who followed Lord Killanin as president of the IOC. The Latino mafia also included the Italian Primo Nebiolo, notorious boss of the International Amateur Athletic Federation. The General Assembly of International Sports Federations (GAISF) had been born out of Keller's desire to have a body closer to sport and its developments than the IOC. The IOC, after all, presided over one meeting every four years, whereas bodies like FISA had responsibilities all the year round year in, year out. The rise of the Latino mafia increasingly isolated Keller in the mid-eighties, but he did not bend in his opinion. And he was 'by far the best president of any federation I encountered,' according to Killanin, who was his friend as well as a president of the IOC with whom he had to negotiate. Killanin shared Keller's dislike of anthems and flags, mistakes over which gave him more trouble than anything else, and he regarded Keller's principles with respect, even though he was sometimes in dispute with him. He points out that, unlike the federations which make the rules for their sports, the IOC is not democratic, while conflict between the IOC and the federations is as inevitable as it is between the IOC, the federations and the organizing committees of the Games. Keller's strength, Killanin says, is that he knew every athlete by his nickname.

There was one conflict which Keller had to reconcile with himself concerning the Olympics: his dislike of commercialism and the erection of costly structures for the Games was at odds with his passionate interest in building new rowing courses to get the best for the athletes in his own sport. Building a piece of flat water large enough to take six 2000-metre lanes and all the necessary infrastructure is a huge undertaking even if a lake or gravel pit is available for adaptation. The Bosbaan in Amsterdam was dug manually during the depression of the thirties partly to relieve unemployment. The Holme Pierrepont course in Nottingham was a conversion from gravel pits, and the Strathclyde course near Glasgow was created by diverting and then damming the river Clyde. The Xochimilco course was the first purpose-built for an Olympic regatta. It was designed by Keller himself and created from the canals of Mexico City. Four years later the course in Munich was specially constructed for the Games; Montreal's was created beside the St Lawrence; Moscow's was specially constructed in 1980 and Seoul's in 1988. The setting in the mountains on the fringe of Seoul is as aesthetically satisfying as Xochimilco. Neither would exist if the Olympics had not been hosted there. Keller liked the Seoul course, returning to it on the day after the regatta ended to view it from a road which rises to the hill behind it. 'It was as if he were saying goodbye to it,' his son Dominik, who accompanied him on this little pilgrimage, says.

Keller was especially fond of Xochimilco because it was his first and because he struck such a rapport with the Mexicans. The 1968 regatta left behind it a band of able administrators and an active North American continental representative for FISA in Pablo Span. But people in the Olympic movement began to question the expense involved in setting up such facilities, and organizing committees and controllers of budgets of future events began to show concern. Keller revealed to the 1967 FISA congress that he had sent an ultimatum to the president of the IOC on 7 December 1966 insisting that the race course be ready for use no later than October 1967. This had been prompted by unanswered requests for progress reports, and it concluded with the threat that if the demand was not met, FISA would renounce its participation in the Games. 'Moreover,' Keller told congress, 'I demanded that if these conditions were not met, the IOC permit this regatta to take place somewhere else. A copy . . . was sent to the president of Mexico City organizing committee.' The main worry over courses such as Seoul and Mexico was that they would be little used after the event for which they had been built (see chapter 19). The feeling grew within Keller that the continued use of such a facility must be an integral part of the scheme, just as the trend has been for accommodation built for Olympic athletes to be easily adaptable to other users when the Games are over. Even where artificial courses have been built in places where there is a lot of rowing activity, there are problems over the amount of use and the cost thereof.

Sometimes Keller gave the impression that he would like to wash his hands of the whole Olympic paraphernalia. But he knew in his heart that it was essential for rowing to stay inside the Games. For one thing, FISA could not support itself without Olympic funds, even though its president personally spent much of his own wealth on his federation's business. Secondly, the athletes are wedded to the Olympics. They enjoy taking part in them and regard them as the pinnacle of achievement, despite the fact that athletically there may be little or no difference between an Olympic regatta and a world championship. Thirdly, the appeal, glamour and charisma of the Olympics is a lifeline to the member federations of FISA. 'Olympic' is often the only magic word which will extract sponsorship, both from governments and commercial interests. So Keller never seriously considered removing FISA from the Olympics. On the contrary, he watched its back and encouraged it to join with other sports to make their voice known. He would not have minded if the Olympic Games had ceased to exist. But while they existed, Keller ensured that his federation maintained its place as a founding Olympic sport.

A Good Spurt

Rowing has always had a close relationship with the modern Olympics. As we have seen, Pierre de Coubertin, the founder, was an anglophile who admired the educational ideas and ethos of team sport which he found on visits to England. One connection between the French father of the Olympics and rowing was his acquaintance with a Cambridge rowing Blue who was prime minister of France for a short time in 1879, William Henri Waddington, an Englishman who took French nationality and was ambassador to the Court of St James in 1883. Coubertin watched the stewards running Henley and implanted some Henley habits into his Games. Rowing was scheduled in the first Olympics at Athens in 1896 but abandoned due to bad weather. But it has featured ever since. In defending its special qualities in an article in 1911, Coubertin identified some of its problems. It was not a sport full of technical innovation like many others at the time, he said, and not many new clubs are opening (although there had been an enormous boom in rowing clubs during the last twenty years of the nineteenth century). 'Everywhere, the same regattas continue to attract more or less the same entries . . . The members remain practically the same and so do the performances.' He opined that the basis of good performance had not changed:

> The position of the rower before the stroke, the stroke, the release and the return to the forward position do not succeed fully except by applying the same principles which have been the secret of the success of all the best rowers for over forty years. If you start with a hunched back, your shoulders forward, your arms drawn in and your hands too low; if you lean too far back at the end of the stroke and let your elbows stick out and then come back forward sharply, jolting your spine, you have always been, still are, and always will be a bad rower.

As for spectators:

> If they are on the stands they complain that they only see the finish. If they are following along behind they complain that they see nothing. Not to mention the fact that the river is not usually very accessible, and the banks rarely lend themselves to the construction of comfortable stands. There are hardly any rivers suitable for regattas in the world apart from the Thames . . . The public does not come in large numbers, and if . . . people are lured they tend to go away disappointed. For all they really manage to do is catch a few quick glimpses of a spectacle that only the initiated can fully appreciate. In between are a lot of long, boring intervals.

But Coubertin identified, albeit with mixed metaphors, the underlying strength of rowing under these considerable handicaps, the band of faith which binds its congregation, even those members of it who have hung up their oars. 'All this just goes to prove what a powerful, superior sport rowing is,' the baron wrote.

> Given that it is so handicapped, why has it not simply died out, particularly nowadays when the idea is to make the least effort possible and the love of publicity and the hatred of discipline are so overtly predominant?

Rowing is a rigorous, tough cult, which is all about obedience and self-denial. There is no artificial sense of satisfaction to be had from it. Yet, not a single one of its followers has abandoned it. This should give you some idea of its value and endurance. Furthermore, at the end of the day, those who love rowing and practise it as a sport will be tempted to congratulate themselves on this state of things, which has done much to preserve the sport from the threefold corruption hanging over the world of sport, namely, money, show, and hangers on . . . Rowing clubs are in some way like the convents of sport, always a little isolated and insular with their harsh training, enforced camaraderie, egalitarian spirit and obligatory discipline. Now, a convent that wants to safeguard its position has to be careful about recruitment. It looks for quality rather than quantity. It looks for 'first-class monks', intelligent, learned, strong in character and with plenty of willpower. Rowing clubs should do the same. They should not seek to swell their membership numbers indiscriminately. Instead, they should try and attract the cream of those with a sporting spirit and a 'vocation' for intensive, healthy muscular work. They should try and win robust, fair-minded young people who are neither braggarts nor prone to envy, but who are capable of putting on a good spurt not just in the water but in life too.

Here, to conclude our voyage through the story of rowing, are some who responded to the cause and joined the order, taking part in both Coubertin's Games and FISA's championships.

In 1900 in Paris there were rowing events for single sculls, coxed pairs and fours, and eights. The Dutch pair dropped their cox, Hermanus Brockmann, after the first heat on the grounds that he was too heavy. The substitute was a French boy who was thought to be as young as seven. His name has been lost, but he remains the youngest Olympic competitor ever. Incompetent officials caused two finals to be held in the fours. They first said that the winners of the three heats plus the second crew in the third heat, which contained four boats against the others' two, would contest a four-boat final. When the second boats in heats two and three returned faster times than the winner of heat one, an extra qualifying heat was announced, but the authorities failed to notify all the crews. They then announced a six-boat final composed of heat winners and the three fastest losers, but the heat winners refused to participate because the course had only four lanes. So the three-boat final included no heat winners, and another final had to be run for the heat winners. Roubaix of France won the first in 7 minutes 11 seconds, and

Germania of Hamburg the second in 5 minutes 59 seconds. In 1908 races were held for four-oared inriggers, for the first and last time. In 1924 the repechage system was introduced whereby losers in heats are given another chance to avoid elimination. Jack Beresford reached the final of the single sculls by this method and won the gold medal on a very hot day, about which he wrote: 'when . . . I was making a supreme effort to grasp victory, a kindly breeze swept across the Seine, carrying a strong but pleasant scent from a per-fumery which was not within sight. It was truly so strong that it first gagged me, but in a moment I was rowing on as if in a flowing river of the perfume itself.' In the same year Bill Havens had dropped out of the victorious American eight from Yale because his wife was expecting a baby. Twenty-eight years later the mite Frank won the 10,000-metre Canadian canoeing gold medal.

In 1928 in Amsterdam, after another American victory in the eights, this time by the University of California at Berkeley, the *New York Times* described the cox, Don Blessing, as giving 'one of the greatest performances of demoniacal howling ever heard on a terrestrial planet.' Bobbing up and down in his seat, he was like a 'terrier gone mad', beating his toggles on the side of the shell and rising above the roar of the crowd in 'magnificent flights of rhetorical vituperation'. Alongside the American crew were the British, a Thames RC eight strengthened by some Leander men, stroked by the future publisher Hamish Hamilton and including Donald Gollan who was impervious to Blessing's blessings because he was deaf and dumb. 'Compared with the sullen British cox,' Wythe Williams continued in the *New York Times*, 'immaculate in blue and red blazer, white shirt and tie, Blessing, in a torn and worn shirt and old flannel trousers, looked like a young tough – but it was just that young tough who was necessary today to ensure the American victory.' The British cox's name was Arthur Sulley. The Americans won by two seconds, and Blessing was baptised in the Sloten Canal. Paul Costello (USA) in the double sculls became the first man to win a gold medal at three Games. The Australian Bob Pearce won the singles despite checking his boat in the final to allow a family of ducks to pass in front of him.

In 1948 the Olympic regatta came to the Henley course for the second time. The course was shortened to 2000 metres and widened to three lanes, and Ran Laurie and Jack Wilson came home from the Sudan to win the coxless pairs on six weeks' training after no rowing since 1938.

There was a special poignancy to the 1952 Games in Helsinki. The Soviet Union was taking part for the first time, and the Finns, at the height of the Cold War, had arranged two villages, one for the socialist countries and one for the rest. The defeated Soviet eight invited the victorious American eight from the US Naval Academy to their village for drinks. Protocol was involved; the Russians obtained permission but the Americans were having trouble with their minders. Evenually their cox, Charles Manring, led his crew to the other village and fraternal greetings were cemented in Russian champagne beneath the portraits of Lenin and Stalin which the Finnish hosts had hung round the dining area. The Russians remember this defiance of officialdom by the American cadets with affection. Contact is supposed to be an integral part of the Olympic idea.

In 1956 the Russian Vyasheslav Ivanov was so excited at winning the sculls by a sensational spurt which ditched the Australian seventeen-year-old *wunderkind*, Stuart Mackenzie, that he dropped his medal into Lake Wendouree. Frogmen failed to find it, and the IOC eventually gave him a replacement. He won the gold again four and eight years later, the last time after blacking out, according to his account of the occasion. 'I don't know how long it was before consciousness gradually returned . . . I wondered whether it was a case of delirium and that I was having hallucinations.' He gathered his last ounce on seeing clear water with nobody in front of him for the last 50 metres: 'I managed to find an extra bit of strength, picked up the oars and crossed the line first.'

Part Three on the ebb and flow of coaches and technique covers much of the ground of the Games from the sixties onwards, as well as the rift and fusion of styles between the world wars. Suffice it to say here that the East Germans were very much to the fore in the seventies, Soviet crews and, in the case of women, Romanians being their nearest challengers. Siegfried Brietzke and Wolfgang Mager won the Olympic coxless pairs in 1972, a crew discovered some years earlier when they answered a television appeal for tall lads to go and row. Frank Forberger, Frank Rühle, Dieter Grahn and Dieter Schubert completed eleven years together and six years without defeat when they won the coxless fours in 1972. In 1976 the twins Bernd and Jörg Landvoight beat the Americans Coffey and Staines in the coxless pairs, and retained their Olympic title in Moscow four years later against the Russian twins Yuri and Nikolai Pimenov. Brietzke was in the gold medal coxless four and became the fourth man to win three golds; the fifth was the Finnish sculler Pertti Karppinen, who was champion in 1976, 1980 and 1984.

From the sixties there is a diminishing difference between Olympic regattas and European and world championships. As FISA expanded, so its members increasingly entered all three categories of regatta. FISA members held European championships each year from 1893 until 1973, with the exception of 1914–19, 1939–46, the Olympic years when the Games were located in Europe (1928, 1936, 1948, 1952 and 1960, plus the Mexico year of 1968), and three years when FISA held world championships (1962, 1966 and 1970). Single sculls, coxed pairs, coxed fours and eights comprised the original European events. Double sculls were added in 1898, coxless pairs in 1924, and coxless fours in 1925. (The Olympic regatta of 1908 included coxless pairs and fours, and the 1924 Olympic regatta included coxless fours.) European championships for women in single, double and quadruple sculls, coxed fours and eights were held each year from 1954 to 1973. From 1974 the championships were designated 'world' each year for men and women and held in the three years between Olympic regattas. Coxless pairs were added for women, and quadruple sculls were included for men in the following year. Some Olympic boycotts, notably those in 1980 and 1984, have reduced the number of final-class competitors, and so several world championships have surpassed Olympic regattas in both number of entries and competitive excitement, though not necessarily in the quality of the medal winners. In men's rowing a rising standard has been accompanied by a narrowing of the margins between finalists. This has been less marked in women's rowing where the Eastern Europeans maintained an almost exclusive grip on medals until the demise of Communism and its accompanying generous state support for sport. Perhaps the pattern will now change. The addition of events for lightweight men in the mid-seventies and lightweight women in the mid-eighties at world championships has extended the opportunity of winning medals to athletes who may lack height and weight but nevertheless excel in technique and performance.

We have come a long way from the great Paris regatta of 1867, when the fishermen from New Brunswick showed the English and the Europeans a thing or two about how to row. Olympic regattas have reached Lake Wendouree in Australia, Toda in Japan, Xochimilco in Mexico, the St Lawrence in Montreal, Casitas in California, and the course near the Han River in South Korea. World championships have been held in St Catharine's in Canada, Karapiro in New Zealand, and Lake Barrington in Tasmania. The annual international regatta in Lucerne has been the biggest and most prestigious event apart from championship regattas since the 1960s. Crews race in six lanes on the 2000-metre Rotsee course, a beautiful god-given sheltered lake behind the old Swiss city. Here wooden boats are rare, honeycombed fibre and epoxy resin mixtures ruling the day; here oars are perfectly matched from pieces, only the handles being of wood; here uniforms are of one-piece lycra and coxes speak softly into miniature microphones connected to transistorized speakers as they watch electronic stroke-timers and stopwatches which give them split times to a hundredth of a second. The water is usually mirror-like; the only thing that the Brunswickers would recognize is the mechanically operated steering mechanism from the foot-stretcher in coxless boats. Bums slide on nylon wheels and runners; lightweight alloy outriggers are strong and slim; swivels, minutely adjustable in pitch and height, have replaced tholepins. Some boats have tiny cameras mounted on stalks behind the cox to send close-up images of 'grunt and sweat' to television sets; coaches lean against trees with video cameras, photographers aim lenses like bazookas at those straining at the oar, and an electronic scoreboard records results a few seconds after crews have completed their race. And participants come from several continents, swept in by air to Zürich and by train alongside the Rotsee course to hotels beside the Lake of Lucerne, where an old rowing club has pride of place near the steamer quays. Professionals of the 1867 variety are no more, but the Brunswickers would probably feel at home in the cosmopolitan Lucerne crowd of the 1990s. Beer-and-sausage prevails over wine-and-pâté, and when the weather is good, the under-dressed prevail over the over-dressed. Prizes are medals and trophies; there are flags and a band and a party on Saturday night.

Like Paris in 1867, Lucerne is for the Olympians and the ambitious, hightech fanatics. But an abundance of club life and wooden boats remains in old haunts and new. We have glimpsed some worlds and times when rowing meant war and peace, trade and commerce; we have traced the progression from the working ship to the racing boat with the philosophers and geniuses who understand the relationship between wood and water; we have attended class with the professors of speed; and we have journeyed through time and place, through the hinterland of recreation and racing. As the world keeps rowing, each can choose where to ship oars. For me, rowing is a fellowship which is more than winning races, so on my way back to its spiritual home, Henley and the River Thames, I am going to pause in Paris in 1926 with another journalist, the *New Yorker* writer A. J. Liebling, who was recruited into the debutante crew of La Société Nautique de la Marne to take on the Rowing Club de la Seine in their annual race. This was serious business, as Liebling explains:

'I learned from a young man named Morin . . . that the crews of the Société practised only on Sundays when the weather was pleasant; there was consequently no time for elaborate dinners . . . So we had, as *hors d'oeuvre*, only a crock of duck pâté, a crock of pâté of hare, a few tins of sardines, muzzle of beef, radishes, and butter. Morin, who sat next to me, was abjectly apologetic.' Two little girls in pigtails served the lunch, daughters of the caretaker and his wife the cook. 'After *hors d'oeuvres* we had a potato soup, then a *buisson de goujons*, a mound of tiny fried fish . . . a leg of mutton with roast potatoes, a salad, cheese, and fruit. Red and white wine were there to take *à discrétion*, and most of the *sociétaires* had a brandy with their coffee as a digestive. Naturally, one did not attempt violent exercise after such a meal. It would not be healthy, M. Parisot [the coach] explained.' They went for a walk and watched the shell of the Femina Sports being towed upstream by motorboat. 'The girls sat with their feet on the gunwales in order not to wet their slippers; their thighs were ravishing . . . When the girls got about a quarter of a mile above the island they decided not to row anyway, so the motorboat towed them back to their own float . . . We of the Nautique were disappointed.' But down there at the Nautique as the rowing world was waking up to the awkwardness of Orthodox and the comfort of Fairbairn, Liebling learned a lot about '*le long layback*'.

Glossary and conversion table

Academic rowing: *see* English rowing

Beat: *see* Rating

Best boat: long, narrow development from whiff with sliding seat and long outriggers for competitive sculling

Blade: flattened or spoon-shaped end of oar or scull; often used as term for oar

Bore: to encroach on another boat's course

Bow: forward end of boat

Bow (man): the rower in the seat nearest the bow

Bow ball: safety ball fitted to sharp stem of racing boat

Bowside (starboard): all the rowers whose oars are in the water on the right hand side of the boat when viewed from the stern

Button: leather or plastic sheath on oar to prevent it slipping through the rowlock; adjustable on modern oars

Canvas: the canvas on fore and aft decks of a boat; in race verdicts, the distance between the bow ball and the bow man's stateroom

Carvel: planking in which the edges are flush with one another to give a smooth-surface boat

Catch: the part of the stroke when the blade is put in the water

Challenge prize: a prize which becomes the property of the winners after certain conditions have been complied with

Classes of boat: international classes of racing boat are eight (8+), coxed four (4+), coxless four (4-), coxed pair (2+), coxless pair (2-), quadruple sculls (4x), double sculls (2x), single sculls (1x)

Clinker: planking in which the lower edge of a plank overlaps the upper edge of the one below it

Cock and hen: a skiff in which the bow position is much narrower than the stroke position

Cockpit: space for a person in a racing boat

Coxed four, pair: a four-oar or pair-oar with a coxswain; sometimes known as four with, pair with

Coxless four, pair: a four-oar or pair-oar without a coxswain; sometimes known as four without, pair without, straight four, straight pair

Coxswain (cox): steers the boat from a seat in the stern or a lying position in the bow

Crab: occurs when rower fails to get the oar out of the water at the end of the stroke; can result in the rower being ejected from boat to water

Crew: rowers who man a boat; American college term for rowing

Deck: covered-over areas at bow and stern of boat

Dodger: a short half-outrigged fixed-seat boat used for pleasure boating at Eton

Double: two scullers without cox

Double-banked: two rowers on one seat

Double ended: boat in which bow and stern are the same shape

Drive: *see* Pull-through

Eight (VIII): eight rowers with cox

English rowing: rower sits and faces the back; competition rowing using shells with outriggers in eights, fours, pairs, quads, doubles and singles

Feather: to turn the blade parallel with the water surface at the start of the recovery to reduce wind resistance

Fin: small flat plate perpendicular to the bottom of the boat to aid steering a straight course

Finish (release): the part of the stroke just before the blade is taken out of the water

FISA: Fédération Internationale des Sociétés d'Aviron (the International Rowing Federation)

Fixed pin: a rowlock in which the oar slides between two fixed vertical wooden thole pins

Four (IV): four rowers with or without cox; *see also* Coxed four, Coxless four

Frontloader: a boat in which the coxswain lies in the bows

Funny: a double-ended sculling boat

Galley: a heavy boat of four oars or more

Gate: bar across a rowlock to retain the oar

German rig: an eight rigged so that the outriggers for seats Nos. 4 and 5 are on the same side, while the others alternate

Gig: inboard- or outboard-rigged pleasure or racing boat with straight gunwales

Gunwale: horizontal strips running the length of the boat

Hands away: the act of turning the oar handle at the finish of the stroke so that the blade leaves the water and is feathered at the start of the recovery; sometimes referred to as 'out of bow'

Inboard: the distance between the far end of the handle of an oar or scull and the face of the button. The remainder is called the outboard

Italian rig: an eight rigged so that the bow seat and stroke seat outriggers are on the same side, with the others alternating from side to side in pairs

Keel: member running along the centre line of a wooden boat to which all other parts are attached

Keelson: a support between keel and seat braces

Knee: wooden support connecting keel, gunwale, washboard and outrigger

Lapstreak (lapstrake): *see* Clinker

Layback: the amount of backward lean of the rower's body towards the bow at the finish

Leather: *see* Button

Lightweights: maximum weight for a rower or sculler is 72.5 kilogrammes (men), 59 kilogrammes (women); average weight of a crew shall not exceed 70 kilogrammes (men) and 57 kilogrammes (women)

Loom: the shaft or part of the oar between the blade and the handle

Modern rowing: *see* English rowing

Oar: a lever approximately 12 feet long by which the rower pulls against the rowlock to move the boat through the water; sometimes used as shortened form of oarsman

Oarlock: *see* Rowlock

Octuple: eight scullers with cox

Olympic rowing: *see* English rowing

Outboard: *see* Inboard

Outrigger (rigger): a metal framework or a carbon-fibre-reinforced arm to support the rowlock which is placed approximately 30 inches (76 cm) from the centre of the boat

Pair (II): two rowers with or without cox; *see also* Coxed, Coxless

Perfect: a fixed-seat, fixed-pin, clinker coxed pair used at Eton

Port (larboard): stroke side, the left-hand side of the boat when facing the bow

Puddles: whirls left in the water caused by the blade as the rower pulls

Pulling: rowing or sculling (freshwater); working one oar with both hands (salt water)

Pull-through: the part of the stroke between the catch and the finish

Quadruple (quad): four scullers with or without cox

Randan: a three-person boat with a rower (one oar) in the bow and stern and a sculler (two oars) between them

Rating (beat): the rate of striking, or the number of strokes per minute that a crew is rowing

Recovery: the part of the stroke cycle between the finish and the catch in which the oar is feathered and the seat is returned to the aft end of the slide

Regatta: a competitive event raced in boats (*regata*, Venetian, perhaps from *riga* (line), *aurigare* (to compete in a race), *ramigium* (rowing))

Release: *see* Finish

Rhythm: the proportion of time occupied on the recovery to the time taken on the pull-through

Ribs: members between keel and gunwale for supporting the hull

Rig: *see* German rig, Italian rig, Standard rig

Rigger: *see* Outrigger; Eton name for a sculling boat

Rob Roy: a kayak type of canoe

Rowing (sweep rowing): using one oar or sweep (freshwater); using two oars (salt water); *see also* Crew

Rowlock (rollock, oarlock): a bracket which swivels on the end of the outrigger to support the oar

Rudder: steering device attached to the stern or under the hull of a shell

Rum-tum: a short, wide clinker sculling boat

Run: the distance a boat travels in one stroke

Saxboard: the top strake of a boat, usually of heavier planking, which carries the rowlocks; *see* Gunwale

Scull: *see* single

Sculling: using two oars or sculls (freshwater); using one oar over stern (salt water).

Sculls: short oars used in pairs for singles, doubles, and quads

Shell: smooth-bottomed racing boat; 'light shells made of wood' (Samuel Hearne, 1776); 'light narrow racing boat' (USA, 1873); 'the floating part of a racing boat' (*Oxford English Dictionary*, 1895); *see also* Eight, Four, Pair, Quadruple, Double, Single

Shoulder: reinforcement for thole pins or outriggers

Single: shell for one sculler

Single-banked: one rower on a seat

Skiff: racing boat for single sculler (North of England); clinker pleasure boat for several passengers, sculled by one, two or three persons (River Thames)

Slide: a seat which moves on wheels on parallel rails

Standard rig: uniform alternation of outriggers (and therefore oars and rowers) in the boat; the rower in the seat nearest the stern is usually on stroke side

Starboard: bow side, the right-hand side of the boat when facing the bow

Stateroom: *see* Cockpit

Stem: extention of keel in bow

Stern: the back of the boat

Stern post: upright post in stern
Strake (streak): planks forming the hull
Stretcher: a frame with straps or shoes to anchor the rower's feet
Stroke: the complete cycle of moving the boat through the water using oars; the rower seated nearest the stern
Stroke side (port): all the rowers whose oars are in the water on the left-hand side of the boat when viewed from the stern
Sweep: long oars with narrow blades; *see also* Rowing
Swivel: a square or round rotating rowlock
Thole (thowle) pin: *see* Fixed pin
Thwart: a fixed seat
Tub: half-outrigged gig for training
Varsity: the first crew of an American university
Voga inglese: English style of rowing (sit and face the stern)
Voga Veneta: Venetian style of rowing (stand and face the bow)
Wale: rounded piece of wood fixed to saxboard; *see also* Gunwale
Washboard: a narrow strake placed round a boat to keep water out
Washing out: occurs when the blade comes out of the water during the pull-through before the finish
Wherry: Thames ferry
Whiff: half-outrigged sculling boat

Conversion table

Imperial to metric

1 mile	1760 yards	1.6093 kilometres
1 nautical mile	6080 feet	1.852 kilometres
1 knot	1 nautical mile per hour	
1 yard	3 feet	0.914 metres
1 foot	12 inches	0.3046 metres
1 inch		2.54 centimetres

Metric to imperial

1 kilometre	1000 metres	0.62137 mile
		1093.6 yards
1 metre	100 centimetres	1.0936 yards
100 centimetres		3.281 feet
1 centimetre	100 millimetres	0.3937 inch

Weight

1 cwt		50.8 kilogrammes

1 stone	14 lb	6.3504 kilogrammes
1 lb	16 oz	0.4536 kilogrammes
1 kilogramme		2.20462 lb

Rowing distances

Henley distance: 1 mile 550 yards (2112 metres)
Olympic and FISA championship distance: 2000 metres
Oxford and Cambridge Boat Race distance: 4 miles 374 yards

References

J. J. Cox and M. L. Edwards, *Glossary of Boat Terms*. Eton: Thames Traditional Boat Society, 1988

Thomas C. Mendenhall, *A Short History of American Rowing*. Boston: Charles River Books, 1980

Neil Wigglesworth, *Victorian and Edwardian Boating from Old Photographs*. London: Batsford, 1987

Selected Chronology

Entries refer to earliest recorded organized regatta or club unless otherwise stated; locations are England unless otherwise stated; countries are as 1991. FISA members are listed at the end.

BC

5800: Lehtojävi, Finland – Elk-head boat

4000: Egypt – boats with single steering oar and crew facing forward, either paddling or rowing

3500–500: Finland – Stone Age rock paintings of boats

3100: Late Gerzean pot shows Mesopotamian-type craft with rectangular sail, first evidence of sail

3000: Abydos, Egypt – 12 wooden ships

2560: Cheops ship with flat bottom, no keel, and forefoot at bow. At same period there were narrow oared craft

2500–500: Tigris and Euphrates – shell-built plank boats using dovetail clamps and mortice and tenon joints. Sail and oars

2400: Egypt: oars replaced paddles for river craft

8th century: Mycenae – two levels of oars

8th century (end) or **7th century** (middle): Corinth – first trireme/*trieres* built

7th century: Forefoot converted to ram; Assyrian reliefs show round boats probably made of sewn hides with two oarsmen, one at each end, one pushing, one pulling

6th century: Ram armoured with metal sheath; Sennacherib palace relief at Nineveh shows ships with up to 120 oarsmen in two tiers; leads to design of *trieres*.

5th century: Dünberg – logboat model has pivoted oars, first indication of their use in Northern Europe. Logboats from this time are in Shapwick, Holme Pierrepont, Poole (England), France, Sweden, Netherlands

482: Themistocles and Athenians built 200 *triereis*
480: Battle of Salamis – Persian fleet destroyed by Athenians and allies using *triereis*
300: Stockholm – Als boat, oldest known Nordic boat
1st century: Broighter, Co. Derry, Ireland – gold model has nine thwarts with oar grommets for oars through holes in hull, steering oar, currach shape, possibly a skin boat

AD

Six boats found in England and Scandinavia from pre-Viking period. Nydam and Sutton Hoo boats propelled by oars
400: Schleswig (southern Jutland, Denmark) – Nydam oak boat, oldest known Nordic rowing boat
5th–10th centuries: Byzantine warships called *dromons* with one or two tiers of oars
6th century: Gotland (Baltic) – boat depicted on Sanda stone with bearded oarsmen rowing vigorously
700: Kvalsund (western Norway) – rowing boat with keel
793–c. 1200: Viking period, thirty boat finds
8th and 9th centuries: Scandinavia – sail begins to feature in stone carvings
800: Oseberg (Norway) ship combines sail and oars
10th century: Eksar (Bombay) – naval battles in oar- or paddle-powered ships depicted on the hero stones
1274: Venice – first reference to *regata*
14th century: Genoa and Venice had similar ships to Byzantium in 5th–10th centuries
1315: Venice – first competitive *regata*
Ming dynasty (1368–1644), late period: China – raft buoyed by skin floats propelled by oars
1454: London – Lord Mayor's water procession (until 1856)
1462: Lake Bolsena, Umbria (Italy) – regatta in homage to Pope Pius II
1493: Venice – races for women
16th century (early): Bay of Bengal – mention of oarpowered *fusta*
1521: Indonesia – *prau* with three rows of oars on each side (doubtful – it may be that described below under 1544–1668)
1544–1668: Indonesia – Moluccan *kora kora* paddled and/or rowed from crossbeams and two outrigger platforms
1553: Chile – sewn *dalea* made of three planks, presumably paddled. Spaniards later modified them to take oars
1571: Battle of Lepanto – Venetian galleys supreme in defeat of Turks

1579: Race in Istanbul

1588: Spanish Armada included *galleases*

1642: Regatta in Malta

1682: Lord Dunblane and Duke of Grafton plus two others row from London to Erith

1740s: Rowing at Winchester

1768: Regatta at Walton-on-Thames

1775: Regatta at Ranelagh Gardens, London

1778: First eight-oared race, *Chatham* versus *Invincible*, from Westminster Bridge to Richmond, London

1805: First race in Australia

1806: Organized rowing at Eton College

1811: New York (USA) – Race between Whitehall fours *Knickerbocker* (NY) and *Invincible* (Long Island)

1816: Durham regatta starts; Newfoundland (Canada) – race in St John's Harbour

1817: Sweden – first church boat competition

1818: Sydney, New South Wales (Australia) – Captain Piper's crew versus other ships' boats
Leander Club (London)

1819: Sydney, NSW (Australia) – Captain Piper's crew beat crew from USA ship *General Gates*

1820: Australia – race in Van Diemen's Land (Tasmania)

1821: Barcelona (Spain) – Regatas Club, Barcelona

1825: New York (USA) – Whitehall *American Star* beats *Sudden Death*, gig of British frigate *Hussar*

1827: Hungary – two Englishmen and a Hungarian row from Vienna to Pressburg (Bratislava)
Sydney, NSW (Australia) – regatta

1828: Newcastle-on-Tyne – outriggers by Antony Brown

1829: Henley-on-Thames – first Oxford versus Cambridge University Boat Race, eight-oared cutters
Portsmouth, Southsea and Gosport regatta

1830: Hamburg (Germany) – English Rowing Club
London – Wingfield Sculls for amateur championship of the Thames

1831: London – first professional sculling championship, C. Campbell (Westminster) versus J. Williams (Hammersmith)

1832: Sydney, NSW (Australia) – regatta
Canton (China) – regatta

1833: Australia: inter-colonial race, Sydney versus Hobart Town

1834: Singapore – New Year's Day watersports
Budapest (Hungary) – Count Széchenyi founds club

New York (USA) – Castle Garden Amateur BC Association
Paris (France) – regatta
1835: Sydney, NSW (Australia) – club
Philadelphia (USA) – regatta
1836: Ringsend, Dublin (Ireland) – Pembroke Club
Hamburg RC, first German club for Germans
1836 or 1837: New Brunswick (Canada) – St John regatta
1837: China – Canton Regatta Club
1838: France – Société Havraise de l'Aviron
Hobart (Tasmania) – Regatta
1839: Henley regatta (became Henley Royal Regatta in 1851)
USA – Detroit BC
1840: Rio de Janeiro (Brazil) – regatta
Chester – race for women in coracles
1841: Melbourne, Victoria (Australia) – regatta
1842: St Petersburg (Russia) – pleasure rowing
1843: New Haven (USA) – Yale University Boat Club
1844: Hanover (Germany) – Deutsch RC
Putney (London) – racing single with outriggers and inboard keel
1845: Dover–Boulogne crossing by six-oar
1846: Belgium – Ghent club
St Petersburg (Russia) – Arrow Club
France – Regatta Society of the Somme
1848: USA – Cincinnati Turnverein
1849: Hong Kong – Victoria Regatta Club (ex-Canton); Hong Kong BC
c. 1850 New Brunswick (Canada) – *The Experiment*, first outrigger to be
raced
1851: Sweden – Gothenburg RC
1852: USA – Harvard versus Yale race
1853: France – RC de Paris founded by French and English
Philadelphia (USA) – Bachelors' Barge Club
1854: France – Lyon RC; Reims Rowing Society
1855: Outriggers reach Australia
1856: USA – purpose-built racing boat at Williamsburg, Long Island
London RC
1857: Argentina – English row at Buenos Aires
Round loom for oar introduced
1858: India – Calcutta RC
France – first race between French and English clubs in Paris
1859: Australia – Melbourne University BC
1860: Belgium – Sport Nautique de la Meuse
Czechoslovakia – English Crew (later English RC) in Prague

London – City of London RC (later Thames RC)
Sweden – regatta
1861: Cape Province (South Africa) – race in Table Bay; Civil Service RC
in Cape Town
Christchurch (New Zealand) – Canterbury RC
British Rowing Almanack first published
1862: Zürich (Switzerland) – race on Zürichsee
1863: Austria – Lia RC (Vienna)
Berlin – Dr Schiller claims invention of slides using small wheels
Piedmont (Italy) – Cerea club (Turin)
Switzerland – See-Club Zürich
Trieste (Italy) – Triestina club
1864: Germans rowing in Schleswig Holstein, then part of Denmark
Hungary (later Romania) – Society of the Little Boats in Timisoara
1865: Germany – Frankfurter Ruderverein
1866: Sind, Karachi (Pakistan) – Sherwood Foresters win regatta on China
Creek
Portugal – Oporto British RC
Denmark – clubs for Danes at Kvik and Copenhagen
Japan – Yokohama Barge Club
1867: Switzerland – Zürich regatta
1869: Frankfurt and Wurzburg clubs found Central German Federation
Australia – first eight launched on Yarra
1870: Argentina – rowing at Tigre, Buenos Aires
Australia – Sydney RC
1871: USA – J. C. Babcock's sliding seat
1872: Poland – Warsaw River Yacht Club (for Germans)
Austria-Hungary (later Croatia, Yugoslavia) – Zagreb Rowing and Fish-
ing Association
English clubs meet to draw up Laws of Boat Racing
1873: Argentina – Buenos Aires RC
Peru – Chorrillos Club of Rowing and Shooting, Lima
Poland – Rowing Circle of University Youth, club for Poles in Warsaw
1874: Uruguay: Montevideo RC
USA – Michael Davis's swivel oarlock
1875: Finland – race
Japan – international regatta at Nagasaki
1876: Germany – Berliner Ruderverein founded
Gibraltar – Calpe RC
London RC versus Frankfurter RC at Putney
1877: Norway – Fredriksstad club
1878: American crews at Henley

Australia – eights championship at Melbourne for King's Cup

North German Regatta Association adopted 2000–metre distance

1879: Barcelona (Spain) – Club Catalan de Regatas (later Real Club Maritimo de Barcelona); Royal Club of Mediterranean in Malaga

Singapore – Singapore RC

1880: Canada – Canadian Association of Amateur Oarsmen

USA – cox in the bow proposed at Yale

1881: Sind (Pakistan) – Karachi BC

1882: Amateur Rowing Association (ARA)

1883: Netherlands – Netherlands Student Federation

Germany – Deutscher Ruderverband

USA – Intercollegiate Rowing Association (IRA)

1884: Finland – Helsingin Soutuklubi

1885: Greece – RC Piraeus

Philippines – Manila BC

1887: Cuba – Santiago da Cuba

1888: Brazil – Club de Regatas Guaiba Porto Alegre

Mexico – rowing on Lake Chalco

1890: French federation founded

First European championship in single sculls

National ARA splits from ARA

1892: International federation (Fédération Internationale des Sociétés d'Aviron – FISA)

USA – Zlac for women, San Diego

1893: European championships organized by FISA at Lake Orta, Italy

1895: USA – Poughkeepsie regatta

1896: Chile – Club de Regates Valparaiso

Norwegians George Harbo and Frank Samuelson row Atlantic from New York to Scilly Isles

Olympic Games in Athens. Rowing scheduled but did not take place

1898: Austria – patent taken out for sliding rigger

1899: USA – California versus Washington race

1900: Paris – first Olympic Games to stage rowing events

1901: Germany – Frauen RC, Berlin

1902: Argentina – international regatta at Tigre (Buenos Aires)

1903: USA – American Rowing Association

1904: Paraguay – Club de Regatas El M'Bigua

1905: Rhodesia (Zambia/Zimbabwe) – regatta on Zambesi

1906: Germany – women's races at Hamburg

1909: Germany – Hamburg women's RC

Germany – workers' clubs form Free Rowing League

1910: Scandinavian championships

1912: Mozambique – Club Naval Lourenço Marques
1916: Korea – Choong Ang High School Rowing Team
1923: Burma (Myanmar) – Rangoon University BC
1924: Bulgaria – marine officers start rowing
  USSR – Sportni Morski Legioni in Warna (Black Sea)
  Olympics adopt repechage system
1926: London – Head of River Race
1927: North Borneo (Brunei) – Miri BC
1931: South American championships at Montevideo (Uruguay)
1933: Amateur Rowing Association of the East
1937: Iceland – participates in Scandinavian championships for only time
  Netherlands – Bosbaan opens in Amsterdam, first man-made course
1938: Palestine (Israel) – Tel Aviv RC
1939: Guatemala – rowing introduced
1942: Match between Assuncão, Buenos Aires and Montevideo universities
1944: Benito Romero rows 1200 kilometres from Avellaneda (Argentina) to Porto Alegre (Brazil)
1945: South American federation
1950: German Democratic Republic – championships at Leipzig
  FISA accepts women
1951: Pan-American Games, Buenos Aires
1953: West Germany – Ratzeburg Rowing Academy
1954: European championships for women, Amsterdam
  Far Eastern Rowing Association
  Head of River Race for Scullers, Putney
1956: ARA and NARA unite
  Front-loaded cox at European championships
1962: FISA world championships
1966: German Democratic Republic competes under own name
1967: FISA junior championships
1972: Pan-American rowing federation and Pan-American regatta
  National championships of Great Britain
1973: FISA veterans' regatta
1974: FISA women's world championships
1975: Italy – Vogalonga (Venice)
  FISA Match des Seniors (for under-23s)
  FISA lightweight championships
  Oxford versus Cambridge Ladies' Boat Race
1976 West Bengal RA and Rowing Federation of India
  Women in Olympics
1981: Asian Rowing Federation
1982: Venezuela – Club Margarita

Cuba – Central American Games include rowing
India – Asian Games include rowing
1983: FISA women's junior championships
1985: FISA women's lightweight championships
Asian championships
1990: East and West German federations unite

FISA Members

1892   Belgium, France, Italy, Switzerland

Ordinary members (date order)

1904   Germany (leaves 1914; rejoins 1934; leaves 1939; rejoins 1951)
1913   Netherlands
1920   Spain
       Czechoslovakia
1921   Hungary
1922   Portugal
1924   Yugoslavia
       Poland
1929   USA
1930   Denmark
       Greece
1938   Finland
1946   Sweden
1947   Great Britain
       Australia
       Austria
1948   Canada
       Cuba
1951   Federal Germany
       Japan
       Mexico
1952   USSR
       New Zealand
1955   Bulgaria
1956   Democratic Republic of Germany
1965   Korea
1973   China
1979   India

Extraordinary members (date order)

1925 Egypt
1927 Romania
1928 Argentina
1931 Turkey
     Brazil
1932 Uruguay
1946 Norway
1948 South Africa
1948 Ireland
     Cuba
     Chile
1959 Peru
1961 Morocco
     Israel
1967 Algeria
     Paraguay
1968 Guatemala
     Ecuador
1969 North Korea
1971 Lebanon
1976 Nigeria
1977 Cayman Islands
1979 Pakistan
1981 Zimbabwe
     Hong Kong
1982 Sri Lanka
1983 Tunisia
     Chinese Taipei
1984 Gibraltar
     Puerto Rico
     Kuwait
1985 Venezuela
     Panama
1986 Indonesia
     Singapore
1988 Philippines
1989 Cyprus
1991 Bangladesh
     Estonia
     Latvia
     Lithuania
     Malaysia

Myanmar (Burma)
Uganda

Ordinary members (alphabetical order)

Australia   1947
Austria   1947
Belgium   1892
Bulgaria   1955
Canada   1948
China   1973
Cuba   1948
Czechoslovakia   1920
Denmark   1930
Finland   1938
France   1892
Germany (East – Democratic Republic)   1956
Germany (West – Federal Republic)   1951
Great Britain   1947
Greece   1930
Hungary   1921
India   1979
Italy   1892
Japan   1951
Korea (South)   1965
Mexico   1951
Netherlands   1913
New Zealand   1952
Poland   1924
Portugal   1922
Spain   1920
Sweden   1946
Switzerland   1892
USA   1929
USSR   1952
Yugoslavia   1924

Extraordinary members (alphabetical order)

Algeria   1967
Argentina   1928
Bangladesh   1991

Brazil   1931
Cayman Islands   1977
Chile   1948
Chinese Taipei   1983
Cyprus   1989
Ecuador   1968
Egypt   1925
Estonia   1991
Gibraltar   1984
Guatemala   1968
Hong Kong   1981
Indonesia   1986
Ireland   1948
Israel   1961
Korea (North)   1969
Kuwait   1984
Latvia   1991
Lebanon   1971
Lithuania   1991
Malaysia   1991
Myanmar   1991
Morocco   1961
Nigeria   1976
Norway   1946
Pakistan   1979
Panama   1985
Paraguay   1967
Peru   1959
Philippines   1988
Puerto Rico   1984
Romania   1927
Singapore   1986
South Africa   1948
Sri Lanka   1982
Tunisia   1983
Turkey   1931
Uganda   1991
Uruguay   1932
Venezuela   1985
Zimbabwe   1981

Further Reading and Chapter Sources

Paul Kennedy's *The Rise and Fall of the Great Powers* (Unwin Hyman, 1988) goes a long way towards explaining how Britain came to be in the van of the Industrial Revolution, and Jan Morris's triptych – *Heaven's Command, Pax Brittanica,* and *Farewell the Trumpets* – is a wonderfully entertaining account of the rise and subsequent retreat of the British Empire (Faber and Faber 1973, Penguin, 1979). Until very recently social historians have made only passing reference to sport and recreation in Britain, but Richard Holt has done more than anyone to set this right in his book *Sport and the British* (1989). Holt explains many complexities of sport and its development in British society. Tony Mason supplements this in his polemic *Sport in Britain* (1988) and in essays by various authors in his social history of the same title (1989). There are many accounts of the Olympics, but John J. MacAloon's *This Great Symbol* (1981) is a thorough investigation into Coubertin and the influences which inspired him to revive the Games.

Narrowing sport in society down to rowing matters, Eric Halladay's *Rowing in England* (1990) tackles the vexed question of the amateur definition very thoroughly. Many insights into rowing's history can be gleaned from the best of the Victorian and Edwardian rowing books, notably W. B. Woodgate's *Boating* (1888) and R. C. Lehmann's *The Complete Oarsman* (1908). The most recent history of the Oxford and Cambridge University Boat Race is the present author's (1983). Henley is laid bare by the present author's social history, *Henley Royal Regatta* (1989), Richard Burnell's official history (1989), and the regatta's official souvenir for its 150th birthday, which contains a package of lively articles and shares the same title. The stewards also publish complete records of crews and results from 1839. The reconstruction of the trireme is documented in Frank Welsh's *Building the Trireme* (1988) and in *The Athenian Trireme* (1986) by John Morrison and John Coates. The classics of coaching books are Gilbert Bourne's exposé of the English Orthodox in *A Text-book of Oarsmanship* (1925) and Steve Fairbairn's collected works, which drove a coach and eight through Orthodox rowing, and Karl Adam's work in

German (see sources for chapter 12). Just as interesting is Archibald's Maclaren's *Training in Theory and Practice* (1866), a very early fitness and health guide by an author with plenty of common sense.

For American history, Thomas C. Mendenhall's *A Short History of American Rowing* (1980) gives an excellent outline. Peter King's *Art and a Hundred Years of Canadian Rowing* (1980) is quirky and error-prone here and there, but it is a good supplement to Mendenhall. There is much of interest, too, in Samuel Crowther's contribution to *Rowing and Track Athletics* (1905) and Robert F. Kelley's *American Rowing* (1932). But the best and most recent information is the series of articles Mendenhall wrote for the magazine *American Rowing* in its previous incarnations as *The Oarsman* and *Rowing USA* during the 1970s and 1980s (see sources for chapters 14 and 20). Anything of Mendenhall's is worth reading, and so are books and articles by John Gardner whose realm is sea-going craft. He is the Keeper of Small Boats at Mystic Seaport. Mendenhall's forthcoming history of the Harvard versus Yale race will add further to the history of college sport. A very rare treat is the Waters, Balch *Illustrated Catalogue and Oarsman's Manual* (1871) which has detailed plans of racing boats.

Horst Überhorst edited the excellent German centenary history, *Hundert Jahre Deutscher Ruderverband*, which is a readable and well-illustrated account acclaimed among histories of German sport for putting no gloss on the turn of events during the Nazi period.

For a small sport, rowing is well endowed with literature. Virtually everything published about it before 1930 is listed in Freddie Brittain's *Oar, Scull and Rudder*, and this list of 943 books and articles was reproduced and updated to 1939 in *Red Top, Reminiscences of Harvard Rowing*, edited by Robert F. Herrick. Some of the best sources are club histories of which there are hundreds worldwide. Those which contain memoirs of members are almost always worth the effort, and some, such as *Sampan Pidgin* (1938) about Shanghai Rowing Club, are gems. Schools such as Eton are well endowed with volumes of history and memoirs. *The Eton Book of the River* (1952) repays attention, as does *Rowing at Westminster* (1890). Memoirs, biographies, and autobiographies particularly of academics and people who attended schools and colleges with a rowing history, are always worth investigating for anecdotes and news of their contemporaries. There are one or two refreshing accounts of rowing from inside the boat, such as Stephen Kiesling's *The Shell Game* (1982) and Brad Lewis's *Assault on Lake Casitas* (1991). Finally, local newspaper archives are often a good source of rowing history.

Many books and articles in languages other than English and about places other than Britain are listed in the chapter sources. First there follows a general bibliography of books in English, including details of those mentioned above. Inclusion is granted on the basis of the importance of the subject or of the book's entertainment value. Some qualify under both.

The Fédération Internationale des Sociétés d'Aviron (FISA) published an official history for its centenary year (1992). FISA is the best source of international records (FISA, 3653 Oberhofen am Thunersee, Switzerland).

General

The Annual Illustrated Catalogue and Oarsman's Manual for 1871. Troy, NY: Waters, Balch, 1871

The Aquatic Oracle, or Record of Rowing 1835–1851. London: Simpkin, Marshall, 1852

H. Armytage, *The Cam and Cambridge Rowing*. Cambridge: W. P. Spalding, *c*. 1886

William J. Baker, *Sports in the Western World*. Totowa, New Jersey: Rowman & Littlefield, 1982

Frans G. Bengtsson, *The Long Ships, a Saga of the Viking Age*. New York: Knopf, 1954

John Rickards Betts, *America's Sporting Heritage 1850–1950*. Reading, Massachusetts: Addison-Wesley, 1974

John A. Blanchard, *The H Book of Harvard Athletics*. Cambridge, Massachusetts: Harvard Varsity Club, 1923

Gilbert C. Bourne, *A Text-book of Oarsmanship*. London: OUP, 1925

E. D. Brickwood ('Argonaut'), *The Arts of Rowing and Training*. London: Horace Cox, 1866

F. Brittain, *Oar, Scull and Rudder*. London: Oxford University Press, 1930

Bruce C. Brown, *Open Water Handbook*. Camden, Maine: International Marine Publishing, 1991

Richard Burnell, *Henley Royal Regatta, A Celebration of 150 Years*. London: William Heinemann, 1989

R. D. Burnell and H. R. N. Rickett, *A Short History of Leander Club 1818–1963*. Henley-on-Thames: Leander Club, 1968

A. F. Ryder Bird, *Boating in Bavaria, Austria, and Bohemia, down the Danube, Moldau, and Elbe*. Hull: William Andrews, 1893

L. S. R. Byrne and E. L. Churchill, *The Eton Book of the River*. Eton: Alden & Blackwell, 1952

John Chandos, *Boys Together, English Public Schools 1800–1964*. London: Hutchinson, 1984

W. A. Clark and F. E. Prothero (eds.), *A New Oarsman's Guide to the*

Rivers and Canals of Great Britain and Ireland. London: George Philip & Son, 1896

Hylton Cleaver, *A History of Rowing,* London: Herbert Jenkins, 1957

Sir Theodore Cook, *Rowing at Henley.* London: Oxford, 1919

W. B. Coventry, *The Racing Eight.* Cambridge: Heffer, 1922

S. Crowther and A. Ruhl, *Rowing and Track Athletics.* New York: Macmillan, 1905

Charles Dickens Jr, *Dickens's Dictionary of the Thames.* London: Macmillan, 1885

Christopher Dodd, *Boating.* Oxford: Oxford University Press, 1983

Christopher Dodd, *Henley Royal Regatta,* London: Stanley Paul, 1981; revised edition 1989

Christopher Dodd, *The Oxford and Cambridge Boat Race.* London: Stanley Paul, London, 1983

G. C. Drinkwater and T. R. B. Sanders, *The University Boat Race Official Centenary History 1829–1929.* London: Cassell, 1929

Kenneth and Helen Durant, *The Adirondack Guide-boat.* Camden, Maine: International Marine Publishing, 1980

Steve Fairbairn, *The Complete Steve Fairbairn on Rowing.* London: The Kingswood Press, 1990

J. David Farmer, *Rowing Olympics* (catalogue of exhibition at University Art Museum), University of California, Santa Barbara, 1984

FISA Coaching Development Programme Course, Levels I, II, and III. Oberhofen: FISA.

J. V. S. Glass and J. Max Patrick, *The Royal Chester Rowing Club Centenary History 1838–1938.* Liverpool: James Laver, 1938

P. Haig-Thomas and M. A. Nicholson, *The English Style of Rowing.* London: Faber and Faber, 1958

T. F. Hall, *History of Boat Racing in Ireland.* Dublin: Irish Amateur Rowing Union, 1937

Eric Halladay, *Rowing in England, a Social History.* Manchester: Manchester University Press, 1990

Louis Heiland, *The Undine Barge Club.* Philadelphia: Undine Barge Club, 1925

Ernst Herberger *et al., Rowing, The GDR Text of Oarsmanship.* Toronto: Sports Book Publisher, 1990

Robert F. Herrick, *Red Top, Reminiscences of Harvard Rowing.* Cambridge, Mass: Harvard University Press, 1948

Robert J. Higgs, *Sports, a Reference Guide.* Westport, Connecticut: Greenwood, 1982

Lucille E. Hill, *Athletics and Out-door Sports for Women.* New York: Macmillan, 1903

Timothy Holme, *Gondola, Gondolier*. London: Gentry Books, 1971

Richard Holt, *Sport and the British, a Modern History*, Oxford: Oxford University Press, 1989

Richard Holt, *Sport and Society in Modern France*. London: Macmillan, 1981

Robert S. Hunter, *Rowing in Canada since 1848*. Hamilton, Canada: Davis-Lisson, 1933

Alan N. Jacobsen, *Australia in World Rowing, the Bow-waves and Strokes*. Melbourne: Hill of Content, 1984

John Keats, *The Skiff and the River, the story of the St Lawrence River Skiff*. Nantucket: Herrick Collection, 1988

Robert F. Kelley, *American Rowing, its Background and Traditions*. New York: G. P. Putnam's Sons, 1932

Peter King, *Art and a Century of Canadian Rowing*. Toronto: Amberley House, 1980

John Langfield, *The Eton River Book*. Eton: Eton College, 1987

T. C. Lethbridge, *Boats and Boatmen*. London: Thames & Hudson, 1952

R. C. Lehmann, *The Complete Oarsman*. London: Methuen, 1908

R. C. Lehmann, *Rowing*. London: Innes, 1897

A. J. S. Lewis, *History of Rowing in Table Bay 1861–1912*. London & Cape Town: Whitehead, Morris, 1912

London Rowing Club, 125 Years of Rowing 1856–1981. London: London Rowing Club, 1981

John J. MacAloon, *This Great Symbol, Pierre de Coubertin and the Origins of the Modern Olympic Games*. Chicago & London: University of Chicago Press, 1981

A. A. Macfarlane-Grieve (ed.), *A History of Durham Rowing*. Newcastle-upon-Tyne: Andrew Reid, 1922

Eric McKee, *Working Boats of Britain, their Shape and Purpose*. London: Conway Maritime Press, 1983

John McPhee, *The Survival of the Bark Canoe*. New York: Farrar, Strauss Giroux, 1975

Herbert Manchester, *Four Centuries of Sport in America 1490–1890*. New York: Benjamin Blom, 1931

J. A. Mangan, *Athleticism in the Victorian and Edwardian Public Schools*. Cambridge: Cambridge Univerity Press, 1981

J. A. Mangan (ed.), *Pleasure, Profit, Proselytism, British Culture and Sport at Home and Abroad 1700–1914*. London: Frank Cass, 1988

Robert B. Mansfield, *The Log of the Water Lily During Three Cruises on the Rhine, Neckar, Maine, Moselle, Danube, Saône and Rhône*. London: J. C. Hotten, 1873

Tony Mason, *Sport in Britain*. London & Boston: Faber & Faber, 1988

Tony Mason (ed.), *Sport in Britain, a Social History.* Cambridge: Cambridge University Press, 1989

Roy Meldrum, *Coach and Eight.* London: Country Life, 1932

Thomas C. Mendenhall, *A Short History of American Rowing.* Boston: Charles River Books, 1980

John Ed. Morgan, *University Oars, a Critical Enquiry into the After Health of the Men who rowed in the Oxford and Cambridge Boat Race 1829–1869.* London: Macmillan, 1873

J. S. Morrison and J. F. Coates, *The Athenian Trireme.* Cambridge: Cambridge University Press, 1986

Geoffrey Page, *Hear the Boat Sing, the History of Thames Rowing Club and Tideway Rowing.* London: Kingswood Press, 1991

Peter Parker, *The Old Lie, the Great War and the Public School Ethos.* London: Constable, 1987

Charles A. Peverelly, *American Pastimes.* New York: New York News, 1868 (second edition)

Colin Porter, *Rowing to Win.* London: Stanley Paul, 1959

Richard A. Proctor, *Rough Ways Made Smooth, a series of familiar essays on Scientific Subjects.* London: Longman, Green, 1893

Isabel Quigley, *The Heirs of Tom Brown, the English Schoolboy.* London: Chatto & Windus, 1982

Reports of the London Rowing Club, 1856–1868. London: London Rowing Club

R. T. Rivington, *Punting.* Oxford: R. T. Rivington, 1983

R. P. P. Rowe and C. M. Pitman, *Rowing.* London: Longman, Green, 1898

Rowing at Westminster 1813–1883. London: Kegan Paul, 1890

Bill Sayer, *Rowing and Sculling, the Complete Manual.* London: Robert Hale, 1991

A. C. Scott and J. G. P. Williams (eds.), *Rowing, a Scientific Approach: a Symposium.* London: Kaye & Ward, 1967.

A. T. W. Shadwell, *The Principles of Rowing and Steering.* Oxford: Slatter & Rose, *c.* 1857.

W. E. Sherwood, *Oxford Rowing, a History of Boat-racing at Oxford from the Earliest Times.* Oxford: Henry Frowde, 1900

Sixty Years of the Union Boat Club 1851–1911. Boston: Union Boat Club, 1976 (reprint)

L. C. Smith, *Annals of Public School Rowing.* Oxford: Blackwell, 1919

Arthur W. Stevens and Eugene A. Darling, *Practical Rowing and the Effects of Training.* Cambridge, Mass: Massachusetts University Press, 1921

Robert Louis Stevenson, *An Inland Voyage*. First published 1878; London: Dent, 1925

J. T. Swann, *Trinity Hall BC, 1928–1949*. Cambridge: Trinity Hall, 1949

R. E. Swartwout, *Rhymes of the River*. Cambridge: W. Heffer & Sons, 1927

Colin Thubron, *The Venetians*. New York: Time-Life Books, 1980

Anthony Trollope (ed.), *British Sports and Pastimes*. London: Virtue, Spalding, 1868

D. Walker, *Manly Exercises*. London: T. Hurst, 1834 (2nd edition)

Edmond Warre, *On the Grammar of Rowing*. Oxford: Oxford University Press, 1909

Frank Welsh, *Building the Trireme*. London: Constable, 1988

Rt Hon. The Earl of Wilton, *On the Sports and Pursuits of the English, as bearing upon their National Character*. London: Harrison, 1869

Neil Wigglesworth, *Victorian and Edwardian Boating from Old Photographs*. London: Batsford, 1987

W. B. Woodgate, *Boating*. London: Longman, Green, 1888

W. B. Woodgate, *Oars and Sculls, and how to use them*. London: George Bell, 1875

Biography

Scott Bennett, *The Clarence Comet, the Career of Henry Searle 1866–1889*. Sydney: Sydney University Press, 1973

Gilbert C. Bourne, *Memories of an Eton Wet-bob of the Seventies*. London: Oxford University Press, 1933

Hylton Cleaver, *Sporting Rhapsody*. London: Hutchinson, 1951

Martin Cobbett, *Sporting Notions of Present Days and Past*. Edinburgh: Sands, 1908

Martin Cobbett, *Wayfaring Notions*. Edinburgh: Sands, 1906

T. A. Cook, *The Sunlit Hours, a Record of Sport and Life*. London: Nisbet, 1925

T. A. Cook and Guy Nickalls, *Thomas Doggett Deceased, a Famous Comedian*. London: Archibald Constable, 1908

Frank Cosentino, *Ned Hanlan*. Don Mills, Ontario: Fitzhenry & Whiteside, 1978

Bern Cuthbertson, *Around Tasmania in a Whaleboat 1986*. Hobart: Artgraphic, 1986

H. R. A. Edwards, *The Way of a Man with a Blade*. London: Routledge & Kegan Paul, 1963

Steve Fairbairn, *Fairbairn of Jesus*. London: Bodley Head, 1931

John Fairfax, *Britannia: Rowing alone across the Atlantic*. London: William Kimber, 1971

Lewis R. Farnell, *An Oxonian Looks Back*. London: Martin Hopkinson, 1924

Paul Gallico, *Farewell to Sport*. London: Simon & Schuster, 1988

David Haig-Thomas, *I Leap before I Look*. London: Putnam, 1936

David Halberstam, *The Amateurs*. New York: William Morrow, 1985

Elizabeth Johns, *Thomas Eakins, The Heroism of Modern Life*. Princeton: Princeton University Press, 1983

Stephen Kiesling, *The Shell Game, Reflections on Rowing and the Pursuit of Excellence*. Chicago: Contemporary Books, 1982

Robert C. Leslie, *A Waterbiography*. Southampton: Ashford Press, 1985

Shane Leslie, *The End of a Chapter*. London: William Heinemann, 1916

Brad Alan Lewis, *Assault on Lake Casitas*. Philadelphia: Broad Street Books, 1990

Tom McClean, *I Had to Dare, Rowing the Atlantic in Seventy Days*. London: Jarrolds, 1971

Devon Mahony, *The Challenge*. Chicago: Contemporary Books, 1989.

F. Markham, *Recollections of the Town Boy at Westminster 1849–1855*. London: Edward Arnold, 1903

Arthur E. Martin, *Life in the Slow Lane*. Portsmouth, Maine: Peter E. Randall, 1990

Eric Newby, *Something Wholesale*. London: Secker & Warburg, 1962

Gordon Newell, *Ready All! George Yeoman Pocock and Crew Racing*. Seattle: University of Washington Press, 1987

G. O. 'Gully' Nickalls, *A Rainbow in the Sky*. London: Chatto & Windus, 1974

Guy Nickalls, *Life's a Pudding*. London: Faber & Faber, 1939

Eric Parker, *Floreat, an Eton Anthology*. London: Nisbet, 1923

John Ridgway and Chay Blyth, *A Fighting Chance, how we rowed the Atlantic in 92 days*. London: Paul Hamlyn, 1966

A. L. Rowse, *Quiller Couch, a Portrait of 'Q'*. London: Methuen, 1988

Peter H. Spectre, *Different Waterfronts, stories from the WoodenBoat Revival*. Gardiner, Maine: Harpswell Press, 1989

Leslie Stephen, *Sketches from Cambridge*. London: Oxford University Press, 1932

S. F. Wise and Douglas Fisher, *Canada's Sporting Heroes*. Don Mills, Ontario: General Publishing, 1974

W. B. Woodgate, *Reminiscences of An Old Sportsman*. London: Eveleigh Nash, 1909

C. V. P. Young, *Courtney and Cornell Rowing*. Ithaca: Cornell Publications, 1923

Fiction

Allan Aldous, *McGowan Goes to Henley*. London: Oxford University
  Press, 1949
Max Beerbohm, *Zuleika Dobson*. London, William Heinemann, 1911
Edward Bradley (Cuthbert Bede), *Adventures of Mr Verdant Green, an
  Oxford Freshman*. London: James Blackwood, 1900
Thomas Hughes, *Tom Brown at Oxford*. London: Macmillan, 1861
A. P. Garland, *A Yank at Oxford*, London: Collins, 1938
Kenneth Grahame, *The Wind in the Willows*. 1908
Jerome K. Jerome, *Three Men in a Boat*. Bristol: Arrowsmith, 1889

Chapter Sources

1: **The Greeks**

Michael Budd, 'Trials and Tribulations', *Regatta* (Amateur Rowing
  Association, London) November 1987
Lionel Casson, *Ships and Seamanship in the Ancient World*. Princeton:
  Princeton University Press, 1971.
John F. Coates, 'The Trireme Sails Again', *Scientific American*, April 1989
John Coates, 'Trireme – 9.5 knots under oars', *Regatta* (Amateur Rowing
  Association, London), October 1988
John F. Coates, 'Research and Engineering Aspects of Reconstructing the
  Ancient Greek Trireme', *American Society of Naval Architects and
  Marine Engineers*, 1990
J. F. Coates, 'The Athenian Trireme', *Ancient History*, 15 May 1987
J. F. Coates, *et al.* 'The 1987 Trials of *Olympias*', *British Archaeological
  Reports*, May 1989
J. F. Coates *et al.* 'The 1988 Trials of *Olympias*', Oxbow Books, June
  1990
Christopher Dodd, 'Poros-by-the-sea', *Regatta* (Amateur Rowing
  Association, London), October 1987
Christopher Dodd, 'Battering Ram with a Human Engine', *The Guardian*,
  6 August 1987
Graeme Fife, 'An Oarsman's View', in Welsh's *Building the Trireme* (see
  below)
Vernard Foley and Werner Soedel, 'Ancient Oared Warships', *Scientific
  American*, April 1981
G. S. Kirk, 'Rowing into Battle' (review of J. S. Morrison and J. F. Coates,
  The Athenian Trireme), *Ancient History*, 15 May 1985
Andrew Moncur, 'Hard Labour', *Regatta* (Amateur Rowing Association,
  London), October 1987

John Morrison, *Long Ships and Round Ships, Welfare and Trade in the Mediterranean 3000 BC–500 AD.* London: Her Majesty's Stationery Office, 1980

J. S. Morrison and J. F. Coates, *The Athenian Trireme.* Cambridge: Cambridge University Press, 1986

J. S. Morrison and R. T. Williams, *Greek Oared Ships 900–322 BC.* Cambridge: Cambridge University Press, 1968

Roy Perrott, 'OK Xenophon, you win', *Sunday Times*, 26 April 1981

Byron Rogers, 'Sailing the Tides of Scholarship', *Telegraph Sunday Magazine*, 11 December, 1983

W. L. Rodgers, *Greek and Roman Naval Warfare.* Annapolis, 1937 (reprinted 1980)

The Trireme Controversy, letters from *The Times* and the *Financial Times*, 1975–1987. The Trireme Trust.

Christian Tyler, 'Three Men and a Boat', *Financial Times*, 11 July 1987

Frank Welsh, *Building the Trireme.* London: Constable, 1988

Ford Weiskittel, 'Below Athenian Decks', *Regatta* (Amateur Rowing Association, London), November 1987

2: The Vikings

Frans G. Bengtsson, *The Long Ships, a Saga of the Viking Age* (translated from the Swedish). New York: Knopf, 1954

Einar Gjessing, 'Rowing, the Physiological Background', in *Sailing into the Past* (proceedings of Seminar on Replicas of Ancient and Medieval Vessels). Roskilde: Viking Ship Museum, 1986

T. C. Lethbridge, *Boats and Boatmen.* London: Thames & Hudson, 1952

Magnus Magnusson, *Vikings!* London: Bodley Head & BBC, 1980

3: The Venetians

Canottieri Bucintoro 1882–1982, S. C. Bucintoro

Felipe Fernandez-Armesto, *The Spanish Armada, the Experience of War in 1588.* London: Oxford University Press, 1989

Christopher Hibbert, *Venice, the Biography of a City.* London: Grafton, 1988

J. F. Guilmartin, *Gunpowder and Galleys.* Cambridge: Cambridge University Press, 1974

F. C. Lane, *Venetian Ships and Shipbuilders of the Renaissance.* New York, 1934. Baltimore: Johns Hopkins University, 1979

F. C. Lane, *Venice – a Maritime Republic.* New York & Baltimore: Johns Hopkins University, 1979

J. G. Links, *Venice for Pleasure*. London: Bodley Head, 1966; 4th edition 1984

James Morris, *Venice*. London: Faber, 1960

Jan Morris, *The Venetian Empire*. London: Rainbird, 1980; Penguin Books, 1990

Frederick Rolfe/Baron Corvo, *The Desire and Pursuit of the Whole*, 1934

A. J. Symons, *The Quest for Corvo*. London: Cassell, 1934

Colin Thubron, *The Venetians*. New York: Time-Life Books, 1980

Mark Twain, *The Innocents Abroad*, 1869. London: Century, 1988

André Zysberg and René Burlet, *Gloire et Misère des Galères*. Paris: Decouvertes Gallimard, 1987

La Voga alla Venezia. Venice: Office of Tourism and Sport

4: Traditional Rowing

Edward Abbey, *Down the River*. New York: E. P. Dutton, 1982

John Bielinski, 'San Francisco's Oldest Rowing Clubs', *WoodenBoat 40*, 1981

Martin Cobbett, *Sporting Notions*. Edinburgh: Sands, 1908

R. H. C. Gillis, *The Pilot Gigs of Cornwall*. Isles of Scilly Museum

Arthur Grimble, *A Pattern of Islands*. London: John Murray, 1952; Penguin Books, 1981

Stephen Jones, *Backwaters*. New York: Norton, 1979

T. C. Lethbridge, *Boats and Boatmen*. London: Thames & Hudson, 1952

José M. Martínez-Hidalgo, *El Museu Maritim de Barcelona*. Barcelona: Silex, 1985

Robert Rivington, 'Cornish Gig Racing, a Reviving Sport', *ARA Club News,* December 1986

Joseph Serracino, *Tal-Vitorja u Tigrijet Ohra* (Victory Regatta). Malta: Printwell, 1988

W. and W. J. Walker, *Friendship 1879–1951, the History and Records of over Seventy Years of Rowing by the Whitby Friendship Amateur Rowing Club*. Whitby: Whitby Friendship ARC, 1954

Howard Williams, *The Diary of a Rowing Tour from Oxford to London in 1875*. Gloucester: Alan Sutton, 1982

Traineras

Luis Azcue Aldaz, *Orio en el Remo,* Ediciones de la Caja de Aborros Provincial de Guipúzcoa, 1974

Rafael Aguirre Franco, *Donostia/San Sebastian* (introduction to San Sebastian in Basque, Spanish, French, English, German and Italian). San Sebastian: Industria Gráfica Valverde

Rafael Aguirre Franco, 'Estropadak – Regatas de Traineras', from *Enciclopedia General Ilustrade del Pais Vasco*, 1972

Gorka Reizabal Arruabarrena, *Santos Pasajes e Remo,* Junta del Puerto de Pasajes, 1989

5: Workboat to Racing Boat

The Annual Illustrated Catalogue and Oarsman's Manual for 1871. Troy, New York: Waters, Balch, 1871

Gilbert C. Bourne, *A Text-book of Oarsmanship*. London: Oxford University Press, 1925

A. W. Brøgger and Haakon Shetelig, *The Viking Ships*. Oslo: Dreyers Forlag, 1951

Howard I. Chapelle, *The Search for Speed under Sail*. New York: Norton, 1967

Kenneth and Helen Durant, *The Adirondack Guide-boat*. Camden, Maine: International Marine Publishing, 1980

John Gardner, *Building Classic Small Craft*, vol I. Camden, Maine: International Marine Publishing, 1977

Jerome K. Jerome, *Three Men in a Boat*. Bristol: Arrowsmith, 1889

John Keats, *The Skiff and the River: the Story of the St Lawrence River Skiff*. Nantucket: Herrick Collection, 1988

John Leather, 'Skiffs of the Thames', *Classic Boat*, April 1990

T. C. Lethbridge, *Boats and Boatmen*. London: Thames & Hudson, 1952

Eric McKee, *Working Boats of Britain, their Shape and Purpose*. London: Conway Maritime Press, 1983

John McPhee, *The Survival of the Bark Canoe*. New York: Farrar, Strauss Giroux, 1975

Peter C. Newman, *Company of Adventurers, The Story of the Hudson's Bay Company*. Markham, Ontario: Penguin Books Canada, 1985

D. J. Smith, *Discovering Craft of the Inland Waterways*. London: Shire Publications, 1977

Neil Wigglesworth, *Victorian and Edwardian Boating from Old Photographs*. London: Batsford, 1987

6: Nineteenth-Century Innovators

The Annual Illustrated Catalogue and Oarsman's Manual for 1871. Troy, New York: Waters, Balch, 1871

Gilbert C. Bourne, *A Text-book of Oarsmanship*. London: Oxford University Press, 1925

Howard I. Chapelle, *The Search for Speed under Sail*. New York: Norton, 1967

R. J. Charleton, *A History of Newcastle-on-Tyne*. W. H. Robinson, 1885

Hylton Cleaver, *A History of Rowing*. London: Herbert Jenkins, 1957

Sir Theodore Cook, *Rowing at Henley*. London: Oxford, 1919

W. B. Coventry, *The Racing Eight*. Cambridge: Heffer 1922

S. Crowther and A. Ruhl, *Rowing and Track Athletics*. New York: Macmillan, 1905

Christopher Dodd, *The Oxford and Cambridge Boat Race*. London: Stanley Paul, 1983

Christopher Dodd, 'Rowing', in Tony Mason (ed.) *Sport in Britain*, Cambridge: Cambridge University Press, 1989

J. V. S. Glass and J. Max Patrick, *The Royal Chester Rowing Club Centenary History 1838–1938*. Liverpool: James Laver, 1938

A Historical and Descriptive View of the County of Northumberland. Mackenzie & Dent, 1811

Robert S. Hunter, *Rowing in Canada since 1848*. Hamilton, Canada: Davis-Lisson, 1933

Peter King, *Art and a Century of Canadian Rowing*. Toronto: Amberley House, 1980

Herbert Manchester, *Four Centuries of Sport in America 1490–1890*. New York: Benjamin Blom, 1931

Victor M. Mansell and W. B. Woodgate, articles in *British Sports and Sportsmen (Yachting and Rowing)*, The Sportsman, 1916

Thomas C. Mendenhall, *A Short History of American Rowing*. Boston: Charles River Books, 1980

C. M. Pitman, *Record of the University Boat Race*. London: T. Fisher Unwin, 1909

Joachim Schult, *Aus der Jugendzeit des Motorbootes,* Berlin: Delius, Klasing, 1971; English edition Paul Elek Books, 1974)

K. A. Williams, 'The Problem of Designing a Fast Racing Eight', *British Rowing Almanack*. London: Amateur Rowing Association, 1963

7: Twentieth-Century Innovators

Willy Empacher, *Der Bau von Kuststoff Booten*. Berlin: Delius Klasing, 1972

Thomas C. Mendenhall, *A Short History of American Rowing*. Boston: Charles River Books, 1980

8: Atlantic Treatise

L. S. R. Byrne and E. L. Churchill, *The Eton Book of the River*. Eton: Alden & Blackwell, 1952

Bernard Horton, 'George Yeoman Pocock', *The Oarsman*, May-June 1976

Thomas C. Mendenhall, 'The Pococks', *The Oarsman*, April-May and June-July 1981

Gordon Newell, *Ready All! George Yeoman Pocock and Crew Racing*. Seattle: University of Washington Press, 1987

9: Plastic to Heat Cure

Alec N. Brooks, Allan V. Abbott and David Gordon Wilson, 'Human-powered Watercraft', *Scientific American*, December 1986

10: Thor, God of Enlightenment

FISA Coaching Development Programme Course, 3 vols. Oberhofen: FISA, 1990

Kurt Jensen, Thor Nilsen and Matt Smith, 'Analysis of Italian National Training Programme for Rowing', *FISA Coach*, vol. 1, no. 2, 1990

A. C. Scott and J. G. P. Williams (eds.), *Rowing, a Scientific Approach*. London: Kaye & Ward, 1967

11: World Master Class

Rolf Blanke, *Zur Geschichte des Rudersports in Deutschland von ihren Aufängen bis zum 1945*. Magdeburg: Pädagogischen Hochschule Erich Weinert, 1987

Christopher Dodd, 'East German lab that concocted a winning formula', *The Guardian*, 28 March 1990

Peter Klavora (ed.), *Rowing*. Toronto: Sports Book Publisher, 1990 (edited translation of Ernst Herberger *et al.*s *Rudern*, fourth edition of East Germany's rowing manual, 1977)

John Langfield with Bruce Grainger, edited translation of the original edition of Herberger's *Rudern*. Private circulation

Peter Sutcliffe, 'Sport in the German Democratic Republic', *Coaching Focus*, no. 8, Summer 1988. Leeds: National Coaching Foundation

Jörg Winkler, *Die geschichtliche Entwicklung des Rudersports auf dem Territorium der DDR 1945–81*. Magdeburg: Pädagogischen Hochschule Erich Weinert, 1987

Zur Geschichte des Ruderns in Dresden 1872–89. Dresden: BFA Rudern, 1989

12: Adam and Steve

L. S. R. Byrne and E. L. Churchill, *The Eton Book of the River.* Eton: Alden & Blackwell, 1952

Hannes Strohmeyer, 'Natural Gymnastics', paper for the Institute for Sports Sciences of Vienna University, 1985

Horst Überhorst (ed.), *Hundert Jahre Deutscher Ruderverband.* Minden: Albrecht Philler, 1983

Karl Adam

Karl Adam, 'The Development of the Modern Ways of Training', *Rudersport 31* coaching supplement, 1962 (English translation by K. M. Engelbert)

Karl Adam, *Kleine Schriften zum Rudertraining.* Berlin: Bartels & Wernitz, 1982

Karl Adam, *Leistungssport als Denkmodell.* Munich: Wilhelm Fink, 1978

Karl Adam, Hans Lenk, Paul Nowacki, Manfred Rulffs, Walter Schröder, *Rudertraining.* Bad Homburg: Limpert, 1977

Hans Lenk *et al.*, *Handlungsmuster Leistungssport* (a memorial to Karl Adam). Schorndorf: Karl Hofmann, 1977

Steve Fairbairn

Steve Fairbairn, *The Complete Steve Fairbairn on Rowing.* London: Nicholas Kaye, 1951; London: Kingswood Press, 1990. Includes *Notes on Rowing*, 1904; *Rowing Notes*, 1926; *Some Secrets of Successful Rowing*, 1930; *Chats on Rowing*, 1934; *Rowing in a Nutshell*; *Don't Exaggerate*; *The Endless Chain Movement*, 1937

Contributions in *The Complete Steve Fairbairn on Rowing* (1990 edn):

F. Brittain, Obituary of Steve Fairbairn

F. Brittain, 'Slowly Forward, 366 points for oarsmen and coxswains selected from Fairbairn's writing'

Alan Burrough, Foreword to 1990 edition

Ian Fairbairn, General Introduction

Ian Fairbairn, 'Rowing Results of Steve's Teaching'

R. S. de Havilland, 'Elements of Rowing'

Geoffrey Page, Introduction to 1990 edition

Steve Fairbairn, *Fairbairn of Jesus.* London: Bodley Head, 1931

13: Hitler's Games

Victor de Bisschop, *Rowing, Memoirs d'un Starter Olympique*. Gand: Royal Club Nautique de Gand, 1946
Ernest A. Bland (ed.), *Olympic Story*. London: Rockliffe, 1948
Hylton Cleaver, *A History of Rowing*. London: Herbert Jenkins, 1957
Hylton Cleaver, *Sporting Rhapsody*. London: Hutchinson, 1951
Duff Hart-Davis, *Hitler's Olympics*. London: Century Hutchinson, 1986
John Kieran, *The Story of the Olympic Games*. New York: Frederick A. Stokes, 1936
Richard D. Mandell, *The Nazi Olympics*. New York: Macmillan, 1971
Gordon Newell, *Ready All! George Yeoman Pocock and Crew Racing*. Seattle: University of Washington Press, 1987
Die Olympischen Spiele 1936 (official book of the 1936 Winter and Summer Olympic Games, 2 vols.). Berlin: Cigaretten-Bilderdienst Altona-Bahrenfeld, 1936
Horst Überhorst (ed.), *Hundert Yahre Deutscher Ruderverband*. Minden: Albrecht Philler, 1983

14: Conibear Myth and Magic

Malcolm R. Alama, *Mark of the Oarsmen, a Narrative History of Rowing at Syracuse University*. Syracuse, New York: Syracuse Alumni Rowing Association, 1963
Joe Burk, 'The Coach's Column', *Rowing News*. Philadelphia: National Association of American Oarsmen
Emory Clark, 'Al', *The Oarsman*, July-August 1974
Samuel Crowther and Arthur Ruhl, *Rowing and Track Athletics*. New York: Macmillan, 1905
Negley Farson, *The Way of a Transgressor*. London: Victor Gollancz, 1935
Robert F. Herrick, *Red Top, Reminiscences of Harvard Rowing*. Cambridge, Mass: Harvard University Press, 1948
Bernard S. Horton, 'George Yeomans Pocock', *The Oarsman*, May-June 1976
Interview: 'Joe Burk', *The Oarsman*, July-August 1978
Interview: 'Harry L. Parker', *The Oarsman*, May-June 1978
Robert F. Kelley, *American Rowing, Its Background and Traditions*. New York: G. P. Putnam's Sons, 1932
Thomas C. Mendenhall, 'The British are Coming', *The Oarsman*, January-February 1979
Thomas C. Mendenhall, 'The British are Still Coming!' *The Oarsman*, March-April 1979

Thomas C. Mendenhall, 'Cornell's Old Man' (Courtney), *The Oarsman*, July-August 1978

Thomas C. Mendenhall, 'Ed Leader I', *The Oarsman*, December 1981-January 1982

Thomas C. Mendenhall, 'Ed Leader II', *Rowing USA*, April-May 1982

Thomas C. Mendenhall, 'Rusty Callow I', *The Oarsman*, September-October 1980

Thomas C. Mendenhall, 'Rusty Callow II', *The Oarsman*, December 1980-January 1981

Thomas C. Mendenhall, 'Rusty Callow III', *The Oarsman*, February-March 1981

Thomas C. Mendenhall, 'The Dour Dane I' (Ulbrickson), *Rowing USA*, June-July 1982

Thomas C. Mendenhall, 'The Dour Dane II' (Ulbrickson), *Rowing USA*, October-November 1982

Thomas C. Mendenhall, 'The Old Man in the Felt Hat I' (Bolles), *The Oarsman*, September-October 1979

Thomas C. Mendenhall, 'The Old Man in the Felt Hat II' (Bolles), *The Oarsman*, November-December 1979

Thomas C. Mendenhall, 'Coaches and Coaching', *The Oarsman*, March-April 1978

Thomas C. Mendenhall, 'Training, Technology, Technique I', *The Oarsman*, March-April 1976

Thomas C. Mendenhall, 'Training, Technology, Technique II', *The Oarsman*, May-June 1976

Thomas C. Mendenhall, 'Training, Technology, Technique III', *The Oarsman*, January-February 1977

Thomas C. Mendenhall, *A Short History of American Rowing*. Boston: Charles River Books, 1980

Colin Porter, *Rowing to Win*. London: Stanley Paul, 1959

Allen Rosenberg, 'A Discussion of Rowing Styles', *The Oarsman*, 1967

Frank Strong: 'A Glimpse of Bolles & Co in the Late Forties', *Rowing USA*, December 1982-January 1983

R. P. P. Rowe and C. M. Pitman, *Rowing*. London: Longman, Green, 1898

Benjamin Spock, 'The Mother's Boy and the New Coach', in Diana Dubois (ed.) *My Harvard, My Yale.*, New York: Random House, 1982

W. B. Woodgate, *Boating*. London: Longman Green, 1888

C. V. P. Young, *Courtney and Cornell Rowing*. Ithaca: Cornell Publications, 1923

Andra Zezelj, 'Fact and Fiction about Conibear', *Rowing Magazine*, February 1967

15: Made in Britain

Henry Bond, *A History of the Trinity Hall Boat Club*. Cambridge: Heffer, 1930

F. Brittain, *A Short History of Jesus College*. Cambridge: Heffer, 1940

Richard Burnell: 'The Amateur Rowing Association 1882–1982', *British Rowing Almanack*, 1982. London: Amateur Rowing Association.

Christopher Dodd, 'Rowing', in Tony Mason (ed.), *Sport in Britain, a Social History*. Cambridge: Cambridge University Press, 1989

Christopher Dodd, *Henley Royal Regatta*, London: Stanley Paul, 1981; revised edition 1989

T. F. Hall, *History of Boat Racing in Ireland*. Dublin: Irish Amateur Rowing Union, 1937

Eric Halladay, *Rowing in England, a Social History*. Manchester: Manchester University Press, 1990

Der Hamburger und Germania Ruder Club, 150 Jahre Rudern in Deutschland. Hamburg: Hamburger & Germania, 1986

Richard Holt, *Sport and the British, a Modern History*. Oxford: Oxford University Press, 1989.

R. C. Lehmann, *The Complete Oarsman*. London: Methuen, 1908

W. A. Locan, *The Agecroft Story*. Salford: Agecroft RC, 1960

Peter Lovesey, *The Official Centenary History of the Amateur Athletic Association*. London: Guinness Superlatives, 1979

John J. MacAloon, *This Great Symbol, Pierre de Coubertin and the Origins of the Modern Olympic Games*. Chicago & London: University of Chicago Press, 1981

Tony Mason, *Sport in Britain*. London & Boston: Faber & Faber, 1988

R. N. Rose, *The Field, 1853–1953*. London: Michael Joseph, 1953

Neil Wigglesworth, *Victorian and Edwardian Boating from Old Photographs,* London: Batsford, 1988

16: Birthplaces and Channel Crossing

A. F. Ryder Bird, *Boating in Bavaria, Austria, and Bohemia, down the Danube, Moldau, and Elbe*. Hull: William Andrews, 1893

L. S. R. Byrne and E. L. Churchill, *The Eton Book of the River*. Alden & Blackwell, 1952

Charles Dickens Jr, *Dickens's Dictionary of the Thames*. London: Macmillan, 1885

Jerome K. Jerome, *Three Men in a Boat*. Bristol: Arrowsmith, 1889

Robert B. Mansfield, *The Log of the Water Lily During Three Cruises on the Rhine, Neckar, Maine, Moselle, Danube, Saône, and Rhône*. London: J. C. Hotten, 1873

Howard Williams, *The Diary of a Rowing Tour from Oxford to London in 1875*. Gloucester: Alan Sutton, 1982

Belgium
E. Desloovere, 'Onstaan, instituionalisering en evolutie van de roeisport in België 1858–1987' (thesis). Catholic University of Leuven, 1987
Jubileumboek van de Koninklijke Roeivereniging Sport Gent 1883–1983. Gent; KRSG, 1983
Léon Lewillie et Francine Noël, *Le Sport dans l'art Belge*. Antwerp: Crédit Communal de Belgique, 1982
Francine Noël et Stéphane Vandenberghe, *Sportaffiches in België 1890–1940*. Brussels: Crédit Communal de Belgique, 1981
Robert Louis Stevenson, *An Inland Voyage*. First published 1878; London: Dent, 1925
100 Jaar Universitaire Sport de Leuven. Leuven: Universitair Centrum voor Lichamelijke Opleiding en Sport, Katholieke Universiteit Leuven, 1981
Tijdschrift vor Geschiedenis van Techniek en Industriële Cultuur. Vereniging voor Industriële Archeologie en Textial, 1985

France
Joë Bridge et René Chincholle, *Rowing-Club de Paris, 1853–1953*. Paris: Rowing-Club, 1953
Un Ex-Champion (P. Fleuret et A. Seurin), *Le Sport d'Aviron*. Paris: Librairies-Imprimeries Réunies, 1985
Fédération Française des Sociétés d'Aviron 1890–1990. Paris: FFSA, 1990
Richard Holt, *Sport and Society in Modern France*. London: Macmillan, 1981
Michel Riousset, *Les Environs de la Marne et leurs Peintres*. Le Mée-sur-Seine: Editions Amatteis, 1986
Société d'Encouragement du Sport Nautique, 1879–1979. Paris: SESN, 1979

Italy
Società Canottieri 'Armida' 1869–1969. Turin
Mario Bazzi, *Il Buon Gigante a la sua Società* (undated life of Sinigaglia)
Beppe Bracco e Laura Schrader, *Torino un Fiume, Canottieri Caprera 1883–1983*.
Giorgio Croppi, *A Remi, a Vela e a Vapore*. Milan: Ulrigo Hoepli, 1898
Esperia: un secolo sul Po, Società Canottieri Esperia-Torino 1886–1986
Alberto Marchesi e Gianfranco Tobia, *Storia del Circolo Canottieri Aniene*. Rome
75 Anni di Giovent., Società Canottieri 'Firenze' 1911–86.

Lario 1891–1981, Canottieri Lario G. Sinigaglia Como

Netherlands
R. R. J. Davilar en P. Schierbeek, *Toerroeien in Nederland* (touring guide with maps and routes). Haarlem: De Vrieseborch, 1990
De Nederlandse Roeisport. Amsterdam: Nederlandsche Roeibond, 1987

17: Viking Trail

Norway
Matti Goksøyr: 'Popular Pastimes or Patriotic Virtues? The role of Sport in the National Celebrations of Nineteenth-Century Norway', *International Journal of the History of Sport,* vol. 5. no. 2., September 1988
Rolf Manskow (ed.), *Norges Roforbund 1900–1950.* Oslo: Fabritius & Sonner, 1952

Soviet Union
Maxim Knopmuss, 'The Birth and Growth of Rowing in Russia', *Rowing Magazine* (London), May 1956
Yury Tyukalov, *Ot odnogo do vos'mi, Greblya na Olimpiadakh* (From a Single to an Eight, Rowing at the Olympics). Moscow: Sovetskaya Rossiya, 1979

Sweden
Äe Svahn and Sten Thunvik, *En Bok om Rodd.* Stokholm: Sohlmans, 1944
Post boats Broge Witen Liber, *Postfärder över Naudshav* (in Swedish)
Church boats – Albert Eskeröd, *Kyrkbätar och Kyrkbatsfärder.* Stockholm: LTs.

18: Rhine and Danube

Austria
100 Jahre Erster Wiener Ruder-Club Lia 1863–1963
110 Jahre Linzer Ruderverein Ister 1876–1986
120 Jahre Ruderklub Lia, 130 Jahre Rudern in Österreich
Victor Silberer, *Handbuch des Ruder-Sport.* Vienna, Budapest, Leipzig: A. Hartleben, 1897
100 Jahre Wiener Regatt-Verein 1882–1982

Czechoslovakia
*Jubilejni Rocenka ke Vyroci Vzniku Veslarske Organizace v
    Ceskoslovensku 1884–1984* (Hundred years of rowing in
    Czechoslovakia 1884–1984). Prague: Czech rowing federation, 1984

Germany
*Der Hamburger und Germania Ruder Club, 150 Jahre Rudern in
    Deutschland.* Hamburg: 1986
Wilhelm Heichen, *Des Ruderers Fdjönfte Lieder.* Breslau: Franz Görlich,
    n.d.
Gustav Kopal, *Vom Hamburger Wasserport, Erinnerungen aus dem
    Allgemeinen Alster-Club.* Hamburg: M. Glogau Jr, 1912
Georg von Opel (ed.), *Wir Rudern dürch die Zeit.* 1950
Heinrich Pfeiffer, *Der Schiedsrichter und das Regattarecht des
    Rudersports.* Minden: Albrecht Philler, 1964
Horst Überhorst (ed.), *Hundert Jahre Deutscher Ruderverband.* Minden:
    Albrecht Philler, 1983

Hungary
István Birly, *A Csolnakászat Különos Tekintettel A Versenyevezésre.*
    (based on a book by 'Stonehenge' [J. H. Walsh]). Pest: 1866
Kornélia Pap, *Vizek Szabadia Lettem* (I obtained the Freedom of the
    Waters). Budapest: Sport Budapest, 1983
Dr László Siklóssy, *Képek A Hunnia ötvenéves Multjából 1882–1932.*
    Budapest, 1932
Dr László Siklóssy, *A Magyar Sport EzerÉve* (vol. I pre-1820; vol. II
    1820–74; vol. III 1874–96). Budapest, 1928
István Soós, *A Szegédi Evezes Története* (History of Szeged Rowing).
    Szeged, 1979
Ferenc Végh, *SzázÉves a Györi Evezés 1977–1977.* Szeged, 1977

Poland
Ryszard Kobendza, 'Roots and Branches of Polish Rowing' (unpublished
    research paper), June 1990
Roger Verey, *40,000 Kilometrów Skifie.* Warsaw: Sport i Turystyka, 1957

Switzerland
Marc M. Meyer, *50 Jahre Belvoir Ruder-Club Zürich 1928–78*
100 Jahre Seeclub Biel 1886–1986
100 years of Seeclub Zürich

19: Spanish Inquisition

Argentina
Andrew Graham-Youll, *The Forgotten Colony, a History of the English-speaking communities in Argentina*. London: Hutchinson, 1981
James McGouth, *On Rippling Water, the Story of Rowing in Argentina*. Buenos Aires: Buenos Aires Herald (unpublished)
Michael G. Mulhall, *The English in South America*. Buenos Aires: Standard, *c.* 1878

Brazil
Henrique Lichte, *O Remo Através dos Tempos*. Porto Alegre: Confederação Brasileira de Remo, 1986
Raul Leme Monteiro, *Um Pouco de História do Tietê São Paulo*, 1944
Do RV Freundschaft ao Grêmio Náutico União 1906–81. Porto Alegre, 1981

Cuba
Raul Castro Asunsolo, *Memorias del Club Nautico de Varadero 1910–62*
Norge Marrero, 'Rowing in Cuba' (thesis, University of Havana)

Mexico
Jose Luis Gutierrez, 'Memoria de la Seccion de Remo del Club España 1924–74' (unpublished)

Portugal
Gerald Cobb, *Oporto Older and Newer*. Chichester Press, 1966
G. M. A. G. (Max Graham), *OBC Notes on Rowing*. Oporto, 1925

Spain (for traineras see chapter 4)
Banyoles, al costat de Barcelona (official bid of Banyoles for the regatta of the Barcelona Olympic Games with French and English summaries). Banyoles, 1987
La Concòrdia Sobre les Aigües de l'Estany 1685–1985. Ajuntament de Banyoles Centre d'Estudis Comarcals de Banyoles
Luis G. Constans, *Bañolas, Edicion Patrocinada por el Ecmo*. Gerona, 1951
José María Martínez-Hidalgo, *Los Deportes Náuticos en Cataluza 1821–1936*. Barcelona: Silex, 1978
José M. Martínez-Hidalgo, *El Museu Maritim de Barcelona*. Barcelona: Silex, 1985
Antoni Maria Rigau and Jordi Gimferrer, *El pintor Pigem 1862–1946*. Figueres, 1987

Rafael Sardà i Llorens, *80 Anys d'Esports de la Mar 1902–1982*.
  Barcelona: Real Club Maritim de Barcelona/Edicions Barcelona, 1982

20: Coast to Coast America

Canada
John Arthur Carver, *The Vancouver Rowing Club, a History 1888–1980*.
  Vancouver: Aubrey F. Roberts, 1980
Frank Cosentino, *Ned Hanlan*. Don Mills, Ontario: Fitzhenry &
  Whiteside, 1978
Robert S. Hunter, *Rowing in Canada since 1848*. Hamilton, Ontario:
  Davis-Lisson, 1933
Peter King, *Art and a Century of Canadian Rowing*. Toronto: Amberley
  House, 1980
H. O'Brien, *Historical Sketch of the Argonaut Rowing Club*. Toronto:
  Scott Printers, 1912
C. S. Riley, *Autobiography*. Winnipeg: private publication, 1971
S. F. Wise and Douglas Fisher, *Canada's Sporting Heroes*. Don Mills,
  Ontario: General Publishing, 1974

United States
Sarah Bradford, *Princess Grace*. London: Weidenfeld & Nicholson, 1984
Christopher Dodd, 'The Harvard-Yale Race – They Row, Therefore They
  Are', *American Rowing*, August-September 1986. Indianapolis: United
  States Rowing Association
Christopher Dodd: 'Rowing' in Tony Mason (ed.), *Sport in Britain*,
  Cambridge: Cambridge University Press, 1989
Charles W. Eliot, 'What a Day for an Oar Race', in William Bentinck-
  Smith (ed.), *The Harvard Book: Selections from Three Centuries*,
  Cambridge: Harvard University Press, 1982
John Gardner, 'Early Days of Rowing Sport', *The Log of Mystic Seaport*,
  Mystic: Mystic Seaport, 1971 (reprinted in *The Oarsman*, November-
  December 1974)
Lloyd Goodrich, *Thomas Eakins*, 2 vols. Cambridge, Mass: Harvard
  University Press for National Gallery of Art, Washington, 1982
Stephen Hardy, *How Boston Played: Sport, Recreation, and Community
  1865–1915*. Boston: Northeastern University Press, 1982
Elizabeth Johns, *Thomas Eakins, the Heroism of Modern Life*. Princeton:
  Princeton University Press, 1983
Thomas C. Mendenhall, 'Rowing on the Schuylkill I', *American Rowing*,
  June-July 1986
Thomas C. Mendenhall, 'Rowing on the Schuylkill II', *American Rowing*,
  August-September 1986

Thomas C. Mendenhall, *A Short History of American Rowing*. Boston: Charles River Books, 1980

Thomas C. Mendenhall, 'Thomas Eakins', *Rowing USA*, April-May 1983

Charles A. Peverelly, *American Pastimes*. New York: New York News, 1868 (second edition)

Jack Seitz, 'A Remembrance, John B. Kelly Jr', *Rowing USA*, April-May 1985

Theodor Siegl, *The Thomas Eakins Collection*. Philadelphia: Philadelphia Museum of Art, 1977

Horst Überhorst (ed.), *Hundert Jahre Deutscher Ruderverband*. Minden: Albrecht Philler, 1983

Thomas E. Weil Jr, 'An Introduction to Rowing Prints', *Rowing USA*, April-May 1983

Women

Marjorie N. Breitenbach, *Lena, a Determined Woman*. San Diego: Zlac Rowing Club, 1967

Pauline Churcher, 'Development of Women's Rowing 1969–79', *British Rowing Almanack 1980*. London: Amateur Rowing Association

Sara Lopez, 'A History of Women's Rowing in the United States' (paper at California State University, Northridge)

Melissa Ludtke, 'A Century of Rowing, History of Crew at Wellesley College', *The Oarsman*, July-August 1975

Kathleen E. McCrone, 'Emancipation or Recreation? The Development of Women's Sport at the University of London', *International Journal of the History of Sport*, September 1990. London: Frank Cass

Kathleen E. McCrone, *Sport and the Physical Emancipation of English Women 1870–1914*. London: Routledge, 1988

Carol Mast, 'Dick's Chicks', *Rowing USA*, December 1986-January 1987

Jan Palchikoff, 'The Development of Women's Rowing in the United States' (paper at University of Massachusetts, Amherst)

Carolyn Reckman, 'The NWRA [National Women's Rowing Association]', *American Rowing*, August-September 1986

Linda K.Vaughan, 'A Century of Rowing at Wellesley 1875–1975', paper delivered to North American Society for Sports History, 1975

21: Pacific Approaches

Australia

John Bach, *A Maritime History of Australia*. Sydney: Thomas Nelson (Australia), 1976

Nehemiah Bartley, *Opals and Agates; or Scenes under the Southern Cross*

*and the Magelhans; being memories of Fifty Years of Australia and
Polynesia.* Brisbane, 1892

Scott Bennett, *The Clarence Comet, the Career of Henry Searle 1866–89.*
Sydney: Sydney University Press, 1973

Scott Bennett, 'Professional Sculling in New South Wales', *Journal of the
Royal Australian Historical Society*, October 1985

Keith Dunstan, *Sports.* Melbourne: Cassell Australia, 1973

Gordon Inglis, *Sport and Pastimes in Australia.* London: Methuen, 1912

Brian and Barbara Kennedy, *Sydney and Suburbs.* New South Wales:
Reed Books, 1982

Robert Hughes, *The Fatal Shore.* London: Collins Harvill, 1987

An Illustrated Guide to Sydney 1882. Sydney: Gibbs, Shallard, 1882

Alan N. Jacobsen, *Australia in World Rowing, the Bow-waves and
Strokes.* Melbourne: Hill of Content, 1984

David G. Lane and Ian F. Jobling, 'For Honour and Trophies: Amateur
Rowing in Australia, 1888–1912', *Journal of the Australian Society
for Sports History*, November 1987

John Lang, *The Victorian Oarsman.* Melbourne: A. H. Massina, 1919

A. L. May, *Sydney Rows, a Centennial History of the Sydney Rowing
Club.* Sydney: Sydney Rowing Club, 1970

Mercantile, a Century of Rowing. Melbourne: Mercantile Rowing Club,
1980

Russel Ward and John Robertson, *Such Was Life, Select Documents in
Australian Social History* (vol. I 1788–1850, vol. II 1851–1913).
Sydney: Ure Smith, 1969

China

N. M. W. Harris, *Sampan Pidgin, a History of Shanghai Rowing Club.*
Shanghai: Mercantile Printing Co., 1938

W. H. Hunter, *The Fan Kwae at Canton, Before Treaty Days 1825–44*
(includes *Old Canton*). Shanghai: Kelly & Walsh, 1925

Michael Levien (ed.), *The Cree Journals, the Voyages of Edward Cree,
Surgeon RN, as Related in His Private Journals 1837–56.* Exeter:
Webb & Bower, 1981

Timothy Mo, *An Insular Possession.* London: Chatto & Windus, 1986

India

Samik Banerjee, *Calcutta 200 Years: a Tollygunge Club Perspective.*
Calcutta: Tollygunge Club, 1981

Sadashiv Gorakshkar and Kalpana Desai, *The Maritime Heritage of India.*
Bombay: Western Naval Command, 1989

L. H. Macklin, *The Calcutta Rowing Club 1858–1932.* Calcutta: Calcutta
Rowing Club, 1932

Southern Africa
A. J. S. Lewis, *History of Rowing in Table Bay 1861–1912*. London & Cape Town: Whitehead, Morris, 1912

22: Coubertin to Keller

Gene Brown (ed.), *The Complete Book of Water Sports*. New York: The New York Times, 1980

Pierre de Coubertin: 'Où en est l'aviron?', *Essais de Psychologie Sportive*, 1911

Nadejda Lekarska, *Essays and Studies on Olympic Problems*. Sofia: Medicina & Fizcultura, 1973

A. J. Liebling, *Between Meals, an Appetite for Paris*. London: Cardinal, 1990

Alan L. May, *Manila Rows, the Story of the Manila Boat Club*. Manila: Manila Boat Club, 1979

David Wellechinsky, *The Complete Book of the Olympics*. New York: Viking and Penguin, 1988

First-hand accounts of British crews in Olympic regattas from 1924 to 1984, *Regatta* (special Olympic edition). London: Amateur Rowing Association, September 1988

Acknowledgements

T HE story of rowing could not have been written without the help of
Peter Coni and Dominik Keller who read the whole of the manuscript,
and John Coates, Bob Janousek, Tom Mendenhall, John Morrison, Thor
Nilsen, Dick Pieper, John Rodda and Richard Way who read parts of it;
the translators, particularly David Cazes, Sue Coombes, Beatrice Seiler and
Andrew Wiseman; the art historians Richard Marks and Tom Weill; and
rowing federations and their officials, virtually all of whom answered
requests for information and introductions. Those who put resources at
my disposal in the form of services and/or hospitality were China, Cuba,
Finland, Hungary, Italy, India, Mexico, USA and the USSR. The Amateur
Rowing Association in London and the stewards at Henley have cooperated. All those connected with FISA, the international rowing federation,
were extremely helpful, including the president, Denis Oswald, the
secretary-general, John Boultbee, the development coaches, Ted Daigneault
and Ricardo Ibbara, the archivist, Jean-Louis Meuret, and commissioners
or former commissioners including Bjørn Haslov, Hans Howald and many
others who appear under other headings below. Michael Killanin, former
president of the IOC, assisted with Olympic matters.

I also owe a debt to Sue Hogg, a superb editor, to Gabrielle Allen who
researched the illustrations, and to Roddy Bloomfield and Dominique Shead
who guided the book from manuscript to publication at Stanley Paul. My
travel agent Gillian Wooldridge, and Duvee Melhuish who runs a remarkable secretarial agency in Herne Hill, London, kept us all in touch. Thanks
also to colleagues in the press in many countries who have fed my obsession,
to family and friends who have put up with it, and to the *Guardian* for
giving me time off to research and write it.

Other helpmates are listed below under the country about which they
gave most assistance:

Argentina: Andrew Graham-Youll, Alberto Madero, Francisco
Mangialardi, Jeremy Morgan, Ana Villa, *Buenos Aires Herald* (Nicholas
Tozer, Eric Weill).

Australia: Scott Bennett, Michael Nicholson, George Parlby, Robin Poke, Bob Towns, Wray Vamplew.

Austria: Ingeborg Diernhofer, Marius Mautner Markhof, Vera Sommerbauer, Professor Hannes Strohmeyer, Alfred Unger.

Belgium: Rob van Mesdag, Professor Roland Renson, Roland Rombaut.

Brazil: Renato Borges da Fonseca, Henrique Licht, Alvair Rogério Rossetti.

Bulgaria: Tchavdar Kaler, Svetla Otzetova.

Canada: Edward A. English, Frank Read, Earl Green, Alan Morrow, Mike McKinley.

Chile: John Trevena.

China: Liu Aijie, Beattie Donaldson, Wang Deying, Joachim Ehrig, Bertie and Norma Rasmussen, Gao Hong-ying, Huang Yongliang.

Cuba: Norge Marrero, Isaac Zabinski Mulkay.

Czechoslovakia: Svetla Hudeōkova, George Justicz, Josef Nesticky, Magdalena Sarbochová, Zdeněk Vaněk.

Denmark: Mogens Sørensen.

Finland: Henry Forssell, Bo and Zita Gammals, Kanko Miettinen.

France: Claude Arnoult, Jean-Paul Fain, Neil McQueen, Philippe Moras, Jean Rodenfuser, Roland Weill.

Germany (* from the former Democratic Republic): Arno Boes, *Herman Buhl, Herbert Buhtz, *Kurt Debus, Hans Empacher, Helmut Empacher, Rainer Empacher, *Klaus Filter, David Gow, *Wifried Hofmann, *Theo Körner, Udo Korgitzsch, Professor Hans Lenk, Henrik Lotz, Helmut Mensch, Volke Nolte, *Helmut Pohlentz, Waltraut Schrittwieser, Professor Walter Schroeder, Suzanne Schulz-Falster, Matthias Schumann, Professor Horst Überhorst, *Georg Winkler, Leo Wolloner, Karin von Wussow.

Gibraltar: Leslie Grech.

Greece: Argyrios Fotis.

Guatemala: Mario Rolando Castio, Carlos Larranaga Gomar, Juan Zanussi.

Hong Kong: John H. Edwards, Chris Perry, David Sorton, Bob Wilson, Royal Hong Kong Yacht Club.

Hungary: László Cserháti, Samády Béla, László Cseke, Anne Domonkos, Rezsó Gallov, Dávid Imre, Professor Tibor Melega, Tibor Mihály, Kornèlia Pap, Pál Schmitt, Ajan Tamas.

Iceland: Anna Bjarndottir.

India: Rajah Bangara, Burun Chanda, Kalyan Ghosh, Professor Dilip K. Ray, Bob and Ann Wright.

Indonesia: Iwan Vanier.

Ireland: Raymond Blake, Micheal Johnston, John McGifferd, Tom Sullivan, Maritime Institute of Ireland.

Israel: Elkana Caspi.

Italy: Francesca d'Aloja, Claudio Annoni, Fernanado Brunamontini, Sergio Califano, Beppe de Capua, Vittorio Caputo, Sir Ashley and Frances Clarke, Nardo Ettore, Lido Filippi, Donato Martucci, Roberto Menici, Paulo Petri, William Pinarello, Elio Santoni, Lydia Sciama, Ambre Strinati, Vittorio Suave, Enrico Tonali.

Japan: Naoki Asakura, Ian Buchanan, Norio Kimura, Masashi Maeda, Ichiro Taniuchi, Hiroshi Toriba.

Kuwait: Soula Faysal.

Latvia: Daina Sveica.

Lithuania: Romas Levitskas, Rimas Rudzionis.

Malta: Joseph Serracino.

Mexico: Horst Baldamus, Oswaldo Borchi, Hugo Enriquez, Toni Enyedi, Jose Luis Gutierrez, Jose Manuel Huerta, Pat O'Hea, Maggie Klapp, Walter Schreiber, Pablo Span.

Netherlands: Marc van der Arenbeemt, Jos Berkhaut, Willem Pijselman, Chris van der Ploeg, Bieps Riemers-Surie, P. Schierbeek, Marc Top, Sjoerd Venema.

New Zealand: A.Johnson, Jim Renaut, Don Rowlands, Tay Wilson.

Norway: Kjell Emblem, Matti Goksøeyr, Jens Kolberg, Lief Ljungqvist.

Paraguay: Luis Muronioguvio.

Peru: Ivan Dibos.

Philippines: Kurt Lenherr, Benjie Ramos Jr.

Poland: Teodor Kocerka, Tomasz Waszczuk, Ryszard Kobendza.

Portugal: Fernando Estima, Dick Wall, Bill Warre.

Romania: Professor Corneliu Florescu, Dan Popper.

Scotland: Mike Haggerty, Peter Haining, Graham Morison.

Singapore: Eng Ghee Goh, Ted O'Morchoe, David Packman, John Pilgrim-Morris, Simon Woods.

South Africa: Kurt Hipper, Angus Robertson.

Spain: Pedro Abreu, Rafael Aguirre, Jesus Catalá, Iñaki Equibar, Stephen Essex, Antonio Fontquernie, Antonio Martin Gómez, Xabier Leibar Mendarte, Jesus Palacin, Dick Pieper, Gorka Reizabal, Patxi Sarasua, Jean Tarcher, Leopoldo Vives.

Switzerland: Melchior Bürgin, Hans Frohofer, Alex Homberger, Daniel Homberger, Hansjakob Keller, Arnold Kettiger, Paul Kolliker, Charles Riolo, Alfred Stämpfli, Susanna Stämpfli, Christian Schweizer.

Sweden: Rajnrar Bodemyr, Jan Niklasson, Mats Hjelm.

Turkey: Nedim Narli, Alpaslan Özlü.

Ukraine: Elaine Keryluk-Austin.

Uruguay: Ruban Pesce.

UK: Neil Allen, Peter Allwright, Penny Chuter, Diana Cook, Bruce Grainger, Tony Mason, Hugh Matheson, John and Karen Millbourn, Geoffrey Page, Tim Radford, David Lunn-Rockliffe, Ivan Pratt, Mike Pullen, Jim Railton, John Vigurs, Rosemary Webb, Ian Wilson.

USA: Debby de Angelis, Daniel Bakinowski, Joe Burk, Frank Cunningham, Dick Erickson, Tina Forde, Jill Fredston, John Gardner, Jeanne Grainger, Charles Grimes, Graeme King, Craig Lambert, Sara Lopez, Edward McCormick, Mo Merhoff, Ted Nash, Paula Oyer, Jan Palchikoff, George Pew, Sam Pocock, Benjamin Spock, Bill Stowe, David Thorndike, Mike Vespoli.

USSR: Richard Davies, Leonid Drachevsky, Igor Fomin, Leonid Gissen, Gwynydd Gosling, Oleg Ivanov, Vladimir Kiesanov, Evgeni Samsonov, Vitali Sapranov.

Vietnam: Ian Purslow, Bill Stowe.

Yugoslavia: Boẓo Benedik.

Photographic acknowledgements

Colour section:
Page 1: (above) Musee d'Orsay, Paris – The Bridgeman Art Library; (below) Christie's Colour Library. Page 2: (above) The Metropolitan Museum of Art; (below) Laing Art Gallery, Newcastle upon Tyne. Page 3: (below) artist's collection. Page 4: (above) Library of Congress Washington; (below) London Transport. Page 5: Roy Miles Fine Paintings – The Bridgeman Art Library; (below) private collection – Fine Art Photographic Library. Page 6: Scala. Page 7: (above left) Rochdale Art Gallery; (above right) Louvre, Paris; (below) The Metropolitan Museum of Art. Page 8: National Gallery, London – The Bridgeman Art Library; (below) Fine Art Society – The Bridgeman Art Library.

Black and white section:
H. W. Nicholls/Royal Photographic Society, Associated Press, Italian Rowing Federation, University of Washington Libraries, Muriel Brittain/ Jesus College Cambridge, photo of Pierre de Coubertin reproduced with the consent of the International Olympic Committee, Tommy Flanagan, University of Pennsylvania Archives, Olin Library/Cornell, Christopher Dodd, Cuban Rowing Federation, Reuter, Fotograms/Smith College Archives, Popperfoto, Dr Messerli/International Olympic Committee, Leonid Gissens, Vaclav Svoboda, Hulton-Deutsch Collection, Mary Evans Picture Library, St Andrews University Photographic Collection, Nils Jotgensen/Rex Features and Fred Mayer.

INDEX

Index